D1221273

THE NEW SCHOOL HEALTH HANDBOOK

THIRD EDITION

A Ready Reference for School Nurses and Educators

JERRY NEWTON, M.D. ♦ RICHARD ADAMS, M.D.
MARILYN MARCONTEL, R.N.

JOSSEY-BASS
A Wiley Imprint
www.josseybass.com

Published by Jossey-Bass
A Wiley Imprint
989 Market Street, San Francisco, CA 94103-1741   www.josseybass.com

This book is a reference work based on research by the authors. The opinions expressed herein are not necessarily those of or endorsed by the publisher. The directions stated in this book are in no way to be considered as a substitute for consultation with a duly licensed doctor.

Permission is given for individual classroom teachers to reproduce the pages and illustrations for classroom use. Reproduction of these materials for an entire school system is strictly forbidden.

Jossey-Bass books and products are available through most bookstores. To contact Jossey-Bass directly call our Customer Care Department within the U.S. at 800-956-7739, outside the U.S. at 317-572-3986 or fax 317-572-4002.

Jossey-Bass also publishes its books in a variety of electronic formats. Some content that appears in print may not be available in electronic books.

Library of Congress Cataloging-in-Publication Data

Newton, Jerry
    The new school health handbook : a ready reference for school nurses and educators
/ Jerry Newton, Richard Adams, Marilyn Marcontel : illustrations by John Martini.—3rd. ed.
     p. cm.
    Includes bibliographical references and index.
    ISBN 978-0-7879-6628-7
    1. Pediatrics—Handbooks, manuals, etc. 2. School health services—Handbooks, manuals, etc.
I. Adams, Richard M. (Richard Martin. II. Marcontel, Marilyn. III. Title.
[DNLM: 1. Pediatrics—handbooks. 2. School Health Services—handbooks. WS 39 N564s 1997]
RJ48.N48 1997
618.92'0008837—dc21
DNLM/DLC
for Library of Congress   97-7189

FIRST EDITION
HB Printing 10 9 8 7 6 5

CONTRIBUTORS TO THE THIRD EDITION

Sue Watkins, R.N.C.S.
Vision/Hearing Testing Programs
Dallas Public Schools

Roscoe C. Lewis Jr., P.A.-C.
Specialist-Special Education/Health Services
Dallas Public Schools

Kenneth Lee Matthews, M.D.
Professor of Psychiatry
Director, Residency Education Program
University of Texas Health Science Center at San Antonio

Lois Oquin, M.S.N., R.N.C.S., C.S.N.
Continuing Education Programs
Health Services Department
Dallas Public Schools

ACKNOWLEDGMENTS

Additional individuals who made suggestions, reviewed chapters, or were otherwise supportive include James Bennett, M.D., Darlene English, BSN, RNCS, CSN, Emita Garcia, BSN, RN, CSN, Elizabeth Gregory, Ph.D., R.N., Charles Haley, M.D., Joanne Lisk, R.N., M.S.N., Lois Oquin, R.N.C.S., and David Weakley, M.D.

ABOUT THE THIRD EDITION

Enlarged and updated to accommodate new challenges faced by school nurses and other health caregivers, this third edition of *The New School Health Handbook* contains new material on special education, computers, teen pregnancy, and employee health. There is expanded coverage of mental health issues and psychoactive medications, as well as the addition of National Association of School Nurses standards and position statements.

Additional new information includes:

- Health education tips at the end of each section
- List of abbreviations and acronyms used by ophthalmologists
- Food poisoning at school
- Meningitis and encephalitis
- Traumatic brain injury
- *DSM-IV* criteria for many mental health diagnoses
- Unproven therapies for learning disorders
- Identifying the suicidal student
- School-linked clinics
- Expanded section on program administration
- Detailed suggestions for planning for acute emergencies
- Overview of nursing diagnosis and health management plans
- Health service responsibility chart defining nurse and paraprofessional activities
- Plan for school health program evaluation
- Expanded and updated references

We hope this resource will be even more valuable than previous editions for school health professionals and school administrators

Jerry Newton
Richard Adams
Marilyn Marcontel

ABOUT THE AUTHORS

Jerry Newton

Jerry Newton, M.D., a pediatrician with a wide variety of experiences, conducted a busy private practice in San Antonio, Texas, for 23 years, and served as medical supervisor for the Peace Corps Public Health Program in Paraguay for 3 years, where he was also personal physician to 75 Peace Corps volunteers. Upon returning to the United States, he became full-time medical director of the San Antonio independent school district and has served in that position for over 15 years.

He has consistently applied his efforts to improve the quality of health care offered to students. To increase the effectiveness and expand the services provided by school nurses, he developed an active school nurse practitioner program, which has resulted in many new and innovative school health programs and clinics dealing with learning disabilities and behavior problems.

Dr. Newton is clinical professor of pediatrics at the University of Texas Medicine School in San Antonio and has been active in school health committees of his local and state medical associations as well as the American School Health Association and the American Academy of Pediatrics. He is the author of the first two editions of *School Health Handbook: A Ready Reference for School Nurses and Educators* (Prentice Hall, 1984 and 1989) and *Complete Book of Forms for the School Health Professional* (Prentice Hall, 1987). He is the editor of *School Health Alert*, the only monthly newsletter that deals solely with comprehensive school health—services, education, and environment—that is read by over 3,000 school nurses and health educators.

Richard Adams

Richard Adams, M.D., serves as director of health services for the Dallas public schools and for the past 10 years has been a consultant to the High School for Health Professions. He is also clinical associate professor of Pediatrics at Southwestern Medical School in Dallas.

Dr. Adams is a diplomate of the American Board of Pediatrics, and a member of the American School Health Association (former vice-chairman of the Physician's Committee and assistant editor for Medicine of the *Journal of School Health*), the American Medical Writer's Association, and other organizations. He also has served on a number of boards and committees of health agencies, including vice-chairman, Advisory Committee on the Comprehensive School Health Program of the Texas

State Board of Education. He is past chairman of the Texas Council of Urban School Districts' Health Advisory Committee.

The author of numerous articles published in professional journals and textbooks, Dr. Adams was honored in a ceremony at the White House in May 1992 for his immunization efforts in Dallas.

Marilyn Marcontel

Marilyn Marcontel, R.N., is the coordinator of nursing for the Dallas Public Schools and a leader in the development of continuing education programs for school nurses and paraprofessionals. She is assistant clinical professor of the College of Nursing at Texas Woman's University in Dallas.

Ms. Marcontel is a certified school nurse and a certified nurse administrator and is the recipient of two distinguished service awards from the National Association of School Nurses (1987 and 1990) and numerous state and local awards for school nursing leadership activities. She has served as president of the Texas Association of School Nurses, president of the Texas Association of School Nurse Administrators, Texas director of the National Association of School Nurses, Board of Directors, and is currently serving on several boards and committees of regional health agencies and professional organizations.

In 1991, Ms. Marcontel was recognized as one of the Great 100 Nurses of the Dallas–Fort Worth Metroplex. She is a member of the editorial board of the *Journal of School Nursing* (National Association of School Nurses) and has authored numerous articles published in professional journals and books.

CONTENTS

SECTION I
ADMINISTRATION OF THE HEALTH SERVICES PROGRAM
I

SECTION 2
ACUTE ILLNESSES AND EMERGENCIES
21

SECTION 3
INJURIES
45

SECTION 4
HEALTH SCREENING PROGRAMS
75

SECTION 5
SKIN CONDITIONS, INFECTIONS, AND DISEASES
93

SECTION 6
DISEASES OF THE EARS, NOSE, AND THROAT
121

SECTION 7
EYE PROBLEMS
135

SECTION 8
DISEASES OF THE LUNGS
151

SECTION 9
DISEASES OF THE HEART
169

SECTION 10
DIABETES
181

SECTION 11
INFECTIONS OF SPECIAL SCHOOL RELEVANCE
193

SECTION 12
SEVERE PHYSICAL DISABILITIES
215

SECTION 13
DISEASES OF THE BRAIN
235

SECTION 14
DISORDERS OF LEARNING
253

SECTION 16
PSYCHOACTIVE MEDICATIONS
305

SECTION 17
SPECIAL EDUCATION ISSUES
319

SECTION 18
TEEN PREGNANCY
337

SECTION 19
EMERGING CONCEPTS
353

ADMINISTRATION OF THE HEALTH SERVICES PROGRAM

Scope of the Program

Goals and Objectives

Budget and Funding Sources

Personnel
• Program Managers
• Medical Consultants
• Registered Nurses
• Unlicensed Assistive Personnel
• Volunteers

Health Advisory Committees

Data-Driven Decision Making

Employee Issues

Liability Issues

Program Evaluation

School Relevance
• Communicating with Physicians

Role of the School Nurse

References

We must remember that we cannot separate health from the ability to learn. The two must go together.
Surgeon General Antonia Novella, 1992

The complex process of promoting health and wellness for students, faculty, and staff is a challenge to school nurses and other school health care providers. Children often come to school with a variety of health needs, problems, and conditions, and students may require first aid or attention to minor health problems during the school day. In the early 1900s, the emphasis on preventive medicine and control of communicable disease fostered the development of visiting nurse associations, which resulted in some nurses specializing in school populations.

SCOPE OF THE PROGRAM

A successful school health program focuses on school and community needs and attempts to fill those needs as much as possible. Frequently performed activities include first aid; managing the illnesses of students and school staff; controlling communicable disease; assisting in crisis and high-risk situations such as child abuse, suicide threat, or attempts, and substance abuse; evaluating severe trauma and medical emergencies; administrating medication during the school hours; and providing nursing procedures and necessary care for students with special health needs. Figure 1-1 gives an overview of school health services.

Registered nurses with varying degrees of advanced training may perform specialized functions:

- Evaluating the medical aspects of children with learning and behavior problems. School nurses have knowledge of health and education, they are able to evaluate a child's medical history, socio-economic status, physical condition, and the relationship of these factors to that student's learning style and behavioral pattern.
- Special screening programs, such as complete physical examinations when starting school and spinal curvature (scoliosis) screening in early adolescence.
- Special vision screening procedures, such as tests for eye muscle imbalance, excessive hyperopia, and color blindness, in addition to the standard visual acuity testing.
- Liaison between educational and medical personnel, especially with regard to special education placement and development of the individual educational plan.

SCHOOL HEALTH SERVICES
(An Overview)

Personnel in the Health Services Department work collaboratively with students, parents, teachers, and other school and community professionals to remove health barriers to learning.

The school health service staff may include registered nurses, nurse practitioners, certified school nurses, and trained paraprofessionals. Student and adult health room volunteers may assist this staff in promoting and safeguarding the health of the school population.

Health services include:

- Evaluating student illness. School health service personnel determine which students are able to return to class, which should go home, and which require medical referral.
- Administering emergency care and first aid to students and staff. All school health service personnel are skilled in emergency care and first aid techniques and are certified in cardiopulmonary resuscitation.
- Teaching first aid and cardiopulmonary resuscitation to school staff designated by the principal to assume responsibilities for health services in the absence of a nurse.
- Providing an effective communicable disease control program, including immunization surveillance and protective measures.
- Administering physician- and dentist-prescribed medications and special procedures in school when required by the prescribed schedule.
- Identifying health problems that may interfere with learning. Students in selected grades receive a health appraisal annually (vision testing and hearing testing are included).
- Providing physical evaluation of students eligible for Title XIX Early Periodic Screening, Diagnosis and Treatment Program (EPSDT).
- Assessing the unique health needs of handicapped students and providing specialized medical procedures where needed.

HEALTH COUNSELING

Students are counseled regarding potential or identified health problems. Teacher/nurse and parent/nurse conferences are held to interpret medical information and to define health needs, educational implications, and needed adjustments in the school environment.

HEALTH EDUCATION

School nurses utilize each student contact as an opportunity for health education. Students are encouraged to develop responsibility for their personal health. Nurses also serve as resource persons to classroom teachers in conducting health education sessions.

Figure 1-1. School health service (overview).

- Developmental screening that assesses functional levels of young children (because standard educational pencil-and-paper psychometric testing is frequently inaccurate and difficult with very young children).
- Working with occupational and physical therapists in the care of disabled children.

Nonmedical persons, nursing assistants, and trained community volunteers can assist in the school health program by giving basic health care to the child. These individuals generally provide first aid for minor injuries or illnesses, clerical , help, and mass screening for vision, hearing, and spinal problems. Special attention to their training and continued monitoring of their activities by a registered nurse is necessary. Some states and local school health programs require a specific course of study for those who provide routine screening tests and other health service activities. The American Red Cross first aid and cardiopulmonary resuscitation (CPR) courses are essential, and in-service education on policies, procedures, and public relations will help prepare these nonmedical persons to provide selected health care activities in the school.

GOALS AND OBJECTIVES

School health service personnel and the school administration determine and write program goals and objectives based on identified health needs. These policies must fill service gaps; ensure access to community treatment resources; meet the health needs of students in the community; coordinate with community values; comply with federal, state, and local requirements; and meet standards of nursing and the medical profession. The primary goal of any school health program is to remove health barriers to learning; see Figure 1-2.

BUDGET AND FUNDING SOURCES

The allocation of funds is of great significance to a health service program. Goals, objectives, and activities are accomplished when an adequate budget is provided for the program. Most budgets assign dollar amounts to goals; thus the budget becomes a financial plan for carrying out the goals of an organization.

Personnel is the major cost (80%–90%) of the school health program. Equipment and supplies make up the remainder.

In recent years, several school health programs have started to bring funds back to the school through services provided by nurses and other health personnel.

GOAL AND OBJECTIVES
School Health Services

Goal:

To enhance the educational process by removing health barriers to learning.

Objectives:

1. To reduce the incidence of student morbidity and absenteeism related to accidents and illnesses.
2. To decrease the incidence of student absenteeism due to communicable disease.
3. To provide health assessment or physical examination of students to promote early referral of health problems.
4. To assist with the identification, placement, and management of students with special health needs.
5. To coordinate health services to students in collaboration with other district departments.
6. To perform selected activities that promote employee health and wellness.
7. To serve as liaison among school, home community health agencies, and other health care professionals.
8. To provide staff development and other informational support for department personnel, faculty, staff, and clinic volunteers.
9. To serve as a resource to the administration on environmental health and safety issues.
10. To provide technical assistance, health personnel, clinic supplies, furniture, and equipment to local schools.
11. To conduct all departmental affairs in a cost-effective manner, with appropriate quality control and accountability.

Figure 1-2. Goals and objectives.

Programs that will reimburse the school district for selected services or activities performed by nurses and other health personnel include school health and related services (SHARS), Medicaid administrative, and early and periodic screening, diagnosis, and treatment (EPSDT) programs funded by the federal government through Title XIX Medicaid. Ideally, this money is used to fund health services. Thus, health services in schools continue and are strengthened in this time of the shrinking educational dollar. If these services are to remain a part of the educational program in many schools, school health personnel must be aware of programs that return money to the provider and be willing to learn how to access these funds.

PERSONNEL

Program Manager

Most often, the person employed to manage the school health program is a registered nurse; sometimes it is a physician. Management skills along with clinical knowledge are essential. Nonhealth professionals are usually not effective health service managers.

Physician Consultants

A paid or volunteer physician consultant is essential to a successful health service program. Often the nurse needs to consult with the physician to assist the student with an acute or chronic health problem. The ongoing development of protocols and procedures also require input from the physician consultant.

Registered Nurses

A registered nurse (R.N.) is generally responsible for planning, implementing, and monitoring health services in a specific school or schools. The legal title R.N. can be used only by persons who have completed an accredited educational program and who have passed examinations required by each state. Following these two steps, an R.N. is registered to practice nursing in the state of his or her residence. The titles registered nurse, nurse, and R.N. maybe used.

The American Nurses Association, the National Association of School Nurses, and other national and state professional groups interested in school health and school nursing have written the Standards of School Nursing Practice; see Figure 1-3. These standards are the core of the school health program and define the role of the school nurse.

Unlicensed Assistive Personnel

The title and job description of an unlicensed assistive personnel (UAP) in schools varies greatly. People in this position are frequently called nurse assistants, nurse aides, or clinic assistants. Many school health departments employ, train, supervise, monitor, and evaluate UAPs so as to provide health services deemed appropriate in

STANDARDS OF SCHOOL NURSING PRACTICE
National Association of School Nurses

I.   The school nurse utilizes a distinct knowledge base for decision-making in nursing practice.

II. The school nurse uses a systematic approach to problem-solving in nursing practice.

III. The school nurse contributes to the education of the client with special health needs by assessing the client, planning and providing appropriate nursing care, and evaluating the identified outcomes of care.

IV. The school nurse uses effective written, verbal, and nonverbal communication skills.

V.   The school nurse establishes and maintains a comprehensive school health program.

VI. The school nurse collaborates with other school professionals, parents, and caregivers to meet the health, developmental, and educational needs of clients.

VII. The school nurse collaborates with members of the community in the delivery of health and social services, and utilizes knowledge of community health systems and resources to function as a school- community liaison.

VIII.The school nurse assists students, families, and the school community to achieve optimal levels of wellness through appropriately designed and delivered health education.

IX. The school nurse contributes to nursing and school health through innovations in practice and participation in research or research-related activities.

X.   The school nurse identifies, delineates, and clarifies the nursing role, promotes quality of care, pursues continued professional enhancement, and demonstrates professional conduct.

Figure 1-3. Standards of school nursing practice.

their district. UAPs may be trained to perform selected clerical activities, first aid, and basic health care under the supervision of a registered nurse and may be responsible for assisting a nurse with implementing health services in assigned schools.

Clearly defined responsibilities for the registered nurse and the nurse assistant (see Figure 1-4) will assist school principals and faculty to understand the functions and limitations of these position. In addition, a position or job description that describes or defines the knowledge, skills, and abilities required to perform this job, the working conditions of the job, and the educational requirements of the employed individuals is essential. This position description is updated when a significant change occurs.

RESPONSIBILITY CHART
Health Services for Students and Employees

Services Offered	Staff Nurse	Nurse Assistant
1. First aid (illness/injury)	X	X
2. Health appraisal	X	
3. Mandated screening (vision, hearing, scoliosis)	X	X[a]
4. Immunization monitoring	X	X
5. Administration of prescribed medication	X	X[b]
6. Special procedures (i.e., urinary catheterization)		
Teaching	X	
Monitoring	X	
Service delivery	X	X
7. Pregnancy case management	X	
8. Drug toxicity assessment	X	
9. Management of communicable disease	X[c]	
10. Individual health counseling	X[c]	
11. Referral of medical problems	X	
12. Follow-up of referred medical problems	X	
13. Participation on the interdisciplinary team	X	
14. Records/reports	X	X

[a] **With successful completion of course of study and Certification from Texas Department of Health.**
[b] **District policy includes course of study in Administration of Medication to the School Age Child, and first dose of medication given by R.N.**
[c] **Includes employees.**

Figure 1-4. Responsibility chart.

Under delegation rules outlined in most state nursing practice acts, unlicensed assistive personnel are responsible to the registered nurse.

Volunteers

Guidelines, policies, and procedures for volunteers in a school health program vary from school to school. In rare instances, state laws address areas of volunteer functions. In most schools, the administration outlines activities that volunteers (non-employees) may perform.

Some of the American Red Cross area chapters provide a course of study for school clinic volunteers. These programs provide training of participants and ongoing support. American Red Cross–trained volunteers are required to follow local school policy and the guidelines of the American Red Cross. Some schools develop their own program and training for volunteers, giving consideration to tasks that will assist the nurse and that are within policy and legal guidelines.

HEALTH ADVISORY COMMITTEES

The purpose of a health advisory committee or council is to involve persons to provide breadth and focus to the health program and to assist in gaining support from the school administration and the community. The major functions of such committees are to make recommendations regarding the program, to ensure implementation of program components, and in some cases, to assist with evaluation. Positive feedback to the community and updated information regarding program status adds to the committee's overall success. Members should be able to work as a team to accomplish identified goals and objectives. The makeup of a health advisory committee often includes the following individuals:

- Faculty members (elementary and secondary)
- Students (elementary and secondary)
- School board member or board of trustees member
- Campus administrator
- Food service administrator
- Member of the clergy
- Physicians (family practice, ob/gyn, sports medicine, opthimologist, otolaryngologist, etc.)
- School nurse (staff)

- Social or community agency members
- Parents (member of a parent-teacher organization)
- Department of Human Services and other service agency representatives
- School at-risk coordinator
- School counselor
- Business community members
- Police force and/or fire department representative
- Faculty members from nursing schools

The number of members of an advisory council will vary according to program needs and community resources. A small advisory council may not provide adequate representation of the community, but a very large one may be unmanageable. An advisory council member's term of office and criteria for joining the advisory council should be determined prior to organizing the group. Some advisory councils implement a rotation system in which members leave the advisory council at different times and new members are added. The success of the council depends on many factors, but most important is the program manager, who oversees the organization and ongoing activities of the group.

DATA-DRIVEN DECISION MAKING

Data gleaned from reports and other sources are of major importance to a school health program because they objectively show efforts to achieve the goals. By allowing the retrieval of compiled statistics at any time, computer programs make many reporting activities less burdensome than they used to be. The model summary page from an annual report in Figure 1-5 may be useful to those developing a reporting process. An important figure is the per-pupil cost per school year. In addition to this page of the report, narratives about specific projects in a particular school health program should be included; examples are student pregnancy and parenting related service programs, CPR and first aid training for nonmedical school personnel, school-based or school linked clinics, summer school activities, hearing and vision screening programs, school health and related services (SHARS) and reimbursement, Medicaid administrative outreach program (MAOP) reimbursement, nurse recruitment, student nurse clinical training programs, and special education activities. Attachments may be included in the report to show program details. The entire report becomes a comprehensive summary of the year's activities.

MODEL ANNUAL REPORT
(Summary Page)

I. Activities of Health Professionals
A. General
  1. Clinic visits
    a. Student

Illness/health maintenance	659,184
Minor trauma	149,690
Major trauma	259
Other student visits	533,015
Total student visits	1,342,148

    b. Adult

Employees	25,748
Other adults	223,983
Total adult visits	249,731
GRAND TOTAL CLINIC VISITS	1,591,879
Enrollment =	149,749
Clinic visits per student/year =	10.6

  2. Health screening

Health Screening	Screened	Referred	Completed
Health appraisal	36,734	648 (1.8%)	393 (60.6%)
Dental	36,998	5,255 (14.2%)	1,509 (28.7%)
Vision	85,480	6,056 (7.1%)	2,974 (49.1%)
Hearing	73,771	2,766 (3.7%)	1,513 (54.7%)
Spinal screening (grades 5, 8)	20,244	302 (1.5%)	83 (27.5%)

  3. Immunization protection levels (%)
    (TEA Annual Report)

Measles #1	99.3%
Measles #2	97.4%
Mumps	99.3%
Rubella	99.3%
Polio	98.0%
Diphtheria/tetanus	97.8%
Hib	97.9%
District compliance level	98.4%

  4. Pediculosis

Student cases identified and treated	5,562
Family cases identified and treated	15,058 > 20,620
Cost of pediculicide	$ 53,012
Cost per treatment	$ 2.60

  5. Child Abuse

Cases	Year Reported
285	1995/96
412	1994/95
258	1993/94
389	1992/93
335	1991/92

B. Vision examination (35 clinics)
  1,184 @ 1.70 = 2,016.00
C. Communicable diseases
  (school nurse reported)

1. Chicken pox	1,663
2. Hepatitis, type A	18
4. Hepatitis, non-A/non-B	
5. Influenza	5,296
6. Measles, rubella	
7. Measles, rubeola	
8. Meningitis, viral	
9. Meningitis, bacterial	1
10. Mumps	1
11 Pediculosis	5,562
12. Rheumatic fever	
13. Ringworm, scalp	293
14. Scabies	243
15. Scarlet fever	38
16. Amebiasis	
17. Encephalitis	
18. Shigellosis	
19 Tuberculosis	1
Total	13,122

D. Technical procedures

Tracheostomy care	13
Tube feedings (N/G and gastromy)	37
Catheterization (bladder)	28
Ostomy care (colostomy/ileostomy)	4
Continuous oxygen	1
Bronchodilator aerosolizatrion (asthmatics) Pumps/nebulizer with medication only	53
Insulin injection/glucose monitoring	78
Oral/nasal suction (no trach)	1
Urinary bag care	2
Epi-pen®	1
Respirator	1
Miscellaneous	1
Total	220

E. Cost analysis

95-96 health services central budget	$417,424
Nurse salaries	3,855,355
Nurse assistant salaries	666,319
Clinic attendant salaries	556,050
Total expenditure	5,495,148
Enrollment	149,749
Per pupil expenditure/year	$36.69

Figure 1-5. Model annual report.

Copies of the annual report are distributed to the superintendent, principals, health advisory council members, health service staff, and community agencies as well as administrators in other school departments (special education, physical education, food services, personnel, psychological and social services, environmental control, and so forth) who work closely with the health services department. Throughout the following school year, the report is used to describe the school health program, to increase public awareness, and to gain support in a variety of ways.

EMPLOYEE ISSUES

Although student health is the focus of most school health service programs, faculty and staff inevitably seek first aid and advice on other health matters from school nurses and other school health care providers. Managers of employee assistance programs (EAPs) designed for employees dealing with stress, substance abuse, and excessive absenteeism often ask the school nurse to participate in the treatment program of troubled employees (see Section 19). Risk management departments are in larger school districts. They usually carry out an umbrella function of reducing financial losses through safety education and prevention programs, management of workers' compensation cases, and securing cost-effective insurance coverage for high-cost items. Information on these activities is in Section 19.

LIABILITY ISSUES

Persons in the education and health care fields are familiar with the high-risk liability issues in school nursing. These include reporting child abuse and neglect, delegation, minor consent for health services, individual right for privacy, confidentiality, and do not resuscitate (DNR) orders. To prevent (or to deal effectively with) a lawsuit, the nurse needs to follow the state nursing practice act and the standards of school nursing practice (Figure 1-3), federal and state laws, and local board of education policies.

The best protections against legal liability are to stay current in the profession, to focus on the client, to practice within the framework of the law, and to document actions and recommendations. The nurse is responsible for remaining qualified for the job; being and remaining certified in school nursing through the National Association of School Nurses (NASN) or the American Nurses Association (ANA); seeking to understand and adapt to cultural, religious, and ethnic differences in the workplace; joining and becoming active in the American School Health Association

(ASHA), NASN, and ANA; attending professional seminars; reading professional journals; maintaining records of continuing education and training received; maintaining a professional library; keeping letters or memos of appreciation; documenting, in writing, unsafe practices and notifying appropriate persons of such practices; and maintaining a level of professionalism that enhances student safety and contributes to the overall quality of care.

The employer also has responsibilities to the nurse. These include providing written job descriptions that are updated to reflect professional and educational changes, training (orientation) of new staff, encouraging or providing in-service education to update information and review policies and guidelines, developing and updating protocol and procedure manuals, evaluating employees, and developing a line of communication to keep management and staff informed.

PROGRAM EVALUATION

Many school health programs today are fighting for their existence. Some school administrators, faced with less money and a demand for new and improved educational programs, are eliminating nursing positions and cutting the costs of health programs to a minimum.

By defining program goals and objectives and then measuring the extent of accomplishment, a program evaluation enables an administrator to determine the usefulness and effectiveness of a program. An annual report is not only valuable to the health service personnel in determining accomplishments, but may also influence the continuation of an adequate budget for the program (see Figure 1-6).

SCHOOL RELEVANCE

Communicating with Physicians

When there is a clear-cut medical illness for which a child is receiving adequate medical attention by the family physician, school personnel are usually informed of the progress and nature of the disease, and there is no need for additional direct communication. Sometimes, however, the school nurse or other caregiver may need to talk to the physician directly. Two examples of such conditions are as follows:

- Children with a chronic low-grade illness who continue school attendance, but whose various symptoms (poor appetite, failure to play) cause the teacher to suspect that the child is not doing well.

PLAN FOR EVALUATING A SCHOOL HEALTH PROGRAM

Items may be rated on a scale from one (not met) to five (fulfilled):

I. Administration

   A. School board philosophy and policies provide for an effective school health program.
   B. Administrative guidelines facilitate the implementation of effective school health services.
   C. Budgetary resources are adequate.
   D. Activities and services are based on student need.
   E. Measurable goals are set.
   F. Objective evaluation is performed.
   G. Program adjustments are made based on evaluation results.
   H. Legal standards of health care are met.
   I. The student: school nurse ratio is determined by student health needs, legal requirements, number of individuals with special health care needs, mobility of population, and other relevant factors.

II. Health Services

   A. A health history is obtained on entering students and updated periodically.
   B. A health appraisal or physical examination is performed on entering students and updated periodically.
   C. Selected screening procedures are performed to identify health barriers to learning.
   D. Immunization monitoring and other communicable disease control programs are in place.
   E. Provisions exist for emergency care and first aid.
   F. Appropriate referral and follow-up care are carried out on identified health problems.
   G. Effective parent communication is established.
   H. Networking with community agencies is developed.
   I. Technical currency is maintained through appropriate staff development.
   J. School personnel are encouraged to observe students for possible health problems and are given in-service training on recognizing such problems or emergencies.
   K. Ethical standards of health care practice are met.
   L. Provisions exist for the administration of medication and special procedures.
   M. Child abuse reporting is comprehensive.
   N. Health services personnel recommend necessary school adjustments for students with health problems.
   O. Health services personnel make home or hospital visits related to student health problems.
   P. Accidents are analyzed to determine their cause; safety hazards are reported.
   Q. Health services personnel assist families in obtaining free or partial-pay health services when necessary.
   S. Clinical research is conducted to determine efficacy of activities and procedures (optional).
   T. An annual report is prepared.

III. Health Education

   A. Health services personnel cooperate with other school professionals to meet formal and informal health education goals.
   B. Health service personnel serve as consultants to health educators.
   C. All health service activities are utilized as teaching/learning opportunities.
   D. Health services personnel conduct programs for parent-teacher organizations and community groups.

IV. School Environment

   A. The district provides a physical plant and equipment that meet the educational needs of its students and staff.
   B. School health personnel assume shared responsibility for the safety and comfort of the school environment.
   C. Mechanisms exist for addressing potential environmental health hazards.
   D. Safety education and injury prevention are given high priority.
   E. Federal, state, and local regulations on environmental safety are observed.
   F. A smoke-free environment is provided.
   G. Fire and disaster plans are established.
   H. The school lunch program is utilized as a learning laboratory for good nutrition.

(Adapted from the Texas Education Agency)

Figure 1-6. Plan for evaluating a school health program.

- Children with learning and behavior problems serious enough to require medical intervention. In such cases, school nurses often need to give information to the physician to supplement that of the parents or to seek advice that will help in the child's management and education.

Because of laws governing medical confidentiality, a physician will require written parental consent to disclose information to the school. The nurse must obtain permission from a parent to contact the physician. Most parents cooperate with the school to help their child. After obtaining the necessary permission form, the nurse mails it to the physician. The nurse then calls to make sure the release form has been received and explains the nature of the call. If this procedure is followed, the school nurse will usually have the physician's cooperation.

As experienced school nurses know, these contacts do not always go smoothly. Some of the obstacles are created by:

- An uncooperative or poorly informed parent
- The absence of a reliable and regular source of medical care
- Physicians who cannot be reached by phone (often employed by large city, county, or military hospitals or by health care businesses)
- An uncooperative doctor; some physicians have very little or no familiarity with the administrative and professional operation of a school

ROLE OF THE SCHOOL NURSE

Because almost all states have laws that prohibit nurses from making a medical diagnosis and prescribing treatment, there are differing opinions among school nurses concerning the legality of diagnosing and identifying obvious medical conditions or illnesses. For example, school nurses do not hesitate to identify (or diagnose) head lice; some feel competent to identify impetigo, scabies, or chicken pox; but most will not diagnose diseases such as hepatitis or scarlet fever.

In the early 1970s, school nurses began to expand their scope of activities. Since then, frequently seen skin conditions and minor illnesses have been identified by the school nurse.

The school nurse practitioner movement began in the early 1970s and received impetus a few years later from a Robert Wood Johnson Foundation grant. In addition, the school-based clinic movement, which began in Dallas, Texas, and St. Paul, Minnesota, in 1967, continues to expand. At this time, there are numerous school-based and school-linked clinics. In these clinics, a nurse practitioner, under a physician's supervision, diagnoses and treats minor illnesses commonly seen in schools. The nurse practitioner follows protocols or standing orders dated and signed by the physician supervisor (see Figure 1-7). The nurse practitioner's judgment is required for giving medication under protocols or standing orders. Medical and nursing practice laws permit these special arrangements in some states.

Some school districts with part-time, full-time, or consulting physicians have developed their own standing orders for certain conditions. This helps the school nurse to provide more efficient and effective health services and also gives the nurse legal protection while providing for minor common complaints. In this process, each school district, with input from nurses, doctors, and school administrators, develops its unique protocols and standing orders.

Some conditions frequently described in school health services protocols and standing orders for the school nurse to treat include abrasions, acne, anaphylaxis, asthma, blunt injury (abdomen), blunt injury (chest), boils, burns, cellulitis and lymphangitis, common colds versus allergic rhinitis, conjunctivitis, contact dermatitis, dog bites, eczema, foreign bodies, head trauma, herpes simplex, hives, human bites, laryngeal edema, impetigo, lacerations, nosebleed, ringworm, scabies, seizures (epilepsy), sprains (ankle or knee), sties, and urticaria. School districts without physician directed protocols restrict nursing practice to treatments without medications. In these cases, nurses refer to physicians or health agencies.

Nursing diagnosis is defined by the North American Nursing Diagnosis Association as "a clinical judgment about individual, family or community response to actual or potential health problems/life processes. Nursing diagnosis provides the basis for selection of nursing interventions to achieve outcomes for which the nurse is accountable." Nurses in most settings are using or are beginning to use these standardized statements to communicate with each other and, in the schools, with other school professionals. School nurses use nursing diagnosis (see Figure 1-8) when developing health management plans and other student health records. Recommended reading for school nurses in the 1990s includes *Nursing Diagnosis: Definitions and Classifications*, published by the North American Nursing Diagnosis Association; *Using Nursing Diagnosis in the School Setting* and *Quality Nursing Interventions in the School Setting: Procedures, Models and Guidelines*, published by the National Association of School Nurses; and *The School Nurse's Source Book of Individualized Health Care Plans*, edited by Mary Kay Hass and published by Sunrise River Press.

PROTOCOL FOR IMPETIGO

Definition

Superficial infection of the skin manifested by vesicular or pustular lesions that rapidly become crusted.

Etiology

Caused by certain strains of streptococci, staphylococcus, or by a combination of both.

Epidemiology

Can occur at any age; both sexes and all races equally vulnerable. It is often associated with poor hygiene and is contagious. Infection is spread by contact with material from skin lesions.

Clinical Manifestations

Onset usually sudden; may be prolonged with new lesions developing over several months if child is not treated.

Lesions tend to occur at site of previous injury (scratch) and at mucocutaneous junctions (corner of lip, nasal folds); common on figures.

Red macule-vesicle-pustule-crust lesions vary in size. Multiple sites can appear readily and diffusely. Lesions are superficial because bacteria invade upper skin layers.

May have pruritus, regional adenopathy, low-grade fever.

Diagnosis

Culture of material from pustule on blood agar, rarely necessary. Lesions as described above.

Treatment

1. Antibiotic therapy for 10 days (only necessary for severe cases)
    a. Pen-Vee-K 50—100 mg/kg/day x 10 days
    b. Erythromycin 20—40 mg/kg/day x 10 days if allergic to penicillin and no history of erythromycin sensitivity
2. Wet compresses to crusts with careful removal t.i.d. by parent
3. Bacitracin ointment
4. Urinalysis 2—4 weeks after prescription ends or as need arises
5. Heart exam 2—4 weeks after prescription
6. Throat culture of patient and family if impetigo recurs

Prognosis

1. Ecthyma—more serious form of impetigo with deeper invasion of streptococcus into dermis—results from neglect and poor general physical resistance.
2. Cellulitis.
3. Acute glomerulonephritis. Efficacy of penicillin therapy in preventing acute glomerulonephritis (AGN) is questionable but strongly advocated at present.

Education

1. Explain carefully to parents dosage of antibiotic and importance of compliance (A.G.N.).
2. Stress importance of child's fingernails being kept short and clean.
3. Discourage scratching.
4. All involved in child's care should wash hands carefully.
5. Child's towel and wash cloth must be isolated.
6. Classmates, relatives, siblings should be observed carefully to suspicious lesions.
7. Report any change in condition (antibiotic intolerance, lesions, urinary complaints, etc.).
8. Child may attend school if under treatment for 24 hours.

Read and approved by: _____   Date: _____
                            Physicians Signature

Figure 1-7. Model protocol. (Adapted from the Texas Education Agency.)

NURSING DIAGNOSES
of the North American Nursing Diagnosis Association

Activity intolerance
Activity intolerance, high risk for
Adjustment, impaired
Airway clearance, ineffective
Anxiety
Aspiration, high risk for
Body image disturbance
Body temperature, altered, high risk for
Bowel incontinence
Breastfeeding, effective
Breastfeeding, ineffective
Breastfeeding, interrupted
Breathing pattern, ineffective
Cardiac, output, decreased
Caregiver role strain
Caregiver role strain, high risk for
Communication, impaired verbal
Constipation
Constipation, colonic
Constipation, perceived
Coping, defensive
Coping, family: potential for growth
Coping, ineffective family: compromised
Coping, ineffective family: disabling
Coping ineffective individual
Decisional conflict (specify)
Denial, ineffective
Diarrhea
Disuse syndrome, high risk for
Diversional activity deficit
Dysreflexia
Family processes, altered
Fatigue
Fear
Fluid volume deficit (1)
Fluid volume deficit (2)
Fluid volume deficit, high risk for
Fluid volume excess
Fluid volume excess
Gas exchange, impaired
Grieving, anticipatory
Grieving, dysfunctional
Growth and development, altered
Health maintenance, altered
Health-seeking behaviors (specify)
Home maintenance management, impaired
Hopelessness
Hyperthermia
Hypothermia
Incontinence, functional
Incontinence, reflex
Incontinence, stress
Incontinence, total
Incontinence, urge
Infant feeding pattern, ineffective
Infection, high risk for
Injury, high risk for
Knowledge deficit (specify)

Management of therapeutic regimen (individuals), ineffective
Mobility, impaired physical
Noncompliance (specify)
Nutrition, altered: less than body requirements
Nutrition, altered: more than body requirements
Nutrition, altered: high risk for more than body requirements
Oral mucous membrane, altered
Pain
Pain, chronic
Parental role conflict
Parenting, altered
Parenting, altered, high risk for
Peripheral neurovascular dysfunction, high risk for
Personal identity disturbance
Poisoning, high risk for
Post-trauma response
Powerlessness
Protection, altered
Rape-trauma syndrome
Rape-trauma syndrome: compound reaction
Rape-trauma syndrome: silent reaction
Relocation stress syndrome
Role performance, altered
Self-care deficit, bathing/hygiene
Self-care deficit, dressing/grooming
Self-care deficit, feeding
Self-care deficit, toileting
Self-esteem disturbance
Self-esteem, chronic low
Self-esteem, situational low
Self-mutilation, high risk for
Sensory/perceptual alterations (specify) (visual, auditory, kinesthetic, gustatory, tactile, olfactory)
Sexual dysfunction
Sexuality patterns, altered
Skin integrity, impaired
Skin integrity, impaired, high risk for
Sleep pattern disturbance
Social interaction, impaired
Social isolation
Spiritual distress (distress of the human spirit)
Suffocation, high risk for
Swallowing, impaired
Thermoregulation, ineffective
Thought processes, altered
Tissue integrity, impaired
Tissue perfusion, altered (specify type) renal, cerebral, cardiopulmonary, gastrointestinal, peripheral)
Trauma, high risk for
Unilateral neglect
Urinary elimination, altered
Urinary retention
Ventilation, inability to sustain spontaneous
Ventilatory weaning process, dysfunctional
Violence, high risk for: self-directed or directed at others

Figure 1-8. Nursing diagnosis (NANDA). (Adapted from"Protocols for Nurse Practitioner," Robert Wood Johnson School Health Project, New York.)

REFERENCES

Adams, Richard M. "Planning and Management of School Health Services." In *Principles and Practices of Student Health*, vol. 1, 291–301. Oakland, Calif.: Third Party Publishing, 1991.

————. *School Nurse's Survival Guide*. Englewood Cliffs, N.J.: Prentice Hall, 1995.

Ellis, Janice K., and Celia A. Hartley. *Nursing in Today's World: Challenges, Issues, and Trends*, 5th ed. Philadelphia: J. B. Lippincott, 1995.

Igoe, Judith. "Community Health Nurse in the Schools." In *Community Health Nursing: Promoting the Health of Aggregates, Families, and Individuals*, 4th ed., edited by Marcia Stanhope and Jeanette Lancaster, 879–906. St. Louis: Mosby, 1996.

Igoe, Judith, and Beverly Giordano. *Expanding School Health Services to Serve Families in the 21st Century*. Washington, D.C.: American Nurses Publishing, 1992.

Kim, Astroth, Gertrude McFarland, and Audrey McLane. *Pocket Guide to Nursing Diagnosis*, 5th ed. St. Louis: Mosby, 1993.

Nader, Philip R., ed. *Organization and Staffing of School Health Services in School Health: Policy and Practice*. Elk Grove Village, Ill.: American Academy of Pediatrics, 1993.

National Association of School Nurses. *Resolutions and Policy Statements*. Scarborough, Maine: National Association of School Nurses, 1990.

National Association of School Nurses. *Position Statements*. Scarborough, Maine: National Association of School Nurses, 1990.

Proctor, Susan T., Susan Lordi, and Donna Zaiger. *School Nursing Practice: Roles and Standards*. Scarborough, Maine: National Association of School Nurses, 1990.

Schwab, Nadine. *Guidelines for School Nurse Documentation: Standards, Issues, and Models*. Scarborough, Maine: National Association of School Nurses, 1991.

Schwab, Nadine, and M. Gelfman. "School Health Records: Nursing Practice and the Law." *School Nurse* 7(2): 26–34.

Sullivan, E. *Effective Management in Nursing*. Redwood City, Calif.: Benjamin-Cummings, 1992.

SECTION 2
ACUTE ILLNESSES AND EMERGENCIES

Fainting
- Symptoms
- First Aid and Treatment

Nosebleeds (Epistaxis)
- Causes
- First Aid and Treatment

Stomachaches
- Symptoms and Recommendations for Care

Vomiting
- Causes
- First Aid

Diarrhea
- Symptoms
- First Aid and Treatment

Food Poisoning
- Symptoms
- Questions to Ask the Student

Poison Ingestion and Drug Overdoses
- Symptoms
- First Aid
- Poison Control Center

Appendicitis
- Symptoms and Recommendations for Care

Menstrual Problems
- Symptoms
- Premenstrual Syndrome
- Treatment

Headaches
- Symptoms

Cardiopulmonary Resuscitation (CPR)
- Personnel Training
- Resuscitation Methods
- Precautions

Hyperventilation
- Symptoms
- First Aid and Treatment

Foreign Bodies: Eye, Ear, and Nose
- Eye
- Ear
- Nose

Heat-Related Illnesses
- Adverse Physical Reactions to Excess Heat: Symptoms
- First Aid and Treatment
- Prevention

School Relevance

Role of the School Nurse

Health Education Tips
References

Throughout my youth I was assailed by an astounding variety of weird diseases that invariably sent my doctor hunting through medical texts.

Ambidextrous, 1985
Felice Picano

When children or adults become ill or are injured during the school day, they are generally seen in the school clinic. The school nurse or another school health caregiver is the person first called upon to determine if a significant health problem exists and if further assessment is required. Caregivers must be aware of signs and symptoms of illness, the type and extent of the injury, and the immediate care that may be given in the school. Recommendations for ongoing care at school or home and referral for medical care are also given by the health caregiver. The student may be able to go back to class, may need to go home, or may need to be referred to a physician or emergency room. Unfortunately, parents are not always available. Following an assessment, it may be necessary either to provide care for the student at the school until a parent can assume this responsibility or call for an immediate transport via an ambulance to an emergency facility. A comprehensive plan of action (see Figure 2-1) approved by the school administration, board of trustees, and the school medical advisor should be available in each school.

FAINTING

Fainting can occur for a variety of reasons. Strong emotional reactions, hunger, pain, or the onset of illness may be the cause. A serious health condition such as diabetes or hypoglycemia may cause fainting when the blood glucose levels dip too low. It is important to try to establish the cause of the faint before dismissing it. Additionally, frequent fainting should be taken seriously, and the person should be referred to a physician for evaluation.

Symptoms

Before fainting, a person may be pale, weak, dizzy, and nauseated and may experience sweating. The person becomes limp, falls to the ground, and is unconscious for a few seconds. Usually the pulse is weak and rapid.

Fainting is associated with a sudden decrease in blood supply to the brain and may or may not be associated with low blood pressure and slow pulse. A sudden change in position, especially from lying or sitting to a standing position, can cause dizziness or fainting.

EMERGENCENCY PLANNING FOR ILLNESS OR INJURIES

I. Require immediate treatment and call for emergency medical system (EMS) services
- Notify administrator
- Get nurse or trained staff person to assist student or adult
- Call ambulance
- Notify nurse if he or she is not with victim
- Administrator or nurse notifies parent

    Illness/injury

    A. Acute airway obstruction
    B. Cardiac or respiratory arrest
    C. Near drowning
    D. Massive external hemorrhage and internal hemorrhage
    E. Internal poisoning or external poisoning
    F. Anaphylaxis
    G. Neck or back injury
    H. Chemical burns of the eye
    I. Heat stroke
    J. Penetrating/crushing chest wounds and pneumothorax
    K. Gunshot wounds

II. Require immediate evaluation and referral to treatment facility
- Notify administrator
- Get nurse or trained staff person to assist/evaluate student or adult
- Call ambulance, if necessary, notify nurse if he or she is not with student or adult
- Administrator or nurse notifies parent

    Illness/injury

    A. Internal bleeding
    B. Coronary occlusion
    C. Dislocations and fractures
    D. Unconscious states
    E. Heat problems
    F. Major burns
    G. Drug overdose
    H. Head injury with loss of consciousness
    I. Penetrating eye injuries
    J. Seizure—cause unknown
    K. Diabetics

III. Medical consultation is desirable as soon as possible (within 1 hour)
- Contact nurse or, in nurse's absence, administrator
- Nurse or trained staff person assesses extent of injury
- Notify parent and refer to medical facility if necessary

    Illness/injury

    A. Lacerations
    B. Bites and stings—animal, insect, and snake (without anaphylaxis)
    C. Burns with blisters
    D. Accidental loss of tooth
    E. Acute emotional state
    F. Moderate reactions to drugs
    G. High fever (above 103°F)
    H. Asthma/wheezing
    I. Nonpenetrating eye injury

IV. Attention by a trained staff person with school nurse/parent consultation needed
- Contact nurse or, in nurse's absence, administrator
- Nurse or trained staff person assesses extent of injury
- Notify parent and refer to medical facility if necessary

    Illness/injury

    A. Convulsion (in known epileptic)
    B. Insulin reaction (in diabetic)
    C. Severe abdominal pain
    D. Fever 100°–103°F
    E. Sprains
    F. Frostbite

V. Minor injuries/illnesses—can be handled by a trained staff person following standard procedures
- Refer student to trained staff person
- Child may remain in school in most instances

    Illness/Injury

    A. Abrasions
    B. Minor burns
    C. Nosebleeds
    A. Abrasions
    E. Stomachache
    F. Colds

If condition worsens with the passage of time, reassessment of student or adult may call for a change of decision regarding further care.

Figure 2-1. Emergency planning for illness or injuries. (Modified from School Health: Policy and Practice American Academy of Pediatrics)

First Aid and Treatment

First aid and treatment of fainting are as follows:

- Place the person in a horizontal position with the head on level with or lower than the chest. *Allow a person who has fainted and is lying on the floor to remain there until recovered.* Maintain body temperature (i.e., if the weather is cool, cover with a blanket; if the weather is hot, leave uncovered).
- Check pulse and respiration. If these are normal, you can be reassured that the child (or adult) will soon recover.
- Measure blood pressure. If it is not excessively low (below 90/60), the fainting spell is usually not serious.
- Attempt to awaken the person. If this brings no response, it is better to observe the person for a short time and check the blood pressure, pulse, and respiration periodically. Moving or groaning is an indication of consciousness. If signs point to deepening unconsciousness or if recovery is prolonged (more than 2 minutes) or the person has difficulty breathing, call the emergency medical service (EMS) system.

Always advise parents of a fainting episode and recommend evaluation by the medical care provider.

NOSEBLEEDS (EPISTAXIS)

Causes

Hemorrhage from the nose may be secondary to an infection, such as a cold or sinusitis, or may be due to drying of the nasal mucous membrane, trauma (including picking the nose), hypertension, or a bleeding disorder. Children and adults with colds or nasal allergies have more nosebleeds than healthy people because the lining of the nose is irritated and they blow their noses frequently.

Because most colds occur in winter, nosebleeds often occur then. Vigorous exercise in hot weather can also bring on nosebleeds in children without colds, however. Repeated nosebleeds in one child are not uncommon.

First Aid and Treatment

Encourage the child to sit with the upper body tilted forward so that the blood does not run down the throat and be swallowed. Swallowed blood can cause vomiting. For comfort, the forehead can rest against the wall. Apply firm pressure near the tip of the nose, pinching the end of the nose. Children who are old enough can apply pressure with their thumb and index finger to stop the bleeding. If the blood is coming from one side, apply pressure only against that nostril. Most nosebleeds will stop in 5 minutes, but occasionally 15 minutes may be necessary. Allow 15 to 20 minutes of rest after the bleeding stops before resuming activities, and advise the child to use caution or avoid blowing the nose.

Very few children with nosebleeds need referral for medical care; parents need to be notified, however. A referral to the physician is needed when (1) bleeding is noted in or from other parts of the body (bruises, blood in the urine, etc.), (2) bleeding occurs almost daily, and (3) bleeding has not stopped in a reasonable amount of time.

STOMACHACHES

Most children (and adults) have an occasional stomachache. The causes of stomachache are numerous: overeating, gas, constipation, food intolerance, intestinal infections, food poisoning, urinary tract infections, and appendicitis. The condition is often minor, needs no special treatment, and goes away by itself. Anxiety or other emotional distress also causes stomachaches. This does not mean the person is emotionally disturbed; it is simply that person's particular reaction to stress. Common emotional causes of stomachaches at school are academic failure, not liking the teacher or the subject, being harassed by a bully, sibling rivalry, child abuse or other home problems, and school phobia. Although some older children can describe the cause of the stomachache, it is unrealistic to expect it of younger children.

Symptoms and Recommendations for Care

The symptoms and recommendations for treating a stomachache are as follows:

- *Fever.* The presence of fever indicates an organic (as opposed to emotional) cause and is a reason to send the child home. A child with a stomachache and no fever could still have something serious, but it is not as likely.

- *Facial expression.* A child who complains of a stomachache, looks alert, does not seem worried or uncomfortable, or does not "frown" as if in pain usually does not have a serious condition. This child may need to rest in the school clinic and may need reassurance from the caregiver for a while. If no fever is present and the pain is gone in 10 or 15 minutes, the child may return to class. The nurse may suggest that the student comes back later if the pain begins again. Frequent complaints of stomachache with clinic visits or stomachaches that occur at about the same time each day (i.e., at the same time as math class) should be noted and discussed with the parent.

- *Position of comfort.* If the child is just as comfortable sitting in a chair as lying on a cot, it generally indicates a less serious type of stomachache.
- *Vomiting or diarrhea.* If either vomiting or diarrhea is present, the child may have a condition that is contagious and should be sent home. (See the discussion of vomiting and diarrhea below).
- *Progression of pain.* With serious stomachaches, pain is worse in an hour or two; with less serious stomachaches, the pain diminishes within the first hour.

VOMITING

Causes

Almost any illness can cause a child to vomit. One episode of vomiting does not necessarily mean that the child needs to see a doctor or even go home. Vomiting one time can be caused by too much exercise in the hot sun, strong emotional factors (fear, anxiety, etc.), or other causes that soon pass. The nurse should assess facial expression, an important sign, after a 5- to 10-minute wait. Fever, as measured by a thermometer, is probably the most important factor to consider in assessment. When fever is present, or if there is continued or increased discomfort, the child should be sent home.

First Aid

If no other significant signs or symptoms are present and the child has vomited only once, allow a brief rest in the clinic; take the child's temperature, reevaluate the child's condition in 10 to 20 minutes, and decide whether the child should return to class or if the child's parents should be called. If the decision is to return to class, send a note to the teacher explaining the situation and suggest that the child return to the clinic if vomiting resumes.

DIARRHEA

Symptoms

School-aged children who develop diarrhea often have a specific intestinal disease. Diarrhea is also caused by a virus, diet, gastrointestinal infections, certain drugs, or emotional turmoil. Although approximately half of the children with mild diarrhea have a low-grade fever and are ill for 2 or 3 days, many bouts of diarrhea are minor and last less than 24 hours. Treatment is not usually necessary, but the child's diet and activity should be limited.

Children with mild diarrhea may not have fever. Those with severe diarrhea usually do and are likely to have a stomachache from intestinal cramping. The stomachache will be most severe before bowel movements. After a bowel movement, the pain will diminish for a while. It is rare for children with diarrhea to have only one loose stool.

The contagiousness of any case of diarrhea depends on the cause, but most cases are contagious. School caregivers should take all appropriate precautions.

First Aid and Treatment

Light foods in small quantities are acceptable; do not urge a child with diarrhea to eat. To prevent dehydration and to maintain the flow of urine, liquids are important and are given at frequent intervals. Most cases of diarrhea in children are mild and will not need treatment. Refer severe cases with fever and cramps to a physician.

FOOD POISONING

Symptoms

If in the school clinic several students are seen at about the same time due to nausea, vomiting, diarrhea, or any combination of these symptoms and if they have eaten at the same location, food poisoning (bacterial contamination) should be considered a cause. Symptoms of food poisoning occur within 24 hours after ingesting contaminated food.

The school medical consultant or the city or county health department can advise if there is an epidemic of gastrointestinal disease in the community or in other schools.

Questions to Ask the Student

To help determine the cause and treatment of the condition, students showing signs of food poisoning should be asked the following questions:

- What was eaten?
- How soon after eating did the symptoms occur?
- Did the food eaten appear, smell, or taste unusual?

- Did anyone else who ate the same food become ill?
- Did vomiting or diarrhea occur?

A student should also be evaluated for fever. All information should be recorded on the referral to the physician.

POISON INGESTION AND DRUG OVERDOSES

Symptoms

A child or adult who swallows poison or takes an overdose of medication needs immediate attention. Signs and symptoms of an overdose or poison injection include nausea, vomiting, diarrhea, abnormal breathing and pulse, unusual breath or body odor, burns around the mouth, changes in the color of the skin, drowsiness, unconsciousness, and convulsions.

First Aid

The student's airway, breathing, and circulation (follow the emergency action principles of cardiopulmonary resuscitation) should be checked immediately and monitored frequently. Call the poison control center for advice and follow their instructions.

Poison Control Center

Throughout the United States, poison control centers provide a 24-hour phone line to answer questions and help people deal with poisoning. The staff of these centers have access to information about most poisonous substances and can advise on how to manage the person who has ingested poison. The telephone number of the nearest center should be posted in each school clinic and office.

When providing specific directions for management of a particular situation, the poison control center may say to give the child syrup of ipecac to induce vomiting or may say that vomiting should not be induced (as with kerosene ingestion). Because vomiting empties only about half of the stomach's contents the center may advise the use of activated charcoal to further neutralize the unvomited poison. Both syrup of ipecac and activated charcoal may be purchased from a drugstore. School personnel need a protocol (physician's order) before using syrup of ipecac. The protocol and both these products should be readily available in every school for use in an emergency.

APPENDICITIS

When a child with a stomachache is seen in the clinic, school personnel are frequently concerned about the possibility of appendicitis. If left untreated, appendicitis can progress rapidly, leading to rupture and *peritonitis* (infection of the entire abdominal cavity). This is an extremely serious condition and is often fatal. Although the school nurse or other school employee are not encouraged to take the responsibility for making such a diagnosis, certain symptoms should make a caretaker suspicious and warrant prompt medical referral.

Symptoms and Recommendations for Care

The symptoms of appendicitis and recommended care are as follows:

- *Fever.* Early in the course of appendicitis, the fever is low, usually 99.6 to 101°F. It is impossible to determine the temperature accurately by feeling a child's forehead; therefore, it is very important to use a thermometer.
- *Location and progression of pain.* The pain characteristically begins in the pit of the stomach—in the center and just below the ribs—and as it increases in severity, it gradually moves to the lower right, halfway between the navel and the groin. The pain progressively gets worse. The rate of progression varies; the younger the child, the faster the pain moves. In general, in a child 6 to 11 years old, the pain moves to the lower right quadrant of the abdomen in 2 to 6 hours. In a 3-year-old child, progress is often faster.
- *Facial expression.* A child with appendicitis looks uncomfortable and will not be smiling.
- *Position of comfort.* In appendicitis, the child prefers to lie down, most often on the left side with the right leg drawn up.
- *Other findings.* Nausea, vomiting, constipation, loss of appetite, and abdominal tenderness may also be present. If appendicitis is suspected, call the parent and advise that the child be taken to a doctor immediately.

MENSTRUAL PROBLEMS

In women, the monthly vaginal blood flow, menstruation, is due to shedding of the lining of the uterus (womb). Each month, after the flow ends, the lining begins to build up again. Then, after an average of 28 to 30 days, in response to hormonal stimulation, the process repeats.

The average age for menarche (start of menstruation) is 12; the normal variation is 10 to 16 years old. Exercise, diet, and stress can delay menarche.

Medical problems associated with menstruation are pain, excessive bleeding, and unexpected bleeding.

Symptoms

Excessive menstrual pain (dysmenorrhea) is common in school-aged girls. It begins 1 to 3 years after menarche (onset of menstruation) and, in most cases, disappears after the birth of a child. The pain can be severe and can be accompanied by vomiting, headache, and backache. Without treatment, the student may miss a day or two of school each month.

Excessive bleeding means bleeding either more frequently than once a month or bleeding once a month but excessively.

With normal menstruation, bleeding does not occur more often than 21 days from the first day of one period to the first day of the next, the bleeding does not last more than 6 days, and not more than 6 well-soaked pads are necessary in a 24-hour period.

Unexpected bleeding can be caused by unanticipated menarche or by the early onset of a period in a previously menstruating girl.

Premenstrual Syndrome

About one third of all women have premenstrual syndrome (PMS), beginning anywhere from the middle cycle to a few days before menstruation. Symptoms vary greatly and may include breast swelling and tenderness, fluid retention, increased thirst or appetite, craving for sweets, headaches, anxiety, restlessness, irritability, depression, hostility, and loss of self confidence. Prevalence increases with age, peaking in the 30s and 40s.

Treatment

Allow the student to rest in the school clinic for a brief period. Safe prescription and OTC medications may be prescribed by a physician for prevention or control of pain. *(Follow the state nurse practice act and school policy regarding medication administration at school.)* If pain is severe, send the student home and recommend physician consultation. Suggest that the student keep a calendar to anticipate the time of her next menstrual period. This is an opportunity to establish rapport, which will make the school nurse a primary resource for future questions relating to menstruation or other developmental concerns. Do not assume that the student knows what is happening to her, how to use sanitary napkins or tampons, or how to keep a calendar. (See the resources for educational information in Health Education Tips later in this section.)

HEADACHES

Headache is a common symptom of organic disease and of emotional anxiety. For students with headaches, a school caregiver must assess many of the same factors seen in children with stomachaches. Fever and facial expression are of equal importance. An active, afebrile (fever free) child who appears to be alert and interested in what is happening in the clinic does not, in most instances, have a serious headache.

Symptoms

Important warning signs of headaches are dizziness, blurred vision, fainting, fever, drowsiness, nausea, or vomiting for an hour or more. If one or more of these symptoms is present, send the child home with suggestions to the parent to monitor further symptoms, or refer the student to a physician for diagnosis and treatment.

A brief rest in the clinic may be all that is necessary for complete resolution of the headache. A small amount of food, especially if the child has missed breakfast, may help. Asking the child what caused the headache is often informative and helpful to the caregiver. The answer given may provide sufficient information to determine whether the child returns to class or is referred to a physician.

Students who are frequently seen in the clinic due to headache or who miss school and complain of excessive pain need a medical evaluation. Medication should be given only when prescribed by a physician. There are multiple causes of headaches, and many indicate serious disease. Treating the symptom without trying to identify the cause may delay diagnosing the condition. Keeping a record or, with an older student, suggesting that he or she keep a diary of information regarding recurrent headaches (see Figure 2-2) may help the parent or physician and may assist in the referral process and in identifying the cause of the headache.

CARDIOPULMONARY RESUSCITATION (CPR)

Personnel Training

The goal of cardiopulmonary resuscitation (CPR) is to provide oxygen quickly to the brain, heart, and other organs of the body until medical treatment can restore nor-

HEADACHE DIARY

for _____
        (Student's Name)

Instructions: Following a headache, answer questions to help describe your headache. Return this form to me in two weeks.

Nurse's name

Date of headache					
Time started					
Time ended					
Activity engaged in when pain started					
Signs/symptoms: Eyes hurt; sleepy; saw flashes of light; other changes of sight, smell, hearing; nausea; stuffy/runny nose; earache; other					
Severity: Rate on a scale of 1 to 10 with 10 as most severe					
Describe pain: Dull, throbbing, pounding, stabbing, constant, other					
Location: All over head, face, or jaw; over one eye or both eyes; front of head; side(s) of head; lower or upper back; back of head; back of neck; other					
Care/treatment: Bed rest, sleep, food, name of medicine (if used)					
Cause (personal assessment of what triggered or caused the pain)					
Medication taken on day of headache for another condition (i.e., infection, colds, allergy, asthma, menstruation, birth control)					
Other comments regarding the headache					

Figure 2-2. Headache diary.

mal heart and lung function. Many school health programs recommend, and some require, CPR training for school nurses, nurse assistants, secretaries, cafeteria managers, teachers, coaches, athletic trainers, and principals. The American Heart Association and the American Red Cross have taken the lead in establishing structured CPR training courses throughout the United States. Although detailed instruction is available in reference books and pamphlets, the training courses leading to certification or recertification and the practice on a mannequin are necessary for nurses and other school health caregivers.

Resuscitation Methods

Heimlich Maneuver (Abdominal Thrust)

Children (and adults) may choke on popcorn, peanuts, a piece of meat or other food, or any object partially or completely blocking an airway. The person may grasp the front of the throat, be unable to speak, and become pale or cyanotic. If coughing is not present, the airway must be opened quickly. A series of quick, hard thrusts to the abdomen will often accomplish this. These abdominal thrusts (Heimlich maneuver) are given with both fists while grasping the victim from behind. Chest thrusts may be used for a pregnant woman or a person who is too large for the rescuer to reach around and give abdominal thrusts.

Finger Sweep

The finger sweep is used on adults after the abdominal thrusts to remove an object in the mouth when air does not appear to be moving. Lift the lower jaw and tongue with finger and thumb; slide a finger down the throat, and attempt to hook the object and bring it out. Care must be given to prevent pushing the object farther down. Thrusts and finger sweeps may need to be repeated.

For infants under 1 year of age, use the heel of the hand and give back blows between the shoulder blades; the infant should be held face down on the forearm, with the infant's face in the palm of the hand.

Rescue Breathing

Choking, electric shock, asthma, anxiety, and reactions to certain poisons, drugs, insect stings, or food, as well as other illnesses or injuries, can cause the absence of spontaneous respirations while the heart is still beating. Mouth-to-mouth resuscitation should be attempted if the person is making no effort to breathe. Blow air into the individual's mouth or nose slowly. Each breath must make the chest rise gently to provide oxygen to sustain life until paramedics arrive.

Chest Compression

When no pulse can be felt in the neck (carotid artery), upper arm (brachial artery), or wrist (radial artery), intermittent chest compression will keep the blood circulating enough to keep body cells alive until the heart resumes a spontaneous beat. Rescue breathing and chest compressions, given together, take the place of heart and lung action. A person has a better chance of surviving cardiac arrest if CPR is started immediately and emergency medical system service personnel follow up rapidly with more sophisticated techniques.

Precautions

The following procedures should be followed when CPR may be needed:

- An immediate call for emergency medical service may be the most important part of saving a life.
- A person who is coughing should be allowed to cough up whatever is causing the cough. The first aiders will not need to help as long as the coughing continues.
- If a pulse is felt, chest compressions do not need to be attempted.
- In some way, the methods of resuscitation are different on adults, children, and infants. The person(s) responsible for providing this service in schools needs to know CPR for each age group represented in the school.
- This information does not replace first aid protocols recommended by the local district, and the material in this book or other books is not a substitute for formal CPR training with mannequin practice. Training and certification should be repeated at intervals, usually each year.

HYPERVENTILATION

Symptoms

Hyperventilation is rapid deep breathing that lowers the level of carbon dioxide in the blood. It may be accompanied by dizziness, chest pain, tingling sensations to the skin, and fainting. The condition is sometimes seen in asthma and certain emotional disorders (anxiety).

First Aid and Treatment

The immediate treatment for the condition is aimed at returning the carbon dioxide level in the blood to normal. This may be accomplished by keeping the child calm and by encouraging slow breathing. Breathing into hands cupped around the mouth and nose, breathing into a paper bag, or breathing through one nostril with the mouth closed may be helpful. If these efforts fail, medical help should be obtained.

FOREIGN BODIES: EYE, EAR, AND NOSE

Eye

An eyelash, piece of sawdust, or another foreign object in the eye will cause sudden discomfort, irritation, and excessive tearing. Chemicals or other liquid irritants can cause lasting damage and need immediate special treatment. (Cuts or bruises of the eye are discussed in Section 7.)

First Aid

If the object is under the lid, the lid can be pulled away from the eyeball (see Figures 2-3 and 2-4). This may loosen the foreign body and allow tears to wash it away. If the object is easy to see on the lid (not on the eyeball), it can be safely removed with a cotton-tipped applicator. In all other circumstances, the student should be encouraged to blink frequently and not to rub the eye. If the foreign body is not gone in a few minutes, an eye specialist should be consulted. If the child is sent to an eye specialist, the affected eye should be covered with a 2-inch by 2-inch gauze flat held in place with criss-crossed adhesive strips.

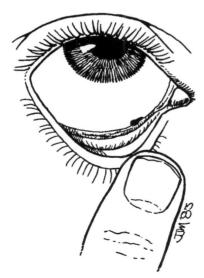

Figure 2-3. Foreign body in the lower eyelid.

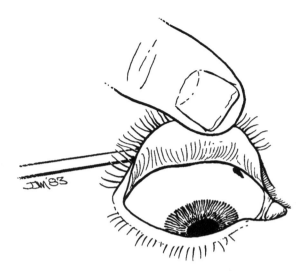

Figure 2-4. Foreign body in upper lid. (Lid is rolled back over a cotton swab.)

Immediately wash acid or alkaline solutions in the eye with copious amounts of plain tap water. Unless special neutralizing solutions are immediately available, it is a waste of time to search for them. Use a large volume of water. Ideally, have the child lie down; then hold the eyelid open to allow a gentle stream of cool water (about 1/4 to 1/2 inch in diameter) to run into the eye at the inner corner and out of the eye at the outer corner. Another way of flushing the eye with water is to have the child stand at the water drinking fountain; then gently turn the water on. Have the child's face (eye) in the stream of water when the water is turned on. The constant flow of water will wash the chemical from the eye. Tilt the head so that the water runs to the outer corner. Cleansing with water should continue for 15 minutes. In any emergency of this nature, never be concerned about a wet bed, floor, or clothing. Continue flushing the eye without interruption. A phone call to an eye specialist will help determine how long to continue irrigation before taking the student to a physician.

Ear

Children often push erasers, paper wads, beans, or other objects into their ears (see Figure 2-5). Because these objects usually cause no pain, a child may not mention it to parents or other adults. Objects in ears are often discovered during a routine checkup when the ear is examined with an otoscope.

Occasionally, an insect will fly into the ear. While the insect is alive, the buzzing and movement cause intense discomfort. Some schools have a protocol to follow in this event; others refer the student for further medical follow-up. Do not use mineral oil to dislodge the insect; it causes the insect to swell and makes it difficult to remove later.

Foreign objects in the ear are quite hard to get out. Nurses or other school personnel are not encouraged to remove any foreign object from the ear unless the object can be easily grasped with the fingers or forceps. Without the proper equipment, special technique, and good lighting, the object will be pushed farther into the ear and will become even more difficult to remove.

Foreign bodies in the ear are not usually emergency conditions, but for removal of the object, refer the student to a physician.

Nose

Children push the same kinds of objects into their noses as they do into their ears (see Figure 2-6). There is no pain, and often the child does not tell parents or school personnel. Because the nose is always moist, however, infection ensues and causes a foul-smelling nasal discharge from only one nostril. (Nasal discharge from a common cold, sinus, or allergy is seen on both sides and is rarely associated with an odor.)

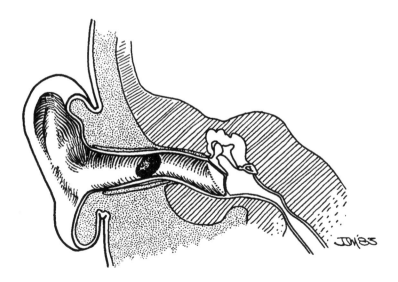

Figure 2-5. Foreign body in the ear.

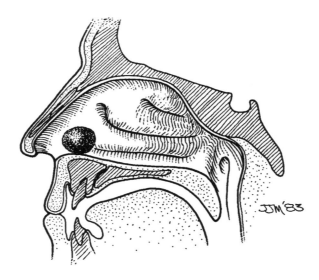

Figure 2-6. Foreign body in the nose.

The same warnings for foreign bodies in the ear also apply to foreign bodies in the nose. When a student does report a foreign body in the nose, attempts to remove it will usually push it in deeper. School personnel should attempt to remove the object only when the object is protruding and can be removed easily. This is not usually an emergency condition, but for removal of the object, refer the child to a physician.

HEAT-RELATED ILLNESSES

There are four types of adverse physical reactions to excess heat: heat syncope, heat cramps, heat exhaustion, and heat stroke. The higher the humidity, the more dangerous high air temperature is because of decreased evaporation of body sweat. Exercise causes increased sweating and body metabolism, which leads to greater loss of body water and electrolytes (sodium, potassium, etc.). If these losses are severe, the effect may be a fatal heat stroke. Although excessive heat and humidity are often the cause of heat-related illnesses, these conditions can occur indoors and in climates that are not excessively hot.

Adverse Physical Reactions to Excess Heat: Symptoms

The following are symptoms of adverse reactions to excess heat:

1. *Heat syncope.* Heat syncope is simple fainting or near fainting caused by mild to moderate overheating. It begins with dizziness, usually while the student is standing or running. The blood pressure falls, and the body temperature rises to 103°–105°F. The skin is usually moist.

2. *Heat cramps.* Cramps, or spasms of active muscles, usually occur during intense, prolonged exercise in hot weather. Heat cramps are associated with low body sodium. There is no loss of consciousness, and the body temperature is normal or only slightly elevated.

3. *Heat exhaustion.* Early symptoms of heat exhaustion are dizziness, weakness, fatigue, headache, disorientation, nausea, and vomiting. The student may become irrational and belligerent. The body temperature is high, and muscle cramps are often present. The skin is flushed and usually moist, but in extreme cases it can be dry. If the symptoms continue, partial or complete unconsciousness may ensue and lead to heat stroke.

4. *Heat stroke.* Heat stroke is a life-threatening emergency. The child or adult will have extremely high fever (106°–108°F), disorientation, twitching, seizures, and coma. The skin is hot and dry.

Heat-related illnesses are not usually seen as clearly separate entities; they represent a continuum or progression, especially if proper treatment is delayed. For example, when there may be clinical doubt about heat exhaustion versus impending heat stroke, always assume the worst and provide care accordingly.

First Aid and Treatment

Heat syncope, heat cramps, and heat exhaustion are all treated by having the student rest, by placing the student in a cool area, by having the student replace water by drinking, and by cooling the skin with cool water, a fan, or both. Loosen or remove the student's heavy clothing and delay exercise. This treatment is usually sufficient.

More severe symptoms such as irrationality or partial loss of consciousness require evaluation by a physician. In heat stroke, fluids can rarely be swallowed. Rapid evacuation to a medical emergency room is mandatory, and, at the same time, the skin should be cooled with water, ice, a fan, or a combination of these treatments. If available, oxygen should be given.

Prevention

All heat-related illness is preventable if proper precautionary measures are taken.

- Exercise preconditioning, heat acclimatization, and water replacement are the most important factors in avoiding heat-related illnesses.
- Wear lightweight, loose, cool clothing.
- Provide cool water. Sometimes athletes require extra water intake.
- Salt and calcium tablets are of no benefit; if a person drinks enough water, the body automatically conserves salt and calcium.
- Commercial electrolyte solutions are not harmful and may be used if desired, but they are no more effective than water.
- People who perspire a lot should salt their food more liberally.
- Conditions predisposing a person to heat illness are cystic fibrosis, vomiting or diarrhea, fever from any cause (even an immunization), obesity, voluntary water restriction, poor acclimatization, and prior heat-related illness.

Athletic trainers are knowledgeable in preventing and treating heat-related conditions in athletes. In addition, it is beneficial that school administrators and all school health caregivers support these additional measures:

1. Schedule rest periods for athletes.
2. Provide accurate scales for weighing. Athletes who lose more than 3% of their body weight (about 5–7 pounds for a 200-pound athlete) because of sweat loss during a practice session are at special risk.
3. Caution all personnel about the dangers of voluntary water deprivation to produce weight loss, especially in athletes.

SCHOOL RELEVANCE

Specific guidelines or protocols for the caregiver are essential for dealing with students and staff emergencies. Emergency information cards for each child in the school should include the following: telephone numbers where parents/guardians may be reached during the day, other persons in the community designated by the parents to be called if parents cannot be located, the name and telephone number of a local physician preferred by the parents, local hospital preference, and the student's medical problems or drug allergies (see Figure 2-7). These forms should be completed by the parent at the beginning of the school year and should be updated when any change occurs. The information in this book or other textbooks does not supplant that information.

STUDENT EMERGENCY CARD (S-12)

This form is to be completed by the parent each year. The school principal is responsible for establishing a procedure for obtaining and maintaining the information. Cards are usually kept in the clinic. Cards are alphabetized by name or grade section.

Figure 2-7. School emergency card.

If an illness or injury requires emergency transportation, a nurse or another designated school employee should accompany the student to the hospital and remain with the student until the parent/guardian arrives. Providing the student's emergency card to the person in charge of the emergency room will assist in obtaining care in the parents' absence. If a private car is used to transport the child, designate two adults to go to the emergency room: one person to drive and the other to attend to the student.

Post the ambulance, police, fire departments, and poison control center phone numbers in the clinic and principal's office, and review this list for accuracy frequently.

ROLE OF THE SCHOOL NURSE

Knowing basic health care principles alleviate a caregiver's anxieties and increase the confidence of the ill child or adult. Because the school nurse frequently is responsible for health care in more than one school, an important task is to plan and to teach others, usually nonmedical persons, in each site to recognize signs and symptoms of illness and to give immediate and temporary care when necessary.

Provide persons assisting in the clinic a way to identify students with known medical problems quickly, such as with an acute problem notebook maintained by the school nurse that lists each student's name and any health problems. Include basic information about any special care or emergencies as well as procedures for providing basic first aid, sending ill or injured students home, referring a student for medical treatment, and notifying parents. Keep a first aid manual and the school district's policies and procedures readily available in the clinic.

Prior to the beginning of school each year, identify persons who can assist with health care, such as nurse aides, nurse assistants, school secretaries, faculty members, or others designated by the principal. The nurse should work closely with these persons to ensure their understanding of the school district's policy and procedures for health care.

The American Red Cross offers a community first aid and safety course that presents information in a video series and requires active participation in learning activities designed to increase knowledge and skills in CPR and first aid. To ensure appropriate action in an emergency or to prevent further problems with illness or injuries, nonmedical persons designated to assist with health care in the nurse's absence may be required to take this or a similar basic first aid course In addition, these persons will need to know the following:

- Specific protocols or instructions for giving medications
- Location of information regarding special medical instructions for students with known health problems
- School policy regarding sending students home
- Universal precautions (hand washing, gloving, proper disposal of contaminated waste, etc.)

HEALTH EDUCATION TIPS

There are numerous types of acute illnesses, and they often have similar signs or symptoms. The child "looks" ill, may complain of dizziness or weakness, or may be confused. The skin color may be pale or flushed, the eyes may look shiny or red, or the cheeks may be rosy or show a rash. In a number of acute illnesses, it is not unusual to have nausea, vomiting, diarrhea, a headache, or difficulty breathing. The illnesses may be mild or severe and may or may not be contagious. Nurses and other adult caregivers can help children learn when self-care is appropriate and when seeking expert medical care is necessary.

In contacts with ill and injured students, the school nurse or caregiver can assist the child to express the signs and symptoms of his or her condition and to use correct terms to describe body parts. Adults often need help with this also.

Very young children recognize when they need help and how to obtain it. A child can learn his or her complete name, address, and when to use an emergency access system, such as 911 or the system available in the community.

Free or low-cost resource materials on menstruation and growth and development to use with individual students or groups may be obtained from numerous companies. To ask for a sample of free materials or a list of materials available, (use school letterhead stationery) and write directly to the company. Some resources are:

American Academy of Pediatrics
Division of Publications
141 Northwest Point Blvd.
P.O. Box 927
Elk Grove Village, IL 60009-0927

Pamprin Educational Program
Chattem Inc.
1715 W. 38th St.
Chattanooga, TN 37409

Personal Products
P.O. Box 529
Gibbstown, NJ 08027-9901

Free copies of excellent illustrations of common rashes (measles, rubella, etc.)
are available on request from:

Merck Sharp & Dohme
West Point, PA
215-652-5000

REFERENCES

American National Red Cross. *Community First Aid and Safety*. St. Louis: Mosby Lifeline,
1993.

Benenson, A. S. *Control of Communicable Diseases in Man*, 15th ed. Washington, D.C.:
American Public Health Association, 1990.

Committee on School Health. *School Health: Policy and Practice*, 5th ed. Elk Grove Village, Ill.:
American Academy of Pediatrics, 1993.

Engel, Joyce. *Pocket Guide to Pediatric Assessment*, 2nd ed. St. Louis: Mosby-Year Book, 1993.

Haas, M. K., ed. *The School Nurse's Source Book of Individualized Health Care Plans*. North
Branch, Minn.: Sunrise River Press, 1993.

Hay, W. W., Jr., et al., eds. *Current Pediatric Diagnosis and Treatment*, 12th ed. Norwalk, Conn.:
Appleton and Lange, 1995.

Lewis, K. D., and H. B. Thomas. *Manual of School Health*. Menlo Park, Calif.: Addison-Wesley,
1986.

Suddarth, D. S. *The Lippincott Manual of Nursing Practice*. Philadelphia: J. B. Lippincott, 1991.

Thomas, C. L., ed. *Taber's Cyclopedic Medical Dictionary*. Philadelphia: F. A. Davis, 1993.

INJURIES

Time heals all wounds.

Ancient proverb

Time wounds all heels.

Modern proverb

INJURIES TO INTERNAL ORGANS

Stab: Penetrating Injury

Stab wounds of the chest or abdomen are rare at most schools. The diagnosis is obvious, and there is never any doubt about what to do: immediate evacuation to the nearest hospital emergency room. If there is sufficient time, a large, padded compression bandage may be applied, but not if it causes a delay in transferring the student to the hospital. With the rise in violence in our schools, many campuses now routinely stock 2 or 3 of these compression bandages in the nurse's clinic.

The parents should be notified after evacuation arrangements are made. If there is reason to suspect that an ambulance will take more than a few minutes, the school principal should take the initiative and have school personnel transport the student to the hospital immediately.

Blow: Blunt Injury

Nature of the Condition

An injury to an internal organ from a nonpenetrating blow with a blunt object such as a rock, fist, or baseball bat is called a blunt injury (see Figure 3-1). There will be a bruise, large or small, on the chest or abdomen where the child was struck, but the seriousness lies in the damage to the internal organs: the abdominal organs, heart, or lungs.

Abdomen   A severe blow to the front of the abdomen can cause rupture or bleeding of the liver, spleen, stomach, or urinary bladder. A blow to the back may cause rupture of the kidneys. The initial blow causes severe pain and often knocks the wind out of the recipient of the blow. The initial symptoms, however, may go away after a relatively short time (less than an hour in most cases). If there is no internal organ damage, no further symptoms will appear.

Rupture of an internal organ, however, can be serious and may be missed if not suspected and watched for. The primary problem caused by a ruptured spleen or liver is bleeding into the abdominal cavity, causing the student to go into a state of shock and die unless an operation is performed to tie off the bleeding blood vessels.

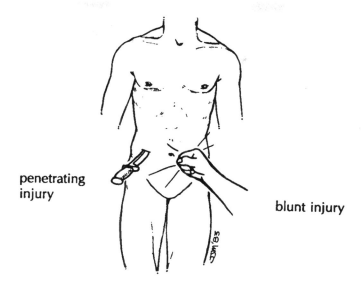

Figure 3-1. Penetrating and blunt injuries.

If the stomach or urinary bladder is ruptured, the problem is aggravated by toxic material escaping into the abdominal cavity and causing peritonitis. This is apt to cause marked abdominal pain sooner than if blood alone is present.

Symptoms of Blunt Injury to an Abdominal Organ The symptoms of a blunt injury include the following:

- History of blow to the abdomen.
- Apparent recovery in a relatively short time
- Gradual onset, 2 to 6 hours later, of symptoms of shock: weakness, dizziness, sweating, rapid weak pulse and respiration, gradual loss of consciousness, dilated pupils of the eye, and deepening unconsciousness leading to coma and death.

Chest The lungs or the heart may be damaged by a severe blow to the chest. The period between the injury and the onset of symptoms is usually less than 10 minutes. The cause of the symptoms is usually the same as in abdominal organ injury: bleeding. In the chest, the excess blood compresses the lung, heart, or both, thus impeding their function. If the blow is severe enough, the lung may actually be torn by a fractured rib; the escape of air from the torn lung then adds to the difficulty. In this case, the wound resembles a penetrating injury.

Symptoms of Blunt Injury to the Chest (Lung or Heart)   The symptoms of a blunt injury include the following:

- Rapid respiration
- Apprehension and fright from not being able to catch breath
- Blueness around the lips
- Rapid pulse
- Gradual loss of consciousness in severe cases

Nonbleeding Cardiac Injury   Recently, there have been numerous reports of a blow over the heart causing death soon after the injury. At autopsy, there is no free blood compressing the heart or any other obviously visible cause of death. Many of the cases reported have occurred in children after being hit by a fast-pitch baseball or after a blow from a bicycle handlebar.

It is thought that the sudden blow over the heart causes a cardiac arrhythmia that leads to cessation of the heartbeat. If no resuscitative measures are taken, sudden, or near-sudden, death soon follows.

Treatment   Treatment of nonbleeding cardiac injuries includes the following:

1. Observe the student in the clinic for 20 to 30 minutes.
2. Place the student in a position of comfort.
3. If no further symptoms appear, allow the student to go to class.
4. Check with the student's teacher in 1 to 2 hours.
5. A ruptured stomach or bladder will usually result from a very severe blow, and the pain will be so severe that the child obviously needs immediate medical attention by a physician.

Injuries to internal organs (see Figure 3-2) result from blows of more-than-average severity. Suspicious observation is necessary to become aware of such a possibility. Delays in diagnosis occur when the student fails to report the accident or if the possibility is not considered at all.

EYE INJURIES

An eye can be injured in many ways: by a blow, a cut, a penetrating injury, or a burn. The student will hold the hand over the eye and will usually cry and complain of pain or will rub the eye excessively. Tape a four-by-four-inch gauze flat over both eyes, and send the student to an eye specialist immediately.

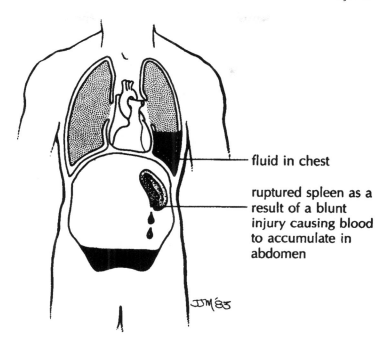

fluid in chest

ruptured spleen as a result of a blunt injury causing blood to accumulate in abdomen

Figure 3-2. Fluid or blood in chest or abdomen.

Two types of eye injury are serious but may escape detection by the school nurse or teacher unless suspected:

1. A blunt blow to the eyeball, such as with a baseball or smooth, round rock, may cause an injury to the cornea and anterior chamber (front part of the eyeball). The pain subsides after a relatively short time, but the cornea may be damaged and a small amount of blood may collect in the anterior chamber (see Figure 3-3). If a significant corneal injury is present, vision will be blurred. The only sure way to detect such an injury is to test the student's visual acuity, preferably on the Snellen test chart. If the test chart is not available, the student should read aloud the letters in a book, one eye at a time. Vision should be equal in both eyes. If vision in the injured eye is poor or blurred, the student should be referred to an eye specialist immediately.

2. A penetrating injury of the eyeball can be caused by a wire or nail. The only thing visible on the outside may be a tiny cut on the upper or lower lid, and a stoic student may not complain very much. If there is any suspicion that penetration could have occurred, immediately refer the student to a doctor.

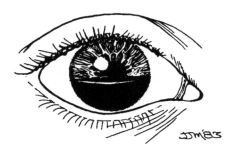

Figure 3-3. Blood (or other fluid) in anterior chamber of the eye.

HEAD INJURIES

Nature of the Condition

Head injuries can be classified as bruises of the scalp, skull fractures, and damage to the brain itself. An objective scale, the Glasgow coma scale (see Figure 3-4), can help the school nurse evaluate the severity of any head injury.

Scalp

A bruise of the scalp is caused by a light blow that usually causes no skull fracture, brain damage, or loss of consciousness. A characteristic and mildly painful *hematoma* ("goose egg" or "pump knot") is seen (see Figure 3-5). Ice is the best treatment; pressure is not necessary. If there is no concussion or loss of consciousness, no further treatment is necessary. The swelling usually lasts several days.

Skull Fracture

Skull fractures are of two principal varieties: linear and depressed. On an X ray, *Linear fractures* look like a cracked eggshell, with both edges occupying about the same level as before the fracture (see Figure 3-6). They are caused by a relatively mild blow to the head. The blow causes pain, but the fracture itself heals with no special treatment. In a depressed skull fracture (see Figure 3-7), such as might occur if someone were hit on the head with a hammer, a fragment of the bone is pressing down on the brain. A depressed skull fracture is serious and requires urgent treatment.

GLASGOW COMA SCALE

This practical method of assessing changes in level of consciousness is based on eye opening, verbal, and motor responses. The response may be expressed by the sum of the scores assigned to each response. The lowest score (bad) is 3, and the highest score (perfect) is 15.

	Examiner's Test	Patient's Response	Assigned Score
Eye opening	Spontaneous	Open eyes on own	4
	Speech	Says yes when asked to do so in a loud voice	3
	Pain	Opens eyes when pinched	2
	Pain	Does not open eyes	1
Best motor response	Commands	Follows simple commands	6
	Pain	Pulls examiner's hand away when pinched	5
	Pain	Pulls a part of body away when pinched	4
	Pain	Flexes body inappropriately to pain (decorticate posturing)	3
	Pain	Body becomes rigid in an extended position when pinched (decerebrate posturing)	2
	Pain	Has no motor response to pinch	1
Verbal response (talking)	Speech	Carries on a conversation correctly and tells the examiner where and who he or she is and the month and year	5
	Speech	Seems confused or disoriented	4
	Speech	Talks so that the examiner can understand words but makes no sense	3
	Speech	Makes a sound the examiner cannot understand	2
	Speech	Makes no noise	1

Figure 3-4. Glasgow coma scale.

Brain Damage

Damage to the brain itself is classified as follows:

1. Laceration. A laceration is an actual cut or crushing injury and is always accompanied by a skull fracture.

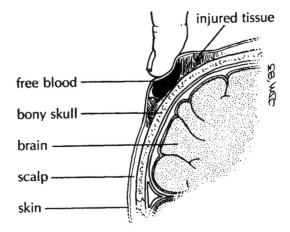

Figure 3-5. Hematoma of the scalp. The free blood under the skin feels soft and mushy. The injured tissue is swollen and hard, and a ridge can be felt (indicated by finger). This is often mistaken for a depressed skull fracture.

2. Contusion. With a contusion, a rupture of small blood vessels inside the brain occurs. The leakage of blood destroys the surrounding brain tissue. A contusion is usually accompanied by a skull fracture.

   Both contusions and lacerations result from severe head injury, are accompanied by loss of consciousness, and are never treated at school. Both injuries require immediate evacuation to the nearest hospital emergency room.

3. Concussion. Of the three types of brain injury, a concussion is the least severe. When a football player or a boxer "sees stars" or "has his bell rung," he has suffered a concussion. A concussion can be mild, requiring only a short rest period, or it can be severe, requiring 1 to 2 days of bed rest. If one were able to look at the brain after a mild concussion, it would appear normal. The symptoms are caused by a shock wave passing through the brain and temporarily disrupting the normal nerve pathways. If the concussion is severe enough, small pinpoint hemorrhages can be seen on microscopic examination.

Symptoms of a Concussion

Severe Concussion

Loss of consciousness is the most important of all symptoms of concussion and must be assessed very carefully. A student who is deeply unconscious and cannot be

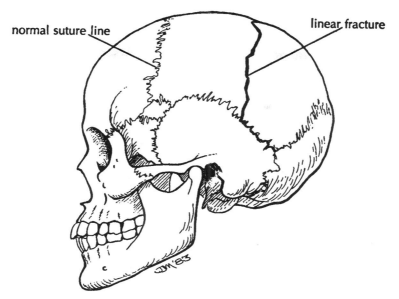

Figure 3-6. Linear skull fracture.

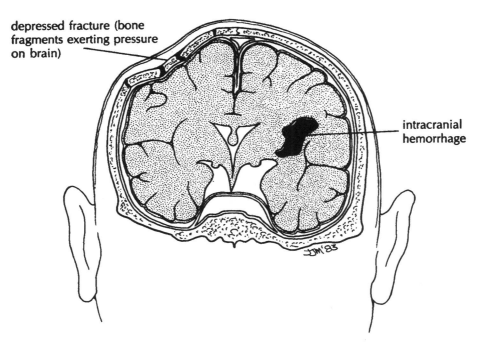

Figure 3-7. Depressed skull fracture with intracranial hemorrhage.

awakened has suffered a severe concussion. The more dilated the pupils, the more severe the concussion. Unequal pupils also have a serious import. At first, the pulse and respiration may be rapid, but with deepening unconsciousness they will become slower. Vomiting always indicates a more severe concussion. Upon awakening, there can also be a loss of memory for recent events (retrograde amnesia). Many children also suffer an anterograde amnesia, or a loss of memory of events occurring shortly after the concussion. Such memory losses must be specifically inquired about or can be missed.

Mild Concussion

With a mild concussion, a brief period of dizziness, disorientation, or both occurs. There is a quick return to normality, and the student may not remember what happened.

Diagnosis

A scalp bruise is diagnosed by inspection, but a skull fracture can only be diagnosed by X ray. Brain contusion and lacerations follow severe head injury, and students with such injuries should always be evacuated to a hospital for diagnosis. Following any blow to the head that causes momentary confusion, dizziness, or temporary unconsciousness, a concussion must always be strongly suspected.

Treatment

A concussion is the only important head injury that frequently requires school treatment. The cardinal principal of treatment is to prevent further injury to the head by an absolute prohibition of further physical activity for the rest of the day, or, in more severe concussion, as the doctor orders. It is well known that a second concussion soon after the first often leads to much more serious brain injury. The student should lie quietly for a few minutes with the head slightly elevated and, if it is a mild concussion, then be allowed to sit. If the child remains asymptomatic, he or she may go back to class with a warning to the teacher to be alert of any further problems.

Students with a more severe concussion with a measurable period of unconsciousness should be evaluated by a physician.

Parents should always be notified in all types of concussion.

SCHOOL RELEVANCE

Usually, a mild concussion causes no special problems; the student will rest and be perfectly normal later. There is, however, one notable exception: contact sports, especially football. It is quite common for a high school player to suffer a mild concussion and continue to play, either because the student does not report it to the coach or trainer or because, if reported, it is not regarded with sufficient seriousness and the student is allowed to play again during the same game.

Several organizations, such as the American Medical Association and the American Academy of Pediatrics, have formulated some fairly simple guidelines that all schools should follow:

> One concussion: out of the game
>
> Two concussions: out for the season
>
> Three concussions: out for school career

This would prevent many deaths from head injuries, which occur every year in the United States during school athletic contests.

Protocol and Parent Form

In the even of a head injury, the following procedures should be followed:

1. Classify the injury as mild, moderate, or severe by the following criteria:
   a. State of consciousness (ranging from complete loss to fully alert)
   b. Vomiting
   c. Unequal size of pupils of the eyes
   d. Unusually rapid or slow pulse rate
   e. Use of Glasgow coma scale
2. If any of the above are distinctly abnormal, the student should be referred to a physician or emergency room immediately.
3. If the child is slightly woozy but all other findings are normal, notify the parents that the student should be taken to a doctor.
4. If all findings are normal, have the student rest in the clinic for 15 to 30 minutes, depending on the severity of the head injury and the student's appearance, then allow the student to return to class.
5. Ask the teacher to give you a report on the student's status in 1 hour.
6. Check the student at the end of the school day.
7. Notify the parents by phone and in writing (see Figure 3-8) of what happened and what to watch for. If, while the student was being observed at school, the symptoms were to any degree more than the bare minimum, insist that the parents get follow-up instructions from a physician.

HEAD INJURY PROTOCOL

1. Classify the injury as mild, moderate, or severe by the following criteria:
   a. State of consciousness (ranging from complete loss to fully alert)
   b. Vomiting
   c. Unequal size of pupils of the eyes
   d. Unusually rapid or slow pulse rate
   e. Use of Glasgow Coma Scale
2. If any of the above are distinctly abnormal, the child should be referred to a physician or emergency room immediately.
3. If the child is slightly woozy, but all other finds are normal, notify parents to take child to the doctor.
4. If all findings are normal, have the student rest in the clinic for 15-30 minutes, the length of time depending on the severity of the head injury and appearance of the child, and then allow child to return to class.
5. Ask the teacher to give you a report on the child's status in one hour.
6. Check child at the end of school day.
7. Notify parents by phone and in writing (see following form) of what happened and what to watch for. While the child was being observed at school, if the symptoms were to any degree more than the bare minimum, the school nurse should insist that parents get follow-up instructions from a physician.

Dear Parent:

Today _____ **received an injury to the head. Your child was seen in the clinic and had no problems at that time, but you should watch for any of the following symptoms:**

1. Severe headache
2. Nausea and/or vomiting
3. Double vision, blurred vision, or pupils of different sizes
4. Loss of muscle coordination, such as falling down, walking strangely, or staggering
5. Any unusual behavior such as being confused, breathing irregularly, or dizziness
6. Convulsion
7. Bleeding or discharge from an ear

If child was a little dizzy or foggy, vomited, or showed any of the other above signs, child should be checked carefully at bedtime and awakened at midnight (if bedtime is between 8:00 and 9:00 P.M.) to be sure he/she can be awakened and seems normal.

CONTACT YOUR DOCTOR OR EMERGENCY ROOM IF YOU NOTICE ANY OF THE ABOVE SYMPTOMS

_____   _____
School Nurse   School phone number

Figure 3-8. Form to be given to parents when child has a head injury.

SUBDURAL OR EPIDURAL HEMORRHAGES

Nature of the Condition

On occasion, a blow to the head will cause rupture of a blood vessel between the brain and bony skull without causing any direct damage to the brain tissue or skull fracture (see Figure 3-9). This is serious because blood can collect rapidly and can cause deeper and deeper unconsciousness from continually increasing pressure on the brain.

Symptoms and Diagnosis

All the symptoms listed under concussion may be present in a subdural hematoma. Subdural or epidural bleeding is characterized by a relatively brief period of unconsciousness followed by awakening and seeming normality. Because of continued slow bleeding, however, several hours or days later the student may exhibit unusual behavior or may slowly lapse into unconsciousness again. This second period of unconsciousness has grave implications.

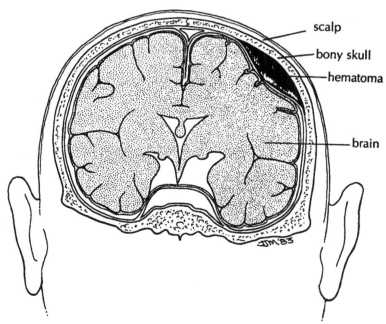

Figure 3-9. Subdural hematoma. There is no skull fracture or brain damage. The blood collects as a result of a blow to the head, which causes rupture of small blood vessels.

LACERATIONS OF THE SKIN

Nature of the Condition

Emergency treatment and later management of skin lacerations depend entirely on the nature of the wound, which may be clean and straight or dirty and jagged. Because of greater blood supply, lacerations of the face and scalp usually bleed more profusely than those on other body parts. This greater blood supply, however, leads to better healing.

Treatment and School Relevance

Pain

Most lacerations seen at school are not very severe and rarely require medication to control pain. If the pain is severe, a physician must be consulted.

Bleeding

The best way to control bleeding is to place a gauze flat directly on the cut and press firmly with a finger or the palm of the hand (see Figure 3-10). After 3 to 5 minutes of pressure, the bleeding will usually stop.

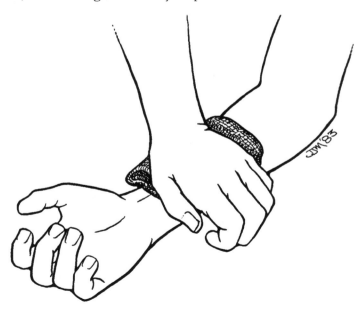

Figure 3-10. Applying pressure to large bleeding surface. The amount of pressure should be only enough to stop bleeding and no more.

Some books on first aid advocate applying pressure over pressure points, but this is rarely effective in slowing the blood flow.

Tourniquet application is controversial because if a tourniquet is applied too tightly and left on too long, the fingertips or toes may become gangrenous from lack of blood supply. On the other hand, for severe bleeding, a tight tourniquet is absolutely essential. What is safe? For severe bleeding, especially arterial bleeding in which blood is spurting, apply a tight tourniquet 1 to 3 inches above the wound, note the time, and never leave it on for more than 10 or 15 minutes. The student must be immediately evacuated to an emergency medical facility.

Prevention of Infection

If the wound becomes infected, the resulting scar will be larger than that resulting form an uninfected wound. Copious amounts of soap and water should be applied to the wound to wash out all dirt and other contaminating materials. This may be a bit painful at first, but it is highly necessary. The water should be lukewarm and may be running from a tap or may be in a soaking basin. Germicidal or plain soap is beneficial.

Merthiolate, mercurochrome, or other skin antiseptics cannot be relied on to prevent infection. Iodine is quite painful, and it and other strong antiseptics such as alcohol impede the growth of fibroblasts, the new cells that grow out from the edges of the wound and heal it.

Dressing

Small cuts, after cleaning, require only an adhesive bandage. The bandage should be changed and the cut should be washed with soap and water daily until it is almost completely healed.

Larger cuts should be covered with a nonsticking gauze flat and adhesive tape and the student should be referred to a physician right away, not at the end of the school day.

To pull the two edges of skin together in place of sutures, cut adhesive tape into a butterfly dressing, so that, when the wound is healed, the scar is narrow. There are two ways to do this; see Figures 3-11 and 3-12). This procedure is especially useful for jagged cuts that are incurred under contaminated, dirty conditions and are likely to get infected. By leaving the wound partly open, an abscess with trapped pus will not form underneath.

Sutures

To determine whether or not a cut will require stitches, several factors must be considered.

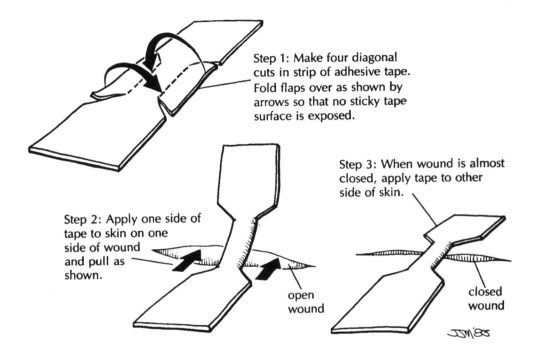

Step 1: Make four diagonal cuts in strip of adhesive tape. Fold flaps over as shown by arrows so that no sticky tape surface is exposed.

Step 2: Apply one side of tape to skin on one side of wound and pull as shown.

Step 3: When wound is almost closed, apply tape to other side of skin.

open wound

closed wound

Figure 3-11. Adhesive tape strip butterfly dressing. The size is usually about 3/4 inch in width and 2 to 3 inches in length.

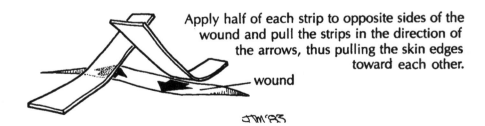

Apply half of each strip to opposite sides of the wound and pull the strips in the direction of the arrows, thus pulling the skin edges toward each other.

wound

Figure 3-12. Alternative type of butterfly bandage. This method uses two strips of adhesive tape about 1/4 to 1/2 inch in width and 2 to 3 inches in length.

1. *Size and shape*

   a. Jagged, irregular cuts or cuts longer than 1 inch with the skin edges separated by 3/8 inch or greater usually need stitches.

   b. Cuts under 1/2 inch long with edges separated by 1/8 inch or less rarely need stitches.

2. *Location*

   a. Cuts on the face, especially on the lip or eyelid, need careful attention regardless of size, sometimes by a plastic surgeon (see Figures 3-13 and 3-14).

   b. Cuts on the scalp should be seen by a physician. Hair tends to mat in the scab, delaying healing and occasionally leading to infection.

   c. Cuts inside the mouth, although the initial appearance may be bad, usually heal excellently with little or no scar.

3. *Age.* Only fresh cuts should be stitched (within 6 hours). Older cuts should be taped loosely with the skin edges apart so that any infection will not be trapped under the skin edges and form an abscess (boil).

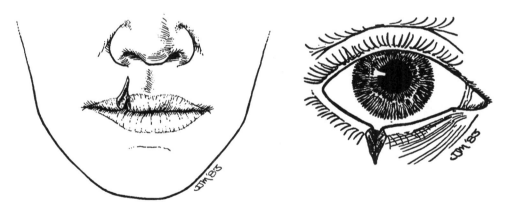

Figure 3-13. Laceration of upper lip.   **Figure 3-14.** Laceration of lower eyelid.

Booster Shots

If a student with a small, clean cut has had a recent dose of tetanus toxoid, a booster shot will probably not be necessary. If the cut is large and dirty or if the child has not had a recent booster shot, however, one may be required. This decision should never be made by school personnel; a physician should always be consulted.

PUNCTURE WOUNDS OF THE SKIN

Most puncture wounds of the skin that are caused by small, clean objects (pins or paper clips), are minor, and need no treatment except cleansing. There is usually no bleeding, and an adhesive bandage should not be applied. (A dab of colored antiseptic may be applied so that the student does not feel neglected.)

If a student steps on a nail or other sharp object, it is apt to be quite painful. In addition, the danger of infection is greater because any germs present will be deposited deeply into the tissues. The foot should be soaked in warm water for 20 to 30 minutes. Epsom salts or another weak antiseptic may be used. This soaking encourages the wound to remain open and to drain as much as possible.

After drying, a loose-fitting covering may be applied so that air can enter. If the sole of the foot has been punctured, a small round pad with a hole in the center may be used to relieve pressure. Deciding whether or not to give a booster shot of tetanus toxoid requires the consideration of many factors. Nurses or other school personnel should not make the decision; a physician should be consulted.

Any puncture wound of the sole of the foot that penetrates 1/4 to 1/2 inch or more should be referred to a physician. The incidence of secondary infection is high, and antibiotics are usually necessary.

A puncture wound caused by the point of a wooden pencil is often seen in the school setting. This kind of wound cannot cause lead poisoning. The so-called lead in a pencil actually contains no lead; it is compressed graphite, completely inert and nontoxic. It does color the skin and tissue immediately beneath and leaves a small bluish dot that is often permanent; it is actually a small tattoo.

Because of the bluish color, it may look as if the pencil tip is broken off under the skin. It is rare that this happens. Unless you can see and feel the actual broken-off point of the pencil sticking up over the skin surface, do not attempt removal since it will usually result in greater tissue damage. Treatment should be limited to cleansing to prevent infection, as in any other small puncture wound. If the mark is on the face and is considered unsightly, it may be removed later by plastic surgery.

FRACTURES

Nature of the Condition

A fractured bone is a broken bone; there is no difference between the two terms. There are numerous different kinds of fractures (see Figures 3-15 through 3-20), but most have one thing in common: the broken bones will not heal properly unless put into some type of cast or splint.

Figure 3-15. Comminuted fracture.

Figure 3-16. Oblique fracture.

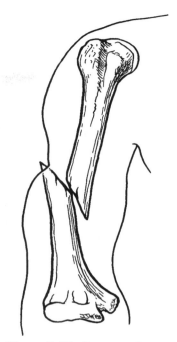

Figure 3-17. Compound fracture.

Figure 3-18. Greenstick fracture.

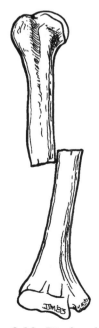

Figure 3-19. Displaced fracture.

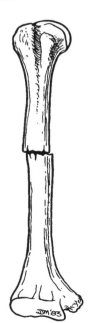

Figure 3-20. Nondisplaced fracture.

Symptoms

Pain, swelling, and sometimes crookedness can be seen in the fractured arm or leg. In many minor fractures, the bones are not out of line, but special treatment such as a cast is usually necessary for proper healing.

During the healing process, new bone is built up around the fracture site; this new bone is called callus. It often causes a knot or bump that goes away after complete healing.

Treatment and Diagnosis

Any suspected fracture should always be referred to a physician. The diagnosis can only be made with certainty by X ray. Emergency treatment at school is by splint and sling.

DISLOCATIONS

Nature of the Condition

In school-aged children, dislocation is most apt to occur in the ball-and-socket joint of the shoulder (see Figure 3-21). This may occur following an injury or from throwing a ball too hard. If the elbow, wrist, ankle, knee, or hip becomes dislocated, it usually follows a severe injury and is often accompanied by a fracture.

Symptoms

Severe pain and noticeable deformity are always present with dislocations.

Treatment

After ice application, the student should always be referred to a physician, preferably an orthopedic surgeon. Definitive treatment (putting the joint back in place) should never be attempted at school. Although this may look easy to do with a dislocated finger joint, school nurses, coaches, and athletic trainers should resist the temptation.

ROLE OF THE SCHOOL NURSE

Sprains, strains, fractures, and dislocations are common occurrences at school. Each school should develop a prearranged plan, with contacts made in advance at a doctor's office or a hospital emergency room, so that hasty decisions need not be made

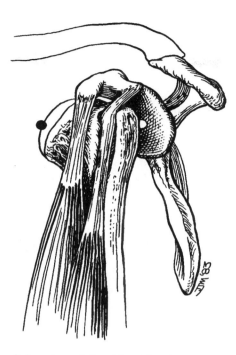

Figure 3-21. Rotation-type dislocation of shoulder. The shoulder is a ball-and-socket joint. The ball is the upper end of the humerus. The ball's apex is shown by the black dot. The socket is at the lateral plate of the scapula, or shoulder blade. When the dislocation is reduced, back in place, the black dot will fit into the white hole.

in an acute emergency situation. These procedures should be written and, if possible, posted in the nurse's clinic, the principal's office, or both.

Parents must always be notified of these types of injuries, but if they are not available, treatment should not be delayed.

ARM AND LEG INJURIES: SPRAINS AND STRAINS

Nature of the Condition

A sprain is a stretching injury of a *ligament* without a tear. A strain is a stretching injury of a *muscle* or *tendon* that does not actually cause the tendon or muscle to tear or rupture. (See Figure 3-22.)

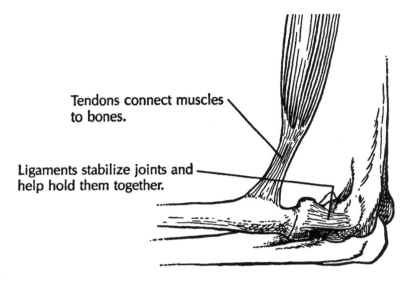

Tendons connect muscles to bones.

Ligaments stabilize joints and help hold them together.

Figure 3-22. Difference between tendon and ligament.

Either of these injuries can be mild, requiring only a little rest, or severe enough to require a plaster cast. They usually occur during athletic contests in secondary school, but may also occur during normal childhood play, especially during recess.

Symptoms

With sprains and strains, there is pain and swelling, of sudden onset, after twisting the ankle, knee, wrist, elbow, shoulder, hand, or foot.

Treatment

Treatment of sprains and strains can be remembered by the acronym RICE:

R = Rest
I = Ice
C = Compression
E = Elevation

Although ice can be safely applied directly to the skin, it is much more comfortable if the ice is first wrapped in a towel. Compression should never be performed by untrained personnel; cutting off the blood supply for too long a time presents a serious danger. Elevation is often helpful.

Refer a student with a sprain or strain to a physician in all but mild cases.

Decision Rules for X Rays of the Leg Following an Injury

Injuries of the knee, ankle, and foot occur often, and in most cases, the injured person is referred to a hospital emergency room. As part of the examination, routine X rays are almost always taken, and fewer than 10%–15% show a fracture. Therefore, the following "decision rules" have been suggested.

An X ray is required for an acute knee injury only if the patient exhibits one or more of the following:

- Tenderness to pressure at the head of fibula
- Isolated tenderness of the patella (knee cap) plus no bone tenderness of the knee other than the patella
- Inability to flex knee to 90°
- Inability to bear weight both immediately and within 2 hours; inability to transfer weight twice onto each leg (take four steps regardless of limp)
- Age 55 or older

An X ray of the ankle is required only if there is reported pain in the inner or outer ankle bone with any of these findings:

- Tenderness to pressure over the medial or lateral malleolus (inner or outer ankle bone) or an area 1 to 2 inches around it
- Inability to bear weight both immediately and in the emergency room

An X ray of the foot is required only if there is reported pain in the midzone of the foot plus any of these findings:

- Tenderness to pressure over the navicular bone (the small protuberance just below the inner ankle)
- Tenderness to pressure over the base of the fifth metatarsal bone (the ankle end of the outside bone of the foot)
- Inability to bear weight both immediately and in the emergency room.

The knee rules have been tested only with older adults; the foot and ankle rules were also tested with young adults. For the school nurse and athletic trainer, however, these rules can all be used as guidelines to determine the severity of injury and to aid in deciding whether or not to urge immediate referral to a physician, who will then decide about the need for an X ray.

BRUISES

Nature of the Condition

A bruise occurs following the sudden impact from a fall or blow by a rock, fist, or other blunt object. The surface of the skin is not broken, but the underlying blood vessels are ruptured and the surrounding tissues are crushed and damaged. In medical jargon, it is called a contusion. A "charley horse" is a bruised muscle.

Symptoms

With a bruise, pain, redness, and swelling are usually seen. If the bruise is minor, no redness or swelling will result. At first, the blood in the tissues causes a reddish discoloration. In a few days, the blood gets older and turns bluish purple and then yellowish green. This color change reflects the age of the bruise. Swelling usually disappears within 4 days, depending on the severity and location of the bruise. With minor bruises, pain lasts a few minutes, but with more severe bruises, tenderness persists for days.

Diagnosis

A bruise is usually obvious from the history and symptoms. A student with a disease that causes a delay in blood clotting may be seen with identical physical evidence without a history of pain or trauma, however. If the history is reliable, the student should be examined to see if any other bruises are present. If so, the student should be sent home at the end of the day with a note to the parent.

Treatment

An ice pack will relieve the pain of a bruise. If no ice is readily available, a towel wrung out with cold tap water will help. Commercially available products that produce instant cold packs are available, and some of these should be stored at each school.

Compression bandages, when indicated, should never be applied by untrained personnel; the danger of cutting off the blood supply is too great. If the injury looks severe, the bruise should be treated with a loose-fitting cold pack and the student should be sent home or to a hospital emergency room

Elevating an injured arm with a sling or propping a leg on a chair is helpful.

The procedure outlined above is commonly referred to as RICE—rest, ice, compression, and elevation. The same treatment that is effective for joint injuries such as sprained ankle or twisted knee, shoulder, or elbow—RICE (rest, ice, compression, and elevation)—should be followed for bruises.

ROLE OF THE SCHOOL NURSE

Assess the severity of the bruise. If it is minor yet needs treatment, it may be treated at school; if it is severe, the student should be sent home or to a medical facility.

Be on the alert for nontraumatic discolorations of the skin that resemble bruises; they sometimes occur spontaneously and are often completely painless. If they are on the body or arms, they may be more serious than bruises, and if more than one is seen, parents should be notified because a blood clotting disease may be present.

Warning: Children often have several bruises on their legs, especially between the ankle and knee, and have no knowledge of any injury. These bruises occur during the rough-and-tumble of normal childhood play and need no treatment at all. Also, some adolescent girls (and older women) bruise very easily, such as from a slight bump on the corner of a desk. Bruises limited to the thighs and legs in these individuals need no treatment.

Bruises are one of the most common occurrences a school nurse is called upon to attend. Most children need only a little reassurance, some need ice for relief of pain, but few need to be seen by a physician.

Be aware that bruises in different stages of healing on various parts of the body may be warning signs of child abuse.

MUSCLE AND JOINT PAINS NOT INJURY RELATED

Nature of the Condition

Pain in the arms and legs occurs in children who have not been injured, but because pain in the legs is much more common than in the arms, pain in the arms must be taken more seriously. The pain may be in the muscles or in the joints; the significance and treatment are quite different.

Neck pain (crick in the neck), commonly seen at school, can result from several factors such as sound sleep with the neck in a stressed or twisted position or excessive cold causing neck muscle tension. Arthritis of a cervical (neck) bone, rare in children, may simulate a crick.

Nontraumatic muscle pain in the legs is almost always caused by excessive use during normal childhood play. This pain results from excessive lactic acid production, a by-product of muscle glycogen metabolism that causes delayed pain by irritation of the muscle. Such muscle pain goes away quickly without intervention. A related condition, "growing pains," occurs for the same reason, is always in the legs, and characteristically awakens a child from sleep.

Nontraumatic joint pain may indicate some type of arthritis. It is rare and should be regarded cautiously if it occurs.

Symptoms

Pain is the usual symptom, although redness and swelling may be seen in certain types of arthritis. It is quite common for the pain to occur 1 to 2 hours following a play period.

Diagnosis

Differentiation between muscle pain and joint pain is important; the treatment is different. The best way to tell the difference is by gentle manipulation. *Any movement or massage of a diseased joint will usually cause increased pain; gentle massage to painful, noninjured muscle usually brings relief. Growing pains hurt* between *joints; arthritis hurts* in *the joint.*

Treatment

By numbing nerve endings and slowing blood circulation, cold applications diminish pain and swelling. By increasing blood circulation, heat applications increase tissue metabolism and thus promote healing and a return to a normal condition. Therefore, most traumatic pains are treated with cold, whereas nontraumatic muscle and joint pains are best treated with heat. In some cases, a heat lamp can provide excellent relief, but care must be taken not to burn the skin. Hot, wet compresses are equally effective.

Gentle massage can sometimes provide relief, especially if the pain is in the calf muscles. If any manipulation increases the pain, it must be stopped immediately.

Athletes are often advised to exercise a painful muscle to work out the pain. This method should not be used in younger children. At best, it should only be used after the cause of the pain is reliably diagnosed.

ROLE OF THE SCHOOL NURSE

If the pain is minor and of short duration, the student can be sent back to class. If manipulation causes increased pain, stop treatment and allow the student to rest in the clinic. Then, if pain goes away, send the student back to class. If pain persists for an hour or more, send the student home.

Emergency evacuation is not necessary unless pain is severe.

BURNS

Nature of the Condition and Classification of Burns

Burns are classified into three categories, depending on what layers of the skin are involved (see Figure 3-23):

First-degree burns show redness with no blisters. Mild sunburn is a good example. First degree burns involve only the upper part of the first layer of the skin.

Second-degree burns show redness with blisters. Severe sunburn or hot liquid are the most common causes. Second degree burns involve the first and second layers of skin.

Third-degree burns affect at least the entire thickness of the skin and may include deeper muscles and even bone in severe burns such as those that occur in some explosions. The remaining skin tissues may be blanched white or charred black. There are usually no blisters; they have already broken.

Treatment

Treatment for burns depends on the type of burn.

For first-degree burns, relieve pain with cool compresses or anesthetic ointment (such as benzocaine or lanacaine); nothing else is necessary. Healing always occurs with no scar. As soon as the pain is gone, clean to prevent infection. A tiny burn can have an adhesive bandage applied. The student need not be sent home.

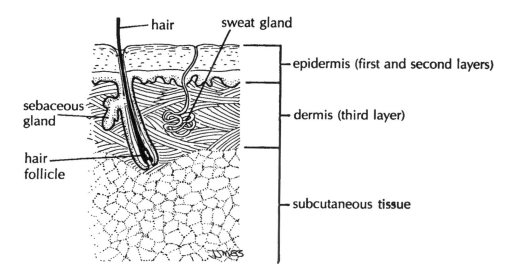

Figure 3-23. Normal layers of skin.

For second-degree burns, relieve pain with cool compresses, but do so gently so as not to break any blisters. If the blister can be kept intact, there will be no danger of infection until it eventually breaks, which blisters usually do within several days. After gentle cleaning with lukewarm water, a bulky padded bandage should be gently and loosely applied as a first aid measure. The student should then see a physician for further treatment. The longer the blister remains intact, the more new skin will grow underneath, so that when the blister does break, there is less likelihood of infection and less pain from raw skin being exposed. A small second-degree burn on the arm or leg can be safely treated at school. After waiting about 10 to 15 minutes for the pain to subside, the burn should be washed gently. Then, after gently patting dry, a small (four-by-four-inch) nonstick gauze flat can be applied and held on with adhesive tape or gauze roller bandage. If in the judgment of the nurse or principal, the circumstances are proper and the parent concurs, the student may stay at school but should not go out for recess or gym class for fear of injury to the new burn. Ointments are not harmful, but they moisten and weaken the blister and are conducive to breaking it. The only reason for applying ointment is to relieve pain; cool compresses do this better. Later, if infection is present, antibiotic ointments are necessary but should be prescribed by a physician.

Third-degree burns are most apt to occur on direct exposure to flames, scalding liquids, or very hot metal. They represent a true medical emergency, not to be treated at school, and students with such burns should be evacuated to the nearest hospital as quickly as possible. The burns should be covered loosely with a sheet or smooth towel. Ointments should not be applied.

HEALTH EDUCATION TIPS

- Educate teachers concerning delayed effects of blunt injury.
- Confer with physical education teachers about all forms of head injury, especially mild concussion.
- Confer with health education teachers and serve as resource regarding head injuries.
- Inform faculty and parents of the potential danger of puncture wounds in the foot.
- Educate parents and faculty about differences between pain *in* joints and pain in muscles *between* joints.
- In health education classes, emphasize the dangers of excess sun exposure.

REFERENCES

Barrett, K., et al. "Sequelae of Minor Head Injury; the Natural History of Post-concussive Symptoms and Their Relationship to Loss of Consciousness and Follow-up." *Journal of Emergency Medicine* 11(2):79-84.

Bratton, R. L., et al. "Preparticipation Sports Examinations. Efficient Risk Assessment in Children and Adolescents. *Postgraduate Medicine* 98(2):123-26.

Budgett, R. "ABC of Sports Medicine: The Overtraining Syndrome." *Journal of British Medicine* 309(695):365-68.

Forman, E. S., et al. "High Risk Behaviors in Teenage Male Athletes." *Clinical Journal of Sport Medicine* 5(1):36-42.

Karjalainen, J., et al. "Blood-Borne Pathogens in Sports."*Annals of Internal Medicine* 123(8):635-36.

Kujala, U. M., et al. "Knee Osteoarthritis in Former Runners, Soccer Players, Weight Lifters, and Shooters." *Arthritis Rheumatism* 28(4):539-46.

Lie, S. H., et al. "Lateral Ankle Sprains and Instability Problems." *Clinical Sports Medicine* 13(4):793-809.

Mast, E. E., et al. "Transmission of Blood-Borne Pathogens during Sports: Risk and Prevention." *Annals of Internal Medicine* 122(4):283-85.

Nastasi, K. J., et al. "Exercise-induced Asthma and the Athlete." *Journal of Asthma* 32(4):249-57.

Sobal, J., et al. "Vitamin/Mineral Supplement Use among High School Athletes." *Adolescence* 29(116):835-43.

Stiell, J. G., et al. "Decision Rules for X-ray of Ankle Following Injury." *Journal of the American Medical Association* 271 (16 March 1994): 827.

Stiell, J. G., et al. "Decision Rules for X-ray of Knee Following Injury." *Journal of the American Medical Association* 275 (28 Feb. 1996): 611.

U.S. Public Health Service. "Physical Activity in Children." *American Family Physician* 50(6):1285-88.

Wight, J. N., Jr., et al. "Sudden Cardiac Death and the 'Athlete's' Heart." *Archives of Internal Medicine* 155(4):1473-80.

HEALTH SCREENING PROGRAMS

Well-planned screening programs are important tools for achieving the objectives of the school health program.

Susan Wold

Screening is a process to determine from a large group of apparently healthy individuals those who have, or are at risk of having, a health condition or problem. The school is an ideal place to accomplish mass screening programs if the screening process is relatively simple and does not disrupt the educational program and if medical diagnosis and treatment of the particular condition is accessible and affordable in the community. The benefit of a screening program is the reduction of morbidity from early intervention and prompt treatment. Problems with hearing, vision, growth, blood pressure, and the spine are frequently identified in school screening programs. The most common evaluations performed in the schools are for hearing and vision. Difficulties with these senses are often subtle, and parents, the student, or the teacher may not recognize that a problem exists. Even minor vision and hearing problems can significantly affect a student's ability to learn.

CHOOSING PROGRAMS

Screening programs are costly and time consuming; therefore, they must be chosen carefully. No school district can perform all the health screening procedures available. Some guidelines to consider are as follows:

1. The condition being screened for should have a precise definition, agreed on by a large majority. Visual acuity of 20/20, for example, is universally accepted as normal. Dyslexia has no universally agreed-on definition; therefore, vision screening tests are valuable. Dyslexia must be discovered through individual diagnostic exams.
2. The condition should be correctable or amenable to improvement.
3. The condition should be clearly established.
4. Referral criteria should be clearly established.
5. Periodic evaluation and comparison with other schools and other testers will minimize over- or under-referrals.
6. There should be adequate public and private referral sources to correct any defects uncovered. If not, efforts should first be directed at resource development. A major example is dental screening. Unless students have access to dental care, screening or dental health education does not improve their mouths or teeth.

VISION SCREENING

A school vision screening generally consists of six parts: visual inspection of the eyes, visual acuity, testing for ocular alignment, excessive or latent hyperopia, depth perception, and color vision.

Before the vision test, history from the parent, teacher, or student will assist the screener in obtaining evidence of visual difficulties. Questions to ask the student might be: Do you see well? Do you need to hold your book near your face to read the print? Can you see the blackboard from your desk? Family history of eye disorder or early use of glasses always needs to be explored. Observations of the teacher and parent often prove correct. A checklist of signs and symptoms of vision difficulties may be completed by the parent, teacher, or student to support the screener's observations further (see Figure 4-1). This checklist will be of help when acuity is normal and when referral to a physician or specialist is based on symptoms observed or on a student's complaint.

VISION PROBLEM CHECKLIST

Student's Name _____ Age _____

Signs and symptoms of vision difficulties noted with this student:

- Frowns when reading
- Avoids close work
- Short attention span
- Excessive blinking
- Rubs eyes frequently
- Squints
- When reading, head close to book
- Tilts head to side
- Eyes crossed

- Crusted eyelids
- Frequent sties
- Frequent headaches
- Says can't see blackboard
- Eyes red
- Sensitive to light
- Short attention span
- Frequent watering (tearing)

Other: _____

_____

Person Completing Checklist _____

Figure 4-1. Vision problem checklist.

Inspection

Inspection is an important part of the vision screening examination. Squinting, sensitivity to light, redness of the eye, discolorations, abnormalities of the white or colored part of the eye (for example, coloboma, a defect of the iris), eczema of the eyelids, mild strabismus, and many other significant problems are often discovered. Inspection can be done quickly while talking to the child without the child being aware of an inspection.

Visual Acuity

The procedure for testing *visual acuity* is described in pediatric physical assessment texts, manuals of state health departments, professional school nursing organizational materials, and school health procedure books. Vision screening guidelines are given in Figure 4-2. A few relevant factors are the following:

1. The 10- or 20-foot Snellen chart is recommended. A measurement of 20/20 means that the person being screened can see the details on a screening chart that a person with average vision can see at 20 feet. Children 4 years of age and younger are thought not to have developed the adult's ability to determine differences in detail at the 20/20 level. Therefore, the Snellen notation of 20/40 is used as an acceptable (passing) level of screening performance for children 4 years or younger. For children 5 years and older, the 20/30 notation is passing If the acuity is 20/30, it means that the child can see and respond to details on the screening chart at a distance of 20 feet that the average adult can respond to at 30 feet.

2. Most states have set standards for referring children to a vision specialist. The American Academy of Pediatrics School Health Guide recommends the following guidelines:
   - Up to the fifth birthdate, children should read a majority of the 20/40 line with each eye.
   - After the fifth birthdate, children should read a majority of the 20/30 line with each eye.
   - A student with a two-line difference between eyes, even in the normal range, should be referred to a specialist.

3. For prekindergarten children, the screening test most often used for young children and retardates is the H:O:T:V: Matching Symbol Chart Set. HOTV or the "preliterate" or "tumbling" E.

4. The titmus vision tester is widely used, and when the person administering this test method is proficient, the reading is accurate. This test can be used for testing convergence ability (required for binocular vision), depth perception, and excessive hyperopia. It is often used in small clinics or other areas of testing where a 10- to 20-foot space is not available. The major disadvantage to the titmus vision tester is that when the eyes of the person taking the test cannot be seen.

The skill of the screener is an important factor in the accuracy of any vision test. Children quickly memorize the chart, peek from the eye covered to see the chart, or in other subtle ways pass or fail the test by their choice. If a failure occurs, a second screening after an interval of a few days is performed to confirm the visual acuity noted from the first screening.

Excessive (Latent) Hyperopia

Small degrees of *hyperopia* (farsightedness) are common in children; 75% of newborns are mildly hyperopic, and 50% continue to be mildly hyperopic at age 16. These children see and read perfectly well without glasses. If the hyperopia is severe, the accommodative power of the lens of the eye is insufficient, vision will be blurred, and the student will fail the vision screening test.

A small group of "borderline" hyperopic children will pass the vision screening test; they can see well but must accommodate so much that their eyes tire, and they sometimes complain about their eyes or prefer not to read. To test these students, use a pair of +2.5 diopter lenses. A normal child will not be able to pass a standard Snellen test wearing these glasses; the chart will be too blurred. A child with moderate to severe hyperopia will pass the test easily because this is the lens type used to correct hyperopia.

Some screeners perform this test on all students as part of the vision screening program. We suggest it be used only with students in kindergarten through third grade, with special education candidates, and with students who are new to the school district.

Muscle Balance Testing for Ocular Alignment

Muscle balance testing for *ocular alignment* may show deviation of the eye toward the nose (cross-eye or esotropia) or away from the nose (walleye or exotropia). Less common is when the deviation is straight up or obliquely up. All forms of ocular alignment are caused by excessive pull of one of the eye muscles. The deviation is often seen when a student gazes into the distance without focusing on a single point.

VISION SCREENING GUIDELINES*

Function	Recommended Tests	Referral Criteria	Comments
Ages 3-5 years Distance visual acuity	Snellen letters Snellen numbers Tumbling E HOTV Picture tests Allen figures LH test	1. < 4 of 6 correct on 20-ft line with either eye tested at 10 ft monocularly (i.e., 10/20 or 20/40) or 2. Two-line difference between eyes, even within the passing range (i.e., 10/12.5 and 10/20 or 20/25 and 20/40)	1. Tests are listed in decreasing order of cognitive difficulty; the highest test that the child is capable of performing should be used; in general, the tumbling E or the HOTV test should be used for ages 3-5 years and Snellen letters or numbers for ages 6 years and older 2. Testing distance of 10 ft is recommended for all visual acuity tests 3. A line of figures is preferred over single figures 4. The nontested eye should be covered by an occluder held by the examiner or by an adhesive occluder patch applied to eye; the examiner must ensure that it is not possible to peek with the nontested eye
Ocular alignment	Unilateral cover test at 10 ft or 3 m or Random-dot-E stereo test at 40 cm (630 s of arc)	Any eye movement < 4 of 6 correct	

Function	Recommended Tests	Referral Criteria	Comments
Ages 6 years and older Distance visual acuity	Snellen letters Snellen numbers Tumbling E HOTV Picture Tests Allen figures LH test	1. < 4 of 6 correct on 15-ft line with either eye tested at 10 ft monocularly (i.e., < 10/15 or 20/30) or 2. Two-line difference between eyes, even within the passing range (i.e., 10/10 and 10/15 or 20/20 and 20/30)	1. Tests are listed in decreasing order of cognitive difficulty; the highest test that the child is capable of performing should be used; in general, the tumbling E or the HOTV test should be used for ages 3-5 years and Snellen letters or numbers for ages 6 years and older 2. Testing distance of 10 ft is recommended for all visual acuity tests 3. A line of figures is preferred over single figures 4. The nontested eye should be covered by an occluder held by the examiner or by an adhesive occluder patch applied to the eye; the examiner must ensure that it is not possible to peek with the nontested eye
Ocular alignment	Unilateral cover test at 3 m or Random-dot-E stereo test at 40 cm (630 s of arc)	Any eye movement < 4 of 6 correct	

*Vision screening guidelines were developed by the AAP Section on Ophthalmology Executive Committee, 1991–92: Robert D. Gross, MBA, M.D., Chairman; Walter M. Fierson, M.D.; Jane D. Kivlin, M.D.; I. Matthew Rabinowicz, M.D.; David R. Stager, M.D.; Mark S. Ruttum, M.D., AAPOS; and Earl R. Crouch, Jr, M.D., AAO.

Figure 4-2. Vision screening guidelines.

When the same eye always deviates, it is called *strabismus;* when the deviation alternates from one eye to the other, it is called *alternating strabismus.* If uncorrected, strabismus that begins at an early age leads to amblyopia; alternating strabismus does not.

Several easy tests detect mild strabismus. Two of the more common tests are the *cover test* and the *pupillary reflex test* (Hirschberg test). In the cover test, each eye is alternately covered while the student concentrates at a point 10 to 20 feet away with the uncovered eye. If the covered eye deviates, it will quickly move back to center when the cover is moved to the other eye. For the pupillary reflex test, a student is asked to look at a light held 12 to 13 inches in front of the face. The light will be reflected as a pinpoint of light in the center of the pupil of each eye. If an eye is deviant, the pinpoint of light in that eye will be significantly off center. If the *visual acuity is normal and equal* in both eyes, referral to a specialist is not necessary.

Depth Perception and Color Vision Testing

Depth perception and *color vision testing* do not adversely affect educational performance. Some educators disagree with this opinion. In any case, these tests are not always a part of school screening programs. Because the student with either of these two conditions may have difficulty in the classroom and because testing is not difficult, we suggest that they both be performed. Color vision needs to be done as early as possible (i.e., prekindergarten or kindergarten) so that teachers and parents will know if a problem exists.

HEARING SCREENING

School Procedures

In many states, audiometric training programs are provided by state health departments and state education agencies. All persons who perform hearing testing and screening should attend training programs and subsequent review sessions to understand the procedures used in the testing and state regulations regarding minimum standards. The quality of any hearing screening program depends on the proper calibration of the hearing testing equipment, properly trained testers using acceptable techniques, and the necessary referral and follow-up services.

The *audiometer* is an instrument used in screening or evaluating the function of hearing. More than 100 models of various types of audiometers are currently available from numerous manufacturers. The pure-tone audiometer, which electronically generates tones for the purpose of measuring hearing, is the instrument most frequently used in hearing testing in schools. An audiometer with a choice of several pure tones (discrete frequencies) as well as a method of precisely controlling the intensity of the tones is recommended for hearing screening.

Another instrument, the *immitance bridge* or *tympanometer*, is useful to assist the audiologist or specially trained registered nurse in the diagnosis of middle ear pathology in individual children. The test results alone should not be used for diagnosis or referral to a specialist, however. Information gained from this test method along with that obtained from otoscopic inspection, pneumatic otoscopy, and pure-tone audiometry form a test battery that reduces the number of referrals to a specialist.

Audiometers and the immitance bridge are delicate electronic machines that must be checked (calibrated) by a specialist at least once a year to determine if they are accurate. It is important to find a credible company or service to calibrate the audiometer and to keep records of the equipment's most recent calibrations.

Measuring Decibel Levels

Intensity (loudness) of sound is expressed in decibels (dB). The level of sound that can barely be heard by a normal young adult is 0 dB. Note that his measurement is not the absence of sound, which is why some children hear pure tones at -10 or -20 dB.

A tone's highness or lowness of pitch is expressed in hertz (Hz; also called frequency or cycles). Low-pitched tones tested are 125, 250, and 500 Hz; high tones are 4,000, 6,000 and occasionally 8,000 Hz.

Sweep Check Screening

With sweep check screening, testing at 20 dB is recommended. Most programs recommend screening at 1,000, 2,000, and 4,000 Hz; some also recommend screening at 3,000 Hz as the final step. Each ear is tested separately. Children who can hear 20 dB in both ears at all frequencies pass the test. If a child fails, screening should be repeated in 2 to 3 weeks before referral to a physician. Minor respiratory infections may temporarily depress hearing. Any child who fails two sweep check tests is given the threshold test.

Threshold Testing

Threshold testing establishes the lowest decibel at which sound can be heard at each hertz level. In school, the usual levels tested are 500, 1,000, 2,000, 4,000, and 6,000 Hz. At each level, the screener starts at 20 dB and gradually goes up until the child first hears the sound. The sound is then decreased in steps of 10 dB until it is no longer heard. The sound is next increased in increments of 5 dB until the child hears it again. This is the threshold for the frequency (Hz level) being tested.

Referral Standards and Procedures

The sweep check is done first. Those who pass are not screened again for 1 to 3 years unless hearing failure is suspected. Those who fail two sweep checks given 3 to 4 weeks apart are given the threshold test. Those who fail the second sweep check and the threshold are referred to a specialist.

The levels at which a child fails the test are not rigidly defined, but all agree that a child who cannot hear 30 dB at any single frequency (Hz) should be referred to a specialist. We do not recommend such referral for a child who hears at 20 dB or better. Most state health departments issue exact referral standards for those tested in schools in that particular state.

There is some disagreement whether a child who can only hear at 20 dB or louder is at higher risk for learning problems. Most pediatricians feel that if a child can hear the spoken voice, learning will be normal, but some audiologists feel that children with a 25–30 dB hearing loss have more learning problems because they do not hear key words or sounds. Because there are so many other variable factors, this question is difficult to answer. For example, poor children have more hearing loss and also more learning difficulties. Is the learning problem associated with the hazards of poverty, or is it due to hearing loss?

Most hearing loss in children is due to middle ear disease (otitis media) and is called a *conductive* loss (see Figure 4-3). In adults, the loss is usually due to repeat-

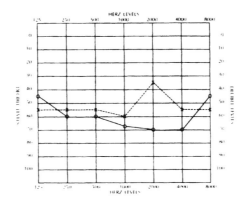

Figure 4-3. Audiogram: Conductive hearing loss.

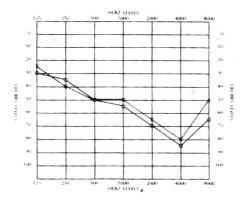

Figure 4-4. Audiogram: Sensorineural hearing loss.

ed exposure to loud noises or to degenerative inner ear disease and is called a *sensorineural* loss (see Figure 4-4). A hearing loss is often due to both causes and is called a *mixed* hearing loss.

Audiograms are used by hearing screeners to show graphically the hearing problem as tested. All screeners need to use this method of recording so as to see any failure repeatedly.

Students who need to be referred should be sent to a physician, preferably a pediatrician or ear specialist who is knowledgeable about children's hearing problems and who is able to deal with children skillfully.

SPINAL SCREENING

Abnormal Curves

The normal spine curves slightly from front to back. *Scoliosis* means a lateral or S-shaped curvature of the spine; it is described as a side-to-side curve of the spinal column with a twisting of the vertebra. The thoracic (chest) or lumbar (lower back) regions are most commonly affected by scoliosis, and most cases are noted between the ages of 10 and 14. Sometimes the condition worsens with time and can result in serious problems of pain, appearance, and interference with heart and lung function. Most cases (85%) have no known cause; such a case is called idiopathic scoliosis. Other causes of scoliosis include conditions that occur prior to birth, congenital scoliosis, and conditions of the nerves and muscles such as muscular dystrophy, cerebral palsy, and poliomyelitis. Injury from fractures, surgery, irradiation, or burns can also result in scoliosis.

Kyphosis is a forward curve of the shoulder area of the spine. This condition usually appears at the time of puberty. Inflammation of the growth plate of the vertebra (Scheuermann's disease), infection (osteomyelitis) in the vertebral bone, or congenital malformation may cause the condition, but frequently the cause is unknown. Exaggeration of the backward curve in the lumbar area is called *lordosis*.

Screening

The spinal screening procedure is described in detail in physical assessment textbooks and in school education agency and public health manuals. The procedure is easy, quick, and if carried out properly, accurate. Several states require nonmedical persons to pass a course of study prior to screening for spinal problems. Medical and nonmedical screeners need to have staff development presentations or reviews of the methods of screening for spinal problems and the opportunity to assist an experienced person with screenings prior to assuming the responsibility for the examinations.

The screening procedure generally follows this routine for scoliosis. The student, dressed in shorts plus bra or halter for girls, stands facing away from the seated examiner, bends over with palms together in a diving position, and touches the fingers to or near the toes. The examiner inspects the back from the neck to the lumbar region to see if one side protrudes (see Figures 4-5 and 4-6). Each student is observed from the front, side, and back while standing straight and while gradually bending forward with the arms hanging down and palms touching. Several specific

View of Back Standing

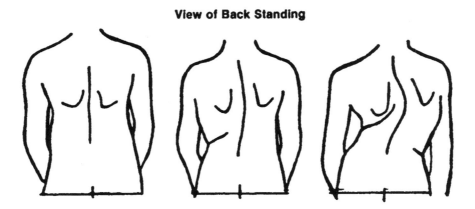

Figure 4-5. Standing view of the back.

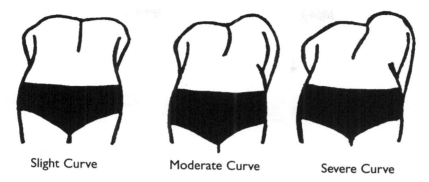

Slight Curve   Moderate Curve   Severe Curve

Figure 4-6. Bending view of the back.

abnormal findings may be noted. For kyphosis, the student is observed from one side while standing and bending over for an accentuated roundness in the upper back.

With experience, the examiner learns what is normal and what is abnormal. All students thought to require referral are rescreened in 2 to 4 weeks. If possible, the second screening is by another screener. If there is a condition that does not appear normal, refer the student to a physician. An experienced examiner can screen 20 to 25 students in an hour.

Some screeners find the scoliometer (see Figure 4-7), a small, handheld device that measures the angle of trunk rotation, helpful in reducing overreferrals and in monitoring small curves in children whose scoliosis is minimal. The advantages of

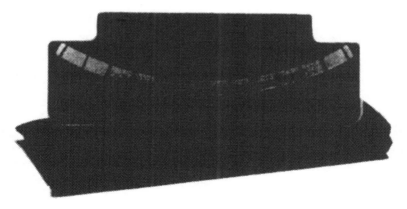

Figure 4-7. Scoliometer.

using the scoliometer are a reduction of overreferrals, a lower false negative rate, and accurate monitoring of small curves. The use of this technique with the scoliometer is easy and convenient.

Referral and Treatment

Two spinal screenings are recommended during the growth spurt years, ages 10 through 14, in fifth through ninth grades. Referrals are based on positive findings from the rescreening that follow the initial screening. Reassure the parent that many referrals from school screenings only require professional observation to ensure that the condition is not worsening.

A 3%–5% overall referral rate after the rescreen is considered acceptable. Consistent variations should be investigated. Not all students referred will require treatment; most only need to be followed by their doctors to see if the degree of curve requires follow-up or bracing. Skilled observation rather than definitive treatment is required because the scoliosis does not progress to the degree that bracing is necessary. Moderate curves may need to be treated with a brace during the growth years. The brace may correct the existing curvature, but its main purpose is to prevent the condition from worsening.

The usual treatment for scoliosis is with a Milwaukee brace worn 23 hours a day until the child's growth is completed. This brace is effective, but as can be expected, compliance is poor. One recently developed brace must be worn only at night. So far, the results with this new brace are equal to the Milwaukee brace, and compliance is excellent. To prevent muscle shrinkages, thoracic pressure, and abdominal cinching and to improve balance, prescribed exercises usually accompany the use of the brace. Sometimes surgery is necessary.

Experimental treatments with a small battery-operated muscle stimulator taped to the skin on the back have been used in the past. Electrical stimulation causes the muscles on one side to contract constantly, and it was hoped that this treatment would gradually pull the spine into a straightened position. Current studies have found that in most cases, electrical stimulation is not effective in stopping the progressive curve.

Value of Screening

Opponents of spinal screening say that some scoliosis is nonprogressive and that referring these children may result in needless parental anxiety. In addition, they say that the yield of children requiring actual bracing is low and that this screening is not cost effective. In addition, some say that students sent to chiropractors or other therapists may receive needless therapy.

HEIGHT AND WEIGHT SCREENING

Program Considerations

Human growth from infancy to maturity involves great changes in body size and appearance. Individual patterns of growth vary widely because of differences in heredity and environment. The rate of growth is more significant than height and weight measured during a single examination and can be determined by height and weight measurements plotted on a standardized growth pattern chart.

The procedure for weight and measuring is simple and need not be described, but consideration of the following information can benefit the program. The typical balance-beam scale found in doctors' offices or health clubs is no more accurate than platform-with-dial spring scales. The important factor is gain or loss; thus the student should be weighed on the same scale every time. If a student appears to have gained or lost 1–3 pounds as measured on a different scale, it is probably meaningless; neither scale is necessarily "correct." Neither balance-beam nor platform scales are scientifically calibrated.

Height measurement is best done with a yardstick attached to the wall and a triangle or square sliding down to rest on the top of the head. When the student moves away, the screener keeps the triangle straight for reading. The sliding rod attached to a foldout flat metal strip that is found on a typical balance-beam scale is not accurate; between readings, it may vary by as much as an inch.

Grids to plot height, weight, and head circumference on a graph are useful. We recommend the use of grids for students who appear, by inspection, to have a problem with height and weight.

A table of normal heights and weights readily available and used when weighing and measuring children is helpful.

Referral Considerations

For height, general considerations for medical referral include but are not limited to the following:

- Ethnicity:
  Anglo/African American: under the fifth percentile (grids show percentiles)
  Hispanic: under the fourth percentile
  Asian: under the third percentile
- Growth pattern: Over 3 years old with fewer than 2 inches growth in 12 months

- Growth percentile: Significant drop in percentile (e.g., 20th percentile to 10th percentile)
- Referral point: Reevaluate in 1 year if measurement is near the referral criteria point

Weight

- Weight/height ratio: Over 95th percentile for weight and ratio inappropriate (e.g., 50th percentile of height and 98th percentile of weight)
- Growth percentile: Significant drop in percentile.
- Unexplained weight loss

Height and weight measurements do not require the professional skills of the school nurse. Nonprofessional health caregivers, physical education or health education faculty, or others can be taught the proper way to weigh, measure, and record the information. Nurse evaluation prior to referring a student identified as experiencing or at risk for abnormal growth pattern for his or her age, weight, and heredity is appropriate.

SCHOOL RELEVANCE

Health screening programs are time consuming and costly; therefore, they must be chosen carefully. The value of early detection made possible through school screening programs must be constantly assessed against the time and personnel required. Questions school administrators should ask prior to selection decisions are: Is this a health problem that affects learning? Is there a treatment or correction for persons with the condition? Are public and private facilities for further diagnosis and treatment accessible and available in the community? Is there an approved and easily administered screening test? Is the screening procedure cost effective? Does the screening program provide a means for providing health education for the students? Can the program be a continuing process through the appropriate age or developmental stages of the students in the school? Is the person conducting the screening well trained, or can the person or other persons be well trained?

ROLE OF THE SCHOOL NURSE

The school nurse is frequently responsible for planning and implementing school screening programs. It is always an advantage to have several other trained persons to assist. The other screeners may be nurses, paraprofessionals, or volunteers who can assist with specific parts of the screening. Vision, hearing, and scoliosis screening requires that screeners receive in-service training and information updates. Testing is more difficult than it appears from simply reading about the testing. In-service training should meet state health department criteria or local guidelines. Such training is given by a consulting physician, vision specialist audiologist, or proficient nurse. Several states require a specific curriculum and a successful completion of an examination to certify screeners and trainers of screeners.

HEALTH EDUCATION TIPS

Each screening program will benefit students more when health information is presented prior to the screening. The health educator, school nurse, or classroom teacher can use this opportunity to provide information about the eye and vision or the ear and hearing. Eye and ear safety information is also important. Demonstrations of the audiometer and Snelling vision test and an explanation of how students are to be screened and what information is identified are valuable information for students.

Three resources for nurses and teachers are the following:

The Good Lite Company
1540 Hanna Ave.
Forest Park, IL 60130
708-366-3860

Texas Department of Health, Bureau of Maternal and Child Health Vision
Audiometric Screening Techniques
Vision Screening Manual
Spinal Screening Program Guidelines

Hearing and Speech Services
1100 West 49th St.
Austin, TX

Texas Society to Prevent Blindness
3211 West Dallas
Houston, TX 77019

REFERENCES

Chauvin, V. G. *Hearing Screening Guidelines for School Nurses*. Scarborough, Maine: National Association of School Nurses, 1993.

Cronk, C., et al. *Growth Charts for Children with Down Syndrome: 1 Month to 18 Years of Age*. Pediatrics 102 (1988): 114.

Greenswag, L. R., and R. C. Alexander, eds. *Management of Prader-Willis Syndrome*. New York: Springer-Verlag, 1988.

Gross, R. D., et al. *Vision screening guidelines, 1991–1992*.

Lewis, K.D., and H. B.Thomas. *Manual of School Health*. Menlo Park, Calif.: Addison-Wesley, 1986.

National Association of School Nurses. *Spinal Screening Guidelines for School Nurses*. Scarborough, Maine: National Association of School Nurses, 1987.

National Association of School Nurses. *Vision Screening Guidelines for School Nurses*. Scarborough, Maine: National Association of School Nurses, 1992.

Proctor, S. T., S. L. Lordi, and D. S. Zaiger. *School Nursing Practice: Roles and Standards*. Scarborough, Maine: National Association of School Nurses, 1993.

Roeser, R. J. *A Guide to the Practice of Audiology, Roser's Audiology Desk Reference*. New York: Theieme Medical Publishers, 1996.

Wold, S.J. *School Nursing: A Framework for Practice*. North Branch, Minn.: Sunrise River Press, 1981.

Yawn, B.P., et al. "Is School Vision Screening Effective?" *Journal of School Health* 66(5).

SKIN CONDITIONS, INFECTIONS, AND DISEASES

Rashes Associated with Common Childhood Diseases
- Rubeola
- Rubella
- Chicken Pox
- Scarlet Fever
- Fifth Disease (Erythema Infectiosum)

Allergic Rashes
- Causes
- Types
- First Aid

Bacterial Infections
- Cellulitis
- Impetigo
- Paronychia (Felon)
- Furuncle (Boil)

Fungal Infections (Ringworm)
- Tinea Capitis
- Tinea Pedis
- Tinea Corporis
- Tinea Curis
- Treatment of Fungal Infections

Parasites (Infestations)
- Pediculosis (Head Lice)
- Pediculosis Corporis (Body Lice)
- Pediculosis Pubis (Crab Lice)
- Scabies
- Treatment of Parasites

Insect Bites and Stings
- Local, Generalized, and Anaphylactic Reactions
- Prevention and First Aid

Spider Bites

Animal and Human Bites
- Rabies Prophylaxis
- Prevention of Infection
- Prevention of Tetanus
- First Aid

Other Common Skin Disorders
- Acne Vulgaris
- Herpes Simplex

School Relevance

Role of the School Nurse

Health Education Tips

References

If you go long enough without a bath even the fleas will let you alone.
Ernie Pyle

Medical and nonmedical personnel who assist in school clinics see dozens of children with skin conditions or rashes. Many of these conditions have a similar appearance: *tinea capitus* often looks like *impetigo, dandruff,* or *alopecia areata;* the rash of an allergic reaction to penicillin may look like the rash of rubella; red measles (rubeola) on occasion is mistaken for scarlet fever. To add to the confusion, rashes that are symptoms of the same contagious disease sometimes look different on different people, and a secondary skin condition such as impetigo or red marks from scratching may add to the difficulty of identification. A variety of allergic rashes is commonly seen in children and adults. Rashes from completely different causes may look alike. At times, the school nurse or other personnel will be able to identify the condition with certainty; on occasion a visit to a doctor may be necessary.

An experienced school nurse or health caregiver often identifies the rash from history, symptoms, and observation of the rash. A physician can almost always say whether or not a particular rash is contagious, even when the cause may escape precise identification. When in doubt, consider that contagion may need to be ruled out or that medication will be required, and refer the child to a physician. In addition, to protect other students, school policy often requires that any rash be deemed "not contagious" by a physician if the afflicted student is to continue in school. This section and reference materials answer some caregivers questions about skin conditions.

RASHES ASSOCIATED
WITH COMMON CHILDHOOD DISEASES

Rash is a term applied to any eruption of the skin. Skin rashes are symptoms of a large number of infectious and noninfectious human diseases. The appearance and distribution of the rash often is distinctive enough to permit diagnosis of the disease. Some noninfectious rashes such as drug reactions mimic rashes and may be mistakenly identified as an infectious disease.

Rashes associated with internal disease include those from red measles (rubeola), German measles (rubella), chicken pox, and scarlet fever. These conditions are all contagious, and the most contagious are chicken pox and red measles. The most contagious period begins 1 to 3 days before the rash appears and continues 1 to 2 days after the rash appears and then rapidly diminishes even though the rash may remain 1 to 2 days longer (see Figure 5-1).

94

	Fever prior to rash (days)	Rash continues (days)	Contagious period after onset of fever (days)
Red measles	2-3	5-8	4-6
German measles	0-1	1-2	2-4
Chicken pox	0-1	5-10	2-4
Scarlet fever	0-1	2-4	2-4 (if not treated)

Figure 5-1. Comparison of four contagious diseases.

Many other childhood viral infections cause a variety of rashes (see Figure 5-2). Two of these diseases, roseola and fifth disease, are only slightly contagious. Roseola generally occurs in children younger than age 4. Measles (rubeola) and German measles (rubella) are becoming rare because of successful immunization programs. Scarlet fever is not contagious after 1 day of proper treatment. If untreated, the child usually recovers spontaneously. A small percentage of children become carriers of the germ (streptococcus) while remaining in good health. Susceptibility to chickenpox is universal among those not previously infected. All these diseases can vary in severity; the more severe cases last a little longer and remain contagious longer than others. Contagion does not end abruptly; the child slowly becomes less contagious.

Rubeola

The rubeola (red measles) rash begins on the face and then moves to the upper chest, stomach, back, and finally arms. It begins as red spots about the size of the head of a match. Usually the spots run together. No crusts or scabs are formed. Children with rubeola have red eyes, runny noses, coughs, and high fevers and are quite sick. The incubation period (the interval between exposure to the infection and the first symptom) is about 10 days, varying from 7 to 18 days from exposure to onset of fever and about 14 days until a rash appears. Isolate the child for approximately 1 week after the appearance of the rash.

Rubella

Rubella (German measles) begins and spreads the same way as the rash of rubeola, but the rash is faint pink and sparse and, in most cases, is gone by the third day. Children with this disease usually have a low-grade fever and may have a headache, mild conjunctivitis, and swollen lymph glands behind and below the ears. The diagnosis is often missed because it is similar to many other conditions and often is very mild. The incubation period is about 16 to 18 days.

	Rubeola (Measles)	Rubella (German measles)	Roseola	Scarlet Fever (Scarlatina)	Erythema Infectiosum (Fifth disease)	Varicella (Chicken pox)
Etiology	Rubeola virus	Rubella virus	Not yet identified; probably several viruses	Group A Streptococcus	Parvovirus	Varicella-zoster virus
Characteristics of rash	Severe red maculopapular; becomes confluent	Mild, red maculopapular; remains discrete	Mild, red maculopapular; remains discrete	Reddish blush, "goose flesh"; fades on pressure	Red (like slapped cheek); Lacy and reticulated later	Tiny clear blister with redness around it; soon forms crust and scab
Part of body on which rash first appears	Forehead, behind, ears, face, neck	Forehead, cheeks, neck	Face, chest, abdomen	Upper chest, face	Cheeks	Scalp, face, chest, abdomen
Spreads to	Chest, abdomen, arms, legs	Chest, abdomen	Very slight spread	Lower chest, abdomen, arms	Chest, abdomen, arms, legs	Arms, legs
Progression and time intervals for diagnosis	Fever, then red eyes, then cough; rash at end of 2nd day or onset of 3rd day during height of fever	1st day, fever; 2nd day, fever and rash; 3rd day, all gone	1st-3rd days, fever; end of 3rd day or onset of 4th day, fever goes away and rash appears	Rash and fever begin on 1st day; 5-7 days later, skin peels or flakes	Fever for 2-3 days 1 week prior to onset of rash on cheeks; 1-4 days later, lacy rash appears on body	Rash and fever begin at about same time on 1st-2nd day; when fever stops, new blister formation stops
Severity of illness	Usually severe	Usually mild	Mild but high fever	Mild to moderate	Mild	Mild to moderate; severe in older adolescents and adults

96

	Rubeola (Measles)	Rubella (German measles)	Roseola	Scarlet Fever (Scarlatina)	Erythema Infectiosum (Fifth disease)	Varicella (Chicken pox)
Associated symptoms other than rash	High fever, red eyes, severe cough, mild itch	Low fever, lymph nodes, back of neck and suboccipital	Usually none	Exudative tonsillopharyngitis, sore tongue	Fever mild to moderate	Fever, itching
Complications	Otitis media pneumonia, encephalitis	Usually none, occasional arthritis	Usually none	Nephritis, carditis	Painful joints, arthritis	Usually none
Period of Infectivity	From 1 day before onset of fever to 2 days after appearance of rash, except in atypical cases	From 1 day before onset of fever to 1 day after rash appears	Duration of fever	From 1 day before fever to cure with antibiotics, or 1 week after onset of rash	For 2-3 days about 1 week prior to appearance of facial rash	From 1 day before onset of fever to drying of all crusts, or 5 days after first appearance of rash
Additional information	Preventable with immunization; atypical cases frequent since advent of immunization	Preventable with immunization; because virus may infect fetus, notify pregnant teachers	Does not occur after age 3-4	Curable with penicillin or antibiotics; complications rare but severe, return to school with doctor's premission; Scarlet fever and scarlatina are synonymous	Because virus may infect fetus, notify pregnant teachers; not contagious when rash appears; may return to school when fever subsides and feels well	Lengthy school exclusion not necessary; 4-7 days usually sufficient

Figure 5-2. Rashes: Differential diagnosis of common childhood diseases associated with rash.

Chicken Pox

Chicken pox (varicella) begins with a tiny clear blister (vesicle) that rapidly breaks and forms a loose crust or red scab. It begins on the back and chest and spreads to the face and extremities. The rash continues to erupt for 2 or 3 days, so all stages of the sores—blisters to loose crusts—may be seen at any one time. The incubation period is about 2 to 3 weeks. A child is generally able to return to school about 1 week after the appearance of the vesicles.

Scarlet Fever

Scarlet fever almost always begins on the face, neck, and upper chest. In more severe cases, it then spreads to the trunk and arms. It starts as a diffuse reddish blush, with no discrete spots, and the reddish skin feels rough to the touch. The child may or may not feel sick, depending on the severity of the disease. The incubation period is 1 to 3 days.

Inexperienced observers often mistake scarlet fever for red measles. This is a serious mistake because the treatment is completely different. Untreated scarlet fever can result in serious kidney or heart disease. Scarlatina and scarlet fever are the same disease.

Fifth Disease (Erythema Infection)

Erythema infectiosum is called fifth disease because it was identified after four other rashes: rubeola, rubella, scarlet fever, and roseola. It is a very mild skin disorder caused by a virus. About 1 week after exposure, the child develops a low-grade fever that lasts 5 to 7 days and then recovers with no additional symptoms in about another week. A distinctive rash may then appear. This faint, lacy rash on the trunk, arms, and legs resembles a slapped cheek. Adults, especially women, may have joint pain and swelling at this stage. Occasionally, the rash recurs after days or weeks, but promptly subsides. Often there is neither fever nor rash with this disease. The child may return to school when he or she feels well and when the fever (if present) subsides.

ALLERGIC RASHES

Causes

Contact dermatitis is an inflammation of the skin due to touching an irritating or sensitized chemical. The most common of these chemicals is poison ivy or poison oak. Many other plants can cause a rash in susceptible individuals. Substances that frequently cause contact dermatitis are fiberglass, wool, animal fur, cosmetics, soaps, detergents, scouring compounds, hair dye, metals, and chemicals.

Allergies to food are common, and rashes take various forms on different people. Sensitivity to any food or chemical can occur. Fish, shellfish, nuts, seeds, eggs, cow milk, soy, wheat, and corn are frequently cited as the cause of a rash.

Some individuals develop allergic rashes due to dusts, pollens, or other inhaled substances. Environmental allergies are more difficult to control than food allergies or contact dermatitis.

Types

Hives (urticaria) usually appear as round or oval pale reddish spots with slightly raised borders. They are usually the size of a dime or a quarter and occasionally come together to form irregular shapes. The spots fade and reappear, sometimes several times in an hour. In addition, eyelids, lips, or other parts of the body can occasionally swell.

Eczema is an allergic rash and is commonly seen in the bends of the elbows, on the back, behind the knee joints, and on the cheeks. It can, however, appear almost anywhere on the body except the palms of the hands and soles of the feet. It is often rough and scaly and bleeds from scratching. Areas may be dry or have a watery discharge. Eczema is a noninfectious chronic condition.

There are innumerable other types of allergic rashes, some have large red splotches some scaly, scabby pinpoint sores, some spread and join other sores to form larger areas of rash. Rashes caused by an allergy can last from a few minutes to many days.

First Aid

A variety of over-the-counter ointments and lotions are available to control itching or to soothe skin conditions caused by an allergic reaction or contact with an irritant. To find out what the rash is, what caused it, and how to prevent future exposure, it is best to have a physician see the student. The physician will usually prescribe an oral antihistamine to control itching and an antibacterial medication to prevent infection. If a secondary condition such as impetigo develops (sometimes due to the child's scratching), advise the parents to consult a physician to ensure effective treatment of both conditions.

BACTERIAL INFECTIONS

Cellulitis

Cellulitis is an infection most often secondary to a cut, abrasion, impetigo, boil, or other infection or trauma. It is first seen as a tiny edge of redness encircling the primary lesion. The red area spreads, which indicates that body defenses are not limiting the infection. Pain, tenderness, swelling, fever, and possibly a red streak (lymphangitis) beginning at the primary lesion indicate progression of the infection.

If the condition appears to be mild, encourage parents to watch the child closely to be sure healing is taking place and to seek medical care if any symptoms persist or become more severe. If the cellulitis is on the face, is over a joint, or progressively becomes more reddened, swollen, tender, or painful or if a red streak is noted, make an immediate medical referral.

Impetigo

Impetigo is a contagious skin infection caused by streptococcus and staphylococcus bacteria. The bacteria usually enter the skin through a scratch, cut, or insect bite. The lesion formed is covered with a brownish yellow (honey-colored) crust and first appears near the entry site. Lesions often spread to other parts of the body.

The most characteristic features of impetigo are the brownish yellow crust covering all or part of each sore. Sores may be single and isolated, about 1/2 inch in diameter, or several may coalesce and form a larger, irregularly shaped sore. Sores are most common where children scratch themselves: on the face, on the fingers, and around the nose.

Impetigo is contagious on direct contact. A student with few sores can be treated by covering the sores with an adhesive bandage and may remain in school. It is preferable to keep a child with many exposed lesions at home.

Without proper treatment, impetigo will continue to spread. Most physicians advise parents to treat the infected lesions by soaking the area with water, then removing the crust. The crusts are easy to pick or rub off. Slight bleeding usually occurs when this is done. A topical antibacterial ointment should be applied to each sore. It takes only a few days for the condition to heal after this treatment.

Paronychia (Felon)

A paronychia is an abscess that occurs at the junction of the fingernail and the cuticle. It is almost always associated with nail or cuticle biting or picking.

Symptoms include pain, redness, swelling, and pus around the edge of the nail. When the pus is still under tension, prior to rupture of the abscess, the tip of the finger may be throbbing and painful. After the abscess ruptures, the pain diminishes and a crust forms. Occasionally, the abscess circles all around the cuticle, encompassing both sides plus the bottom. This is called a runaround.

Healing is usually spontaneous. Sometimes the infection heals without formation of pus. In some cases, infection spreads to the deeper tissues of the finger or hand and can be most serious and disabling. Prior to the formation of pus, applying hot compresses or soaking the finger in warm water relieves pain and accelerates healing. After the formation of pus, it may be necessary to refer the student to the physician so that the abscess can be drained by gently inserting a sharp blade between the cuticle and the nail. This is a sterile procedure and is not appropriate for school personnel to handle. If the whole tip of the finger is red and swollen, emergency referral to a physician is mandatory with follow-up to make sure the parent complies. The student is often given antibiotics to assist the healing.

Furuncle (Boil)

A furuncle is the medical term for a skin abscess or boil. The infection usually starts below the skin and expands. The deeper below the skin the infection begins, the larger the boil will be when it reaches the surface.

Skin abscesses vary in size from 1 centimeter to the size of a golf ball. Possible causes of an abscess include an insect bite or a puncture wound that deposits germs below the skin surface. These wounds are usually small. Initially, there is only pain with minimal swelling and redness at the site of the boil. Within 24 hours, however, the redness, swelling, and pain increase; the center of the boil appears pale yellow, indicating pus formation. The yellow area enlarges, becomes soft to the touch, and may drain spontaneously. In larger abscesses that do not drain properly, the pus gradually becomes thick and waxy, and when drainage finally does occur, the pus is apt to come out in one lump. This is known as a *core*.

Prior to the abscess becoming fluctuant and purulent (soft with pus), some physicians recommend warm compresses or soaks and an application of an antibiotic ointment. We do not recommend that school health personnel squeeze or open the abscess. In addition to causing needless pain, squeezing may introduce new infection or may spread the infection and delay healing. Refer the student to a physician to have the boil opened to allow the pus to drain properly. The student will need medication (usually antibiotics) and will require medical care.

FUNGAL INFECTIONS (RINGWORM)

Ringworm (tinea) is a fungal infection of the skin commonly found in four areas of the body:

- Scalp: tinea capitis
- Feet: tinea pedis
- Trunk, face, and limbs: tinea corporis
- Genital area: tinea curis

Although ringworm in all four areas is caused by similar fungi, the appearance and treatment depend on the location.

Tinea Capitis

Tinea capitis, ringworm of the scalp, is an infection caused by a fungus that can be acquired from contact with infected persons, animals (including household pets), or soil. The affected areas of the scalp are noted as scaly patches where hair has broken off or fallen out. Often there is no discomfort with ringworm of the scalp, but some individuals develop an allergic response with resulting inflammation, itching, and secondary bacterial infection.

Ringworm of the scalp is treated with antifungal medication (Griseofulvin®) that is taken orally for 4 to 8 weeks. In addition, a topical ointment may be applied. With adequate treatment, most children will have negative cultures in 4 to 6 weeks and be 95% clear by two months. The most common cause today is the fungus *trichophyton tonsurans*, and the condition is increasing in the United States.

The most common type of tinea capitis resembles dandruff and causes no bald spots. A culture is required for diagnosis.

Other types of tinea capitis resemble impetigo with crusted, weeping sores, appear as bald spots with short, broken-off hair, or appear as a kerion, a large, boggy, puss filled, weeping, painful area on the scalp. Some of these types of conditions require culture for diagnosis, but some can be diagnosed by inspection.

Although the fungus is not readily transmitted, close contact with other students is not advisable until treatment is successfully completed. When the condition is suspected by history or by observation of scalp, refer the student for medical evaluation and treatment. Exclude the student from school pending:

Physician's statement that treatment (medication) has been prescribed and started or

Physician's statement that the condition is *not* ringworm

Tinea capitis is sometimes confused with another condition called *alopecia areata*, which also causes round bald spots. In the latter case, the bald spots are absolutely smooth with no broken hairs; the hair falls out by the roots. The differentiation is important because alopecia areata is noncontagious, whereas tinea capitis is highly contagious and can spread through a school rapidly if not controlled.

Students who have ringworm of the scalp should be seen by the school nurse at regular intervals to be sure that the prescribed treatment and management is followed. A management plan to ensure that the student continues medical care and is taking the medication until the fungus is no longer active is needed. Periodic inspection of the student's head by the nurse or other caretaker and the recording of dates and findings will be required to ensure that treatment is continuing and that the condition is improving. It is generally recognized that many individuals act as carriers of ringworm of the scalp without actually showing a clinically identifiable lesion. When children who are properly treated have recurrences or when several children in the family have tinea capitis, the adults as well as the children need to be cultured and, if positive, will need to be treated. Failure to take long-term medications regularly is the main reason that this skin condition is difficult to cure.

Tinea Pedis

Tinea pedis, athlete's foot, is much more common in boys than in girls. It responds easily to treatment with specific lotions or ointments. Unfortunately, it keeps coming back in certain susceptible individuals. Many men never completely get rid of it. Tinea pedis is seen most commonly in postpubertal males. It causes blisters on the instep of the foot, and fissuring between the toes is occasionally seen.

Refer students with sores on their feet to the school nurse or their personal physician for advice and treatment.

Tinea Corporis

Tinea corporis, ringworm of the body, is a common ringworm. It appears on the arms, chest, abdomen, and, more rarely, face. It starts as a tiny red spot that slowly grows in a circular fashion, clearing in the center as it enlarges. The edges remain reddish and scaly. No scabs, pus, or crusts are formed. Most children have a single lesion, but on occasion, a child will develop more.

Children often develop small, round, whitish depigmented areas on their cheeks and upper arms. This is definitely not ringworm and is not contagious. Its cause is unknown, but it waxes and wanes without treatment and is completely harmless. If one looks carefully, it is easy to see that the edges of the whitish circular area look the same as the center, thus distinguishing it from ringworm.

Tinea Curis

Tinea curis is found in the folds and creases of the body, especially the groin area, and for this reason it is often called jock itch. Found on both boys and girls, it is more common in obese individuals than others. Tinea curis is usually quite uncomfortable, itches intensely, and is worse in the summer than other times of the year.

Various fungi cause tinea curis. It is easy to cure, but, like athlete's foot, it often comes back. Cleanliness and certain medicated lotions will cure it quickly.

Treatment of Fungal Infections

A physician will treat ringworm of the body, feet, and groin with medications such as tolnaftate (Tinactin®), chlortrimazole (Lotrimin®), and related compounds. They are not greasy and do not sting the skin or smell bad. The first treatment renders students noncontagious so that they can stay in school during treatment until the sores are gone. If the scalp is involved, it is necessary to take prescription medicine internally, usually griseofulvin (Fulvicin®), and it will be 2 to 5 or more days before the student is noncontagious.

PARASITES (INFESTATIONS)

Pediculosis (Head Lice)

A vast resurgence of head lice since the 1970s has placed head lice infestation as the largest and most exasperating health problem in schools today.

The adult head louse (pediculosis capitis) is about 1/16 inch long and gray in color. It crawls fairly quickly but cannot fly and cannot jump like a flea. The adult female louse lays eggs (nits) at the base of the hair shaft next to the scalp. When adult lice are not seen on examination, finding unhatched or hatched nit casings attached to the hair very close to the scalp (3–4 mm) aids in diagnosis of pediculosis. The nit is covered with a tiny bit of gelatinous material that hardens into a semiopaque, tiny, pearly, whitish mass that is stuck tight to the hair shaft. In about 7 to 10 days, the egg matures and hatches into a louse that lives by sucking blood from the scalp. Without a human host, it can live 1 to 3 days. The adult louse lives 1 to 3 weeks, and a female can lay eggs several times before dying of old age.

The biggest problem with lice is *reinfestation*, especially when siblings share the same bed or when friends sleep over. The nits resist treatment and hatch live lice. Products used on the hair vary in effectiveness; those with a smaller kill ratio need to be left on longer. Some treatments kill both adult lice and nits (see Figure 5-3).

In severe cases, the student will have dirty hair that is matted and unkempt. Scratching is likely. Closer inspection reveals nits and often live, crawling lice.

In mild cases, the hair may appear to be clean and combed if one merely views the child from a distance. Suspicion may be aroused by scratching, and on close inspection nits can be seen.

If lice infestation is neglected, the excessive scratching causes a secondary infection from germs normally present on the scalp, such as staphylococcus. These

	Pyrthrin 0.3%	Lindane 1%	Permethrin 1%
Brand Name	RID®	Kwell®	Nix®
Availability	Nonprescription	Prescription shampoo	Nonprescription cream rinse
Application	10 minutes, followed by regular shampoo	4 minutes	10 minutes; used after regular shampoo
Number of applications	2	1-2	1
Cost per 2 oz.	8.04	7.49	10.65

Figure 5-3. Pediculicides. (Average of three pharmacies, Dallas, TX, March 1996.)

infected areas of matted hair will require frequent washing and applications of antibiotic ointment. Occasionally, some of the hair must be cut away. Lymph nodes in the neck are often swollen. Scratching fingers may also transfer the infection from the scalp to other parts of the body.

Severe cases are obvious by examination of the student's head. Mild cases will require a close inspection. If an instrument such as a tongue depressor is used to separate the hair, care must be taken not to convey the message that the student is too dirty to touch; the student has no control over the problem. Perform the examination unobtrusively and privately. When possible, refer the student to the school nurse for diagnostic confirmation.

Teachers may have an aversion to having a student (or students) in their classroom with nits or lice, but there is no reason for the teacher to fear catching them. Lice cannot jump on you, and nits are stuck to the hair. Physicians, nurses, and other health care workers have handled hundreds of infested children without becoming infested.

There are several ways to tell the difference between nits and dandruff. A louse usually lays the egg on the hair close to the scalp; a scale of dandruff may be 1 to 2 inches away (in warm climates, the nits may be deposited farther from the scalp). A nit sticks to the hair shaft and will not shake off like dandruff. An old nit that has hatched leaves behind a shell that can be combed out of the hair with a very fine tooth or special "nit" comb. When there are multiple nit shells, combing each one out is not easy and will take much time, effort, and patience.

Treatment of Pediculosis

All medicines used for pediculosis are applied to the hair; no medication is taken internally. They fall into three categories: lindane lotion, pyrethrin, and permethrin.

The three most often used topical treatments for individuals are listed in Figure 5-3. Note that since RID® requires two applications (7 to 10 days apart), the $8.04 price quoted for 2 ounces (one treatment) needs to be doubled for a true cost comparison. We believe that Nix® is the treatment of choice; it is not only ovicidal, but binds to the hair and remains effective for several weeks, making retreatment unnecessary.

Some schools enforce a "no-nits" policy, excluding students with nits in their hair from school. It is difficult and almost impossible to comb out every nit, and if an effective ovicidal product such as Nix® is used it is unnecessary. School exclusion is not necessary if treatment occurs the evening after diagnosis.

To treat the environment in which pediculosis is present, certain measures are still recommended. Although fomite transmission is much less important than head-to-head transmission, encourage parents to follow these guidelines:

- Wash all bedding in the washing machine on the hot cycle.
- Soak combs and brushes in the same medication solution used on the head or boil for 20 minutes; small nonmetal items can be microwaved for 60 seconds.
- Dry-clean clothing and other items that cannot be washed.
- Items that can be neither washed nor dry-cleaned (and are small enough) can be placed in a plastic bag secured at the top for 5 days. Include pillows, soft toys, hats, and scarves that cannot easily be washed.

A home (or school) should not be "fumigated" with general insecticides by a pest control company. The effort is wasted and possibly harmful. Simple vacuuming is used to clean carpets and furniture.

Refractory Cases

If treatment is not effective, it may be difficult to determine whether it failed because instructions were not accurately followed or because the infestation was caused by resistant lice. Resistant cases have involved students treated with lindane, and it seems likely that less than a 4 minute treatment time may be the cause rather than true resistance of the louse.

When families fail to understand or follow written instructions (due to a language barrier, illiteracy, or other reason), they require help in interpreting and implementing control measures. A school nurse, public health official, or volunteer should make a home visit to assess the problem and assist with correction. One single family can be the source of chronic reinfestation for an entire school.

Many schools provide students with a medicated shampoo in an effort to prevent absences due to this nuisance condition; for many families, the cost of the pediculicide (medicated shampoo) is the major deterrent obtaining treatment. Although it is necessary to treat family members, it is unnecessary to treat all students in the school.

If a student with pediculosis also has a secondary infection (usually due to scratching), referral to a physician is necessary. If a student has many sores and lindane is applied, it could be absorbed into the bloodstream and cause serious complications.

Unfortunately, some families are homeless or lack plumbing. In these cases, finding a source of water or referring them to a shelter becomes the first priority. The school health caretaker will need to obtain more information on students and families when they repeatedly have reinfestation of lice.

Because we will never eradicate pediculosis, management becomes a matter of control that is acceptable to the parties involved. Good control is more than shopping for the "best" pediculicide. It hinges on the thoroughness with which each family carries out individual treatment and household measures, on teaching children not to share hats and combs, and on other hygiene measures. Periodic monitoring by the school nurse who dispenses medication with clear instructions for use is an effective method of dealing with high-occurrence areas.

Pediculosis Corporis (Body Lice)

Pediculosis corporis is due to infestation with the body louse. It is transmitted by direct contact or by wearing infested apparel. It is most often seen in crowded or unhygienic conditions.

Symptoms are intense itching, possibly a generalized skin eruption, mild fever, tiredness, irritability, and in severe cases, weakness and debility. Treatment is the same as for pediculosis capitis. Sterilize clothing and bedding by dry heat (140°F for 5 minutes) by hot water (at least 130°F and/or dry in a hot dryer for at least 20 minutes) or by dry cleaning.

Pediculosis Pubis (Crab Lice)

Pediculosis pubis is due to infestation of the crab louse. It is generally confined to the genital region, but hair of the axilla, eyebrows, eyelashes, beard, or body surface of hairy individuals may be involved. These lice may be acquired from personal contact, wearing contaminated clothes, toilet seats, or bedclothes. Treatment is the same as for pediculosis capitis.

Scabies

Scabies is an intensely itchy skin rash caused by a mite, a small insect in the spider family. In older children and adults, a rash of raised red bumps occur, usually between the fingers and on the wrist, elbows, belt line, thighs, and genitals. The mite's burrow is a short, wavy, dirty line at the center of each cluster of red bumps.

Itching is often intense at night. Diagnosis is based on the appearance of the rash, complaints of itching, or visible scratch marks. When viewed under a microscope, scrapings of affected areas reveal the mite.

Scabies occurs worldwide and affects all socioeconomic groups. It is more common where there is poverty, poor sanitation, and crowding. Transmission can occur as long as the infected person is untreated.

Treatment of Parasites

Treatment consists of applying one of several different kinds of lotions or ointments. The most effective is lindane lotion, Kwell® (a prescription medicine), the same one used for head lice. A newer scabicide is permethrin in 5% cream, Elimite®. Application instructions are always outlined in the package insert or can be obtained from a family doctor or school nurse. These products are left on for 6 to 8 hours (sometimes more for Elimite®), and then the child is given a bath. The average infestation of scabies will be cured by one application. Some children with a severe infestation require two treatments, at least 7 days apart. Bed linens and all the child's clothing should be washed in an ordinary wash cycle in the washing machine to eliminate any live scabies, mites, or eggs.

INSECT BITES AND STINGS

The most common insect stings are those of bees, hornets, wasps, yellow jackets, and fire ants, which are all members of the Hymenoptera family. The mound-building fire ant found mostly in the warmer southern states has a very painful bite that causes a severe local reaction, but it rarely causes a generalized reaction. Many caterpillars cause a sting via venom on their feet. The sting is painful and leaves a row of tiny blisters with a red base. These insects are called urticating (blister-forming) caterpillars. Earwigs, scorpions, and some other insects also bite and sting.

Insect stings often cause severe pain that diminishes in 5 to 10 minutes, and the pain is usually gone in 15 minutes. Itching at the site of the sting may continue for several hours or days. Pain and swelling vary with individual stings; most reactions, however, are on a small, circumscribed area of the body. These are not considered a serious threat to the individual. Stings on any area of the body can result in an *aphylaxis,* a potentially life-threatening emergency for children and adults who have an extreme sensitivity to Hymenoptera stings. Stings on the head and neck are especially serious.

It is estimated that about two million Americans are highly sensitive to insect stings and that more than 50 people die each year from bee or wasp stings in the United States. Almost all are caused by one of the following severe reactions.

Local, Generalized, and Anaphylactic Reactions

Local reactions indicate that the body's immune mechanism is effectively defending against the insect venom and thereby preventing the entire body from reacting adversely. Some examples are the following:

- A sting that leaves a small red painful area that becomes normal in 10 to 15 minutes
- A sting on the hand or foot that causes some pain and swelling of the foot or hand that remains swollen for several days
- A sting on the forehead that causes tissue around both eyes to swell

A *generalized reaction* or *allergic reaction* may occur in a part of the body far removed from the bite. Examples are swelling of the lips, eyelids, or both from a bite on the hand, a rash all over the body from a single sting anywhere, or swelling of the hands from a bite on the leg. Signs of an allergic reaction include the following:

- Itching of the skin and a raised rash (hives)
- Swelling of the tissues of the lips, throat, tongue, hands, and feet
- Sudden redness of the skin (flushing)
- Wheezing, shortness of breath, coughing, and hoarseness
- Headache
- Nausea, vomiting, and abdominal cramps
- Sense of impending doom
- Loss of consciousness

If signs of a generalized or allergic reaction are present or if a student is not breathing normally, call the emergency medical service system (EMS). Allow the student to assume the most comfortable position for breathing. Monitor the level of consciousness, breathing, and pulse until the EMS arrives. Reactions of this nature can be dangerous because they indicate that the body has a weak immune mechanism against the insect venom and signal the possibility of an increasingly severe reaction and anaphylaxis to subsequent stings.

Anaphylaxis is a severe allergic response that occurs when a person is exposed to an allergy-causing substance to which the body has developed a previous sensitivity. When the allergen enters the bloodstream, the release of chemicals throughout the body is an effort to protect the body from the foreign substance causing the severe reaction.

Common causes triggering anaphylaxis are the following:

- Stings of bees, wasps, hornets, yellow jackets, and fire ants (Hymenoptera)
- Foods, including peanuts, other nuts, milk, eggs, shellfish, whitefish, and a variety of food additives
- Medications, including certain antibiotics (most commonly penicillin), as well as seizure medications, muscle relaxants, and even aspirin and nonsteroidal anti-inflammatory agents
- Exercise

Awareness and avoidance of the triggering substances by the individual are key to avoiding severe allergic reactions. In addition, on the advice of their physicians, susceptible persons can keep medications and learn how to self-administer their medications for the treatment of anaphylaxis, whether caused by insect stings, foods, medications, or other allergens.

Prevention and First Aid

Inspect the school playground and buildings periodically for bee hives, wasp nests, and fire ant mounds. Instruct students and faculty to report any signs of these insects they find. Insecticide sprays may be used to eradicate insects nests. In addition, cover food taken outside, clean outdoor eating areas and garbage areas regularly, and cut or trim hedges in a way that discourages insect habitation. An individual with a known sensitivity can avoid areas where stinging and biting insects congregate and nest.

Local reactions to stings (i.e., pain and itching) are best treated with cool water or an ice cube placed on the area. Although painful for a few minutes, the pain soon subsides and no further treatment will be necessary. Itching may continue for a few hours or intermittently for several days.

If a bee or wasp stinger is present, scrape it away with a plastic card or a knife blade. The stinger usually has a tiny venom sac attached, and care must be taken not to squeeze it. Removal with tweezers is not recommended because they cannot be used without squeezing.

Generalized reactions are potentially serious. It is advisable to explain this to the parent and student and refer the student to a physician. Allergists frequently recommend a series of desensitization shots and may also request that the individual carry a syringe containing the drug epinephrine (adrenaline). Two pharmaceutical companies package kits containing epinephrine in the prescribed dosage in a syringe ready for immediate use. If prescribed for a student or adult, keep the kit readily accessible in the clinic. The student, the school nurse, or a person so designated in the school can give the injection if necessary. Physicians orders must be kept in the clinic to address individual student needs. If the student is stung, the order will be to give the epinephrine injection immediately and to transport the student by ambulance to the emergency room. If the ambulance is delayed, the order will tell the caretaker what the physician wants done. With prevention or prompt treatment, almost all severe or fatal reactions can be avoided.

SPIDER BITES

Spiders (technically not insects) rarely bite humans. Two that have significantly harmful bites are the brown recluse spider and the black widow spider. Perspiration, abdominal cramps, nausea, headaches, and dizziness of various levels of intensity often follow a bite of the black widow spider; pain, nausea, fever, and chills follow a bite of the brown recluse spider. Should a student receive a bite while at school, apply ice to the bite and refer for immediate care by a physician. An antivenin is available for black widow bites; no antivenin is available for brown recluse spider bites. A physician will prescribe corticosteroids and supportive measures to aid healing.

ANIMAL AND HUMAN BITES

Students are often bitten by a pet or other animal, at school or at home. Most animal bites are from cats and dogs. Ignoring the wound may be extremely harmful because serious infections can come from bites of any animals. Most animal bites have puncture wounds or lacerations with jagged edges; in severe bites, there may be pain and bleeding, and tissue may be torn away.

Rabies Prophylaxis

Rabies is an acute, usually fatal viral disease of the central nervous system of animals. It is transmitted from animals to people by infected blood, tissue, or most commonly, saliva. Common carriers of rabies are dogs, cats, foxes, skunks, bats, and raccoons. Although it is theoretically possible for any mammal to develop rabies, rodents have not been implicated in transmitting the disease; therefore, squirrel, rat, mouse, or rabbit bites are not considered to infect with rabies. Tetanus or other bacteria may need to be considered. Always refer to a physician.

Unprovoked bites (especially from a dog) raise greater suspicion than if an animal is provoked or teased. The biting animal must be confined and observed 10 days. Notify the health department or police. A biting dog, cat, or bat that cannot be apprehended must be presumed to have rabies. A student who is bitten will require preventive rabies shots.

Prevention of Infection

Dog bites are more likely to be open, jagged lacerations that can be thoroughly irrigated, have a low infection rate, and usually not require prophylactic antibiotics. Cat bites are usually deep puncture wounds and have a high infection rate. They often require prophylactic antibiotics. Human bites have the greatest potential for infection. With human bites, consider transmission of hepatitis B or, in rare cases, human immunodeficiency virus (HIV).

Prevention of Tetanus

Due to each individual's requirements, advise the parents to obtain medical advice. A school nurse or a physician may choose a particular type of tetanus toxoid for a particular bite:

- No previous active immunization with tetanus toxoid: tetanus immune globulin and begin a series of tetanus toxoid
- Active immunization 10 years ago or longer: booster of adult tetanus toxoid (Td)
- Active immunization within the past 5 years: mild bite requires no booster; severe bite requires a booster adult Td
- Severe, neglected, old (over 24 hours), or dirty bites: adult Td, unless patient has had one in the previous 12 months

The student's most current tetanus immunization information should be noted on the school health record on the medical referral form.

First Aid

In addition to observing universal precautions for wound care, animal bites should be treated as follows:

1. Wash the wound with soap and running water for at least 5 minutes.
2. Apply a sterile dressing only if bleeding is present. Advise removal of the dressing when the bleeding stops.
3. Notify the parent, and recommend a medical evaluation.

Obtain the description and location of the biting animal: breed, color, size, owner's name if known, and owner's home address if known. The animal will need to be confined for 10 days. Also notify the police or animal control center. If the bite is from a classroom pet, follow first aid suggestions and ask the animal control center, health department, or police department for advice regarding confinement of the animal.

For human bites, observe universal precautions for wound care and do the following:

1. Wash the wound with soap and running water for at least 5 minutes.
2. Apply a sterile dressing if there is bleeding. Remove the dressing when the bleeding stops. Leave the wound open to the air to dry.
3. Notify the parent, and recommend medical evaluation.

Human bites have a high potential for infection and may need prophylactic treatment with antibiotics by a physician. Note: Covering a nonbleeding wound caused by an animal or human bite with a dressing can create a dark, warm, moist area in which germs thrive. When at all possible, leave the wound open to air dry after cleaning.

OTHER COMMON SKIN DISORDERS

Acne Vulgaris

About 85% of teenagers have some degree of acne. It is most severe in girls between age 14 and 17 and in boys between age 16 and 19. It begins to subside at about age 22. A student with a single pimple is self-conscious. A teenager with moderate to severe acne feels severely socially handicapped. Students do not initiate discussions about these concerns, so they may not know that methods exist to alleviate this condition.

Acne is caused by the action of androgens (male hormones) upon the sebaceous (wax) glands of the skin. The adrenal glands of both boys and girls secrete small amounts of androgen. Acne is usually worse in boys, however, because the testicles secrete large amounts of androgen during puberty. The sebaceous glands are found in largest number in the skin of the face, chest, and back. These skin glands secrete sebum or wax, and when they overreact to hormonal stimulation, "whiteheads" or "blackheads" occur. The medical term for these blemishes is *comedo.*

A whitehead is a closed comedo and cannot drain out onto the skin surface. It slowly enlarges and bursts out of its capsule under the surrounding skin, gets secondarily infected, and causes a small pimple or abscess (boil). The deeper the original breakout, the larger the boil becomes before it finally ruptures out onto the skin surface or, occasionally, heals without rupturing. In either case, scarring results if the abscess is large enough.

A blackhead is an open comedo that easily drains out onto the skin surface and rarely causes abscesses. The blackened tip is not from dirt or poor hygiene; it is the result of a combination of dead skin cells and skin pigment.

Mild acne is limited to open comedones (blackheads), closed comedones (whiteheads), and occasionally a small inflamed protuberence of the skin (pimples.) The lesions are found mainly on the face, with a smaller number on the chest and back.

With moderate acne, comedones, pimples, small nodules (hard lumps), and abscesses appear. The shoulders, back, and chest are involved the most. The lesions on the face are more numerous. Healing lesions remain red for a long time, but eventually normal skin color returns.

With severe acne, the abscesses are larger and more widespread and are often congruent, with several small ones joining to form a large one. There is more reddish discoloration. Larger abscesses heal by scarring and leave a pitted, irregular skin surface.

Management Considerations

Current treatment for acne offers many new, effective medications. Successful therapy requires careful and sustained patient cooperation. Support and encouragement by a school nurse can be a key factor in a student's continuing therapy and eventual recovery. Other information and suggestions are as follows:

- There is no good evidence to suggest that any food, even chocolate, makes acne worse. If parents or doctors prohibit certain foods, make an effort in the school to accommodate those wishes. If a student is on a bizarre or obviously unhealthy diet, the health caregiver may intervene through the nurse, principal, counselor, parent, or physician.
- Facial applications commonly used are liquids, special soaps, topical prescription antibiotics, and drying lotions (warn against those containing mercury).

Common medicines a physician may prescribe for mild acne are Fostex® cream and shampoo, 5% benzoyl peroxide, vanoxide, and Komed®.

- Internal (oral) medications prescribed by a physician are antibiotics and vitamin A derivative (tretinoin) for severe acne. They require prolonged usage and are only for cases with many pustules and abscesses. Antibiotics can have significant adverse side effects, so careful follow-up and patient cooperation are necessary. With newer topical medications, oral antibiotics are not used as much as in previous years.

- Recommend avoiding oily or greasy hair or facial preparations, and advise the use of only water-based preparations.

- Warn against the use of Retinoin® during pregnancy; it is known to cause birth defects.

Modern treatment offers many new, effective medications, but successful therapy requires careful and sustained patient cooperation. Counseling, support, and encouragement by the school health caregiver can be a key factor in a student's continuing therapy and eventual recovery. A supply of reliable pamphlets for information should be kept in the clinic; see the resources listed in the Teaching Tips in this section.

Herpes Simplex

Herpes simplex, also called fever blisters, is caused by the herpes simplex virus. There are two types of herpes simplex virus.

Type I herpes usually occurs around the lips and nose but can also occur in other facial and body areas (see Figure 5-4). It is extremely common in children; tests show that 70% to 90% of adults have had it at some time in their lives. Type II herpes usually occurs in the genital area and is a common sexually transmitted disease.

Symptoms and Transmission

The active sore of herpes simplex is the well-known, small fever blister seen on the lip. When the external sore heals, usually in 6 to 10 days, the virus remains latent in the nerve trunks and may be reactivated due to excess sunlight, fever, menstruation, or other forms of physical or emotional stress.

The incubation period for either type of herpes varies from 2 to 12 days after exposure. Symptoms begin with a burning, tingling, or itching sensation at the site where the characteristic sores later appear. Generalized symptoms such as fever,

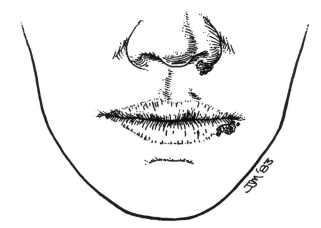

Figure 5-4. Some typical locations of herpes simplex.

malaise, sore throat, and headache can accompany the initial sores, which last no more than 3 weeks; after healing, no scars remain.

Recurrent sores tend to be less severe than the initial infection and persist for a shorter period of time, about 4 ½ days. Some children have no recurrent outbreaks, but others may experience several recurrences each year.

Both types of herpes are only contagious when the active lesions are present on the skin, *not* during the latent period when the virus is in the nerve trunks.

Type I herpes is usually transmitted by direct contact with infected saliva or the active herpetic lesion itself, whereas type II herpes is transmitted primarily through sexual contact. As in impetigo, autoinoculation of either type from active lesions on the lips or genitals to other body sites is possible. Because the virus can survive only a short time outside the body, it is unlikely that herpes can be contracted from toilet seats, hot tubs, or other inanimate objects.

Treatment

Many students may come to school with fever blisters (herpes simplex type I). They do not need to be excluded any more than a student with a common cold is excluded from normal activities. Individual counseling about hand washing and abstinence from close-contact sports, such as wrestling, is helpful.

Currently, there is no medical treatment proven to be completely effective against genital or oral herpes; therefore, medical management focuses on symptomatic relief of pain and discomfort. To enhance healing and prevent secondary infection, clean the affected area with warm water and soap and dry it thoroughly.

Prevention

It is important for herpes patients to be careful when handling their lesions to avoid the possibility of transferring the infection to other parts of their bodies or to others by kissing or close contact. Thorough hand washing and use of a disposable napkin or paper towel to dry an area where lesions are present helps. Caution individuals who wear contact lenses to be particularly conscientious with hand washing so as not to transmit the virus to their eyes.

SCHOOL RELEVANCE

Numerous over-the-counter medications for skin and scalp conditions are available. Any medication may cause a reaction in individuals who are allergic to that drug. School personnel are urged to use caution in making suggestions to students and parents regarding medication or treatments. Different individuals need different medications, and what helps one may not help another. In addition, with some skin conditions, relief may be obtained and symptoms subside, but the condition will not be cured.

ROLE OF THE SCHOOL NURSE

With any skin rash or skin condition, there are three concerns for school nurse:

- Is the condition contagious?
- Should the student be excluded from school, and if so, for how long?
- Is the condition harmful to the fetus of a pregnant woman?

Rashes associated with internal diseases are almost always contagious; until released by a physician to return to school, the student must remain at home. Impetigo, ringworm, and scabies are also contagious.

Some students with common childhood diseases are excluded from school longer than necessary. An American Academy of Pediatrics publication entitled *Report of the Committee on Infectious Diseases,* commonly known as the Red Book, can assist nurses in finding current and accurate information; it is available through:

Academy of Pediatrics
P.O. Box 927
Elk Grove Village, IL 60009
(847) 228-5005

Children with chicken pox and mumps are commonly excluded from school for too long. Neither condition requires exclusion for more than 7 days, unless complications develop.

Sometimes we respond to common childhood diseases with indifference, but they are quite threatening to pregnant women and unimmunized (religious and medical exempted) children. It is important that the nurse know in advance who these vulnerable people are. See Section 11 for more information on neonatally transmitted infections.

HEALTH EDUCATION TIPS

The school nurse is frequently responsible for providing or arranging in-service education on communicable disease for teachers and school staff. State and local health departments can usually provide charts showing incubation periods, symptoms, communicable periods, course of the disease, and precautions for teachers to use in the classroom.

Instruct students and staff in proper hand-washing techniques. This important method for prevention of skin disease and other communicable disease is often only casually mentioned in health education classes and in one-to-one health teaching with children. The use of the Glo Germ (see the Bevis Corporation listing below) for hand-washing experiments in classes is a dramatic way to teach students and adults about proper hand washing.

A school nurse or other school healthcare provider or teachers will find numerous resources for excellent materials on skin conditions, including the following:

American Academy of Dermatology
P.O. Box 681069
Schaumburg, IL 60168-4014
(847) 330-0230
Pamphlets: "Acne," "Skin Care under the Sun," "Black Skin," "Atopic Eczema/Dermatitis," and "Athlete's Foot "

A single copy of each pamphlet is free with a self-addressed, stamped, business-size envelope.

Brevis Corporation
3310 South 2700 East
Salt Lake City, UT 84109
800-383-3377
801-466-6677
Request "Germbuster Flier" educational material, promotional incentives, and Glo-Germ for hand-washing experiments.

American Academy of Pediatrics
Dept. C—Acne
P.O. Box 927
Elk Grove Village, IL 60009-0927
Pamphlet: "Acne Treatment and Control," single copy free

Centers for Disease Control
AIDS Hotline: 800-342-AIDS; 800-344-7432 (Spanish); 800-243-7889 (hearing impaired)

Consumer Information Center
Dept. 552Z
Pueblo, CO 81009
FDA Consumer Report: "No Safe Tan," single copy free

American Cancer Society
800-ACS-2345
Brochure: "Definitely a 15," single copy free

The National Pediculosis Association (NPA)
P.O. Box 149
Newton, MA 02161
617-449-6487
617-449-8129 (fax)

American Academy of Allergy & Immunology
611 East Wells Street
Milwaukee, WI 53202
Pamphlet: "Atopic Dermatitis," single copy 50¢

Walt Disney Educational Media Co.
500 South Buena Vista St.
Burbank, CA 91521
Video: "Advice on Lice"

REFERENCES

Anderson, Richard D. *Infections in Children*, 2nd ed. Gaithersburg, Md.: 1994.

Behrman, R., ed. *Nelson Textbook of Pediatrics*, 15th ed. Philadelphia: W. B. Saunders, 1996.

Benenson, A. S. *Control of Communicable Diseases in Man*, 15th ed. Washington, D.C.: American Public Health Association, 1990.

Committee on School Health. *School Health: Policy and Practice*, 5th ed. Elk Grove Village, Ill.: American Academy of Pediatrics, 1993.

Engel, J. *Pocket Guide to Pediatric Assessment*, 2nd ed. St. Louis: Mosby-Year Book, 1993.

Glanze, W. D., ed. *Mosby's Medical Dictionary*. St. Louis: Mosby.

Haas, M. K., ed. *The School Nurse's Source Book of Individualized Health Care Plans*. Noch, Minn.: Sunrise River Press, 1993.

Hay, W. W., ed.*Current Pediatric Diagnosis and Treatment,* 12th ed. Norwalk, Conn.: Appleton and Lange, 1995.

Lewis, K. D., and H. B. Thomas. *Manual of School Health*. Menlo Park, Calif.: Addison-Wesley, 1986.

Thomas, C. L., ed. *Taber's Cyclopedic Medical Dictionary*. Philadelphia: F. A. Davis, 1993.

DISEASES OF THE EARS, NOSE, AND THROAT

The Common Cold
- Nature of the Condition and Diagnosis
- School Relevance and Role of the School Nurse
- Treatment

Colds versus Nasal Allergies

Complications of Common Colds
- Middle Ear Infections
- Tonsil and Adenoid Infections
- The Dilemma of Tonsillectomies
- Sinusitis

Health Education Tips

References

Nutmegs and ginger, cinnamon and clove, They gave to me this jolly red nose.
T. Ravenscroft, 1609

THE COMMON COLD

Nature of the Condition and Diagnosis

A common cold is a viral infection that usually begins in the nose as a rhinitis. It may begin in the throat as a pharyngitis or farther down the respiratory tract as a laryngitis or bronchitis. The virus then usually spreads to other parts of the upper respiratory tract.

Because the lining of the nose joins that of the sinuses, almost everyone with a cold also has a certain degree of sinusitis, even though they may not have any recognizable sinus symptoms. What we call a cold can be caused by some 50 to 60 different types and strains of viruses, each of which causes a slightly different set of symptoms. Some examples are the following:

- The shortest is a runny nose for 1 to 3 days, with no other symptoms, that goes away rapidly and completely.
- Next is a runny nose for 7 to 14 days with a slight sore throat and a little cough. There may be a low-grade fever the first day or two. The nasal secretions start clear and runny and gradually thicken and become greenish in color.
- Another strain has the same symptoms as given above, with some hoarseness caused by the extension of the virus to the larynx (voice box).

With all the above, the patient may have a little fever the first day or two, a slight feeling of malaise, and some loss of appetite.

- A fourth strain has similar symptoms but with more fever, ranging from 102°–104°F in children and 100°–102°F in adults. This type of cold causes the most concern and may be associated with some secondary infection requiring specific treatment with antibiotics.

All colds are more common in children than in adults. Having a cold usually leaves some immunity to that particular virus, but because there are many others, it takes many years to develop a substantial immunity to the majority of respiratory viruses. Many children seem to catch one cold after another or to have a cold all winter long, especially after they start school or day care. Colds are also more severe in children than adults, usually last longer, and cause higher fever and more complications.

School Relevance and Role of the School Nurse

Students continue to attend school with colds. Obviously, they are quite contagious, but it would be folly to try to keep all students with colds at home; the schools would be half-empty. Students are not harmed by attending school with a cold, provided they do not have fever or excessive cough and do not feel sick.

Treatment

Cold medications do not seem to alter the course of the disease, although they are usually harmless and may make the student more comfortable. Some commonly used medications are the following:

- Acetaminophen (Tylenol®) and similar types of medication are the most widely used medications for low-grade fevers and general malaise. They are safe if used in moderation. Aspirin is no longer recommended because of Reye's syndrome. Many doctors believe that fever is a natural body mechanism that helps combat infections.

- Nose drops may be necessary, but a student may experience the negative effects of a rebound reaction that leaves the nose more stopped up than before. Nose drops are advisable only if used in moderation and for short periods.

- Vaporizers are commonly used and do provide symptomatic relief for some children. Most doctors recommend room-temperature vaporizers rather than steam.

- Ibuprofens, such as Motrin® and Advil®, are commonly used. These medications are now available without a prescription and are available in tablet or capsule form or as a suspension. They are advertised as relieving the discomfort of a cold as well as reducing fever. Ibuprofens are relatively new for use in colds, although they have been used for many years as nonsteroid anti-inflammatory agents and for relief of pain associated with arthritis, backache, and other conditions. As a class of medications, they are commonly referred to as Non Steroid Anti Inflammatory Drugs (NSAID). Their most common and serious adverse side effect is irritation of the lining of the stomach, and in some cases, their use causes bleeding ulcers. It is rare that short-term, low-dose treatment causes serious side effects. But because some parents subscribe to the common belief that "if some is good, more is better" and because the medication is available without a prescription, parents must be cautious when giving these medicines to children.

- Decongestants usually contain adrenalin-like substances such as ephedrine or phenylpropanolamine. They are supposed to shrink the nasal lining to provide easier breathing. Some common brands are Sudafed® and Entex®. All well-controlled studies have not shown any beneficial effects of decongestants as a cold medicine, yet they are widely used. Because all decongestants are also cardiac stimulants, athletes who may have their urine tested should be warned that if these substances are detected, the athlete may be barred from competition.

- Antihistamines are usually combined with decongestants. Again, controlled studies show no beneficial effects of antihistamines as a cold medicine, although the combinations, often containing acetaminophen, are available over the counter and their use is also widespread.

- There are two types of cough medicines. One type is an expectorant, which loosens the secretions and makes it easier to cough. This can relieve dry, hacking coughs that may be very troublesome. A student who cannot rest because of a continuous severe cough may require the second type, a sedative cough medicine. This type usually contains codeine or related substances that suppress the cough. Because of their nature and mode of action, sedative cough medicines usually require a prescription and should be used only under a doctor's guidance. If a cough is sedated too much, the retained excess secretions may lead to complications in the lungs.

A cough is nature's way of clearing undesirable secretions from the lungs and bronchial tubes. If the cough does not excessively bother the student, it is better not to treat it. Parents and teachers often worry because children swallow these secretions. This is also how nature intended; it does no harm whatsoever.

In summary, there are dozens of so-called remedies on the market today, and many people are convinced that they help , although about as many people are convinced that they do not help. Most of the remedies contain varying combinations of acetaminophen and an antihistamine, and occasionally, a decongestant.

All well-controlled large studies in respected medical journals agree that no medications can "cure" a cold. Nobody disputes that some medications (such as Tylenol® or aspirin) offer temporary relief from distressing symptoms such as fever.

Of particular concern is the excess use of antibiotics; for two reasons:

1. There is a potential for adverse reactions such as nausea, vomiting, diarrhea, or allergies such as hives and anaphylaxis.
2. The emergence of antibiotic-resistant bacteria is a concern. This is rapidly becoming a major problem in many infections, including some common ones such as otitis media and pharyngitis and some (so far) less common ones such

as tuberculosis. A fairly safe rule with a few exceptions is that for a common cold, if there is no fever, antibiotics should not be used.

Good medical practice dictates that "the less medicine, the better." Students who are not excessively uncomfortable should be left alone for 1 to 2 weeks to get well by themselves. If some of the symptoms (cough or runny nose) cause particular discomfort, follow the recommendation of a doctor or school nurse.

Figure 6-1 lists common cold remedies and is helpful in management of children with colds.

COLDS VERSUS NASAL ALLERGIES

Colds are acute respiratory infection that begin, run their course, and end. A cold lasts from 2 or 3 to 14 days, depending on the virus. At onset, the nasal secretions are thin and clear, then gradually get thicker before going away.

Allergies, on the other hand, last a full season, usually spring or fall, or may commonly last all year. The secretions usually stay thin and clear. A cough is less likely to develop with an allergy than with a cold, although sneezing can be severe. The student usually does not feel bad or have fever.

Unfortunately, many children with nasal allergy get colds more easily and more often than nonallergic children, so they present a mixed picture of a cold implanted on an allergic nasal mucous membrane (inner lining). When this happens, the student who has a runny nose all year will begin to feel bad, perhaps develop a little fever, and often develop a cough. In many cases, it is difficult to tell one from the other, even for a physician. Figure 6-2 gives ways to distinguish a cold from an allergy.

COMPLICATIONS OF COMMON COLDS

Middle Ear Infections

Acute Otitis Media

Symptoms and Diagnosis   A middle ear infection (otitis media) is usually a complication of a cold. The younger the child, the greater the incidence of otitis media. By school age, this complication becomes less common than in babies and toddlers. Acute otitis media typically begins with high fever and earache.

Type/Dosage	Brands	What It Does	Common Possible Side Effects
Aspirin 325 mg 500mg	Anacin[1] Ascriptin[2] Bayer Bayer Plus[2] Bufferin[2] Ecotrin[3]	Relieves mild to moderate pain from headaches, sore muscles, menstrual cramps, and arthritis; reduces fever.	Prolonged use may cause gastrointestinal bleeding, especially in heavy drinkers; may increase the risk of maternal and fetal bleeding and cause complications during delivery if taken in the last trimester; can cause Reye's syndrome if given to children and teenagers who have the flu or chicken pox.
Acetaminophen 325 mg 500 mg	Anacin-3 Excedrin[1] Pamprin[4] Midol[4] Tylenol	Relieves mild to moderate pain from headaches and sore muscles; reduces fever.	May cause liver damage in drinkers and those taking excessive amounts (more than 4,000 mg daily) for several weeks.
Ibuprofen 200 mg	Advil Motrin-IB Nuprin Pamprin-IB	Relieves mild to moderate pain from headaches, backaches, and sore muscles; relieves minor pain of arthritis; provides good relief of menstrual cramps and	Gastrointestinal bleeding, especially in heavy drinkers; stomach ulcers; kidney damage in the elderly, people who have cirrhosis of the liver, and those taking diuretics. toothaches; reduces fever.
Naproxen sodium 200 mg	Aleve	Relieves mild to moderate pain from headaches, backaches, and sore muscles; relieves minor pain of arthritis; provides good relief of menstrual cramps and toothaches; reduces fever.	Gastrointestinal bleeding; stomach ulcers; kidney damage in the elderly, people who have cirrhosis of the liver, and those taking diuretics.

[1] Contains caffeine.
[2] Contains buffers.
[3] Enteric coated.
[4] Contains ingredients other than analgesics.

(FDA Consumer. p 13. Jan/Feb 95)

Figure 6-1. Common cold medications. (From *FDA Consumer,* January/February 1995, p. 13.)

PHYSICAL FINDINGS:

Allergy	Cold
Nasal discharge remains watery. More sneezing. Little or no cough.	Nasal discharge gradually thickens and crusts. Less sneezing. Cough starts dry and becomes loose. Worse with exertion.
Comes and goes during entire season. Eyes usually red. Fewer lymph nodes in neck.	Duration 1-3 weeks. Eyes usually not red. More neck nodes.

REMEMBER: Children with allergic rhinitis may also "catch cold."

MANAGEMENT:

1. Limit exercise if cough is troublesome. Coordinate with physical education teacher.
2. Exclude from school if student has fever or severe dough.
3. Educate about picking and blowing nose.
4. Encourage high fluid intake.
5. Do not encourage to eat but allow to set own limits.
6. Use vaporizer if necessary and feasible.
7. Do not use aspirin under age 18.
8. When giving Tylenol®, use 1 grain (65 mg) per year of age up to grade 5 (or 300 mg for elementary school age), and 5-10 grains for secondary school students. May be repeated in 4 hours.
9. Discourage use of over-the-counter cold and cough medicines. None of them have been proven beneficial. If parent insists, watch for adverse side effects: antihistamines can cause drowsiness; decongestants such as Sudafed can cause excitability. Plain Robitussin® is safe cough medicine if something must be used.

FOLLOW UP:

1. Refer to physician for complications: earache, fever, vomiting, headache, loss of appetite, sore throat, etc.
2. See in clinic as necessary.

IS IT A COLD OR THE FLU:

Symptoms	Cold	Flu
Fever	Rare	Characteristic High (102°-104° F) Sudden onset: lasts 3-4 days.
Headache	Rare	Prominent
General Aches and pains	Slight	Usual: often quite severe
Fatigue and weakness	Quite mild	Extreme; can last 2-3 weeks
Prostration	Never	Early and prominent
Runny, stuffy nose	Common	Sometimes
Sneezing	Usual	Sometimes
Sore throat	Common	Sometimes
Chest discomfort, cough	Mild to moderate; hacking cough	Common; can become severe

Figure 6-2. Common cold versus allergic rhinitis.

Treatment and School Action   The proper management of otitis media has long been controversial as to the number of days that treatment should be continued, the type and frequency of antibiotic of choice, and whether or not the eardrum should be incised for drainage. In the past few years, however, authoritative guidelines for treatment and standards of care have been developed. These guidelines and standards are available for about $15 from:

The American Academy of Pediatrics
P.O. Box 927
Elk Grove Village, IL 60009-0927
800-433-9016

In general, treatment of otitis media includes the following:

- Antibiotics are almost always necessary.
- The older and less expensive antibiotics are usually just as effective as the newer, more expensive ones, although not always.
- Almost all antibiotics can be given three times a day: at breakfast, after school, and around 6 to 8 P.M. Some are given twice a day and some once a day.
- It is usually necessary to continue antibiotics for 7 to 14 days, even if the pain and fever go away sooner.
- Incision and drainage of the eardrum is rarely necessary.

Otitis Media with Effusion

Symptoms and Diagnosis   An acute inflammation of the middle ear usually causes fever and earache, but with proper treatment, the patient gets well completely and the middle ear and eardrum return to preillness normality. Serous otitis media (SOM) (also called otitis media with effusion, or OME), however, is a frequent complication. In this condition, a small collection of serum (straw-colored, thin, watery fluid derived from blood plasma) fills the middle ear cavity and causes a small hearing loss. This fluid collection usually *does not cause pain* or other symptoms. Although the effusion is usually absorbed and disappears by itself in 1 to 3 weeks, it occasionally persists, and the fluid thickens and may impede the mobility of the eardrum. This can cause permanent, mild, conductive hearing loss. Proper medical management can prevent this complication; antibiotics and a small incision in the eardrum to drain the fluid are usually sufficient. Occasionally, a tympanotomy tube must be inserted.

The same disease process, OME, can occur following a common cold even when there is no acute ear infection with its accompanying earache or fever. Without these symptoms, the condition is apt to be overlooked, because the child is not aware of any hearing loss and does not complain of pain.

The diagnosis of OME usually requires a combination of audiographic and tympanometric testing plus the use of a pneumatic otoscope to test for mobility of the eardrum. This is usually done by an otologist or pediatrician or by a school nurse practitioner who is trained to do this testing.

Treatment and School Action   There are three components to proper therapy of OME:

- In most cases, the fluid disappears by itself in 1 to 3 weeks. Therefore, it is important not to rush quickly to the next phase.
- Antibiotics with or without tympanotomy are usually prescribed.
- Tympanotomy with placement of small plastic tubes to provide drainage can be performed.

The details of treatment vary in each student, but treatment obviously requires management by a pediatrician or otologist. In 1994, the Agency for Health Care Policy and Research of the U.S. Public Health Service published a pamphlet entitled "Management of OME in Young Children." It provides details of diagnosis, risk factors, and treatment plus an easy-to-follow algorithm for managing children under age 3, but the algorithm is also useful for school nurses. It shows, in schematic detail, the clinical course of OME and what to do each step along the way. It is available for $14.95 from:

The American Academy of Pediatrics
P.O. Box 927
Elk Grove Village, IL 60009-0927
800-433-9016

Relevance for the School Nurse   To determine the severity of a student's middle ear inflammation, and audiogram should be made and compared with an audiogram made previously. If OME is a present, this new audiogram would show a mild conductive loss in the ear with the effusion. The loss will be small, 30–50 dB, and equal across all frequencies.

Obviously, a nurse cannot do an audiogram on all students with a common cold, but for a student who is recuperating from an acute middle ear infection, the teacher should be alerted to the possibility of hearing loss and the need for an audiogram.

If the audiogram shows a mild conductive loss, the student should not be referred to the doctor unless the hearing loss persists for 3 weeks. Most middle ear effusions resolve spontaneously in that period of time.

Tympanometer and Tympanogram A tympanometer is also called an impedance bridge. It measures the health of the eardrum by testing how well sound waves bounce off of it. Tympanometers range from small screening types that are built into an otoscope to large, sensitive tabletop models. At one time, it was thought that the tympanometer might replace the audiometer as the hearing screening instrument in the school nurse's office. It is now clear that this instrument should only be used by a pediatrician or otologist as an adjunct in the diagnosis and management of the various types of otitis media. Otoscopy, both simple and pneumatic, audiometry, and careful clinical judgment may all be necessary. In our opinion, the tympanometer should not be used by a school nurse for screening, diagnosis, or management. Although it can aid in the diagnosis of OME, reliance on a tympanometer alone will lead to overreferral and the needless placement of too many tympanotomy tubes.

Tonsil and Adenoid Infections

Cause, Symptoms, and Diagnosis

With tonsil and adenoid infections, in addition to large, red, painful tonsils, the glands (lymph nodes) in the neck become swollen and tender. The adenoids usually get infected at the same time. Such infections are usually a complication of a cold, although sometimes the runny nose and cough follow the sore throat and fever.

Tonsillitis can be caused by many bacteria or viruses. The most important is the group A beta hemolytic streptococcus (GABHS), which may be a precursor to rheumatic fever with subsequent severe heart damage. Sufficient and correctly chosen antibiotics can prevent this complication. Referral to a doctor may be necessary for bacterial cultures and clinical judgment to determine the correct antibiotic to use.

Rapid Strep Tests

Rapid strep test kits are inexpensive, readily available, easy to use, and fairly reliable. They can be used easily in the school nurse's clinic with results available in 5 to 20 minutes, depending on the test. Because of a new law called the Clean Laboratories Investigative Act, however, it is questionable whether these tests can be performed in the school nurse's clinic. Each school district will have to consult with its physician consultant. The administrative proccess required to get a permit is excessively burdensome.

The Dilemma of Tonsillectomies

Whether or not to remove tonsils is a complicated decision that only an experienced and conscientious physician can resolve properly. In the past, tonsillectomies were one of the most commonly overperformed operations, so much so that some insurance companies pay for a consultant in an attempt to reduce the number of procedures. On the other hand, there are certain children for whom tonsillectomies are essential:

- A child with recurrent tonsillitis, to the extent that the child fails to grow and thrive and misses school once or twice every month for 2 to 5 days, despite adequate antibiotics, can benefit from a tonsillectomy. This child often does exceptionally well after surgery.

- A child with frequent middle ear infections should be evaluated for a tonsillectomy. Otitis media is often associated with tonsillitis. Persistent ear infections that do not respond to medication can result in permanent hearing loss. In these cases, tonsil removal, adenoid removal, or both must be considered.

- A tonsillectomy should be consider for a child with severe mouth breathing that actually causes that child to be noticeably odd-looking, have some difficulty in swallowing, and snore loudly at night. Children so afflicted are usually underweight and sickly because of chronic tonsillar infection and are easily susceptible to all infections.

- Other rare severe condition such as peritonsillar abscess may indicate a need for a tonsillectomy.

Many years ago, doctors felt that most children would do better without tonsils and adenoids. As time went by, it was realized that most of this surgery was unnecessary and that there were significant surgical risks and complications of a tonsillectomy. The pendulum swung so far the other way that some children who really needed their tonsils and adenoids removed were denied surgery, especially by younger doctors who were trained in accordance with the newer medical beliefs and who had not had time to see the deleterious effects of long-term tonsillitis.

Today, fairly specific guidelines and standards for doctors to follow are in place. In case of doubt, another doctor, preferably an experienced pediatrician, should be consulted. Responsible doctors do not resent a request for consultation.

Sinusitis

Symptoms

Although the sinuses are always somewhat involved in any cold, sometimes the cold seems to settle in the sinuses. In these cases, the secretions become thick and greenish yellow, and the cough becomes more prominent and is especially pronounced in the morning. During the night, the secretions collect in the upper air passages after draining from the sinuses into the nose and down the throat. Headache is common, usually over the eyes, but sometimes involving the entire head and increasing in the afternoon. The cough may last a long time, occasionally all winter.

Treatment

Treatment of sinusitis takes a long time. Decongestants, antihistamines, nose drops, and antibiotics are all used for different types of sinusitis. Vaporizers may provide symptomatic relief at night. The long-term outlook is good. Most individuals get completely well, but occasionally, people with nasal allergies develop chronic sinusitis that may last several years.

HEALTH EDUCATION TIPS

- Emphasize the importance of hand washing.
- Discourage the administration of unnecessary medication, especially antibiotics.
- Discourage excess absences because of minor colds.
- Inform teaching staff about the importance of low-grade hearing loss.
- Defuse teachers' fears about contagion.
- Educate faculty concerning differences between common colds and nasal allergy.

REFERENCES

Berman, S. "Otitis Media in Children." *New England Journal of Medicine* 32(23):1560–65.

Gravel, J. S., et al. "Early Otitis Media and Later Educational Risk." *Acta Otolaryngology* 115(2):279–81.

Hemila, H., et al. "Vitamin C and the Common Cold: A Retrospective Analysis." *Journal of the American College of Nutrition* 14(2):116–23.

McGuffey, E. C. "Treatment of the Common Cold in Children." *American Pharmacy* NS34(9):19–20.

Oluwole, M., et al. "Methods of Selection for Adenoidectomy in Childhood Otitis Media with Effusion." *International J ournal of Pediatric Otorhinolaryngalogy* 32(2):129–35.

Paradise, J. L. "Treatment Guidelines for Otitis Media: The Need for Breadth and Flexibility. *Pediatric Infectious Disease Journal* 14(5):429–34F.

Reuler, J. B., et al. "Sinusitis: A Review for Generalists." *Western Journal of Medicine* 163(1):40–48.

Spector, S. L. "The Common Cold: Current Therapy and Natural History." *Journal of Allergy and Clinical Immunology* 95(5):1133–38.

Wald, E. R. "Chronic Sinusitis in Children." *Journal of Pediatrics* 127(3):339–47.

EYE PROBLEMS

A small hurt in the eye is a great one.

An ophthalmologist follows procedures and practices that are highly specialized, more so than almost any other specialty of medicine. A cross section of a normal eye is shown in Figure 7-1. A glossary and a list of abbreviations of the abnormalities eye specialists see and the procedures they perform is given below. This glossary can help a school nurse understand an ophthalmologist's report and some of the reasoning behind a doctor's suggestions.

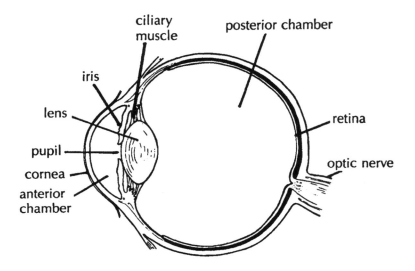

Figure 7-1. Cross section of the normal eye.

GLOSSARY OF EYE TERMINOLOGY

Accommodation. Contraction of the ciliary muscle, causing the lens to become rounder and therefore thicker. Accommodation causes light rays entering the eye to be focused for close reading.

Amblyopia. Blindness of an eye caused by disuse; also called *amblyopia ex anopsia or lazy eye.*

Anisometropia. A difference in the acuity or refractive index between the right and left eyes, causing double or blurred vision unless one eye is closed or unless

136

the vision in one eye is subconsciously suppressed by the brain. Anisometropia can also cause amblyopia.

Astigmatism. Irregular shape of the cornea (clear center of the eyeball), causing blurred vision.

Cataract. An opacity (cloudiness) of the lens that usually impairs visual acuity but may be amenable to surgical removal.

Conjunctivitis. Inflammation of the thin layer of transparent tissue (conjunctiva) covering the eyeball and inner surface of the eyelids; it may be infectious or noninfectious in origin.

Convergence. Both eyes pointing toward the nose simultaneously. Convergence occurs automatically when reading or looking at close objects.

Diplopia. Double vision, seeing two blurred objects rather than one clearly defined image.

Divergence. Both eyes deviating away from the nose simultaneously.

Emmetropia. The normal state of refraction in which light rays are focused exactly on the retina; the absence of refractive error.

Esophoria. One or both eyes deviating toward the nose only in special circumstances (when tired, gazing into the distance, or under certain testing conditions).

Esotropia. One or both eyes permanently deviating inward.

Exophoria. Same as *esophoria* but with deviation away from the nose.

Exotropia. One or both eyes permanently deviating away from the nose.

Fusion. Process by which the brain combines two retinal images to form a single mental impression.

Glaucoma. Increased pressure within the eye, usually caused by impaired drainage of aqueous humor; impaired vision eventually results.

Hyperopia. Farsightedness. The eyeball is shorter than normal, light focuses behind the retina, and vision is blurred.

Myopia. Nearsightedness. The eyeball is longer than normal, light focuses in front of the retina, and vision is blurred.

Nystagmus. Rapid involuntary movements of the eyeball; movement can be horizontal (most common), vertical, rotary, or mixed; functional significance on vision varies with severity and associated abnormalities.

Phoria. A tendency for either eye to deviate inward or outward under special circumstances (not always present).

Pinkeye. See *conjunctivitis*.

Proptosis. Protuberance of the eyeball.

Ptosis. Drooping of the upper eyelid.

Strabismus. Any condition in which the two eyes do not look at the same object at the same time. Also called squint because lack of proper fusion causes *diplopia* so that one eye must be closed to see clearly. Phorias and tropias are types of strabismus.

Stye. Hordeolum; acute, purulent inflammation of the hair follicle of the lid margin.

Tropia. One or both eyes deviate inward or outward most of or all the time; the deviation may alternate between the left and right eyes.

Uveitis. Inflammation of all parts of the vascular coat of the eyeball, that is, iris, ciliary body, and choroid; seen in systemic diseases such as rheumatoid arthritis.

Reports from an eye specialist may also contain a number of esoteric abbreviations. A few of the more common ones are the following:

AC	anterior chamber
A/P	assessment and plan
cc	with correction
Cl	clear
Cr	cycloplegic refraction
csm	central, steady, and maintained (refers to fixation of eye gaze)
c/scl	cornea/sclera
CVF	confrontation visual fields
d/v/m	disc/vessels/macula
EOM	extraocular muscle
ET	esotropia
F	fundus
K	cornea
Mr	manifest refraction
nl	normal
OD	right eye
OS	left eye
OU	both eyes
P	pupils
PLE	penlight exam
sc	without correction

SLE   slit lamp exam
T   tonometry/pressures (test for glaucoma)
V   visual acuity
XT   exotropia

REFRACTIVE ERRORS

Visual Development

Visual acuity does not reach 20/20 in many children until age 6. By age 7, any acuity less than 20/20 can be considered clearly abnormal. It is abnormal at any age to have different acuities in the right and left eyes.

There are three kinds of refractive errors: hyperopia, myopia, and astigmatism (see Figure 7-2).

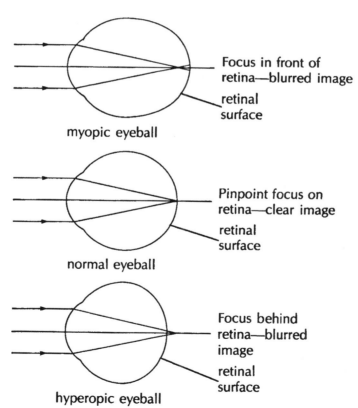

Figure 7-2. Refractive errors.

Hyperopia

In farsightedness (hyperopia), distant vision is better than close vision. In mild cases, distant vision is normal and only a small amount of accommodation is required during reading to cause the light to focus farther forward exactly on the retina; glasses are not needed. In moderate cases, distant vision may also be normal, but to achieve clear vision while reading close to the face, the student must accommodate so much that eyestrain develops. This can cause headache, eye pain, fatigue, and a disinclination to read. In severe cases, clear vision for reading is impossible. Glasses are necessary for a student with moderate to severe hyperopia.

Myopia

Nearsightedness (myopia) means that close vision is better than distant vision. It exists in varying degrees of severity, but glasses are always necessary because the light rays already focus in front of the retina and accommodating efforts would merely focus the rays farther forward. Myopic children cannot see distant objects clearly but do not know it (never having had normal vision). The problem is often first discovered during school screenings. These students usually hold reading material very close to the face to be able to see clearly, and they often squint or frown, which can cause eye strain.

Astigmatism

In cases of astigmatism, vision is blurred at any distance. Caused by a congenital irregularity of the cornea, astigmatism cannot be influenced by accommodation, so glasses are necessary. Holding reading matter close to the eyes, squinting, and frowning are also seen in moderate to severe degrees of astigmatism. See Section 4 for vision screening procedures.

DISORDERS OF ALIGNMENT

Strabismus and Amblyopia

Deviation of the eyes (strabismus) may take one of several forms:

- *Exotropia:* persistent out-turning of an eye
- *Esotropia:* persistent in-turning of an eye
- *Exophoria:* intermittent out-turning of an eye
- *Esophoria:* intermittent in-turning of an eye

Tropias refer to constant deviation; thus, one eye is always favored. The lazy eye loses its visual acuity from disuse. Loss of vision can be complete by age 6. This functional blindness is called amblyopia.

Another cause of amblyopia is unequal visual acuity in the right and left eyes (anisometropia). In this condition, the student favors the best eye and suppresses the image from the other one. The end result is the same as with strabismus. It is said that the overall incidence of anisometropia is 0.5%–1.0% of children.

Treatment

The treatment of strabismus includes patching the good eye to force use of the other one until the condition improves spontaneously or corrective surgery is performed.

Once amblyopia is fully established, restoration of vision is impossible. Prevention consists of diagnosing the antecedent conditions—strabismus or anisometropia—at a young enough age. If treatment is begun by the age of 3 or 4, almost all amblyopia can be prevented. With each year of advancing age, the amount of vision remaining becomes less, so that by age 7, permanent blindness has developed in the amblyopic eye.

From the above discussion, it is easy to see the importance of preschool eye-screening programs. Most 4-year-old children of average intelligence can be given a reliable vision exam with simple screening tests. Certainly, any student with a squint, abnormal eye movements, or other unusual visual habit should be seen by an eye doctor.

CONJUNCTIVITIS

Nature of the Condition

Conjunctivitis is an inflammation of the thin, transparent outer tissue layer of the eyeball and the inner surface of the eyelids. The inflammation causes redness, tearing, and occasionally the formation of pus. A student may complain of a scratchy feeling or other discomfort. Because of the redness, conjunctivitis is commonly called pinkeye. The most common causes are bacteria, viruses, and allergies. Conjunctivitis caused by bacteria and viruses are quite contagious. Allergic conjunctivitis is usually associated with nasal allergy and rarely causes any pus to form; this can be helpful in differentiating contagious from noncontagious varieties.

Treatment

Bacterial conjunctivitis is the cause of about half the cases of pinkeye. Treatment consists of antibiotic eye drops or ointment, and most cases heal quickly. If the infectious conjunctivitis is caused by a virus, however, antibiotic drops will not help. Therefore, some children with mild pinkeye will be told by their physician that no treatment is necessary, and the condition will go away by itself in a few days. Allergic conjunctivitis can be relieved, not cured, by certain nonantibiotic eye drops that contain antihistamines, vasoconstrictors, or both.

School Management Protocol

If new cases of pinkeye occur at 2-week intervals, they are probably not related because the incubation period is only 3 to 5 days. Each case should be evaluated by the school nurse. If the pinkeye appears infectious, it should be referred to a physician; if allergic, it can be observed for a day or two to see if it goes away. If no medication is prescribed, the student should be observed daily; if the condition worsens, the doctor or parent should be notified.

When new cases begin to occur daily, it is important to contain the epidemic by removing each infected student from the school as soon as possible. Although many cases of pinkeye are contagious, it is not always medically necessary to exclude a student from school for more than a day. Common colds are also contagious, and we do not insist that students with colds stay home.

Figure 7-3 shows a brief protocol for the management of conjunctivitis.

CONTACT LENSES

Many school children are now wearing contact lenses. Problems arise when the student does not know how to exercise the proper care or is too young to feel vulnerable when the rules are not followed. The wonder is that more students do not have serious eye disease, judging by how many contact wearers wash their lenses in their mouths.

Types of Contact Lenses

There are three kinds of contact lenses: hard, soft, and soft extended wear. Each kind has specific benefits and characteristics.

Hard lenses are removed each night. Two types of hard lenses are available:

1. Traditional: nonpermeable
2. Newer: gas (oxygen) permeable. These lenses can be worn longer than traditional lenses each day without discomfort.

PHYSICAL FINDINGS

1. Redness of the whites of the eyes.
2. Purulent or watery discharge.
3. Redness, swelling, or both of the eyelids.
4. Itching and rubbing of the eyes.
5. Crusts in the inner corners of eyes, especially upon waking from sleep.

HOW TO DIFFERENTIATE THE CAUSES

1. Allergic: Discharge remains watery without pus formation.
2. Infectious (bacterial): Usually more severe with pus formation and more crusts. Requires treatment.
3. Viral: Usually less severe, often with no pus; runs a 3- to 5-day course and goes away.

All three types may or may not be associated with the common cold.

MANAGEMENT

1. Bacterial culture is usually not necessary.
2. For the temporary relief of symptoms, wash the eye gently with cool compresses.
3. Check visual acuity. It should be unchanged.
4. Check the fingers and the nose for impetigo.
5. Antibiotic drops or ointments may be prescribed by a physician for infections. Sulamyd 10% is often helpful.
6. Avoid steroid ointments and drops.
7. Topical 4% chromolyn eyedrops are helpful in allergies.
8. May or may not be unusually contagious, so DO NOT exclude from school if this condition is:
   a. Mild with no visible pus and few symptoms
   b. Mild and associated with a common cold
   c. Allergic
9. In other cases, refer the student to a physician and exclude the student from school until under treatment.
10. If subconjunctival hemorrhage is present, refer the student to a physician.

Figure 7-3. Cojunctivitis protocol.

Soft lenses need to be removed each night. When wet, these lenses are soft and supple; when dry they are rigid and fragile. They must be kept moist at all times. Qualities of soft lenses are the following:

- Comfortable almost immediately
- Last about 6–12 months
- Ideal for athletes
- Require meticulous care and weekly sterilization

Soft, extended wear lenses are especially designed to be worn for 1 week to 3 months. They require motivated wearers who will care for them meticulously and comply with the doctor's orders.

Important Facts about Contact Lenses

Myopia is not corrected by contact lenses. Hard lenses do tend to flatten the cornea slightly and thus improve myopic vision, but this is temporary; the cornea resumes its previous shape after the lenses are removed. In sports, soft contacts are the safest. Hard lenses, however, pose no greater danger than regular glasses do. For severe myopia and astigmatism, hard contacts are better than soft lenses.

Lens Cleaning Procedure

Regardless of which type of lens is used, cleaning and disinfecting the lenses are important. Cleaning is done first with a salt or enzyme solution that removes impurities that build up on the lens. Disinfecting is done with a chemical solution, heat sterilization, or both sufficient to kill most bacteria, but this may not kill all germs capable of causing a corneal infection. With soft lenses, disinfection must be done daily.

Amoeba Infections

Increasing reports of eye infections caused by amoebas that are abundant in soil and water have surfaced recently. Amoebas have even been found in nonsterile distilled water, which some wearers use to clean lenses. This infection is particularly serious because no antibiotic will cure it and partial or complete blindness may result. Amoeba infections occur most often in users of soft contact lenses that are not changed as frequently as they should be. Therefore, only commercially prepared sterile cleaning and disinfecting solutions should be used, and the contact lens wearer should follow the cleaning procedures recommended by the doctor.

Proper Use of Contact Lenses

Wearers of contact lenses should follow these procedures:

- Never sleep with lenses in place unless so advised by the doctor (under special conditions).
- Do not use saliva as a "wetting" agent. The risk of bacterial contamination is great.
- Never rinse lenses in hot water or store in an unusually hot or cold place because lens warpage may occur. Do not "flex" the lenses; this can also warp them.
- Eye makeup around the eyelids should be used carefully.
- Avoid swimming when wearing contacts as they can easily be washed out and lost.
- If lenses are not worn for a few days, the corneas may lose their adaptation, and wear will need to be restricted to shorter periods when use is reinstituted.
- Good "blinking" is essential in all forms of contact lens wear. Blinking provides a constant fresh supply of oxygen to the corneas and helps to "wet" the lens surfaces.

When a Lens Is Out of Position

Certain methods should be followed to reposition a contact properly.

Recentering the lens:

1. A lens may be left on the white of the eye indefinitely without injury; discomfort will be minimal to moderate.
2. If movement of the lens seems very difficult, flood the area with wetting solution or normal saline and roll the eye.
3. The lens can be moved to different positions by gentle manipulation through the lids.
4. If the student becomes tense, a rest will restore coordination and a second try will succeed.

Lens under the upper lid:

1. Have the student look down.
2. With a finger on the upper lash margin, pull the upper lid up and press against the white of the eye.
3. Push the lens down to the center and hold it there.
4. Look straight ahead.

Lens under the lower lid:

1. Have the student look up.
2. With a finger on the lower lash margin, pull the lower lid down and press against the white of the eye.
3. Push the lens up to the center and hold it there.
4. Look straight ahead.

Lens in the outside corner of the eye:

1. Place the thumb and first finger on the lash margin near outside corner of eye.
2. Spread the eyelids apart.
3. Look toward the nose.
4. Push the lens with the eyelids to the center and hold it there.
5. Look straight ahead.

Lens in the inside corner of the eye:

1. Place the first finger of each hand on the upper and lower lash margins.
2. Spread the eyelids apart.
3. Look to the outside corner.
4. Push the lens with the eyelids to the center and hold it there.
5. Look straight ahead.

SCHOOL RELEVANCE

As long as a student is performing well in school and has no complaints, it is usually correctly assumed that the eyes are normal. As soon as a student begins to fall behind in school, however, the teacher should suggest having the vision checked.

The best time to check a child's eyes for the first time is at age 3. Some school nurses and teachers see 3-year-old children and should be on the alert for any evidence that a child favors one eye over the other.

ROLE OF THE SCHOOL NURSE

Children who are younger than 5 chronologically or mentally may not be testable even by HOTV chart or Allen cards. Nevertheless, valuable information can be obtained by applying the vision evaluation for developmentally delayed students (see Figure 7-4). Definitions of selected terms contained on Figure 7-4 are the following:

VISION EVALUATION
FOR
DEVELOPMENTALLY DELAYED STUDENTS*

Name of Pupil_____
　　　　　　　　last　　　　　　　　　　*first*　　　　　　　　　*middle*

Birth Date_____Date of Testing_____

School _____
　　　　　　　Home school (or school attended, if different)

Home Phone_____Home Address _____

Office Phone _____

Significant history relative to vision (circle findings):

Note presence of any of the following symptoms:

unequal pupils	red eyes	crusting of lids
shuts or covers one eye frequently	watery eyes or discharges	photophobia
tilts head to one side	excessive eye rubbing	styes or swollen lids
blinks continually	nystagmus	other (explain)
holding work close	ptosis	no abnormalities noted

Estimate of Vision

	Not Examined	Pass	Fail
Fixation on light			
Right eye (left eye covered)			
Left eye (right eye covered)			
Picks up raisin (or similar size object)			

Estimate of Alignment

Symmetrical corneal light reflex (Hirschberg)			

Eye Disease

Gross lens/corneal opacities			
Red reflex			
Fundoscopic			

*Reliable visual acuity not obtainable by tumbling E, or H O V T.

This examination (does, does not) suggest evidence of abnormal vision or other eye problem.

☐ This student is being referred to his physician　　☐ This student will be retested in school_____
　　　　　　　　　　　　　　　　　　　　　　　　　　　　(Approximate date)

_____
Examiner

Physician's Findings

I. Vision:_____

II. Alignment: _____

III. Eye Disease:_____

　Diagnosis: _____

　Recommendations: _____

_____

_____　_____　_____
　　　Date　　　　　　　　　*Office Telephone*　　　　　*Physician's Signature*

Figure 7-4. Vision evaluation form

- *Cover/uncover:* The cover/uncover test is performed by having the child focus on a stationary target. While placing a hand or cover in front of one eye, the examiner observes the other eye. Movement of the observed eye is abnormal and demonstrates the presence of strabismus. As the covered eye is uncovered, the examiner observes it for movement. Movement is abnormal and indicates the presence of heterophoria (latent strabismus).

- *Corneal light reflex:* The corneal light reflex test for detection of strabismus is performed with an ophthalmoscope or other light source. Corneal light reflections should fall symmetrically on corresponding points of the student's pupils. Improper alignment appears as asymmetry of reflections (not at corresponding points on the pupils). This is called the Hirshberg test.

- *Red reflex:* The red reflex exam may be performed with an ophthalmoscope or other light source. In a darkened room, the light source should be held about 3 feet from the student and the student's attention drawn to look directly at the light. Both retinal reflexes should be red or red-orange and of equal intensity.

Nurse practitioners or those with special training can also perform a fundo-scopic exam. A clearly visualized, sharp optic disc (on the examiner's usual ophthalmoscope setting) supports the absence of significant refractive error.

In the case of infants or severely mentally disabled individuals, a "visual evoked response" test can be considered. This test measures brain wave (electroencephalogram, or EEG) activity in the visual cortex (occipital lobes) of the brain in response to flashes of light. A normal test demonstrates a brain wave response to each light stimulus. The absence of any response documents disruption of the visual-neural pathways and total blindness. In these cases, optic nerve atrophy can usually be seen with the ophthalmoscope.

HEALTH EDUCATION TIPS

Vision screening and any student contact regarding an eye problem should be used as a teachable moment. Introduce students to the following brief rules of eye care as part of the learning experience:

- Protect eyes from injury:
  - Keep sharp objects away from the eye.
  - Wear protective glasses or goggles during potentially dangerous activities (lawnmowing, working with shop equipment, and certain sports).

- If you feel something in your eye, ask an adult for help.
- Wear sunglasses outdoors on bright days.
- Protect eyes from infection:
  - Try not to rub or touch the eyes.
  - If you wear contacts, use proper cleaning procedures.
  - If medicine is prescribed for an eye problem, use it all as directed by the doctor.
  - Never use over-the-counter eye medicine on your own.
  - Never use someone else's eye medicine.

REFERENCES

Brodsky, M. *Pediatric Neuro-Ophthalmology*. New York: Springer, 1996.

Cassin, B. *Dictionary of Eye Terminology*. Gainesville, Fla.: Triad Publishing, 1990.

Dain, N. *Visual Development*. New York: Plenum, 1995.

Gardiner, P. *Vision in Children*. New York: Appleton Century Crofts, 1982.

Goldberg, S. *Ophthalmology Made Ridiculously Simple*. Miami: Medmaster, 1994.

Lewis, K. "Vision." Chapter 2 in *Manual of School Health*. Menlo Park, Calif.: Addison-Wesley, 1986.

Matoba, A. "Ocular Viral Infections." *Pediatric Infectious Disease*. 3(4):358–66.

Metzger, R., et al. "Use of Visual Training for Reading Disabilities."*Pediatrics*. 73(6):824–28.

Olsen, L., et al. "Caring for Your Eyes." In *Being Healthy*. Orlando, Fla: Harcourt Brace, 1990.

Robb, R. *Ophthalmology for the Pediatric Practitioner*. Boston: Little, Brown, 1981.

———. "Learning Disabilities, Dyslexia, and Vision." *Pediatrics* 90(1):124–26.

———. *Physicians' Desk Reference for Ophthalmology*. Des Moines, Iowa: Medical Economics, 1996.

———. "Vision." Chapter 11 in *Children's Handbook of Preventive Services*. Elk Grove Village, Ill.: American Academy of Pediatrics, 1994.

———. *Contact Lenses*. San Francisco: American Academy of Ophthalmology, 1984.

SECTION 8
DISEASES OF THE LUNGS

Pneumonia
- Nature of the Condition
- Symptoms
- School Relevance and Role of the School Nurse
- Treatment

Bronchitis
- Nature of the Condition and Symptoms
- Treatment and School Relevance

Asthma
- Nature of the Condition
- Symptoms
- Prevalence and School Relevance
- Participation in Physical Education
- Physician Involvement

- Acute Asthmatic Emergencies
- Treatment

Tuberculosis
- Nature of the Condition
- Prevalence Rates
- Case Finding
- BCG
- Complications
- Treatment
- Adverse Drug Reactions
- Multidrug Resistance

Pleurisy

Health Education Tips

References

Let everything that hath breath praise the Lord.

Psalms 150:3–6

PNEUMONIA

Nature of the Condition

Pneumonia is an infection of the air sacs of the lungs. Some physicians use the word *pneumonitis* instead of *pneumonia* to describe this condition. Although the two words mean the same thing, it has become common practice to use pneumonitis when one means a small area of infection with minimal symptoms and pneumonia for larger areas of infection with more severe symptoms.

Normal lungs are soft and spongy because they are filled with air. When a child develops pneumonia, the involved portion of the lung becomes very dense and consolidated.

The lungs are divided into separate portions called lobes; there are two lobes on the left and three lobes on the right. An infection of an entire lobe is called lobar pneumonia. When the infection involves smaller patches in one or several places simultaneously, it is called bronchopneumonia.

There are many different kinds of pneumonia. Acute lobar pneumonia with a very high fever can occur suddenly and is still a formidable cause of death in many parts of the world. With proper diagnosis and treatment, however, it is usually one of the easiest diseases to cure. On the other hand, some types of pneumonia caused by certain viruses can be so mild that the child has only a light cough and a very low-grade fever and is hardly sick. This very mild type is often referred to as *walking pneumonia*, or more scientifically, primary atypical pneumonia.

Symptoms

School nurses have reason to suspect pneumonia when the following symptoms are present:

1. Almost all children with pneumonia have some type of cough, the most common being a relatively small loose cough that is not overly troublesome.
2. High fever is present in most children but occasionally it will be low.
3. Lassitude, loss of appetite, drowsiness, and general malaise are present. These symptoms, of course, are common to almost all children's illnesses.

School Relevance and Role of the School Nurse

A student with pneumonia is usually quite sick and thus will not be in school. Teachers and nurses, however, see many children with coughs and temperatures of

152

100°–106°F. When these symptoms are combined with those listed in item 3 above, it is wise to refer the student to a doctor, especially if, after a day or two, the student does not run and play as usual. Because pneumonia presents such a highly variable set of symptoms, it is not wise for a teacher, principal, or parent to wait too long before having the student examined.

Although a few specific varieties of pneumonia are contagious, the types that are most often seen in school are not. Most pneumonia is caused by germs or viruses that are present in healthy children, and those who actually develop disease in their lungs do so because of individual susceptibility, not by catching it from another student who comes to school with pneumonia.

Treatment

All children with pneumonia need a certain amount of rest. Almost all need antibiotics. The treatment should always be managed by a physician.

BRONCHITIS

Nature of the Condition and Symptoms

Bronchitis is an infection of the bronchial tubes. These tubes carry the air down to the air sacs in the lungs where oxygen is absorbed into the bloodstream. This condition can follow a cold, and although the student usually feels well and has no fever, a troublesome cough persists for several weeks after the cold goes away. A winter walk through the school halls sometimes sounds like a small herd of walruses. The cough usually starts out "tight": dry, hacking, and nonproductive of sputum. Later it gets looser, wetter, more productive, and less frequent. It often takes 4 to 6 weeks for the cough to go away. In some students with allergic bronchitis, the cough can last all winter.

Treatment and School Relevance

The only medicines available for bronchitis are cough medicines. Except in relatively large doses of sedative cough medicines, they are not very effective in controlling the cough, which can suppress the cough so much that dangerous amounts of secretions are retained in the lungs. The cough is almost always made worse by physical exertion, so it may help to limit physical education and recess. Although the cough sounds horrible, it is not very contagious during the time when it is severe. Whether or not a student should stay home depends on how much the cough bothers the student and others.

ASTHMA

Nature of the Condition

Asthma is an allergic disease that causes narrowing of the smaller air passages in the lungs, or bronchioles. This narrowing is caused by three simultaneous processes:

- Swelling of the inner lining of the bronchioles
- Excessive mucous secretions from the tiny glands in the inner lining of the bronchioles
- Constriction of the circular muscle contained in the middle layer of the bronchioles

The first two processes are similar to the way the body fights off an infection: Asthma is an inflammatory reaction, but not infectious, and thus can be alleviated by anti-inflammatory medications such as steroids. The third process is more purely allergic in nature and thus relieved by bronchodilators such as the beta adrenergics.

Symptoms

The two hallmark symptoms of asthma are cough and wheeze. The cough comes first; by the time the wheezing begins, the disease has already progressed past the preliminary stage. The symptoms of asthma are shown in Figure 8-1.

Prevalence and School Relevance

Asthma is one of the most common serious childhood illnesses that must be dealt with by the school nurse. It accounts for almost 23% of the days missed from school.

Figure 8-2 shows the death rates for asthma by race and age group from 1980 to 1993. In the 1980s, the prevalence rate of asthma in children increased 29% and the hospitalization rate increased 43%. Most disturbing, the death rate from asthma increased by 46%, since the 1970s. Most of the increase in severe and fatal asthma occurred in poor and minority children. This trend does not seem to be reversing in the 1990s. Although asthma is not often life threatening, a child's entire lifestyle may be affected in many cases. Students with moderately severe asthma miss school often, must visit the doctor frequently, make many trips to hospital emergency rooms, and have probably been hospitalized several times. They take a lot of medicine and get many shots. Also, they are socially limited. They come to be known as sickly and in time think of themselves that way. With all this, it is easy to see why

Sign and Symptoms	Mild	Moderate	Severe
Peak expiratory flow rate [1]	70%-90% predicted or baseline	50%-70% predicted or baseline	< 50% predicted or baseline
Respiratory rate [2]	Normal to 30% above mean	30%-50% increase above mean	> 50% increase above mean
Alertness	Normal	Normal	May be decreased
Dyspnea	Absent or mild, speaks in complete sentences	Moderate, speaks in phrases or partial sentences	Severe, speaks only in single words or short phrases
Accessory muscle use	None to mild intercostal retractions (spaces between ribs)	Moderate intercostal retractions with tracheosternal retractions, use of sternocleidomastoid (neck) muscles, chest hyperinflation	Moderate intercostal retractions, tracheosternal retractions with nasal flaring during inspiration, chest hyperinflation.
Color	Good	Pale	Possible cyanotic
Auscultation with stethoscope	Wheeze only at end of expiration	Inspiratory and expiratory Wheezing	Breath sounds inaudible

1 Each child with asthma should have a resting rate recorded between acute attacks, as measured with a peak expiratory flow meter. (All school nurses should have one.)
2 The non-asthma resting respiratory rate should be assessed and recorded.

Figure 8-1. Symptoms of Asthma.

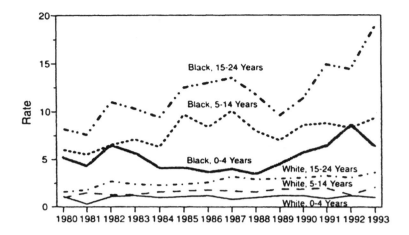

Figure 8-2. Death rates per million population for asthma, by race, age group, and year, in the United States, 1980–1993. (Race-specific analyses were restricted to blacks and whites because numbers for other races were too small to calculate stable estimates.) (From *Morbidity and Mortality Weekly Reports* 45:350–53.)

the disease has an effect far beyond the actual wheezing episode. Fortunately, most children "outgrow" their asthma. Attacks occur frequently in preschool and elementary school children, but by the middle school years, the attacks usually diminish in frequency and intensity.

Treatment is often necessary during the school day. The most common medicine prescribed is an inhaler that must be used as soon as an attack begins. A controversy revolves around allowing children to carry and self-administer their own medication. Many districts have policies that require all medicines to be kept in the nurses' office in a locked cabinet. This dilemma should be resolved at the local school or district level. There are many reasons for allowing or prohibiting a student to carry medicine. A case-by-case decision made by a conference with the parent, doctor, principal, and if appropriate, the student is preferred.

Participation in Physical Education

An asthmatic student's participation in sports is controversial. Until the early 1980s, doctors felt that children with asthma should not be overly active because running and playing usually exaggerate the coughing and wheezing. Children with a condition called *exercise-induced asthma* do not wheeze until they do something that makes them breathe fast. Hard laughing and running will bring on an attack.

Doctors as well as parents prefer that asthmatic children avoid activities known to bring on attacks. An overzealous physical education teacher may insist that all children exercise every day. Lest anyone point a finger at gym teachers for being cruel and heartless, it must be said that many doctors write an excuse from gym for long periods (sometimes all year) on flimsy grounds. In any case, teachers should know that some asthmatic students should limit exercise, and for a certain period in their lives must forgo the pleasures and benefits of active competitive sports. This does not in any way mean that asthma should preclude total participation in all sports, however. Relatively quieter sports such as archery or golf are salutary and maintain body tone without increasing the respiratory rate.

Most students with asthma are perfectly normal between attacks and should be allowed to exercise to the full limits of their tolerance. With today's emphasis on physical fitness, it is current practice to recommend graded exercise for asthmatic children. Thus, they can enhance general body strength and muscle tone in the hope that they will get fewer attacks, be better able to withstand the attacks they do get, and generally lead happier and productive lives. Although this practice has not yet been proven, it seems reasonable.

Many children with asthma are overprotected by parents and doctors to the point that they themselves become convinced that any exercise will bring on an attack. Because of the emotional aspects of asthma, they are often correct. This type of student would probably be helped by graded and carefully monitored physical exercise. Unfortunately, few public school in the United States employ special adaptive physical education teachers to develop special programs for asthmatic children. If encouraged to exercise without guidance, these students typically overexert themselves past their point of tolerance.

Physician Involvement

A student with asthma often ends up in the center of a triangle with parents at one corner, doctor at the other, and physical education teacher at the third. All too often these parties do not work cooperatively. Parents tend to be overprotective, the doctor too casual and unable (or unwilling) to understand the social and psychological implications of the school problem, and the physical education teacher overdemanding. To avoid such a situation, the doctor, parents, and physical education teacher—each respecting and understanding the other—should confer, discuss the situation rationally, and agree on a plan for the year. If this requires more time than they can give, a three-way telephone conference is a useful substitute. This problem usually arises in sixth or seventh grade, and by that time, the methods of coping and the relationships between the student, parents, and doctor have been well established. If a student has a note from the doctor saying that he or she should be excused from physical education for the whole year because of asthma, teachers should not be too insistent on physical education participation. Refer the problem to the principal to deal with as an administrative matter. It is a mistake to equate physical fitness with total health. One or two years without physical education are not crucial in a child's lifetime, and most children outgrow their asthma (or most of it) by high school.

Acute Asthmatic Emergencies

The majority of asthmatic attacks that occur at school are quickly controlled by the use of an inhalant. On rare occasions, the attack will not subside even when the inhaler is used properly, followed by the prescribed brief waiting period, and then used again. If the attack does not subside, the student will begin to get frightened and the anxiety will make the asthma even worse.

A common mistake is overreliance on the inhaler. Most doctors prescribe 2 to 3 puffs, 15 to 20 minutes apart, if the first puff does not cure the attack. If after the third puff the student does not improve noticeably, it usually means that more of the same medicine will not help. Meanwhile, the student's asthma is progressing from mild to moderate, or maybe to severe. Respiratory collapse may be impending.

In this situation, if a parent cannot be immediately located to take the student to the doctor, the best course is immediate evacuation to a hospital emergency room by an emergency ambulance service or by the school nurse and a driver.

Treatment

Treatment of students with asthma can be divided into long-term treatment, treatment of acute asthmatic attacks, and treatment with steroids.

Long-Term Treatment

Environmental control consists of avoiding allergens such as dust, wool, carpet mites, pollens, certain foods, or any other substances to which the individual is known to be allergic. (Allergists often refer to these substances as "triggers.")

Medications are used regularly on a long-term basis for some children to *prevent* attacks from occurring. Examples are medicines containing theophylline (Theodur®, Slo-Bid®, Quibron®), chromium derivatives (Cromolyn®, Intal®), and steroids (see below). A long-acting beta adrenergic drug, Salmeterol®, is also available.

Aminophylline and *theophylline* are distantly related to adrenalin. These mild central nervous system stimulants and bronchodilators are used extensively in the long-term management of asthma. Examples are Theodur®, Quibron®, Slo-Bid®, and Elixophyllin®.

If used regularly in properly adjusted dosage, they are usually helpful, but because of their stimulant qualities, they can cause adverse side effects such as nervousness, nausea, or irritability and have also been suspected of causing learning difficulties. If a student with asthma is receiving any of these medications, the school nurse should be aware of it and should ask the teacher to report any side effects.

Allergy desensitization shots are helpful in some cases. Long-term management should be carried out by the student's primary care physician, but many children, especially in inner-city school districts, do not have an effective "medical home" and receive only sporadic and episodic care of acute attacks in hospital emergency rooms. For these students, a school nurse can obtain literature for children and parents by writing to any of the following organizations:

American Lung Association of Los Angeles
5858 Wilshire Blvd.
Los Angeles, CA 90036
213-935-5864

American Academy of Allergy, Asthma, and Immunology
611 East Wells St.
Milwaukee, WI 532002
800-822-2762

National Heart, Lung, and Blood Institute
National Institutes of Health
Bethesda, MD 20892
800-505-2742
Publication: *Guidelines for the Diagnosis and Management of Asthma*

Some school nurses have organized after-school parent/student asthma groups. These educational sessions can be helpful but, unfortunately, those needing it the most are often single working parents who are unable to attend, because they are usually lower socio economic and their children have more severe asthma and more deaths from asthma.

Treatment of the Acute Attack

Beta adrenergics are available as liquid suspensions, tablets, or capsules or as a metered does inhaler (MDI). Two common examples are Proventil® and Ventolin®, whose action is as a bronchodilator. The MDI is most commonly prescribed in a dosage of 2 to 3 puffs about 15 to 25 minutes apart until the attack has subsided.

School nurses often have to teach the correct use of metered dose inhalers with spacers. When the end of the MDI is placed *directly* into the mouth, the chamber is squeezed, and the student inhales, a relatively large amount of the medicine sticks to the inside lining of the mouth (see Figure 8-3). Spacers are simply hollow containers that fit between the end of the MDI and the child's mouth. Their purpose is to ensure that more of the inhaled medication gets down into the child's lungs, rather than sticking to the inside of the cheeks, palate, and tongue. The inside of the spacer is usually a smooth, nonabsorbing plastic surface; when the cloud of mist is first squeezed into the spacer and then the student takes a deep breath, a wind-tunnel effect is created and a larger volume of medicine goes deeper into the bronchial tubes, rather than sticking to the mouth.

A similar effect (without a spacer) is created if the child first *exhales* deeply (see Figure 8-4), squeezes the MDI about 2 inches in front of the mouth, and then inhales deeply. Using the spacer is more efficient than this method because none of the medicine escapes to the outside air.

Many children continue to put the end of the MDI into their mouth and in most cases obtain relief from their attack. Those children who use their MDIs to *pre-*

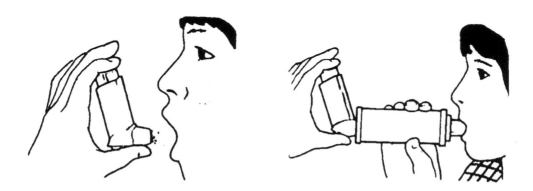

Figure 8-3. Inhaler.   **Figure 8-4.** Inhaler with holding chamber.

vent attacks, such as before a physical education class or other exercise, may not know if the medicine helped them or not.

Steroids, specifically some nonabsorbable (so-called) inhaled steroids, are now being used to treat acute attacks in addition to being used to prevent attacks. Examples are flunisolide and fluticasone. Their action is anti-inflammatory.

Ephedrine- and adrenalin-type inhaled medications are available without a prescription. These are effective rapidly acting bronchodilators, but because they raise blood pressure and increase the heart rate suddenly, they can be dangerous and should not be used. They are heavily advertised on TV. Primatene® is an example.

Adrenaline by injection relieves acute attacks but should only be used in an emergency room or doctor's office where resuscitation equipment and blood oxygen measurements are available.

The American Academy of Pediatrics has published a short and easy-to-follow pamphlet called "Office Management of Acute Exacerbations of Asthma in Children." It contains a schematic diagram that outlines a step-by-step process to managing an acute asthma attack. Although written for use in a doctor's office with a minimal amount of equipment available—peak flow meter (Figure 8-5), oxygen,and so forth—the diagram can give a school nurse an excellent picture of the progression of an asthma attack, what to do at each step, and practically ensure that a student in trouble will be referred before respiratory collapse occurs. This pamphlet is available for $15 from:

Figure 8-5. Peak flow meter.

American Academy of Pediatrics
P.O. Box 927
Elk Grove Village IL 60009-0927
800-433-9016

Treatment with Steroids

It is now believed that a major factor in the development of an acute asthmatic attack is the allergic inflammatory reaction in the bronchioles. Therefore, there has been a development of steroids that, when inhaled via an MDI, are designed to be nonabsorbable into the general body circulation. Flunisolide (Aero-bid®) is an example. But even though the short-term use of these steroids may be safe, the long-term use may still result in systemic absorption. Students who use steroids prophylactically, to prevent attacks, should be watched for weight gain, acne, and other signs of steroid side effects.

TUBERCULOSIS

Nature of the Condition

There are two types of tuberculosis (TB): primary, which usually occurs in childhood, and secondary, which usually occurs in adults. The primary type represents the body's first encounter with the tuberculosis germ

If a child gets TB, he or she is usually 5 to 7 years old and acquires it from an adult living in the same house. The germs are coughed into the air and inhaled by the youngster. They settle in the lymph nodes surrounding the area where the trachea branches into the left and right lung (hilar nodes). The germs (tubercle bacillus) cause some inflammation of the hilar nodes, usually remain in the nodes, cause no discernible illness in the child, and slowly heal with scarring and occasional calcification. This hilar node infection changes the way the body reacts to the tubercle bacillus, so that 3 to 8 weeks after infection, a tuberculin skin test reads positive. Children so infected are not considered to have active TB; they are called skin converters (SC). They are not sick, do not cough, and are not contagious. They may remain in school, and their presence in school presents no need to skin test the other students in the classroom. However, because of teacher and parent concerns, some schools request that the rest of the class be skin tested.

Prevalence Rates

Beginning in the middle of the 1980s, the prevalence rates of tuberculosis began to rise. This has been a cause of concern, because in the previous 20 to 25 years, the prevalence rates in the United States had been dropping steadily. Most of the increase in TB has been in children who are merely skin converters; that is, although their tuberculin skin test changed from negative to positive, these children show no evidence of active disease in their lungs or other areas of the body. There has also been more active adult-type TB, however.

Certain groups of people seem to be predisposed to catch TB easier than others and to have more severe disease with more complications when they do get it. Alaskan and American Indians, blacks, Hispanics, and immigrant groups (from countries in Southeast Asia and some African countries) with a high prevalence rate of TB are considered high risk.

Between 1992 and 1995, a small decline in the number of TB cases was reported.

Case Finding

An important function of metropolitan health departments is keeping track of known tuberculosis cases and locating new sources of active tuberculosis in the community. This is done through direct case findings and through skin testing.

Direct Case Finding

If a student is infected with tuberculosis, it is important to trace the person, usually a family member, who transmitted the infection to the child. In addition, school personnel should be checked for infection. If the infected adult worked in the school, all students who had contact with that person should be skin tested. In the case of cafeteria personnel, the entire school may need to be tested. The local health department should be notified, and they will work with the school authorities to take appropriate action.

Skin Testing

There are two main types of skin tests, the Mantoux test and the tine test.

The Mantoux test is an intracutaneous injection (just under the top layer of the skin of the forearm) of a measured amount of tuberculin material. To perform this test properly, training and practice are required. If the injection is not administered properly, the result is unreliable, but if properly administered, it is highly reliable.

Tine testing is much simpler to perform than the Mantoux test and can be done properly by almost anyone. A small, 1/2 inch plastic cap with four metal points on it is merely pressed onto the skin of the forearm. Unfortunately, this test is not reliable; there are many false positives and false negatives. All experts recommend the Mantoux test instead, but if no one with expertise is available to administer it, some professionals believe it is better to use the tine test than not to test at all.

A skin test may be performed at the same time the dose of measles-mumps-rubella vaccine is given. If they are not both done at the same time, however, then the skin test should be delayed 4 to 6 weeks because the measles vaccine may suppress tuberculin reactivity of a skin test. Red measles and influenza also suppress TB skin test reactivity, so skin testing should be delayed 2 to 3 weeks after recovery from these diseases.

Most experts do not feel that once-a-year TB testing will cause a child to become a skin converter. How often children should be skin tested depends on the area of the United States and the specific population in which they live. In south Texas, children should probably be tested once a year, but in northern Minnesota, much less frequently. In poor, crowded areas and in areas with high immigrant population with higher prevalence rates of TB, it may be necessary to test more than once a year. Local health departments should set the standards for their community.

BCG

BCG is the commonly used acronym for the bacillus of Calmette and Guerin, French physicians who developed a weakened strain of the tuberculosis germ used to "immunize" children against the disease. Children who receive BCG become skin converters and actually have less chance of developing adult-type TB later than those who do not receive BCG. In many European countries and in Mexico, BCG is still the primary method of TB control.

In the United States where the prevalence rates have remained low, BCG is not used. Instead, identification of adult infectious cases and treating all SCs with isoniazid hydrochloride (INH) is preferred.

Skin positivity from BCG slowly wanes over variable periods of time, so that when reading a Mantoux test, any history of whether the student in question has had BCG or not should be disregarded; any student with a positive skin test should receive prophylactic INH.

Complications

Pulmonary tuberculosis is the most common form of the active disease and is not considered a complication. Other complications can develop, however, including the following:

- *Tuberculous meningitis* is the most serious complication, and children who recover from it are often left with severe neurological sequelae.
- *Miliary tuberculosis* occurs when the germ enters the bloodstream and seeds itself throughout the body. This is fatal if untreated, but treatable if caught early.

- *Kidney tuberculosis* is a rare but serious complication.
- *Bone tuberculosis* is usually due to the bovine (cow) tubercle bacillus; this is why people should never drink raw milk.

Treatment

Treatment of tuberculosis depends on the type of TB contracted.

For students who are asymptomatic childhood skin converters, the usual regime is INH once a day for 9 months, although some professionals feel that 6 months is enough. For some disorganized families, the health department may order a dose given at the school 3 times a week under directly observed therapy (DOT). This is the only way to ensure that the student receives full protection and results in a tenfold decrease in the occurrence of later, serious adult-type TB. Although this increases the school nurse's workload, the increase is only slight because such small numbers of children in any one school will require DOT. Many school nurses now do administer this regimen.

Those with active pulmonary TB, which may occur in adolescents or adults, should receive rifampin and pyrazinamide in addition to INH, for a total of three drugs.

Those whose TB is resistant to INH (by lab test) should have ethambutol added, for a total of four drugs. If high doses of ethambutol are necessary, optic neuritis is a possible adverse reaction, and an ophthalmologist must see the patient periodically.

Adverse Drug Reactions

INH or pyrazinamide may cause liver damage. Symptoms of this reaction resemble those of infectious hepatitis: loss of appetite, nausea, jaundice, dark-colored urine, or light-colored bowel movement. This clinical observation is more reliable than the transaminase blood tests. Children on INH do not need pyridoxine (vitamin B6) to protect against liver damage, except in rare cases.

Rifampin may render oral contraceptives inactive, so sexually active females need to be warned. Rifampin also increases the possibility that INH will cause liver problems.

Multidrug Resistance

The incidence of drug resistance is still low in the United States and Canada, but in certain areas and situations, it is increasing. It is most common in New York City, Los Angeles, California, Miami, FL, in the homeless, in those previously treated for tuberculosis, and children whose parents are in one of the aforementioned groups. NY, LA, MI, homeless and the prevously treated. All students with suspected resistance to INH should be given ethambutol or streptomycin. The latter is usually given for 4 to 8 weeks but never longer than 12 weeks because of the possibility of inner ear damage, resulting in deafness or loss of balance.

PLEURISY

Pleurisy, an infection of the thin outer skin of the lungs, can occur as an infrequent complication of pneumonia or tuberculosis. Pleurisy causes chest pain, a higher fever, and occasionally an outpouring of fluid between the lung and the chest wall, a condition called *pleural effusion*. Intensive treatment is required.

Pleurisy caused by some of the other viruses can also be present, independently of pneumonia. This type of pleurisy almost never causes effusion, although it can cause a moderately severe, constricting pain in the chest. Therefore, it has come to be known as the grippe or devil's grippe. It is self-limiting, going away in 7 to 14 days, and requires no antibiotic treatment.

HEALTH EDUCATION TIPS

- Educate the school faculty about the early signs of mild pneumonia.
- Emphasize the minimal contagiousness of ordinary mild childhood cough.
- If possible, organize asthma education periods with an emphasis on:
  — Proper use of metered-dose inhaler and peak flow meter
  — Importance of reporting failure to respond to MDI
  — Exercise-induced asthma
  — Search for "triggers"
- Involve the physical education teacher with the management of a student with moderately severe asthma.
- Notify teachers about the possible side effects of aminophyllin medications.
- Emphasize the noncontagiousness of childhood tuberculosis.

REFERENCES

American Thoracic Society. "Treatment of Tuberculosis and Tuberculosis Infection in Adults and Children." *American Journal of Respiratory Critical Care Medicine* 149:1359–74.

Bierman, C. W. "Allergy." In *Asthma and Immunology, from Infancy to Adulthood*, 3rd ed. Philadelphia: Saunders, 1996.

Buist, A. S., and W. M. Vollmer. "Preventing Deaths from Asthma." *New England Journal of Medicine* 331:1584–85.

Centers for Disease Control and Prevention. "Use of BCG Vaccines in the Control of Tuberculosis: A Statement by the Advisory Committee for Elimination of Tuberculosis." *Morbidity and Mortality Weekly Report* 37:663–64, 669–73.

Centers for Disease Control and Prevention. "Tuberculoses Morbidity—United States." *Morbidity and Mortality Weekly Report* 45:367–70.

Centers for Disease Control and Prevention. "Initial Therapy for Tuberculosis in the Era of Multidrug Resistance: Recommendations of the Advisory Council." *Morbidity and Mortality Weekly Report*, RR7:1–8.

Chaulk, C. P., et al. "Eleven Years of Community-Based Directly Observed Therapy for Tuberculosis." *Journal of the American Medical Association* 274:945–51.

Clark, T. J. H., S. Godfrey, and T. H. Hee. *Asthma*, 3rd ed. London: Chapman and Hall Medical, 1992.

Etzel, R. A. "Indoor Air Pollution and Childhood Asthma: Effective Environmental Interventions." *Environmental Health Perspective* 103:55–58.

Gershwin, E. M., and G. M. Halpern. *Bronchial Asthma: Principles of Diagnosis and Treatment*, 3rd ed. Totowa, N.J.: Humana Press, 1994.

Lehmann, H. P. *Practice Parameters: The Treatment of Acute Exacerbations of Asthma in Children:*. Elk Grove Village, Ill.: American Academy of Pediatrics, 1994.

McKenna, M. T., E. McCray, and I. Onorato. "The Epidemiology of Tuberculosis among Foreign-Born Persons in the United States, 1986-1993." *New England Journal of Medicine* 332:1071–76.

DISEASES OF THE HEART

Gladness of the heart is the life of us all,
And our joyfulness prolongeth our days.

Ecclesiasticus (Apocrypha) 30:22

ACQUIRED HEART DISEASE

Nature of the Condition

Acquired heart disease can occur in children of school age. It may be caused by infectious agents such as viruses, bacteria, or, rarely, fungi, and it can attack a perfectly healthy child. It may occur as a complication following some other serious primary disease like diphtheria or a mild generalized viral infection, and children born with heart defects are more susceptible to these infections.

The heart has three distinct layers: outer, middle, and inner. An infection of the outer layer, or pericardium, is called *pericarditis*. In the middle layer, or myocardium, an infection is called *myocarditis*. And in the inner layer, or endocardium, it is called *endocarditis*. The word *carditis* means infection of the heart.

Symptoms and Diagnosis

All acquired heart disease makes children seriously ill. A child with a heart disease will rarely want to get out of bed and will often have fever. The heart rate is usually quite rapid, even faster than one sees with the same amount of fever from other disease. The heart may also beat irregularly, and the electrocardiogram or echocardiogram will often be abnormal. There are often other symptoms specific to the primary disease. Rashes are common.

School Relevance and Treatment

Acquired heart disease of acute onset as described above makes a child so sick that it is unlikely that he or she will be in school. At school, however, a student who appears sicker than the degree of fever would indicate, especially if the heart rate is rapid, irregular, or both, should be allowed to rest in the clinic until parent can pick the student up. Definitive treatment depend on the exact diagnosis and must always be carried out by the student's physician.

RHEUMATIC FEVER

Nature of the Condition

Rheumatic fever is a special type of acquired heart disease that is caused by a particular sensitivity to the same germ that causes scarlet fever and strep throat: group

A beta hemolytic streptococcus (GABHS). After complete recovery from rheumatic fever, a few children are left with heart valves in a damaged condition. Of the four heart valves, the mitral valve is the one most commonly involved. After several years, this valvular damage causes symptoms that can gradually become severe.

Symptoms

The early symptoms of chronic rheumatic heart disease are mild shortness of breath, especially on exertion, occasional mild chest pain, and, occasionally, a slight blue color around the lips. Eventually, the heart enlarges, it weakens, and heart failure ensues. It takes several years after the initial attack for significant valvular damage to occur. Although most cases of valvular disease do not cause noticeable symptoms until young adult life, occasionally symptoms appear in children of secondary school age.

School Relevance

Some children with chronic rheumatic carditis may be in school. If so, the student may have a note from his or her doctor asking for some restriction of physical activity. If so, the teacher should accede to the doctor's request.

Rheumatic fever is a rare disease, especially in southern climates with milder winters, but recently, more cases have been reported in Florida, Arizona, and Utah, and school nurses should be aware of this. Better treatment of early streptococcus infections has brought a welcome decline in the incidence of rheumatic heart disease.

KAWASAKI DISEASE

Kawasaki disease is a relatively unusual acquired heart disease of unknown cause. It is most common in Japan but occurs in sporadic outbreaks in the United States. Kawasaki disease is most common in children under age 2, and 85% of cases occur in children age 5 or under. It begins with fever. Later symptoms are a rash, sore throat, enlargement of the lymph nodes in the neck, and conjunctivitis. The redness of the eyes is caused by uveitis, a distinctive change that can be detected on slit-lamp examination. Early in the disease, arthritis may occur in the small joints, and in 2 to 3 weeks, the ankles, knees, and hips may be involved. (In acute rheumatic fever, large-joint arthritis occurs in the first week to 10 days). About one-fourth of the children with Kawasaki syndrome develop coronary artery disease that may be severe. This is the most serious late manifestation of the disease.

Relevance for the School Nurse

In the first day or two of Kawasaki disease, the student may appear to have a simple viral infection. The most common observable difference is conjunctivitis that seems more severe than is warranted by the general illness. In a child age 5 or under, other factors to arouse suspicion are a rapid or irregular heart rate and a sore throat with swollen neck glands, although some of these latter factors may be seen in other children with a simple sore throat.

Children with Kawasaki syndrome are not contagious. Their disease is serious, however, and they need to be referred to a pediatrician and pediatric cardiologist as early as possible.

CONGENITAL HEART DISEASE

Nature of the Condition

Congenital heart disease is present at birth. It can be inherited or caused by disease or distress of the embryo during its development. It is usually characterized by a hole between the right and left sides of the heart, an abnormal number of heart chambers, abnormalities of the heart valves or major blood vessels near the heart, abnormal placement or twisting of the heart, or a host of other variations from normal. (Figures 9-1 and 9-2 show normal venous and arterial circulation in the heart.) There are two types of congenital heart disease, cyanotic and noncyanotic.

Cyanotic heart disease, arterial blood has a high oxygen content and is bright red; venous blood is dark red because it has a lower oxygen content. As dark red venous blood passes through the lungs, it is reoxygenated and pumped out through the arteries to the body. In most cases of cyanotic congenital heart disease, venous blood escapes through an abnormal opening in the heart and enters into, mixes with, and darkens the arterial blood. This causes cyanosis, a purplish-blue coloration especially visible through the fingernails and in the lips.

Noncyanotic heart disease, arterial blood is abnormally routed into the venous side of the heart. The mixture goes through the lungs to become oxygenated again before going back out to the body, so it becomes bright red again and the skin color is normal.

Symptoms

Cyanotic Heart Disease

Symptoms of cyanotic heart disease include the following:

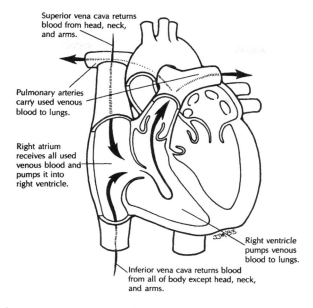

Superior vena cava returns blood from head, neck, and arms.

Pulmonary arteries carry used venous blood to lungs.

Right atrium receives all used venous blood and pumps it into right ventricle.

Right ventricle pumps venous blood to lungs.

Inferior vena cava returns blood from all of body except head, neck, and arms.

Figure 9-1. Normal venous circulation in the heart.

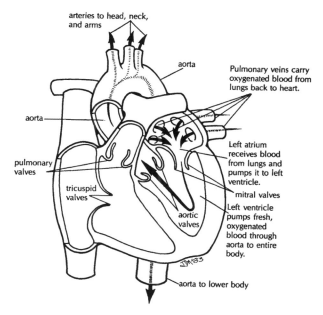

arteries to head, neck, and arms

aorta

Pulmonary veins carry oxygenated blood from lungs back to heart.

aorta

Left atrium receives blood from lungs and pumps it to left ventricle.

pulmonary valves

mitral valves

tricuspid valves

Left ventricle pumps fresh, oxygenated blood through aorta to entire body.

aortic valves

aorta to lower body

Figure 9-2. Normal arterial circulation in the heart.

- A cyanotic child exhibits a bluish tinge around the lips and fingertips. After several years, the fingertips become permanently enlarged. This is called *clubbing*.
- All the tissues receive a poor oxygen supply, impairing body growth. Resistance to infection is low; the child is sickly and frequently absent from school.
- To get sufficient oxygen, breathing is deeper and faster than normal. Very little exercise is tolerated, requiring frequent rest. Chronic shortness of breath makes speaking difficult.
- The brain receives less oxygen, which impairs cerebral processes in many subtle ways.

Many of these children have learning problems.

The extent of the symptoms depends on the amount of the oxygen deficit. Other factors that influence the severity of the symptoms are the size of the heart, regularity of the heartbeat, and blood pressure.

Noncyanotic Heart Disease

In many cases, noncyanotic heart disease causes no symptoms at all, at least not in childhood. As the child grows older, the heart gets abnormally large because of the extra workload of having to pump a larger-than-normal volume of blood. The enlarged heart is a weak heart and eventually decompensates (fails). When this happens, the child begins to show many of the same symptoms as a child with cyanotic heart disease.

Treatment

In both types of heart disease—cyanotic and noncyanotic—in children of school age, treatment consists of surgical repair of the abnormality. Not all congenital cardiac abnormalities can be repaired; some are so severe and complicated that complete cure by surgery is impossible. In these cases, palliative procedures often can be performed that give partial relief. In most cases, however, surgical cure is possible.

The modern-day diagnosis and surgical correction of congenital heart disease are complicated and should be done only by a pediatric cardiologist and skilled cardiac surgeon. If their services are not available locally, the child should be taken to a larger medical center.

School Relevance

Many children with congenital heart disease attend school every day. Most are in mainstream regular classes. Some have had operations to correct their heart defects, and some have not.

Children who visit a doctor for regular checkups are fortunate because this type of heart problem is usually diagnosed with a stethoscope. A murmur, by its sound and location, can guide a cardiologist to perform the kinds of tests that lead to an exact diagnosis. Many children, however, especially in the inner-city schools, rarely if ever visit a doctor. They may go for years with their hearts slowly enlarging and gradually becoming more and more damaged. By the time they start having symptoms, it is usually too late to effect a complete cure.

ROLE OF THE SCHOOL NURSE

Most children with congenital heart disease will be under a physician's care. The school nurse should maintain contact with the doctor's office for any necessary special instructions. The nurse should also act as in intermediary between the educational and medical personnel to make sure the efforts of both are coordinated for the student's welfare. This will be especially true in these instances:

- *Special education.* If the student is not performing at academic potential, it may be because of general weakness or lack of oxygen to the brain. The school nurse may contribute to the development of the student's individual educational plan by pointing out that the student is eligible for special education under the physically handicapped (or "other health impaired") category.
- *Restriction of physical activity.* Almost all children with congenital heart disease can be allowed to regulate their own activity; they will stop when tired.With those students who are exceptions to this, the school nurse may need to reinforce the teacher's efforts to keep the overeager children from exceeding their capabilities.
- *School attendance.* Some principals and teachers are overly fearful when students with symptomatic or cyanotic congenital heart disease attend school. As long as contact can be maintained between doctor, parent or relative, and the school nurse or principal, the student should be encouraged to attend classes as much as possible. Children who have inoperable conditions and a short life span need as much normal activity as they can comfortably tolerate.

HEART MURMURS

A murmur is a prolonged heart sound; it may be moaning and low pitched like a bass note on an organ, high pitched like a soft wind, or harsh and hissing like steam escaping a pipe. A functional murmur is not associated with disease or abnormality of the heart; an organic murmur is.

Most children with congenital heart disease have significant murmurs that can be heard with a stethoscope by a physician or by a school nurse or nurse practitioner with proper training. Caution is necessary, however.

Many children have soft, quiet heart murmurs called *functional* murmurs. These murmurs are very common; about 50% of children have them. They come and go from day to day. *They have absolutely no significance whatsoever. They are normal.*

Functional murmurs are often heard in school screening programs. If proper rechecking is not done, these students, who need not and should not go to a doctor at all, are referred to one. Some of them are subjected to many unnecessary tests, some of which may be risky. Furthermore, the children come to think of themselves as having an abnormal heart and develop an unhealthy attitude toward their own physical capabilities.

Some commonly heard functional murmurs are the following:

- A newborn pulmonary artery murmur disappears after 1 month of age. It is high pitched. This murmur is not heard in school-aged children.
- An aortic valve vibratory murmur is usually heard between 3 and 8 years. The murmur is heard best in the aortic area (second interspace just to the right of the midsternal line) and may be transmitted toward the neck. It is low pitched, groaning, vibratory, and louder when the child is lying down or after exercise.
- A pulmonary valve flow murmur resembles the aortic murmur but is loudest in the pulmonic area (same location but on the left side) and high pitched. It may be soft and blowing or rough and harsh. This type of murmur is more common during late childhood and early adolescence than at other ages. It is louder after exercise and on lying down.
- A venous hum is a continuous whirring sound all through the cardiac cycle, and it can be heard in almost all children by having the child sit up and gently raising the chin. The hum is usually quiet, but in some children it may be loud.

Normal Variation of Heart Sounds

The normal heart produces two sounds: lub´-dub. Occasionally, in an older child, the first sound is prolonged: trrup´-dub. This normal sound can be mistaken for a murmur. Occasionally, if the examiner has extremely good hearing or if the student has a thin chest wall, a third sound can be heard after the dub. This is also normal.

In the rare student who must be referred to a physician, a pediatric cardiologist can sort out most of these murmurs simply by listening to them, thus sparing the child any tests at all, even a simple X ray of the chest. Most of the time, only a chest X ray and electrocardiogram or echocardiogram will be necessary, and these are all entirely harmless and painless. Only about 10%–15% of cases referred to specialists require invasive techniques such as an angiocardiogram (intravenous dye injection) or cardiac catheterization (inserting a long flexible tube through a vein into the heart). These latter tests require hospitalization and carry some small risk, although in the presence of serious congenital heart disease, they are invaluable and necessary. The number of such examinations is gradually getting smaller as a result of the development of new diagnostic techniques.

CHOLESTEROL IN SCHOOL CHILDREN

There is no longer any doubt that increased cholesterol levels are associated with a higher risk of premature coronary artery disease in males under age 50 and females under age 60. Also, it is now a standard part of medical and nursing practice to screen adults for cholesterol and to treat those with elevated levels. Treatment consists of diet, weight loss, exercise, and drugs and is not detailed in this text. There are conflicting opinions concerning the beneficial effects of screening children for increased cholesterol levels.

Proponents of selective screening recommend that children between the ages of 2 and young adulthood have cholesterol measurements (total cholesterol, high- and low-density cholesterol and triglycerides) if there is a positive family history of premature cardiovascular disease, hyperlipidemia, sudden death, or xanthoma. A small number of children themselves have or have had certain diseases or conditions that put them at risk, such as Kawasaki disease or obesity, and they should be screened also. Proponents of selective screening believe that universal screening is:

- Too expensive
- Will mislabel and overrefer too many children and lead to the overuse of cholesterol-lowering drugs for children
- Will have limited value

Universal screening of all children has many advocates, however. Several studies have shown that children with elevated cholesterol levels do not always have a positive family history; a bit less than half of white children and one-fifth of black children do. Therefore, unless we screen *all* children, we will miss many who have elevated cholesterol levels.

Although it is easy and inexpensive to screen for total cholesterol, this measurement does not accurately predict high- and low-density fractions. Currently, most experts feel that there is not enough evidence to recommend routine universal screening for all children.

School Relevance

A question facing many school nurses is, Should cholesterol screening programs be carried out at school for the students, staff, or both?

Quite often, private entrepreneurs or public agencies such as the American Heart Association or local health departments approach a school district with an offer to screen large numbers of school students or staff. This screening will usually be offered at a low cost per person and can be paid for by the individual (or family) or for a contracted sum by the school district. In almost all cases, only the total cholesterol, not the high- or low- density or triglycerides, will be measured. This type of low-cost, universal screening is similar to what is often done in shopping malls.

Almost all medical authorities recommend that this type of indiscriminate, universal, one-shot cholesterol screening not be performed. In the majority of persons, a cholesterol measurement can only have meaning if it is evaluated along with several other factors. Some, but not all, of these factors are:

- Comparison with other measurements (height, weight, age, and other blood tests) of the person tested
- Knowledge of the machine used for the test
- Fasting state of the person tested
- Family and personal history of the person tested

In any case, universal screening, especially in children, will lead to overreferral and inevitably to the overuse of cholesterol-lowering drugs. Therefore, all lipid blood measurements should be done in the context of a full history and physical exam, in the student's or adult's medical home, by a physician or other skilled health care provider who can explain to the individual patient or parents what a particular level of cholesterol means and what should be done about it.

PARTICIPATION IN COMPETITIVE SPORTS

A common list of disqualifications to participation in competitive sports, published by the American Medical Association in 1972, has become obsolete due to changing athletic practices, protective gear, and society's attitudes toward sports. Because all sports are potentially hazardous, athletes, their parents, and their doctors must weigh the risks.

To help in this assessment, the American Academy of Pediatrics Sports Medicine Committee has developed suggestions for participation in contact and noncontact sports concerning children with heart disease (see Figure 9-3). In all cases, these recommendations are guidelines; each athlete should be judged individually. The complete and detailed recommendations can be found in the report of the AAP Committee on Sports Medicine (see the references at the end of this section).

	Contact Sports	Noncontact Sports
Carditis (infection of the heart)	No	No
High blood pressure		
Mild	Yes	Yes
Moderate and severe	Individual assessment for both	
Congenital heart disease		
Mild	Yes	Yes
Moderate and severe	Individual assessment by cardiologist for both	

Figure 9-3. Recommendations for participation in competitive sports.

HEALTH EDUCATION TIPS

- Educate faculty about the rarity of acquired heart disease.
- Hold a conference with the teacher of a student with congenital heart disease concerning
  — the student's ability to self-regulate physical activity
  — Possible learning difficulties in cyanotic children
  — Whether the student may safely attend school
- Discuss the importance of individual versus mass cholesterol screening.

REFERENCES

Bitar, C. N., et al. Use of Prophylactic Antibiotics in Children. *Advanced Pediatric Infectitious Diseases* 10:227-62.

Committee on Nutrition, American Academy of Pediatrics. "Indications for Cholesterol Testing in Children." *Pediatrics* 83:141–42.

Dyment, Paul, ed. *Sports Medicine: Health Care for Young Athletes.* Elk Grove Village, IL: American Academy of Pediatrics, Committee on Sports Medicine, 1991.

Garwick, A. W., et al. "Breaking the News. How Parents First Learn about Their Child's Chronic Condition." *Archives of Pediatrics and Adolescent Medicine* 149(9):991–97.

Gewitz, Michael H. *Primary Pediatric Cardiology.* New York: Futura, 1995.

"Hyperlipoproteinemia." *Scientific American Medicine* 9:1–10.

Nadas, A. S. *Nadas' Pediatric Cardiology.* Philadelphia: Hanly and Belfus, 1992.

Park, Myung K. *Pediatric Cardiology for Practitioners,* 3rd ed. St. Louis: Mosby-Year Book, 1996.

Shiffman, R. N. The Jones Criteria for Diagnosis of Rheumatic Fever; 50 Years Later. *Archives of Pediatrics and Adolescent Medicine* 149(7):725–26.

DIABETES

Nature of the Condition

Symptoms
- Type I: Juvenile-Onset Diabetes
- Type Ii: Adult-Onset Diabetes

Diagnosis

Special Problems at Adolescence and Emotional Problems

Treatment
- Insulin
- Diet
- Exercise
- Strict versus Loose Control

Complications
- Acute Hypoglycemia
- Ketoacidosis
- Urticaria
- Lipodystrophy
- Long-Term Complications

School Relevance and Role of the School Nurse
- Diet and Exercise
- Diabetes Education: Diabetic Educator, Parent, Doctor, and School Nurse
- Monitoring Blood Sugar
- The School Health Record
- Student Carrying Own Insulin
- Family and Physician Contact
- Parent Information Sheet

Health Education Tips

References

NATURE OF THE CONDITION

Diabetes mellitus is a disease or deficiency of the islet cells of the pancreas, a gland located near the stomach. The islet cells produce two hormones, insulin and glucagon, two hormones that regulate the blood's sugar level. Insulin causes the blood sugar level to go down, and glucagon causes it to go up.

Patients with diabetes do not produce enough insulin; therefore, their blood sugar level goes up. As the blood sugar level rises, other changes occur that, in childhood, cause rapidly progressive and severe symptoms. There are two types of diabetes, Type I, or juvenile-onset, diabetes and Type II, or adult-onset, diabetes. On occasion, a person over age 30 will develop type I diabetes and a child will develop type II diabetes. Type I diabetes may be seen at any age in childhood, but there are two ages when it is most likely to develop: ages 5 to 6 and 11 to 13. It is rare in children under 3 years old.

SYMPTOMS

Type I: Juvenile-Onset Diabetes

The classical symptoms of juvenile-onset diabetes are excess thirst and appetite, increased urination, and weight loss. The symptoms usually progress rapidly so that in 2 to 4 weeks, the child becomes thin and dehydrated, progressively weaker, and less responsive, with deep, rapid respirations. If untreated, coma and death ensue. Associated symptoms are blurred vision, bed-wetting (in a previously dry child), itching, and skin infections.

Children who are destined to develop diabetes are rarely overweight; diet or excessive sugar intake is not the cause. Rather, juvenile-onset diabetes is an autoimmune disease and is much more likely to occur in children who have diabetes in the family. Most children who develop diabetes, however, do not have relatives with diabetes.

Type II: Adult-Onset Diabetes

Adult-onset diabetes almost always occurs in middle or later life, is associated with diet and obesity, and progresses slowly. Although rare in children, it is more likely to occur in postpubertal obese girls, especially of Hispanic and African-American origin, and more so if there is diabetes in the family. Because it is so rare in school-aged children, this type of diabetes will not be dealt with in this section.

DIAGNOSIS

Diabetes is a rare disease, occurring in about 1 in 750–2500 children under age 15. In a school of 500 to 1000 students, there is a good chance that there will be a student with diabetes. Although a classical case of childhood diabetes can usually be diagnosed by symptoms alone, blood and urine sugar (and other tests) are always used to confirm the diagnosis and to determine the severity of the disease.

The school nurse should be on the lookout for any student who loses weight, especially if the student continues to eat well. Diabetic children *always lose weight*; they never simply fail to gain. Many preadolescent children gain weight very slowly (2–4 pounds a year), so diabetes need not be suspected if a child simply fails to gain but is otherwise normal.

SPECIAL PROBLEMS AT ADOLESCENCE AND EMOTIONAL PROBLEMS

As with any child with a disability, the rebellious adolescent diabetic presents special problems. It is important for the school nurse to help the student during special situations in school. Teachers may need explanations for restroom excuses for urine and blood testing. Coaches need to know about the importance of regular exercise with little change from day to day (the more exercise, the less insulin required, within limits). The principal needs to make allowances for absences; by communicating with the physician, the school nurse can help determine which absences are necessary.

Diabetic children who develop hypoglycemia (excessively low blood sugar) are likely to exhibit aggressiveness or irritability; become shaky, sleepy, or pale; or develop other behavioral problems as their first symptom. With the current emphasis on strict control of blood sugar, symptoms due to hypoglycemia are now more likely to occur. Any unusual behavior in a student with diabetes should arouse suspicions that he or she may have an imbalance of blood sugar.

TREATMENT

Juvenile-onset (type I) diabetics always need insulin; the condition cannot be controlled by diet alone. Oral antidiabetic medications, so commonly used in type II diabetes, should not be used. The treatment triad consists of insulin, diet, and exercise.

The amount of insulin required varies for each child, but it always depends on the caloric intake and the amount of exercise. The more food eaten, the more insulin required; the more exercise, the less insulin required.

Insulin

Most children with diabetes receive two doses of insulin a day, both at home: one in the morning and the second before dinner. The individual's total daily dose varies from 5 units to 75 or 90 units, depending on many factors. Also, the mixture of regular or short-acting insulin with longer-acting insulins varies with each patient. Today, the emphasis is on the child and family taking responsibility for the control of diabetes, with the doctor and the family and child determining the dose for each patient.

The school nurse should be aware of events that may require a change in or elimination of a dose. *Warning:* It is always safer to give too little insulin than too much. Too little insulin results in *slow* rise in blood sugar with a relatively *slow* onset of serious symptoms. Too much insulin results in a *rapid* decline in blood sugar with relatively *rapid* onset of serious symptoms. Whether or not the school nurse is scheduled to give a student a prescribed dose of insulin each day (a rare situation), the nurse must always be able to contact the doctor or the diabetic educator if a situation arises that requires a change in the daily dose.

Diet

The childhood diabetic needs a carefully prescribed diet. It is important that the child not become obese because this places additional stress on the heart and kidneys. The caloric content should remain steady and should only vary within prescribed limits. The diet should be one that the child enjoys and eats willingly. Special health foods and so-called diabetic foods are never necessary, but low-fat and low-calorie foods that are suitable for the entire family should be chosen. Missing a meal is not a reason for omitting an insulin dose, but it is a reason for finding out why the meal was missed and for consulting with the parents, the doctor's office, or both. It is not good practice for the child to regularly eat too much and take more insulin to control the resultant rise in blood sugar; this makes the diabetes more difficult to control. At the same time, it is not emotionally healthy to forbid the after-the-football-game chocolate ice-cream sundae that "all the other kids are having." This type of exception can be, and usually is, easily worked out in advance.

Because large schools may have unusually early or late lunch periods, the school nurse should help parents and teachers work out a prelunch snack period, which many diabetic children need to prevent prelunch hypoglycemia.

Exercise

In 1935, Dr. E. P. Joslin wrote:

> Exercise tends to lower the blood sugar in the diabetic. . . . The effect is so striking and so beneficial that exercise . . . is now accorded a prominent place in treatment. Through muscular activity, food tolerance improves and higher diets with smaller doses of insulin are possible. This is most strikingly shown in the much lower insulin requirement of diabetic children in summer camp as compared to the larger need when they are in school and relatively inactive.

These words are still true. Although regular exercise is important, the preteen child's normal play activities are usually sufficient. It is not necessary to enroll in special exercise, karate, or soccer classes for the sake of the diabetes alone. On the other hand, a sedentary child needs to be encouraged to run, climb, and jump in normal play. Teenagers more often need organized physical activities. In all cases, common sense, with due regard for the student's physical and emotional health, should prevail. It is impossible to control diabetes with exercise alone; proper diet and insulin are necessary.

Strict versus Loose Control

Strict control means maintaining the blood sugar *at all times* as close to normal as possible. Loose control means keeping the blood sugar low enough to prevent symptoms of ketoacidosis and high enough to prevent hypoglycemia. A useful schema that classifies the types of control is shown in Figure 10-1, and the differences in strict and loose control and given in Figure 10-2.

Degree of Control	Blood Sugar (80% of the time)
Strict	80–130 mg/%
Moderate	80–200 mg/%
Loose	80–300 mg/%

Figure 10-1. Types of blood sugar control.

For many years, the prevailing consensus stated that the long-term results of juvenile diabetes—that is, the incidence of eye, kidney, and microarterial damage—

Management	Strict Control	Loose Control
Daily blood sugar measurements	Frequent	Infrequent
Use of urine sugar test strips	Less frequent	More frequent
Use of ketosis urine test strips	More frequent	Less frequent
Daily doses of insulin	Tend to be more frequent	Tend to be less frequent
Episodes of hypoglycemia	More	Less
Incidence of long-term eye, kidney, and microarterial damage	Less	More
Dietary vigilance	More	Less

Figure 10-2. Differences in management and symptoms of diabetes.

was ultimately the same whether the patient followed a strict or a loose regime. With the advent of better controlled, long-term studies, however, it has become obvious that strict control dramatically reduces the incidence of the serious, irreversible, long-term complications that may lead to blindness, renal failure, or microarterial damage at a relatively early age. Therefore, diabetologists now recommend a strict-control regime whenever possible. With some patients and family situations, however, this much detail in the daily routine of life is impossible. In these situations, the doctor, diabetic educator, patient, and family should decide what is feasible for that family and what compromises can be made in the control regime so that the child has a minimal number of episodes of hypoglycemia and the blood sugar does not rise to excessive levels. In addition, the child's weight must be kept in control and a sufficient exercise level should be maintained. It is in this aspect of diabetes control that the school nurse can play a large role.

COMPLICATIONS

Acute Hypoglycemia

Acute hypoglycemia (low blood sugar) is by far the most frequent complication and the one *most likely to be encountered by the school nurse*. It is caused by excess insulin in relation to diet and exercise. It comes on rapidly and needs to be managed early, before the student loses consciousness.

The early warning signs of acute hypoglycemia are sweating, pallor, trembling, rapid pulse, and blurred vision. Later signs are confusion, disorientation, aggressiveness, and partial or complete unconsciousness. As in adults who are mistaken to be drunk, students may appear drugged. Acute hypoglycemia is also called an *insulin reaction*.

The preferred early treatment is a 4–8 ounce glass of milk or orange juice. Each beverage contains just enough rapidly absorbable sugar to cause a proper and safe rise in blood sugar. If there is no observable response in 5 minutes, the student should chew a package of mints, which contains more sugar. An alternative to mints is commercially available glucose tablets; two or three for an elementary school student, three or four for a middle school student, and four or five for a high school student. If symptoms are not improving in 5 to 10 minutes, the emergency ambulance medical system should be called or the student should be taken to the nearest emergency facility.

An ideal situation is to have a blood sugar testing kit at each school (see below). A blood sugar reading of less than 60 shows that the student is having an insulin reaction instead of early diabetic acidosis (early diabetic coma).

Glucagon is commercially available and is excellent for the treatment of insulin reactions. The usual dose is 1 milligram given intramuscularly, and it is generally considered safe. It is sometimes difficult to differentiate an insulin reaction from *early diabetic coma*, an opposite type of reaction, in which glucagon should not be given, however.

On occasion, a doctor will give a patient a prescription for glucagon and instruct the parent to buy it, take it to school, and tell the nurse to give 1 milligram if the student has an insulin reaction. This instruction alone is insufficient. A school nurse prefers to give the first dose of glucagon when a physician consultant is available, when there are signed standing orders, and when the nurse has demonstrated proficiency in differentiating insulin reaction from diabetic acidosis. Even with all the foregoing criteria, most school nurses would like to give the first dose upon receiving direct telephone orders from the physician. Depending on individual circumstances, the school nurse may exercise independent judgement in giving subsequent doses. Glucagon will never worsen the situation, so in doubtful cases, it is better to give it than withhold it. Having a blood glucose meter available always helps in the decision.

Ketoacidosis

Ketoacidosis refers to a condition that occurs when the blood sugar rises (because of excessive food intake, too little exercise, or not enough insulin) and the child's diabetes begins to go out of control. The early observable symptoms of ketoacidosis are somewhat similar to those of an insulin reaction; the child is somewhat confused, disoriented, and semiconscious. There are differentiating features, however, as shown in Figure 10-3.

Urticaria

Urticaria (hives) at the site of insulin injection occurs infrequently now that insulin is more refined. It usually goes away after a week or two of insulin use.

	Hypoglycemia	*Diabetic Acidosis*
History	Insufficient food, excess insulin, excess exercise	Lack of insulin, stress, gastrointestinal upset, febrile illness
Onset	Relatively rapid, 1 to 3 hours	Relatively slow, 4 to 10 hours or more
Symptoms	Anxiety, sweating, hunger, headache, blurred vision, twitching	Increased thirst and urination, loss of appetite, nausea, vomiting
Physical findings	Pale, moist skin; full rapid pulse; dilated pupils; rsing blood pressure	Red, dry skin; soft eyeballs; deep, rapid breathing; falling blood pressure; dry mucous membranes; lack of tears
Laboratory findings	Low blood sugar, sugar-free urine	High blood sugar, high urine sugar and ketones

Figure 10-3. Hypoglycemia versus diabetic acidosis.

Lipodystrophy

Lipodystrophy, or the breakdown of fatty tissue at the injection site, may occur in students with juvenile-onset diabetes. The long-term prognosis for the complete disappearance of these lumpy, soft skin swellings or depressions is excellent, although they sometimes last 2 to 10 years. The school nurse should encourage the student to use multiple injection sites to lessen this complication.

Long-Term Complications

Long-term complications of juvenile-onset diabetes consist of artery and nerve tract changes that may produce symptoms in the eyes, heart, brain, kidneys, and legs. These changes occur slowly and may become evident after the child has had diabetes for about 10 to 12 years, which is when the student is about 15 to 21 years old. It is rare that a school-aged child will need any treatment for a long-term complication. The better the control of the diabetes, the less severe and later the long-term complications. Some long-term complications may even be reversed by switching to strict control.

SCHOOL RELEVANCE AND ROLE OF THE SCHOOL NURSE

Diet and Exercise

Diabetic school students should be under careful control. They should have a regular regime of insulin, diet, and exercise. Any departures from the daily routine should raise a red flag. The teacher in charge of physical education or recess should understand the diabetic student's need for a steady exercise level. The cafeteria manager needs to know the importance of regular meals and prelunch snacks for students who require them to prevent late-morning hypoglycemia.

The school nurse is the ideal person to correlate all these activities, especially with the cafeteria manager and the physical education teacher, or, in elementary schools with no physical education teacher, the regular teacher. These staff members need to be briefed by the nurse on their roles and on the importance of diet and exercise.

Diabetes Education: Diabetic Educator, Parent, Doctor, and School Nurse

Most diabetic children today are cared for by pediatric endocrinologists with specialized training and experience (diabetologists). They usually employ or work with a diabetic educator who can serve as a valuable resource for the school nurse.

Diabetic educators are often available to give in-service help to school nurses and are also readily available to answer questions about all aspects of diabetes: diet, insulin, glucagon, and exercise as well as the emotional aspects of the disease.

Modern management of type I diabetes emphasizes teaching the child and parents as much as possible about the physiology of the disease so that they can make their own intelligent decisions about the frequent variations in management that occur.

Monitoring Blood Sugar

All children with diabetes will probably use a blood glucose monitor, and the school nurse should also know how to use it. Some monitors use paper strips, and some suck up blood into a capillary tube. In some, a color change on a paper strip, when compared with a sample, indicates the blood sugar level. Other monitors give a direct digital readout; these are more accurate and easier to use, but more expensive, than other types.

In the monitoring of a child with diabetes, the physician may rely on blood tests that measure the long-term stability of the blood glucose and thereby give a better picture of the child's prognosis for the development of the serious late complications. There are two blood measurements used: Hemoglobin A1c and cholesterol.

Hemoglobin A1c is a measure of glucose bound to the red blood cell. A measurement of hemoglobin A1c gives a summary of the average blood sugar for the past 2 to 3 months. The results are read in percent. A reading of 8% or less means good to excellent, a reading of 8%–10% is normal, and a reading of 10% or more is poor. High blood cholesterol is often associated with poor diabetes control.

The School Health Record

Because a student's health records are not safely confidential, record keeping can cause consequences when the student is an adult. (All school distric employees have access to student records, as do school board members.) A person's life insurance, health benefits, other employment, and so on may be affected by the school health record. At this time, the only areas of employment officially closed to diabetics are as an airplane pilot or in the military. Because of the legal, personal, and medical ramifications, school districts should address this concern in a written procedure or policy. (This is also true for epilepsy.) In the case of juvenile diabetics, there is no need to record the diagnosis in the school health record, provided there is open communication between the school nurse and other school personnel, at the current campus and other campuses the student will attend, who may need to know. This is a complicated subject about which there is much discussion, both legal and administrative. Even a whole new chapter would not clarify it.

Students Carrying Their Own Insulin

Practically no school allows a student to carry syringes or lancets, so there is no reason to carry insulin. Besides, insulin should be stored in the refrigerator.

Novopen® is a self-contained insulin-containing syringe that can be used to carry a single dose. It resembles the Anakit® or Epipen® used for anaphylaxis. The school nurse may occasionally have a student who brings a Novopen to school. The nurse should work out the details individually with the parents and doctor.

Family and Physician Contact

Because juvenile diabetes is a relatively rare disease, an individual school nurse will rarely have more than one to three children to monitor at any one time. A small school may not have any students with diabetes.

If there is a diabetic student in the school, it is important to arrange telephone contact with more than one family member and with more than one person in the doctor's office. When diabetic children need help, they need it quickly. To avoid rushing to a hospital, the school nurse needs a telephone network that is reliable and available all during the school day.

Parent Information Sheet

Figure 10-4 on page 192 shows a form letter that has been developed for teachers and school nurses.

REFERENCES

Bergman, J. M., ed. *Principles of Diabetes Management.* New York: Elsevier, 1987.

Jackson, R. L., and R. A. Guthrie. *The Physiological Management of Diabetes in Children.* New York: Elsevier, 1986.

Lowe, E., and G. Arsham. *Diabetes, a Guide to Living Well.* Minneapolis: Chronimed, 1988.

Travis, L. B., and W.W. Gauser. *An Instructional Aid on Insulin Dependent Diabetes Mellitus,* 10th ed. Austin, Tex.: Designers Ink, 1995.

Travis, L. B., B. H. Brouhard, and B. J. Schreiner. *Diabetes Mellitus in Children and Adolescents.* Philadelphia: W. B. Saunders, 1987.

To whom it may concern:

Guillermo has been diagnosed as having Type I insulin-dependent diabetes. In Type I diabetes, the pancreas does not make insulin, and it is necessary for the child to take one or more insulin injections every day; in addition, Guillermo must test his blood sugar to see that the level of sugar in the body is not too high. His insulin injections and blood sugars are administered at home.

Diabetes should not prevent Guillermo from participating in school activities. We encourage involvement in sports and other forms of physical activity since it helps to keep the blood sugar within normal levels.

The important way in which you can help Guillermo is to be alert to signs of low blood sugar (insulin reaction). Symptoms may include pallor, dizziness, sweating, crying or laughing inappropriately, or inability to concentrate or restlessness. In addition, if he complains of being very hungry, shaky, or "having a reaction," he should be allowed to have some form of sugar. These symptoms may appear from midmorning to lunch or after physical activity. He may need a snack or lunch before his physical education class.

Treatment includes providing some form of sugar immediately, such as two sugar cubes, 4 ounces of orange juice, or hard candy. The child should begin to feel better in 10 to 15 minutes. If he does not, repeat the treatment. If the child has provided you with a proprietary gel, give $1/3$ to $1/2$ of the preparation and repeat if Guillermo fails to feel better in 10 minutes.

If Guillermo does not respond or is not able to swallow, then **glucagon** must be injected. Glucagon is packaged with two vials, one containing a diluting fluid and the other containing glucagon powder. To prepare the glucagon solution, draw out the fluid in a syringe, inject it into the powder, mix, and withdraw the solution. Inject in the arms, legs or buttocks.

He should begin to arouse in 5 to 10 minutes. Once he has recovered, offer a slower-acting form of food, such as milk and a sandwich. (If the child does not arouse in 15 minutes, call his parents and **EMS, 911**.)

You will want to notify his parents of all insulin reactions since adjustments may need to be made in his insulin dose or diet.

Guillermo's parents will schedule a conference with you very soon to answer any questions.

If you have additional questions, please feel free to contact us.

Sincerely,

Figure 10-4. Parent information sheet. (Developed by Mark Danney, M.D., Daniel Hale, M.D., and Guadalupe Rupert, R.N. [diabetic educator] at the University of Texas Medical School at San Antonio, Texas.)

INFECTIONS OF SPECIAL SCHOOL RELEVANCES

No one is really safe. But for brief periods you can trick yourself into thinking you're immune.

Stan Levanthal on AIDS, 1995

GENERAL CONCEPTS

Infectious diseases remain the single most common cause of death in the world today: 32.2% of deaths worldwide result from infections and parasitic diseases. In underdeveloped countries, communicable diseases account for more than 70% of mortality, whereas in industrialized countries, the figure is closer to 10%.

In the United States, the rate of death from infections rose by 39% between 1980 and 1992, primarily because of increases in pneumonia, human immunodeficiency virus (HIV), tuberculosis, and septicemia (bloodstream infections). Increased household crowding contributed to a 300% increase in tuberculosis among preschool children in the Bronx during this period.

Children have a special susceptibility to or an increased severity of infections for a number of reasons:

- *First exposure*. Exposure to an agent for the first time (e.g., influenza) often produces fever and severe illness.
- *Small passages*. Smaller bronchi, larynx, and eustachian tubes are more easily obstructed by edema and secretions.
- *Young cells*. There is evidence that the rapid growth rates of cells in young children makes them more susceptible than adults to most viral agents (rapid cell growth allows faster replication of the virus).
- *Immature immune systems*. Many components of the immune system respond less completely in children than in adults.

Exposure to communicable diseases is one of the most important areas that can be elicited in the medical history. Many infectious diseases are first suspected on the basis of information about hobbies, travel, parents' occupation, or the student's spare-time activities, sexual exposures, self-medication or drug exposures, and personal habits. Animal and food exposures can also be important.

VIRAL HEPATITIS

Hepatitis means inflammation of the liver. It can be caused by chemicals, viruses, bacteria, fungi, or other agents. Whatever the cause, the symptoms are the following:

194

1. Early: fever, malaise, loss of appetite, and stomachache
2. One to two days later: continuation of early symptoms, plus nausea and vomiting
3. About the same time or one to two days later: jaundice and enlarged liver

Most children do not have all the above symptoms. The severity of the symptoms is usually age related; children always have a milder form of the disease than adults, including *anicteric hepatitis* (without jaundice). The whites of the eyes offer the easiest and earliest place to detect yellow discoloration. A child with very mild disease may have only a 3- to 5-day illness with low fever, loss of appetite, nausea, and a little stomachache. Many of these children do not stay home from school, and nobody knows they had hepatitis. They are, however, just as contagious.

Varieties of Viral Hepatitis

The two most common types of viral hepatitis of school concern are *infectious hepatitis*, or hepatitis A, caused by the hepatitis A virus (HAV) and *serum hepatitis*, or hepatitis B, caused by the hepatitis B virus (HBV).

Hepatitis A

Almost all cases in school children are hepatitis A. It is caused by the oral ingestion of HAV. Transmission is by the fecal-oral route. Human sewage or fecal material that contains the virus and enters the water or food supply is a source of infection. In addition, people with the virus in their stools transmit it by way of their fingers (failure to wash hands after a bowel movement). A reservoir of viral hepatitis A exists in day-care centers catering to children under age 2 (related to diaper changing).

The incubation period (the time between ingestion of the virus and the earliest onset of symptoms) for hepatitis A is 15 to 45 days. *The most contagious stage is in the late incubation period, so that by the time jaundice develops and the diagnosis is made, the disease has become less contagious, even though the patient may be getting sicker.*

Half of the population over age 50 has antibodies against hepatitis A, meaning that they had the disease at some earlier time in their lives. One attack usually confers lifetime immunity, and there are no chronic carriers. Rarely is the disease severe; the overall mortality rate is less than 1%.

Hepatitis B

Hepatitis B is caused by a different virus than hepatitis A. This virus can be found in blood, urine, feces, semen, vaginal secretions, saliva, breast milk, and other body fluids of infected individuals.

Hepatitis B was previously thought to occur only following blood transfusions and was called serum hepatitis. Now, because of blood screening, it is rarely transmitted this way. The most common methods of spread are by sexual contact and by intravenous drug abuse. Thus, there is a high prevalence of hepatitis B among prostitutes, especially those who are intravenous drug abusers. Homosexual males also have high rates. There is a slightly higher prevalence in health care workers, especially lab technicians, surgeons, and dentists.

In contrast to hepatitis A, hepatitis B has a much longer incubation period—1 to 6 months—and chronic carriers are common; thus, it is thought that there is a pool of about one million active carriers in the United States. Because the symptoms of the active disease are similar to those of hepatitis A, sophisticated laboratory work and good clinical acumen are required to distinguish one from the other.

Figure 11-1 summarizes the major differences between HAV and HBV.

Laboratory Differentiation of Hepatitis A and B

The following laboratory tests are sometimes performed to diagnose the type of hepatitis in a particular child. The hepatitis B antibody profile shown in 2-b will help you interpret lab reports.

1. Liver function tests
   a. Bilirubin level
   b. SGOT (serum glutamic-oxaloacetic transaminase)
   c. SGPT (serum glutamic-pyruvic transaminase)

The transaminase level reflects the degree of liver dysfunction (the more dysfunction, the higher the transaminase). Bilirubin measures the degree of jaundice (more jaundice means higher bilirubin). Because both tests are abnormal in hepatitis A and B, they cannot be used to differentiate between the two types.

	HEPATITIS A	HEPATITIS B
Incubation Period	2–6 weeks	1–6 months
Period of infectivity	Short	May be long
Clinical symptoms	Same	Same
Carrier state	No	Yes

Figure 11-1. Differences between hepatitis A and hepatitis B.

2. Antigen/antibody tests

a. Hepatitis A antibodies (anti-HA) can be detected following the onset of clinical disease (fever and jaundice). Their presence confirms type A infection. Other tests are available for earlier detection, but they are expensive and difficult to do.

b. There are three separate hepatitis B antigens. Each produces its own antibody. Clinical labs refer to them collectively as "Hepatitis B antibody profile."

1. Hepatitis B surface antigen — HBsAg (the test result in an asymptomatic hepatitis B carrier is HBsAg-Positive.)

   Hepatitis B surface antibody — Anti-HBs

2. Hepatitis B core antigen — HBcAg

   Hepatitis B core antibody — Anti-HBc

3. Hepatitis B e antigen — HBeAg

   Hepatitis B e antibody — Anti-HBe

By a judicious selection of antigen/antibody tests and by the clinical condition of the patient (sick versus well, recent versus past illness), a physician can determine whether the patient has active infection, is a carrier, or is infectious and what precautions need be taken. Most physicians will consult with a specialist in infectious diseases.

Unless antigen/antibody studies are performed, it is impossible to be sure whether a person has hepatitis A or B. Because a hepatitis antibody profile is expensive and because the large majority of children with mild hepatitis have the A variety, doctors often obtain only the liver function tests and make a *clinical* diagnosis. Most state health departments require a doctor's diagnosis but do not dictate what criteria must be used in arriving at that diagnosis. Many doctors order hepatitis B antibody profiles only if they suspect child sexual abuse or if the disease is unusually severe.

Other Types of Hepatitis

Hepatitis C, formerly known as non-A/non-B, is currently the greatest challenge of the various types of hepatitis. The incidence of hepatitis C is greater in intravenous drug users than in the general population, but an acute form of the disease is not usually recognized (subclinical) because the symptoms are mild or absent. About 10 years after initial infection, chronic liver disease develops. Hepatitis C is spread primarily by blood, but other routes have been reported.

Hepatitis D is an incomplete virus requiring the presence of HBV to infect and do damage. It has a higher incidence in intravenous drug users than in the general population.

Hepatitis E is an enteric virus similar to HAV. The attack rate is sporadic, and the immunity may not be life long. Infectivity can last up to 6 months in a small number of individuals; this accounts for the large outbreaks that sometimes occur. The mortality rate is 1%-4%, except in pregnant mothers, where it approaches 20%.

The hepatitis F designation was used only briefly until the strain was determined to be a mutant of HBV.

Hepatitis G, the newest of hepatitis viruses, is related to the yellow fever virus and is transmitted by mosquitos. It may result in liver cancer years following initial infection.

Treatment

There is no specific treatment for viral hepatitis, nor does any antibiotic or uniformly effective antiviral medicine actually kill the virus; therefore, preventive measures are paramount. Interferon is being used in hepatitis C, where it has been shown to retard viral replication.

Many supportive measures are helpful in the treatment of hepatitis:

- *Rest*. In the early stages, it is important for children to be in bed or at least indoors, depending on the severity of the disease.
- *Food*. Because loss of appetite and nausea are prominent symptoms, it is difficult for the child to eat the foods necessary to fortify the liver. Small amounts of appetizing carbohydrates at frequent intervals are helpful.
- *Fluids*. All types of liquids are helpful, and in the early stages of the illness, the child may not tolerate much else without vomiting.

Prevention of Hepatitis A

Hand Washing

If everyone always washed hands after a bowel movement and if no one ever put their hands to their faces, childhood hepatitis would diminish markedly. Hand washing is by far the most effective way to prevent the spread of hepatitis A. Unfortunately, despite all exhortations, this practice is rarely followed, and there is no reason to expect that education alone can be relied on.

Hepatitis A can be prevented about 90% of the time if a dose of 0.02 cc of IG per kilogram of body weight is given intramuscularly within 2 weeks of exposure.

This means that a 150-pound individual would require a dose of about 1.5 cc. In some cases, larger doses are used because the doctor may suspect hepatitis B, which requires a dose three times larger, or because exposure occurred more than 2 weeks ago. An effective vaccine is now available, but it is not recommended routinely for all children.

Prevention of Hepatitis B

Prevention of hepatitis B consists of taking the same measures recommended to prevent AIDS (see discussion later in this section). In addition, an effective vaccine that permanently prevents hepatitis B is now available. Although it is expensive—about $150 for the series of three vaccines—it is recommended for high-risk individuals. Most newborns now receive it in the hospital, and some states are beginning to require it at school entry. School nurses should receive the hepatitis B vaccine. After exposure, hepatitis B immune globulin can be used in combination with the vaccine.

TUBERCULOSIS

Tuberculosis is mentioned briefly here because it has been on the rise in United States, although the incidence of new cases began to level out in 1993–96. As in the past, the incidence of tuberculosis is higher in poverty areas due to overcrowding than in other areas. An influx of immigrants from countries with high rates of tuberculosis has also contributed to the increase. The World Health Organization has identified 30 countries with a very high incidence of tuberculosis.

Most alarming is the emergence of drug resistant strains of *Mycobacterium tuberculosis*. These resistant bacteria have arisen in individuals who have the disease and do not complete their course of therapy. Health departments have now begun direct observation of medication (DOM) by public health workers. They are also asking school nurses to administer the antituberculosis drugs at school to ensure that children complete their regimens.

FOOD POISONING

Emetic food poisoning (also called common source vomiting or simultaneous onset vomiting) is the occurrence of vomiting in more than one individual with onset at approximately the same time; diarrhea may also be present. The most common cause is staphylococcal enterotoxin produced in food contaminated by a pustule from a food handler. The onset is rapid: 2 to 4 hours after consuming contaminated food.

A delayed onset (12 to 24 hours) with little or no vomiting, but lower abdominal cramps and diarrhea, suggests *Salmonella* contamination, particularly when suspect foods are involved (eggs, poultry). *C. perfringens* in meat can produce a similar clinical picture.

Food poisoning arises from the ingestion of food that is contaminated with microorganisms, microbial toxins, or chemicals. An outbreak is generally defined by the Centers for Disease Control and Prevention (CDC) as "an incident in which two or more persons experience a similar illness after ingesting a common food, which epidemiologic analysis implicates as the source of the illness."

The number of individual cases of food poisoning that occur annually in the United States is unknown, but each year, about 600 outbreaks are reported to the CDC. Of all outbreaks reported, about 44% are associated with eating at a restaurant, delicatessen, or cafeteria; 23% are associated with meals at home; and the remaining 33% occur at schools, churches, picnics, and camps.

After *Staphylococcus* and *Salmonella,* causes of food poisoning include *Shigella, Clostridium perfringens,* and *Clostridium botulinum.* Other causes include *E. coli* (undercooked bovine meat), *Campylobacter jejuni, Bacillus cereus,* and possibly Norwalk virus. In sum, bacterial causes account for about two-thirds of the outbreaks.

Sources of Food Contamination

At a school, the source of food contamination is most often the food handler in the cafeteria. Even when contaminated, most food, if properly heated or cooked (reaching at least 140°F), is rendered harmless. Uncooked foods such as salads require the greatest care with preparation technique because *E. coli,* Norwalk virus, and hepatitis A can be transmitted.

Food suppliers sometimes have chinks in their quality-control armor. The well-known offending products are eggs and poultry, but ground beef, powdered milk, and instant mashed potatoes are not infrequently contaminated. Using powdered milk in a food that is not cooked poses the greatest risk.

On special occasions (birthdays and holidays), parents and students often bring party food prepared at home to the school. Although no good data exist, this probably is a significant potential risk.

Finally, the water supply may be contaminated, particularly in those schools that have sources other than a municipal water source.

Prevention of Food Poisoning

The single most valuable activity in preventing food poisoning is the training of food handlers. Specific techniques for hand washing and heating food top the list. Also important are wearing vinyl gloves, the proper cool storage of foods (particularly uncooked foods), not using the same sinks for hand washing and preparing food, and plumbing that prevents backflow contamination with sewage. Cough guards are needed for food that is exposed in self-service lines, and ill food handlers should be excluded from work.

It has been well-documented that individual "health certificates" on food handlers are of little or no value in preventing cases of food poisoning, although they can rule out tuberculosis. Most states and counties require food handlers to undergo government-sponsored training for certified food service managers. Cafeteria managers in turn are responsible for training paraprofessionals in the school setting.

In most cities, registered sanitarians make periodic inspections of all establishments that serve food; school cafeterias are treated the same way restaurants are. The primary items on sanitarian check lists are food, garbage, and rubbish disposal; preparation personnel; insect, rodent, and animal control; equipment and utensils; floors, walls, and ceilings; water source; lighting, ventilation, dressing rooms, and other operations (toxic items are properly used, labeled, and stored); plumbing and sewage; and toilet and hand-washing facilities.

The most frequent infraction noted by city sanitarians is inadequate coverage of outside garbage bins (attracting rodents, roaches, and other vermin).

GENITAL SYNDROMES

Modern society talks about and engages in sexual practices more than in the past. Promiscuity has affected the student population as well. More individuals are sexually active at a younger age and with a greater variety of partners. This has caused sexually transmitted diseases (STDs) to leap to epidemic numbers. Whereas in the past STD meant syphilis and gonorrhea, the rapidly rising number of cases has caused previously rare conditions to be added to the list of sexually transmitted diseases. Today, herpes simplex, hepatitis B, and several lesser-known diseases are seen more often than in the past.

Despite the serious threat this presents to school-aged children, there is still widespread opposition to presenting effective education in the schools to offer students information that could protect them from such exposure. The assumption is that if students hear about sex, they will get ideas. In fact, they have already heard about it, and many are past the idea stage. Those students who are not sexually active have made their choice for abstinence despite information on sexuality. Then, methods of reporting and treating existing cases would become more effective, causing the incidence to drop.

Syphilis

Syphilis has plagued humankind since antiquity. It has existed for so many centuries that it seems that the human race has developed a partial immunity to it. Several hundred years ago, *Treponema pallidum*, the bacterium that causes syphilis, was so virulent that it occasionally caused a high fever, delirium, coma, and death within a week. In recent years, the prevalence rates of syphilis have been increasing, and more cases are seen in school-aged children.

Primary Stage

The primary lesion usually consists of a genital sore (chancre) that goes away untreated in 1 to 3 weeks. The chancre is usually located on the glans penis, the labia minora (the inner vaginal lips), or, rarely, on the tonsil or adjacent to the anus. There may or may not be a low-grade fever, but the affected individual is not very sick. Because the chancre is relatively painless, a doctor is often not even consulted, although the disease is highly contagious.

Secondary Stage

The secondary stage of syphilis occurs about 6 to 8 weeks after the primary stage and can manifest itself in various forms. A common finding is a nonitching skin rash that looks like mild measles. Whitish patches that sometimes occur inside the mouth are called mucous patches. They are highly contagious, especially through kissing. This stage is usually accompanied by fever and malaise. It usually goes away untreated in 1 to 3 weeks. There are many other possible manifestations of secondary syphilis, such as acute meningitis or encephalitis, different kinds of skin rashes, bald spots, and arthritis. Occasionally, secondary symptoms continue to reappear for 6 to 9 months or for as long as 2 years.

Tertiary Stage

The first two stages of syphilis are almost always benign and self-limiting. The third or tertiary stage, which has become quite rare since penicillin, occurs 5 to 20 years later. The tertiary stage in untreated syphilis occurs in only about 25%–30% of individuals who have had the primary or secondary stage. It can attack the brain, spinal cord, heart, or other organs. In any case, the illness and damage caused by the tertiary stage are usually serious and sometimes fatal.

Most cases of early syphilis can be cured with a single injection of long-acting penicillin.

Gonorrhea

Gonorrhea, now one of the most common communicable diseases in the world, is also one of the classical venereal diseases of antiquity. Commonly called the clap, it is caused by the bacterium *Neisseria gonorrhea* or, simply, the gonococcus. It settles in the urethra in males and in the cervix in females, producing a purulent discharge and various other symptoms. The time between exposure and first onset of symptoms can be up to 10 days, but in most cases it is 2 to 4 days.

In males, this infection causes burning on urination. In females, the infection is often painless, but if it spreads into the uterus and fallopian tubes, it can cause intense abdominal pain. Further serious complications such as peritonitis may ensue if treatment is delayed. Also, complications can occur in males, especially if the infection travels to the testicles or prostate gland.

In recent years, the gonococcus has been found in the throat and rectum in increasing numbers of patients who regularly indulge in oral or anal sex, both homosexual and heterosexual.

In both males and females, either because of partial natural immunity or partial treatment, the urethral or vaginal discharge can diminish to such a small amount that it is almost unnoticeable and completely painless. It is, however, just as contagious. Gonorrhea is unchallenged as the most prevalent of all serious sexually transmitted diseases, and the incidence of this disease is rising each year.

Treatment

A single injection of penicillin will cure most early cases of gonorrhea, but many physicians prescribe a combination of medications. The gonococcus tends to develop a resistance against antibiotic action, and many strains of the germ are partially or completely resistant to penicillin. If complications ensue, a longer course of treatment is required.

Other Venereal Diseases

In the United States, as in other parts of the world, diseases spread by sexual contact exist in larger numbers than many people are aware. Some experts claim that there are about 20 such diseases. The less common are unknown to most people, and the average doctor rarely sees them because they are treated in STD clinics.

Generally speaking, other venereal diseases cause various kinds of surface lesions (sores, warts, lymph node swellings, etc.) in the genital area, and serious complications occasionally ensue. Some of these diseases are the following:

- Lymphogranuloma venereum
- Chancroid (soft chancre)
- Venereal warts   .
- Granuloma inguinale
- Reiter's syndrome
- Hepatitis B

Some of the less common venereal diseases are readily treatable, and some are not. In all cases, a specialist in venereal diseases should be consulted.

ACQUIRED IMMUNE DEFICIENCY SYNDROME (AIDS)

Current theory has it that the human immunodeficiency virus (HIV) has long existed as a virus in monkeys, not causing any symptoms of illness. The virus then mutated and became capable of infecting humans, and in its mutated form it attacked the human T-cell lymphocytes, the cells responsible for providing immunity to infection. This slow destruction of natural body immunity causes the chain of events leading to full-blown AIDS.

Since 1981, AIDS has been spreading rapidly. It exists in all age groups and both sexes, but because of the methods of transmission it is more prevalent in males. In 1996, the number of cases of AIDS in the United States exceeded 500,000, with deaths approaching 300,000. The number of HIV-positive individuals in the United States is estimated to be about 1.25 million.

The virus can be found in many body fluids but primarily in the blood, since that is where lymphocytes are. It is also found in vaginal secretions and semen in moderate amounts. The amount in saliva, urine, stool, stomach contents, and tears is very small to nonexistent.

AIDS is found mostly in male homosexuals, intravenous drug users, prostitutes, and hemophiliacs. Newborn children of mothers with AIDS often develop congenital AIDS, a condition that may be seen in school-aged children.

Because of its blood-borne nature and because anal intercourse often tears the rectum and causes bleeding, males or females who engage in this practice are at high risk. Prostitutes, male and female, are also at high risk because they have sexual contact with so many different individuals. Intravenous drug users often share unsterilized needles, causing direct blood-to-blood transmission. Hemophiliacs require frequent transfusions of blood products. Any person who received frequent blood transfusions before 1985 is at risk. The incidence of AIDS in hemophiliacs is about

15 per 1,000. Blood used for transfusions is now screened, greatly reducing the chance of an individual contracting AIDS by transfusion. It is estimated there is a 1 in 40,000 chance of acquiring AIDS in this manner.

Clinical Syndrome

Stage I

When HIV first invades the body, it calls forth a normal antibody response. There is a simple blood test that detects this antibody, and persons with a positive test are called HIV carriers. They are completely asymptomatic, but presumably they can transmit the disease and can themselves later develop AIDS.

Stage II

After a period of 2 to 10 years, a high percentage of persons who are HIV positive go on to develop symptoms: low-grade fever, enlarged lymph nodes, night sweats, fatigue, weakness, weight loss, and in some cases, skin and mouth rashes.

Stage III

After another 1 to 3 years, about one-fourth of persons with mild symptoms develop full-blown AIDS. To be officially classified as having AIDS, a patient must exhibit one of a list of "opportunistic infections": diseases caused by germs, viruses, or fungi that are widely prevalent but that normal immunity prevents the disease from invading the body. These germs are relatively resistant to antibiotics, so when they invade a person with no immunity, the disease progresses unchecked and is fatal, but newer medicines are constantly being tried.

Congenital AIDS

Women with AIDS who become pregnant are likely to pass the disease to their fetus. The newborn baby is then actually born HIV positive; symptoms often develop in the first year of life. The most notable finding is brain damage. It appears that the HIV actually attacks the brain cells in addition to the T-cell lymphocytes, thus causing an encephalitis. The children also develop the opportunistic infections if they live long enough.

Congenital AIDS is frequently fatal, but some children may live long enough to attend school. Another group of HIV-positive newborns eventually convert to negative and never develop AIDS. The same policies that apply to any other child with AIDS would be followed, i.e., universal precautions, t-cell monitoring, medications, etc.

The current practice of treating HIV-positive pregnant women with azidothymidine (AZT) is showing promise in preventing congenital AIDS.

Risk Factors

Various factors put an individual at a risk for AIDS:

- Intravenous drug abuse, from sharing unsterilized needles
- Sexual promiscuity. (People who have had only one sexual partner for the past 10 years and who do not fall in other risk categories are at no risk.)
- Anal intercourse, because of anal bleeding and increased susceptibility of the cells lining the inside of the rectum
- Contact with prostitutes of either sex
- Oral sex
- Vaginal intercourse between a bisexual male and his heterosexual partner
- Receiving blood transfusions. (This is low risk now that blood is tested. Giving blood cannot cause AIDS in the donor.)

Prevention and Treatment

Prevention of AIDS consists of avoiding all risk factors. In addition, males should always wear a condom if there is any possibility that a partner has been exposed or if he himself could transmit AIDS.

Treatment during the first two stages consists of preventing any further exposure to the virus. In addition, good nutrition, exercise, adequate rest, and other healthful habits are encouraged.

There are medications used to treat the opportunistic infections that occur during stage III AIDS. Recent evidence suggests that they may actually slow the growth of the virus itself. They are beneficial in that they slow the course of the disease. The most commonly prescribed medication is AZT.

Universal Precautions

In 1985, the Centers for Disease Control and Prevention developed the strategy of "universal blood and body fluid precautions" to address the transmission of HIV and hepatitis B in the health care setting. The concept stressed that all patients should be assumed to be infected with HIV and other blood-borne pathogens. The practice of universal precautions has now been extended to day-care centers, schools, and other settings. The key elements include:

- Proper needle handling and disposal
- Hand washing
- Cleaning, disinfecting, and sterilizing all nondisposable equipment
- Decontaminating spills of blood
- Proper laundry procedures
- Disposal of infective waste
- Personal protection (gloves, goggles, etc.)

These procedures are now well known and should be practiced by all school health personnel.

NEONATALLY TRANSMITTED INFECTIONS

The fetus and newborn are susceptible to many infections during pregnancy, during the birth process, and shortly after birth. A small number of these diseases are capable of causing a long-term illness that may be contagious even as the child grows older and enters school.

Most of these infections are due to viruses:

- Cytomegalovirus (CMV)
- Rubella virus (RV)
- Varicella-zoster virus (VZV)
- Herpes simplex virus (HSV)
- Hepatitis B virus (HBV)

Viral infection calls forth an antibody response, and measuring the antibody level is the usual laboratory method of determining whether a person has had the disease in the past.

When adults are infected by these viruses, it is rarely serious. If a woman gets one of these diseases while she is pregnant, however, she may transmit the virus to her fetus. This is precisely why school personnel have become so concerned about these infections.

Many physically and mentally disabled students, some profoundly so, are now in public schools. It is known that some of the diseases described above can cause infection of the brain and other organs in the fetus and newborn, which may later result in physical and mental retardation. The primary concern of school personnel is *how long these children may remain contagious.* These are legitimate concerns for which there are dependable answers most of the time.

For example, a baby whose brain has been damaged by HSV is contagious as long as there are herpetic skin lesions. On the other hand, a newborn baby with a liver infection due to HBV may become a chronic hepatitis B carrier and be no more contagious than any other hepatitis carrier (of whom there are always several in the school population of students and teachers).

Cytomegalovirus

Cytomegalovirus (CMV) exists worldwide, and antibodies indicating past infection are found in 60%–90% of the various populations tested. It is most commonly contracted during infancy and early childhood from the mother or during young adult life from sexual activity. There are several strains of this virus; immunity to one does not necessarily confer immunity to others. CMV can be recovered from urine, semen, saliva, and vaginal and other body secretions.

Acquisition of the virus rarely results in clinical disease, except in persons with a weak immune system. The groups at high risk of developing symptomatic illness are the fetus and newborn, persons on immune-suppressing drugs such as steroids, and AIDS patients. The remainder develop only an increased blood antibody level. A person who acquires the infection, although asymptomatic, may remain contagious for a long time. In addition, a person who has had the disease and developed antibodies, but whose body fluids no longer contain the virus, can get *reinfected with another strain of CMV and become contagious again.*

Special Precautions in Pregnancy

Because CMV can be so devastating in the newborn, women who are pregnant or may soon become pregnant should take precautions to prevent exposure. In actual practice, this means no unprotected sexual activity, since this is the usual route of transmission in adults.

Women working in day-care centers can acquire CMV from the children. Now that younger and more handicapped children are entering school, there is a greater risk of exposure than in the past. There is, as yet, no vaccine to prevent CMV nor medicine to cure it; the best prevention is hand washing. In-service education programs are useful. When school personnel have a clear understanding of the disease, they cooperate better in hand washing and other preventive techniques.

Of newborns with CMV, 90%–95% are normal at birth. Those few showing signs of disease have a large spleen and liver and overt signs of brain damage. Of the larger number of infants who have appeared to be normal at birth but whose blood test is CMV positive, however, long-term follow-up studies have shown a number of developmental disabilities:

- Microcephaly
- IQ under 90
- Hearing loss
- School failure

Rubella (German Measles)

German measles is, with rare exceptions, a minor 3-day disease with a mild rash. Contracting the disease during pregnancy, especially early pregnancy, often causes severe congenital malformations in the newborn, however. About 75% of the newborns who appear normal at birth but are born to mothers who had rubella during pregnancy develop long-term sequelae (mental retardation, hearing loss, etc.) in the first 5 years of life. Therefore, all females should be vaccinated against rubella in early life. Indeed, now that immunization is required for school entry in all states, there has not been a major rubella epidemic in the United States since 1964, and congenital malformations from rubella are rarely seen.

Recent surveys show that 10%–15% of young women are susceptible to rubella. When a nonimmunized woman becomes pregnant, what should be the course of action if she is exposed to rubella? The vaccine package insert states that it should not be given to pregnant women or women about to become pregnant. About 1,200 such women in the United States have received the vaccine and no rubella babies have resulted, however. When this situation arises, each woman should be individually counseled by a physician.

A baby born with congenital malformations from maternal rubella is contagious; that is, virus is being shed. Rubella babies may shed virus for as long as a year, but rarely longer. Therefore, most school-aged children will not be contagious, but some of those in special programs for birth to 3-year-old children may be.

Varicella Zoster (Chicken Pox and Shingles)

Varicella is chicken pox; *zoster* (also called herpes zoster) is shingles. The virus that causes both diseases is identical. When the body is first invaded by the varicella-zoster virus, (VZV), usually during childhood, chicken pox results. After recovery, the virus may remain in the body in a latent, noncontagious form. On reexposure years later, the latent virus may become reactivated, and because of partial immunity, shingles develops. Shingles is a localized form of chicken pox.

Varicella is one of the most contagious of all diseases; 96% of susceptible contacts develop the disease within 2 weeks of exposure. Shingles is contagious only on close contact; exact figures are unavailable because the disease is uncommon.

Infection of a pregnant woman with VZV results in one of three infant syndromes:

1. *Congenital malformations.* These babies have no skin lesions and are not contagious, although they may have serious malformations of peripheral nerves, spinal cord, brain, and eyes.
2. *Neonatal chicken pox.* These babies may be gravely ill; the mortality rate is high. After they recover and the rash has gone, they are not contagious.
3. *Shingles in infancy or childhood.* These infections are usually not severe; they are mildly contagious only as long as the rash is active.

If a woman of childbearing age is concerned about her susceptibility to chicken pox, blood tests are available to check her antibody level. Because most adults are immune, this is not recommended as a routine measure. A student with chicken pox is not allowed to stay in school. A student with shingles will only be in school if the rash is slight and on a part of the body covered by clothing. An exposed shingles rash or a sick student is also reason for having the student stay at home. Shingles can last several weeks or months, however, and in most cases, the child is not clinically ill with fever or other symptoms. It is safe to allow a student with shingles to attend school provided that care is taken to keep the rash covered by clothing, especially during physical education class.

Herpes Simplex Virus

Cold sores or fever blisters are due to the herpes simplex virus (HSV). HSV and varicella-zoster virus (VSV) both belong to the herpes family of viruses, but they are separate and distinct. There are two types of HSV. Type I causes mouth, nose, and eye lesions (cold sores and fever blisters). Type II is a genital infection. About 10%–20% of the time, genital herpes is caused by type I virus and herpes sores on the face are caused by type II virus.

HSV can be transmitted by a pregnant woman to her baby in one of three ways:

1. *In utero* through the placenta
2. During the birth process from active sores in the genital tract. (Babies who get HSV in utero or during the birth process may develop a very severe form of the disease called disseminated herpes; the mortality rate is high, and those who live often have severe brain damage.)

3. After birth from a mother with active sores, either by direct contact or hand-to-mouth transmission

SCHOOL RELEVANCE

Neonatal Infections

Special education personnel of childbearing age are at greatest risk of exposure to neonatally transmitted infections. The following guidelines are offered to minimize exposure:

- All personnel in special education classrooms should be trained in and employ universal precautions with latex or vinyl gloves when changing diapers or encountering blood. (All students should be treated as if they are HBV, CMV, and HIV positive.) Removal of gloves should be followed by hand washing. Hand washing should also follow contact with saliva or other body fluids before assisting another child.

- Children requiring diaper changes should be placed in classrooms that contain sinks for easy access to hand washing. All diapering should be done in an area separate from the food preparation area; selected classroom surfaces should be sanitized with an appropriate disinfectant.

- Urine cultures on students are of little or no value as the viruses may be shed intermittently.

- Antibody titers on employees fall within the purview of the private obstetrician or primary health care giver.

- Physicians should communicate in writing any accommodations required for their patients in the school setting.

AIDS

Guidelines have also been adopted by most medical and legal authorities that recommend that children with HIV and AIDS be allowed to attend school. Most school districts have accepted these guidelines. Because AIDS has never been shown to be spread by airborne or other nonintimate contact, these guidelines seem reasonable. The following precautions are recommended:

- Children with AIDS who bite, have open sores, frequent nose bleeds, or who drool excessively should be excluded from school.

- All body fluids that are spilled (vomit, urine, etc.) by any child should be wiped up with a 1 to 9 dilution (10% solution) of bleach while wearing plastic gloves.
- Trash cans should have plastic liners.
- Children with AIDS are more susceptible to infection, so they need to be sent home during outbreaks of usual childhood diseases, such as chicken pox or influenza.
- A student's privacy should be respected. Only those personnel with a need to know should be told that the student has AIDS. This usually includes the principal, counselor, teachers, and school nurse, but may include any person whose duties bring him or her in contact with an HIV-positive student.
- The risk of contracting AIDS from a child with a nosebleed or minor skin trauma is minuscule. The following guidelines are suggested:
  - For caretakers with no open sores on the hands, gloves are optional. Hand washing after caring for the child is sufficient.
  - For caretakers with open hand sores, gloves should be worn.
  - In no case should the care of a bleeding child be delayed because of a lack of gloves.
  - Children excluded from school should be provided with an appropriate alternative education.

ROLE OF THE SCHOOL NURSE

In the area of communicable disease, the school nurse should act as the main liaison between the doctor, parents, student, and educational personnel. Many activities such as medications, excused absences, homebound teachers, and calls to the doctor's office need to be coordinated. Many questions will come from faculty, and more and more, calls will come from health and science teachers asking the nurse to act as a resource person for classroom teaching.

New infections are emerging, and old ones are changing. By remaining informed about new developments, the school nurse can be helpful to the entire faculty.

Legal issues are important. Each state has laws governing confidentiality and school attendance for children with contagious diseases. The right of the child to attend school and the perceived right of the school staff to know if a child has a communicable disease are often in conflict. The school nurse can help guide school district policy.

Most available curriculums do not adequately address the benefits of abstinence from sexual intercourse, which is the most reliable way to avoid AIDS and other sexually transmitted diseases. Abstinence is also the only foolproof way to avoid pregnancy. The case for abstinence can be made factually and without moralizing.

HEALTH EDUCATION TIPS

The last two surgeons general of the United States have recommended teaching about promiscuity, homosexuality, heterosexuality, and condoms. They encourage human sexuality courses beginning at the latest in the sixth grade.

Much misinformation and numerous myths still exist in the minds of preteens and early teenagers regarding HIV and AIDS, particularly communicability and testing. The following five questions can serve as a starting point for student discussions or as a "quiz" following a discussion.

1. What percentage of new HIV cases occur in persons age 21 years and younger? *(Answer: 25%)*

2. What are four ways a person can be exposed to HIV? *(Answer: unsafe sex, tattoos or body piercing, being born to an infected mother, and sharing needles)*

3. Why is HIV testing important if the possibility of exposure exists? *(Answer: to avoid unknowing spread of the infection)*

4. What are opportunistic infections? *(Answer: infections caused by microorganisms that do not cause problems in people with normal immune systems, such as Pneumocystis carinii)*

5. How effective is the treatment for AIDS? *(Answer: At the present, multiple drug treatment can prolong life significantly, but the vast majority of cases are still fatal.)*

REFERENCES

Anderson, R. *Infections in Children: A Sourcebook for Educators and Child Care Providers.* Gaithersburg, Md.: Aspen, 1994.

Fineberg, H. "Social Vulnerability and Death by Infection." *New England Journal of Medicine* 334(13):859–60.

Kaplan, S. *Current Therapy in Pediatric Infectious Disease.* St. Louis: Mosby, 1993.

Krugman, S. *Infectious Diseases of Children.* St. Louis: Mosby, 1992.

Moffet, H. *Pediatric Infectious Diseases* Philadelphia: J. B. Lippincott, 1989.

————. *Universal Precautions.* Atlanta: Centers for Disease Control and Prevention, 1990.

————. *Sex Education: A Bibliography of Educational Materials for Children, Adolescents, and Their Families.* Elk Grove Village, Ill.: American Academy of Pediatrics, 1993.

————. *Report of the Committee on Infectious Diseases.* Elk Grove Village, Ill.: American Academy of Pediatrics, 1994.

Nelson, John. *The Pocket Book of Pediatric Antimicrobial Therapy.* Baltimore: Williams and Wilkins, 1995.

————. Centers for Disease Control and Prevention, Bulletin 1702, (Food Poisining) Atlanta, GA, 1994.

SEVERE PHYSICAL DISABILITIES

We must pay particular attention to the mind and heart when the body is disabled. Can you imagine the loss if all children with cerebral palsy were assumed to be retarded?

MacDonald Critchley

More than ever, children with severe disabilities are attending school. It has become apparent to educators and health professionals that smaller classes, complexity of health services, and different types of equipment are necessary to manage these students properly. They also require a variety of health care professionals. A classification system for chronically ill or disabled students, based on the amount and type of health care needed, helps to determine the number of health care personnel required and their necessary level of expertise (R.N., L.V.N., aide).

CLASSIFICATION

The following system classifies students according to the severity and nature of their disability.

Medically complex students are those with long-standing illnesses that may:

- Interfere with education
- Require daily or weekly monitoring
- Require interpretation to educators

These students may not have observable physical disabilities but nevertheless have complex illnesses that often require special attention. Examples are students with asthma, diabetes, or epilepsy, particularly those whose disease is not well controlled.

Medically fragile students are those with serious long-standing, often progressive illnesses that are often life threatening. These students may require extensive schedule and curriculum adjustments, frequent visits to the doctor, and frequent medication. Examples are students with leukemia, muscular dystrophy, sickle-cell anemia, or AIDS.

Medically intensive students are those who require a special health procedure one or more times each day or who are subject to cardiac or respiratory arrest or frequent grand mal seizures. Required procedures may include nasogastric tube feedings, tracheostomy care, or catheterization. These children may be profoundly disabled with severe cerebral palsy or may be bright children with spina bifida. Their distinguishing characteristic is their daily requirement for a trained health professional; a school nurse should be on campus daily.

An alternative, simpler classification has been developed by a group of school administrators, school nurses, and doctors working with the Texas Education Agency. In this system, students are classified as follows.

A medically fragile child is one who has a life-threatening condition and requires a skilled professional nurse on campus at all times. Examples are the following:

- Students who have exhibited severe episodes of cardiac or respiratory arrest and are in imminent danger of recurrence
- Students with severe life-threatening physical deformity, such as extreme hydrocephalus with danger of rupture, extreme scoliosis, or other bone abnormalities that may impair the function of a vital organ
- Students requiring continuous life support, such as cardiac or apnea monitor, or continuous assisted respiration
- Students with severe neurological disorders, such as extreme variations in body temperature, or frequent status epilepticus
- Students with tracheostomy or excess pharyngeal secretions that require suctioning more often than every hour
- Students with any other medical condition that is permanent and considered by the medical staff to be life threatening without constant medical attention

The chronically ill child with special health needs is usually cared for at home by his or her parents. The parent is trained by the doctor or nurse to carry out whatever procedures are necessary, such as tracheostomy suction or catheterization. When the child is well enough to attend school, the usual assumption is that the school nurse will do whatever procedures must be done during the school day. Because each procedure takes only a few minutes and there is rarely a nurse at each school each day, however, health aides and nonmedical personnel (for example, special education teacher or teacher aids) may be trained to perform these tasks.

Although this may seem like a practical solution, it carries some legal risk. The school district may have to prove in court that a health aide is sufficiently skilled to perform these tasks. Therefore, a professional school nurse should be available to perform procedures of this nature if possible. When this is not possible, the nurse is responsible for assessing, planning, teaching, monitoring, and evaluating the nonmedical person in accordance with the state's nursing practice act.

Specialized equipment such as catheters, diapers, ostomy bags, tracheostomy tubes, and suction machines may be required. Some states have ruled that medically related equipment must be furnished by parents; in other states, school districts furnish some and ask parents to provide other equipment. A school district will usually buy a suction machine or a small oxygen tank if the equipment is to remain at the school and be used for more than one child. The parents are expected to furnish supplies that are disposable and used for a single child, such as catheters, suction tips, and diapers.

If specific district policy or state law does not apply, the school district should address each case individually, taking into account parental skills and the severity of handicap. Acting as the child's advocate is always the top priority.

SPINA BIFIDA AS A PARADIGM

Spina bifida, or *myelomeningocele*, is a failure of the vertebral bones (spinal column) to fuse, leaving the enclosed spinal cord unprotected. Although this may occur anywhere from the neck to the lower spine, the most common location is the lumbosacral area. In addition, the skin and spinal cord do not develop properly, and a pouch varying from the size of a walnut to a grapefruit often is present where the bones fail to fuse (see Figure 12-1). This pouch contains all the nerves of the spinal

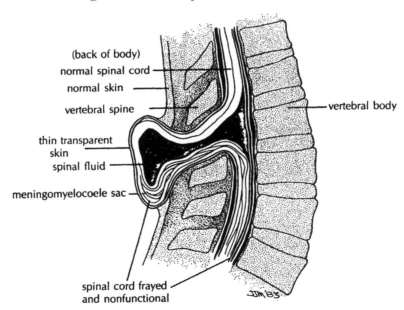

Figure 12-1. Myelomeningocele. The spinal fluid completely surrounds the spinal cord and is immediately below the skin of the sac. The skin consists only of a thin membrane, which often ruptures spontaneously.

cord that are supposed to go to the lower pelvis and legs. In a typical case, the child has no control over bowel or bladder, and both legs are paralyzed.

Hydrocephalus (water on the brain) is often associated with spina bifida. This can be prevented or controlled with proper treatment.

In children with a large pouch, the skin is often very thin and may leak spinal fluid. This can also be surgically corrected.

Spina bifida occulta (hidden spina bifida) is a condition in which the failure of fusion of the lower spinal vertebrae is slight and there is no outpouching of the skin with little or no spinal nerve abnormalities. In most cases, there are no bladder or bowel symptoms or leg involvement.

In the absence of hydrocephalus, children with spina bifida are emotionally and intellectually normal. With proper treatment and training, they should be able to attend school. Indeed, there are now many children with properly treated spina bifida attending school in regular classes.

Spina bifida associations exist in many large cities. Parents of these children, like parents of all handicapped children, have special needs, and organizations of this nature are very helpful.

Upper extremity problems are common with spina bifida. Because the defect is in the lower back, there is a tendency to assume that the arms are normal. Many children with spina bifida have mild weakness, poor fine motor control, poor awareness of the position of their arms and hands, and poor eye-hand coordination. The upper extremity problems may be overlooked, so awareness of them is important.

Manifestations

Because of the size of the pouch, the diagnosis of spina bifida is usually made at birth. There are mild cases in which the bones almost fuse and the visible pouch is very small. In these cases, the nerve damage may be slight, and the resulting bowel or bladder or leg paralysis problem may also be slight (see Figure 12-2). In cases of this nature, urinary or fecal incontinence or clumsiness in walking may be noticeable, and the child should be referred to a physician for evaluation.

Spina bifida occulta often causes no symptoms whatsoever. Symptoms such as enuresis, bowel problems, or sensory or motor lower extremity problems may be caused by a variety of other conditions and must be referred to a physician for diagnosis and initiation of treatment. About 20% of all children who, for unrelated reasons, receive X rays of the lower spine will show a small incomplete closure of the vertebral bones. Some of these children will also have enuresis or encopresis. Spina bifida occulta was formerly thought to be a cause of bed-wetting. Currently, most authorities feel that there is no cause-and-effect relationship between this incidental

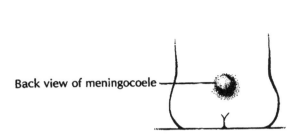
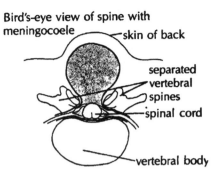

Figure 12-2. Meningocele. The menges or sac that contains the spinal fluid is pouched out between the separated vertebral spines, but the spinal cord itself is normal. The skin is of near normal thickness. The person has little to no paralysis and may have normal bladder and bowel functions.

X-ray finding and a urinary or fecal problem. In questionable cases, investigation by a neurologist or urologist must be made.

Management

The primary treatment of spina bifida is surgical. Because this condition is so complicated and has medical, social, and educational implications, the treatment team must include a pediatrician, a neurosurgeon, a urologist, an orthopedist, a social worker, an occupational therapist, and a physical therapist as well as the school nurse.

Total treatment consists of the following major procedures, which will already have been done by the time the student starts school:

1. Repair of the skin defect in the lower back
2. Shunt procedure in the brain to prevent or arrest hydrocephalus
3. Orthopedic procedures to the legs to enable the child to walk with braces and crutches at an appropriate time
4. Urological evaluation to determine the best method of bladder management

Even after school attendance begins, however, medical consultation and some surgical procedures may be necessary throughout the patient's lifetime.

In addition, many children require diapers and diaper changes for fecal incontinence, urinary incontinence, or both

The school nurse may be asked to monitor and consult with the physician regarding the care of certain areas, such as the skin of the lower back, as detailed below.

Skin of the Lower Back

Usually, very little care is required on the skin of the lower back for children with spina bifida. Occasionally, however, the postsurgical scar may become infected, may be dry and itchy, or may develop crusts. The treatment is to remove the crusts gently, apply antibiotic ointment if necessary for infection, cleanse with antibacterial soap, and occasionally apply softening lotions.

Bowel Care

Because of poor muscular control of the anal opening, fecal soiling is common in persons with spina bifida. Changes of diapers or other appropriate clothing must be kept at school. Privacy and due regard for the student's feelings are essential.

Bladder Care

Because of lack of nerve supply to the bladder with spina bifida, the urge to urinate does not exist. Therefore, the bladder fills until it can hold no more, and eventually urine dribbles out of the urethra and keeps the clothes or diaper constantly wet. Because the bladder never empties, the remaining urine and bladder wall often become infected. Modern management requires that the bladder be emptied periodically to prevent infection and subsequent kidney damage. Some older children have learned to empty their bladders by lower abdominal pressure, but most urologists feel that intermittent catheterization every 4 to 6 hours is the preferred method. Many school nurses now perform this procedure. It is usually performed once a day at school at about noon. The school nurse, parent, and physician must maintain close contact and consultation. School nurses require a little extra in-service training if they have not performed this procedure recently, but the technique is quite simple and can be learned (or relearned) in a short time. Many urologists teach young children self-catheterization. The age at which children can do this depends on individual ability, but it is usually when the child is between 7 and 10 years old. In these cases, the school nurse should work closely with the principal to provide the space and privacy necessary for catheterization.

Care of the Legs, Braces, and Crutches

The school nurse should be aware of possible pressure sores from braces worn by students with spina bifida. Sometimes, extra padding may help. Occasionally, notification to the parents or physician for an adjustment will be necessary. Observing the student while he or she is walking reveals whether the crutches are the appropriate length and whether the student is using them properly. Occupational and physical therapy are usually necessary.

Observation of Head Size

A child with spina bifida should be brought to the school clinic each month or two to have head circumference measured and recorded. Although there may be an intracranial shunt, its valves occasionally malfunction. Therefore, any unusual head growth—more than 1/2 inch in 6 months—should be reported to the parent, the physician, or both.

Class Placement and Learning Problems

Most spina bifida children can be mainstreamed into regular classes. Many, however, have specific learning problems and poor fine-motor control because of subtle cerebral defects (also called perceptual problems). Therefore, psychometric evaluations may be helpful in preparing an individual educational plan (IEP).

Special Problems at Adolescence

As would be expected, depression frequently occurs in students who have spina bifida. Girls worry about childbearing, and boys worry about potency. Normal experiences with children of the opposite sex are lacking. Most adolescents need to know more about their condition; their parents have been told, but they have not. The school nurse and school counselor can be helpful in these situations. A peer group session with other handicapped and normal children may give an adolescent an opportunity to express his or her anxieties. The local spina bifida parents' association is a good resource.

ISSUES COMMON TO CHRONIC CONDITIONS

Generally, each chronic illness or condition is viewed as a separate entity with specific management variables. To a certain degree this is true, but as James Perrin has noted, families whose children have a variety of long-term illnesses face several issues in common:

- Burden of care on families
- Multiple providers and treatments
- Isolation

- Uncertainty
- Mental anguish and fatigue
- Costly treatments

Chronic illness also creates its own stresses and obstacles to normal psychosocial development that physically healthy children do not have. In fact, chronically ill children have about twice the frequency of psychological and behavioral problems found in their healthy peers.

Adolescents are particularly susceptible to embarrassment and negative body image when visible deformities are present. Adolescence is often a time to test the limits of the illness and compliance with recommended therapies. Gradual shifting of responsibility to the young person promotes a greater level of maturity and gets around, at least in part, the built-in struggle against adult authority.

Health professionals at school should help families foster responsibility and encourage students to become increasingly independent.

SPECIAL PROCEDURES

School nurses are increasingly performing nursing procedures previously done only in hospitals. Some school districts are having problems adjusting to this requirement; others have seen it as an opportunity to help normalize the student's life. A partial list of the procedures now being performed include the following:

- Bladder catheterization
- Gastrostomy, nasogastric, or orogastric tube feeding
- Ileostomy or colostomy bag changes and care
- Nephrostomy bag changes and care
- Tracheostomy care
- Pharyngeal and nasopharyngeal suctioning
- Postural drainage with chest percussion
- Peritoneal dialysis
- Oxygen; aerosolization; Intermittent Positive Pressure Breathing (IPPB)

All these procedures are described in step-by-step detail in many nursing textbooks and are familiar to professional nurses. Therefore, here only the parts of each procedure that are relevant to the school setting, as opposed to the home or hospital, are discussed.

A school nurse who has not performed a particular procedure for many years should arrange for refresher instructions from another nurse or doctor who does the procedure regularly. Many hospitals have knowledgeable nurses who teach parents and school personnel new procedures or who conduct refresher courses.

Pharyngeal and Nasopharyngeal Suctioning

Severely disabled children with an impaired swallowing reflex (usually associated with cerebral palsy) often need suctioning when they choke on their saliva.

Suctioning can be done with a soft rubber bulb or a catheter attached to a suction machine. It is best to have both handy: the bulb to keep near each child for frequent, brief suctioning of small amounts, and, less frequently, the machine to clear the deeper nose and throat passages when more thorough suctioning is necessary.

Although it is necessary to go through a brief instructional period, this technique can be mastered only by practice following a demonstration. For many children, it must be performed several times a day, and whoever does it becomes proficient in a short time. As with most procedures, it is best to have a professional school nurse initiate the process in school, instruct the aide or teacher, observe long enough to ensure that the procedure is done well, and monitor at frequent intervals.

Tracheostomy Care

Tracheostomy tubes require special care. They are of two types, a double-walled aluminum tube and a simpler single-walled plastic tube. When a child first has a tracheostomy, the double-walled tube is inserted. The outer sleeve is left in place at all times, only being removed by a doctor on special occasions. The inner tube is removed by the parent or nurse whenever it needs to be cleaned. For children who need to retain a tube for months or years, a simpler single-walled plastic tube is used. It can be removed and cleaned whenever necessary because the hole in the throat is permanently open.

It is unusual for a student to be attending school while wearing a tube inserted in the windpipe. Most tracheostomy tubes are put in place for medical emergencies or other temporary conditions and need to remain in place a few days to a few weeks. When a student comes to school with a tube in place, however, it is for a chronic condition and may need to remain in place for months or years.

What would happen if the tube were to fall out or be coughed out while the student is at school? Would the student choke or die? Fortunately, this would not present an emergency, because the student could continue to breathe through the hole in the throat. There is plenty of time to call the school nurse to replace the tube or to take the student to a doctor. A tracheostomy opening that is relatively new (1 to 3 days old) could close in 3 to 12 hours (but such a child will not be in school); one that has been in place for several months would take days or weeks to close. It is not appropriate or necessary for school personnel to attempt to replace the tube.

To properly care for a school child with a tracheostomy tube, a professional-quality, portable suction machine is needed. The frequency and type of care needed varies with each student. The doctor should prepare detailed protocols and standing orders if the school nurse is expected to participate in the student's care.

Gastrostomies and Tube Feedings

When a patient cannot be fed by mouth, a short rubber or plastic tube may be inserted directly into the stomach through a surgically created opening in the abdominal wall. Liquid or semiliquid foods are given directly through the gastrostomy tube. The surgeon may leave the tube indwelling, or the tube may be inserted each time the child is fed.

Some children are fed with a tube inserted through the nose, down the back of the throat, and into the stomach (a nasogastric tube). A tube that starts in the mouth is an orogastric tube. Nose and mouth tubes are usually changed every 2 or 3 days. If left in place too long, they irritate the lining of the nose and throat.

Whichever type of tube feeding is used, the school nurse should not have to withdraw, insert, or change a tube; this should be done at home by the parent or visiting nurse. The school nurse or health aide will have to give one or two feedings during the school day.

The technique is simple; the liquid food is allowed to slowly run down the tube by gravity, or it can be slowly pushed with a bulb syringe or large (50 cc) syringe. After completion of the feeding, enough water should be added to clear the tube. Then the free end of the tube is clamped shut.

If the tube comes out or gets plugged (a rare occurrence), replacing it is never an emergency. There is plenty of time to take the student home to have it replaced. If the school nurse knows how to replace a tube, it is an extra service to the parent, but written physician orders and parent permission should be obtained in advance.

Colostomy, Ileostomy, Nephrostomy, and Other Ostomy Bags

Changing bags at school is no different from changing them at home or in a doctor's office. The biggest obstacle is getting used to doing this slightly distasteful task in school. After it is done a few times, it becomes as routine as changing a diaper. When the student is old enough, he or she can change his or her own bag and should be provided with the necessary privacy.

The parents should bring all the necessary paraphernalia: bags, cleansing pads, tape, and whatever else is used at home. The frequency of change varies with the student. Some students have a fresh bag applied at home each morning and never require changing at school. Some students require a change of bags at school several times a day, either because the bag fills up or works loose.

A student with an ostomy bag may have no academic deficiencies and may not be in special education. If, for some reason, there is a need for special education or a related service, the student would qualify under the category of "other health impaired."

Clean Intermittent Catheterization (CIC)

The special procedure of clean intermittent catheterization (CIC) is now commonly carried out at school, frequently for students with spina bifida with bladder paralysis, to keep the bladder empty so that stagnant urine will not cause an infection. The name of this procedure comes from the following:

Clean: The catheter need not be sterilized, only clean.
Intermittent: The catheter need not be left in the bladder (indwelling), but merely inserted periodically, the urine in the bladder drained, and the catheter withdrawn.

The usual frequency of catheterization is four times a day, about 6 hours apart. On this schedule, it should be done at school between 11:00 A.M. and 1:00 P.M. The parent should do it at home at 7:00 A.M., at 4:00 or 5:00 P.M., and at bedtime. On occasion, a doctor or parent will request that the student be catheterized twice a day at school, for nonmedical reasons, such as the parent leaving early for work. In these cases, each school district will have to make an administrative decision; once a day at school is usually sufficient for the student's medical needs.

The school should provide a good light and a high, padded table, especially for catheterizing girls. The urethral orifice, when the labia are separated, may look like one of the many tiny folds in the upper vaginal area, and without good light and a firm surface, it is easy to insert the catheter tip into the vagina by mistake.

Catheters, which are usually plastic and disposable, may be used several times until they are no longer soft and pliable. Some parents prefer to use a new catheter each day, but others will not bring a new catheter until the nurse requests it. After each use, catheters should be cleaned with soap and water. Because they are so small, it may be necessary to force water through with a hypodermic syringe to clean the inside. They may be stored in their original paper container until the next use.

The amount of urine recovered from each child will vary from 1/2 to 2 ounces. Usually, the free end of the catheter drains into an emesis basin or other suitable container. If the nurse knows from experience that only a small amount of urine will emerge, the catheter can drain on the diaper, which is usually wet and must be changed anyway.

Clean intermittent catheterization is simple and is easier than giving an injection. Almost all parents, as well as health aides, can be trained in the technique in a short time.

Figure 12-3, special procedure for clean intermittent catheterization (CIC), may be included in the school nurses' procedure book.

SCHOOL RELEVANCE

For schools to serve students with severe physical handicaps, certain specific information is needed. The sources of the following information include existing records, parents, the student's physician, and direct observation of the child.

- What is the diagnosis?
- What is the expected course of the condition? (static; progressive; fluctuating; fatal)
- Does the child understand his or her condition?
- Are there physical limitations or restrictions? (stairs, gym, excessive heat, etc.)
- Is there a need to modify the student's schedule? (short day, homebound instruction, etc.)
- Does the student take medication? Will it affect behavior? What are the side effects? Must it be given at school?
- Does the student need special protective or other equipment?
- Is a special procedure required during school hours? Is the physician, hospital staff, or agency willing to train the school nurse or other staff if necessary?
- Should the student have preferential seating?
- Is a modified diet needed at school?
- Does the student need assistance with toileting?
- Are there emotional or psychological issues to be considered?
- Should the student receive special health counseling?
- Are there special safety precautions? (buses, playground or gym)
- Are there emergency precautions to be taken by the school staff? What hospital emergency room should be used?
- Under what circumstances should the physician be contacted?
- Who is the alternate physician?
- Is there other information important to the student's management at school?

SPECIAL PROCEDURE FOR CLEAN INTERMITTENT CATHETERIZATION (CIC)

I. INTRODUCTION

CIC is a clean (not sterile) procedure that is normally done three or four times a day to empty the bladder. Its aim is to maintain an infection-free urinary tract as well as socially accepted dryness. It is done by the school nurse for students with spina bifida until a student is able to do it for himself or herself. It is an activity of daily living for many children with spina bifida, and self-catheterization should be learned as soon as possible. The school nurse will also serve as liaison between home, school, and health community in matters related to the student's other medical and health care needs.

II. PROGRAM GOALS

A. Decrease the occurrence of urinary tract infection.

B. Regular and frequent emptying of the bladder at planned times.

C. If possible, eliminate the need for diapers.

D. Prevent overstretching of the bladder, and preserve the muscle tone of the bladder wall.

E. Have the student take care of his or her bladder program completely and independently as soon as possible

F. Allow the student normal physical, social, and emotional functioning, free from worry about bladder accidents, thus preserving his or her self-respect.

III. CAMPUS NURSE MANAGEMENT

A. Conduct a parent conference to determine the current health status of the student and to obtain approval to confer with other health care professionals about the student's health needs.

B. Obtain current recommendations from the student's doctor.

C. Design and assist with implementation of the individual health management plan for the student as part of the student's individual education plan (IEP).

IV. GUIDELINES FOR PERFORMING CIC

A. Equipment and supplies

1. Soap and water or prepackaged towelettes

2. Catheter

3. Water-soluble lubricant such as K-Y jelly

4. Storage container for catheter (clean bottle or plastic sandwich bag)

5. Graduated container to catch and measure urine

B. Procedure for girls

1. Wash hands well with soap and water.

Figure 12-3. Specialized procedures for clean intermittent catheterization (CIC).

2. Wash and rinse between labia from front to back.

3. Lubricate the tip of a clean catheter.

4. Insert the tip of catheter into the urethra. Continue to advance the catheter slowly until urine begins to flow. When the bladder is empty, remove the catheter slowly, pausing if urine starts to flow again.

C. Procedure for boys

1. Wash hands well with soap and water.

2. Wash and rinse the penis starting at the meatus (opening).

3. Lubricate the tip of a clean catheter.

4. Hold the penis just behind the glans (where shaft meets head) and stretch slightly. Insert the tip of the catheter and advance slowly until urine begins to flow. If slight resistance is encountered, rotate the catheter with a twisting motion of the fingers while continuing to slowly advance. If catheter will not advance or if the student experiences excess pain, withdraw the catheter and consult with the parent, physician, or supervisor. When urine ceases to flow, slowly withdraw the catheter, pausing if urine starts to flow again.

D. Special information for boys and girls

1. Boys may be catheterized while they are lying on a cot or examining table or in their wheelchair.

2. Girls are best catheterized while lying on a firm examining table. A good light is necessary. The outer lips of the labia majora should be spread apart with the finger and drawn upwards. This maneuver exposes the opening of the urethra (small slitlike opening just in front of the vagina).

3. If no examining table is available and a girl must be catheterized on a cot, place several pads or pillows below her buttocks so that the genitalia are easily visible.

4. It is desirable to teach a child self-catheterization, but it is advisable to proceed slowly and not cause undue fears that ultimately could delay self-catheterization. Each child is ready at a different chronological age, depending on his or her cognitive capabilities and emotional status.

5. smaller children, the amount of urine recovered will usually be small and may be allowed to run into the diaper unless there are specific orders to measure the amount.

6. When the urine stops flowing, press gently over the bladder area for more complete bladder emptying.

V. WARNING SIGNS

A. There are several signs that are considered to be signals of urinary tract infections.

B. Notify parent, supervisor, or school physician if following warning signs are noted:

1. Fever

Figure 12-3. (continued)

     2. Foul-smelling or cloudy urine

     3. Incontinence (constant wetness when fluid intake and the interval between catheterization have been correct)

     4. Bleeding

VI CATHETER CARE

    A. Red rubber catheter: Wash the catheter with soap and water. Rinse well and dry. Store in a dry container (plastic sandwich bag). Replace the catheter when it becomes brittle, frays, or loses its shape.

    B. Plastic catheter: Rinse well with tap water both inside and out. Store tube in a straight container (if not, the tube will kink or break). Replace the tube when it becomes brittle, frays, or loses its shape.

Figure 12-3. (continued)

ROLE OF THE SCHOOL NURSE

The single most important role of the school nurse in the care of students with severe physical disabilities is to be the clearinghouse for all health information entering and leaving the school. For exiting information, the school nurse should be the primary communicator with community health professionals and parents. For incoming information from doctors, physical therapists, and others, the school nurse should be the synthesizer. This synthesis should be reflected in an individualized health plan (IHP) for both special education and nonspecial education students. An example is shown in Figure 12-4.

    In its publication *Students with Special Health Care Needs*, the National Association of School Nurses lists the following activities as appropriate for the school nurse:

- Reviews health information and determines which students require a written health care plan
- Obtains significant health data on identified students
- Completes a nursing assessment and summarizes data. This database should include as a minimum:
  - Description of condition and course of the illness
  - Summary of treatment
  - Significant emergency information
  - Health care procedures, including administration of medication

SCHOOL HEALTH SERVICES INDIVIDUALIZED HEALTH PLAN (HIP)

NURSING DIAGNOSIS/ COLLABORATIVE PROBLEM	GOAL	PLAN OF ACTION	WHO
Intermittent impairment of oxygen exchange related to asthma.	Student will demonstrate self-care procedures to become maximally independent	Daily monitoring with peak flow meter (self-administered and recorded).	R.N., health assistant, parent
		Monitor therapy ordered by M.D. Theophylline capsules Inhaled cromolyn sodium Inhaled abluteral as needed	R.N., nurse's aide
Impairment of physical activities related to suboptimum control of asthma.	Student will tolerate "normal" activities without fatigue or shortness of breath.	Review and monitor side effects of medication (nervousness, inattention, sweating, rash, hives).	Teacher, R.N.
		Encourage and monitor water intake.	R.N., teacher, parent

Figure 12-4. School health services individualized health plan (IHP).

- Secures the release of essential confidential information
- Develops and implements the health care plan to be carried out at school
- Files the health care plan in the student's record and notes on the emergency card that a health care plan is on file
- Ensures that a student-specific emergency plan is in place and has been developed in collaboration with school administration, community emergency personnel, and family
- Sees that the medication and treatment procedures are performed and documented
- Provides general staff training to give an overview of the student's condition and health care needs

HEALTH EDUCATION TIPS

Every child with a severe physical disability should understand and take management responsibility to the extent possible. A grasp of each student's mental age and developmental milestones will allow the formulation of an educational plan that spans his or her school career. A brief outline for formulating such a plan follows. Each area can be addressed in progressively greater depth as the student matures.

- Nature of the disorder
- Routine management
  - Procedures
  - Medication
  - Personal hygiene
  - Eating and nutrition
  - Other self-help skills
- Danger signals
  - How to avoid them
  - What to do when they occur
- What the student can and cannot do now
- What the student may be able to do in the future
- How to explain the condition to friends and classmates
- What to do when feeling down
- When to ask for adult help
- What careers may be open to the student

REFERENCES

American Academy of Pediatrics, Position Statement of the Committee on Children with Disabilities. "Provision of Related Services for Children with Chronic Disabilities." *Pediatrics* 92(6):879–81.

American Academy of Pediatrics, Position Statement of the Committee on Children with Disabilities and the Committee on Psychosocial Aspects of Child and Family Health. "Psychosocial Risks of Chronic Health Conditions in Childhood and Adolescence." *Pediatrics* 92(6):876–77.

Dubowitz, V. *Muscle Disorders in Childhood.* London: W. B. Saunders, 1995.

Haas, M. B. *The School Nurse's Source Book of Individualized Health Care Plans.* North Branch, Minn.: Sunrise River Press, 1993.

Jessop, D. J. "Providing Comprehensive Health Care to Children with Chronic Illnesses." *Pediatrics* 93(4):602–7.

The Medically Fragile Child in the School Setting. Washington, D.C.: American Federation of Teachers, 1992.

Nader, P. R., ed. "Children with Chronic Illness." In *School Health: Policy and Practice*, pp. 188–95. Elk Grove Village, Ill.: American Academy of Pediatrics, 1993.

Passarelli, C. "Case Management of Chronic Health Conditions of School-Age Youth." In *Principles and Practices of Student Health,* vol. 2, pp. 350–59. Oakland, Calif.: Third Party Publishing, 1992.

Perrin, J. " Chronic Illness in Childhood." In *Nelson Textbook of Pediatrics,* pp. 124–28. Philadelphia: W. B. Saunders, 1996.

———. "Prevalence of Selected Developmental Disabilities in Children 3–10 Years of Age." *Morbidity and Mortality Weekly Report* 45(SS-2):1–14.

Walker, D. K. "Children and Youth with Special Health Care Needs." In *Principles and Practices of Student Health,* vol. 1, pp. 185–94. Oakland, Calif.: Third Party Publishing, 1992.

———. *Students with Special Health Care Needs.* Scarborough, Maine. National Association of School Nurses, 1992.

SECTION 13

DISEASES OF THE BRAIN

It must be inconvenient to be made of flesh, said the Scarecrow thoughtfully, for you must sleep, and eat and drink. However, you have brains, and it is worth a lot of bother to be able to think properly.

Wizard of Oz

The brain, as the organ of learning and behavior control, is of primary concern to educators and health care providers for children. Its disorders are legion and range from fatal to subtle. This section takes a look at those diseases of the brain which significantly impact schools.

EPILEPSY

Epilepsy is one of the medical conditions that almost every teacher and school nurse will have to deal with during a school career. It is a relatively common disability and is seen much more often in children than in adults. For unknown reasons, some children outgrow epilepsy during their teenage years. Treatment is effective in most cases, and this too can shorten the natural course of a disease that, untreated, can have serious effects.

Classification of Seizures

The most accepted classification of seizures is that of the World Health Organization (WHO) reflected in the table on page 237.

Each epileptic attack or seizure, especially the tonic-clonic seizure or major convulsion, is frightening to school personnel. But children are unlikely to harm themselves during a seizure. The major cause for concern is brain damage from repeated, uncontrolled convulsions. During a convulsion, the patient stops breathing for a brief period and the body is deprived of oxygen. The brain—the organ most sensitive to lack of oxygen—suffers most, and nerve cells die when the brain is deprived of oxygen for a long enough time. Once a brain cell dies it never regenerates, and eventually, with the death of enough cells, learning disability or mental retardation may result. Certain types of preexisting brain damage are more common in children with epilepsy than with other children, but most children with epilepsy are normal in all respects aside from their occasional seizures.

Students who have severe and frequent attacks, either because of poor compliance with medical treatment or because their disease is severe, often develop a degree of secondary brain damage (recurrent hypoxic episodes). Because pathology in one part of the brain is often associated with abnormalities in other parts, even well-controlled epileptics have a higher incidence of subtle learning and behavior problems as well as a higher incidence of intellectual retardation.

WHO Classification* Other Terminology

I. Partial seizures	
A. Simple partial seizures	
1. With motor signs	Jacksonian seizures or focal motor seizures
2. With somatosensory or special sensory symptoms	Sensory seizures (visual, auditory, olfactory, gustatory, vertiginous)
3. With autonomic symptoms or signs	Abdominal epilepsy or epileptic equivalent
B. Complex partial seizures	Psychomotor or temporal lobe seizures
II. Generalized seizures	
A. Absence seizures	
1. Typical	Petit mal
2. Atypical	Petit mal variant or complex petit mal
B. Myoclonic seizures	[No corresponding term]
C. Atonic seizures	Akinetic seizures or drop attacks
D. Tonic-clonic seizures	Grand mal or major motor seizures

*Modified from the classification of the World Health Organization, the current standard terminology.

Symptoms

Epilepsy is often classified by the nature of the seizure, and different types often respond best to different medications.

Tonic-Clonic Seizures (Grand Mal)

This is a typical hard-shaking convulsion. It may occur at any time, but some authorities think that it is more likely to occur when the child is at rest than when engaged in some sort of mental or physical activity. It sometimes begins with an aura: seeing a light or halo or having an unusual feeling. During the aura, the child is still conscious and may appear frightened. Almost immediately, the motor component will begin with a sudden stiffening of the body, (tonic phase) so stiff and strong that the back is arched. Simultaneously, consciousness is lost and the child falls to the ground. All the muscles of the body are in extreme contraction. The jaw is tightly clenched and no effort should be made to open it. Broken teeth (and lawsuits) have resulted from overzealous efforts.

After about 20 to 40 seconds, the *clonic phase* begins. During this second phase, shaking occurs because of intermittent contractions of body muscles. It is during this period that one may safely insert a padded stick between the teeth, provided it is done slowly and gently.

For many years, doctors recommended the insertion of a padded tongue blade or other object between the teeth during a grand mal convulsion. This was meant to prevent a person from seriously biting the tongue during a clonic convulsion. Instead, it caused broken teeth and cuts and bruises of the lips and mouth. Long-term studies since the early 1990s have shown that patients do *not* bite their tongue during a convulsion. Therefore, most doctors advise not putting anything between the teeth.

The third stage, the *postictal phase*, is one of deep sleep and usually lasts 30 to 60 minutes. Following this stage, the child wakens and, except for possible muscle soreness, is normal.

What has been described here is a typical or average convulsion, although any single convulsion or one of its phases is apt to be slightly different: longer or shorter, more or less severe. Sometimes in a mild attack there is no period of deep sleep. Sometimes the seizure is limited to one side of the body or only one extremity with no loss of consciousness. Such a seizure is called a *Jacksonian* or *partial seizure*.

Absence Seizures (Petit Mal)

Petit mal seizures are now called *absence spells*. They are brief episodes, lasting 10 to 20 seconds, during which the child experiences clouding of consciousness but does not lose body tone and usually does not fall down. If the child is holding something—a pencil or glass—he or she is apt to drop it. During this brief period, the child is completely out of contact. When the episode is over, he or she will resume activity, unaware that anything has happened.

The child with petit mal epilepsy often has 20 to 40 episodes a day. As with grand mal seizures, there is usually some variation in the appearance of the seizures. There may be occasional twitching of the facial or arm muscles. Many seizures are so brief that nobody ever notices they have occurred. Unlike grand mal seizures, this type of epilepsy is not associated with brain damage.

Teachers often wonder if a child has petit mal epilepsy because he or she lacks attention, stares out of the window, or does not hear something, and they often refer such a child to a physician. Many physicians are upset by this because, even though they feel sure from the described symptoms that the child does not have epilepsy, once the suspicion has been raised they are obligated to proceed with expensive tests (EEG, X ray, etc.), which most of the time show normal results. The school nurse can help prevent overreferrals.

It is difficult to give good guidelines about which episodes may be absence attacks and which are simply wandering attention. One important factor is the frequency of occurrence. If the spell occurs only occasionally, it is more likely to be lack of attention. Also, if the teacher looks closely, the pupils of the eyes will be enlarged during a petit mal seizure and will not constrict even if a bright light is shined into them. If the child is touched during an episode, he or she will not notice it. When a pencil is dropped and the child does not react is also suggestive of a petit mal seizure.

In summary, if the teacher or school nurse is not sure and if the attacks are infrequent, it is better to wait and watch until more definitive signs appear. This course of action will result in less anxiety and expense for the family.

Complex Partial Seizures (Psychomotor)

Psychomotor epilepsy is a less common type of epilepsy in which an attack causes the patient to engage in a sudden spurt of coordinated motor activity that may appear to be purposeful and under voluntary control.

The seizures are characteristically of brief duration, lasting from 1 to 10 minutes. Consciousness is often impaired but rarely lost completely, and the eyes may scan back and forth. There may be tonic posturing and coordinated but inappropriate movements may be performed repeatedly in a stereotyped manner (automatism); common examples are fumbling, kicking, swallowing, smacking, chewing, licking, and spitting. Pill-rolling—twisting hand movements—or flinging movements of the arms are less common symptoms. Inhibitory seizures with loss of muscle tone or arrest of motion (freezing) may occur. Emotional outbursts such as laughing or crying are not unusual. When the attack is over, there may or may not be sluggishness or sleep. Amnesia of the attack is the rule.*

Epileptic Equivalents

Episodic vomiting, dizziness, vertigo, headaches, abdominal pain, and even episodes of apparent psychosis have been blamed on epilepsy. Needless to say, these symptoms are rarely caused by epilepsy. A physician can easily rule out epilepsy in more than 99% of cases of this nature. Diagnosis of the remaining 1% is difficult even for skilled neurologists using all the diagnostic tools at their command.

Diagnosis

Certain elements are common to all forms of epilepsy:

1. *Sudden onset and relatively rapid termination.* Epilepsy usually begins when least expected, for no apparent reason, runs its course, and stops.

---

*McLain, L.W. "Epilepsy" in **Pediatrics** (15ed), New York, Appleton Century Crofts, 1994 (Used with permission).

2. *Loss of memory.* Memory loss occurs in all forms of epilepsy except the epileptic equivalent. Remembrance of the episode is very unusual in epilepsy, so unusual that some neurologists are skeptical that it is possible and have doubted that there is a condition called epileptic equivalents. Typically, when epileptic attacks are over, patients awaken in a dazed state wondering what happened to them. If they have suffered many attacks in the past, they will be able to guess what happened but will not remember it.

3. *Repeated attacks.* It is very rare for a person with epilepsy to have a single attack. A child will occasionally be diagnosed and treated after the first attack and never have another, however.

When all three of the above elements are present, the diagnosis of epilepsy is easier to make. Physicians will want to confirm the diagnosis with various laboratory tests, and the most commonly ordered is an electroencephalogram (EEG, or brain wave test). In fairly typical cases, an EEG is all that is necessary. More extensive computerized X rays, blood tests, dye injections, spinal taps, and other tests may be required in complicated cases. Occasionally, when the diagnosis is particularly difficult, a child is hospitalized for round-the-clock monitoring (or given a portable monitoring device to wear).

Figure 13-1 shows the distinction between real and pseudo seizures. The latter type are usually related to malingering or conversion reactions.

Medication

Epilepsy can be either the easiest or the most difficult of all diseases to treat. Some cases respond well to a single anticonvulsant medication. Other cases require as many as three or four types of medicine, all given several times a day. In these difficult cases, because the medicines themselves usually cause some unpleasant side effects and the attending physician must monitor the child frequently, feedback from the school is essential. Epilepsy specialists emphasize the importance of giving as few drugs as possible.

The medicine must be continued for at least 2 to 5 years. Some neurologists have a standing rule that medications must be given for 4 years after the last seizure. If treatment is stopped too soon, the attacks may return with greater severity. For this reason, some think that it is better not to begin treatment after the first attack. Physicians who follow this policy reason that one seizure does not cause ill effects, and it may be possible to save the patient 4 years of drug therapy and emotional trauma. Some children have one typical grand mal seizure and never have another.

SYNCOPE (simple fainting)
1. Situational (e.g., after standing, voiding, or brushing hair)
2. In adolescence or preadolescence
3. No trismus or incontinence
4. May have a few jerking movements

DAYDREAMING
1. Lasts minutes
2. Eyelids do not flutter
3. EEG normal

AGGRESSIVE OR BIZARRE BEHAVIOR
1. No definite beginning or end

2. Does not end in grand mal
3. No aura
4. Is influenced by environment
5. EEG usually normal

PSEUDO OR HYSTERICAL SEIZURES
1. Influenced by environment
2. Serves a psychological role (e.g., attention getting)
3. Patient will not ordinarily hurt self
4. EEG normal even during seizure

GRAND MAL (TONIC-CLONIC)
1. Not dependent on situation (but may be associated with lack of sleep or food)
2. Any age
3. May have trismus or incontinence
4. Jerking movements are prominent

PETIT MAL (ABSENCE)
1. Lasts seconds
2. Eyelids flutter
3. EEG abnormal

PSYCHOMOTOR SEIZURES
1. Clear difference between seizure and nonseizure state
2. May conclude with grand mal
3. Aura is present
4. Usually independent of environment
5. EEG usually abnormal, especially in sleep (24-hour trace may be necessary)

REAL SEIZURES (GRAND MAL)
1. Independent of environment
2. Serves no psychological role

3. Patient may inadvertently hurt self
4. EEG usually abnormal

Figure 13-1. Real versus pseudo seizures.

All forms of epilepsy are treated by oral medication. The schedule can often be arranged so that the student need not take any doses during school hours. This is by far the best arrangement. If the physician has sound medical reasons for requiring the student to take a dose during school hours, the school authorities should cooperate. The psychological effects on the student are so important that the school nurse, principal, or counselor should have a conference with the parent and explore the possibility of giving all doses at home, however.

Athletic Participation

Students with well-controlled epilepsy can participate in almost all activities, but two sports are considered dangerous for children with epilepsy: gymnastics (parallel bars, rings, and trampolines) and swimming, especially under water. Because some children have a history of seizures on hyperventilation, proper preconditioning is essential.

There is more concern and more controversy over the participation of students with epilepsy in football than in any other sport. A seizure on the playing field would be no more harmful than the same seizure anywhere else, but there is a fear that a head injury might aggravate the preexisting epileptic condition and cause more frequent seizures. Actually, there is no good medical evidence to support this. The general feeling prevails that a student should be in top physical condition and free of all illness to play this injury-prone sport, however. A student with epilepsy who is determined and who is a valuable player will probably find a way to play. In such a case, it should be only with full knowledge by all concerned of the risks involved. Sometimes a trial period in middle school can be helpful in deciding future plans so that by high school a decision has already been made and agreed upon.

Emergency Management

The best treatment for grand mal seizures is to let the convulsion run its course and let the child sleep until he or she awakens. Unfortunately, it is almost impossible to keep others from rubbing the chest, loosening the clothing, or doing something else equally ineffective. *The more stimulation the child receives, the longer the seizure is apt to last. The less touching the better.* As the seizure is about to end, it is a good idea to turn the child on the side so that any secretions or vomitus will run out of the mouth and not be aspirated.

It is an often-stated medical dictum that patients never die during a convulsion. There is, however, a condition called *status epilepticus* in which the seizure continues for 15 minutes or longer. Even in these cases the patient does not die, but there is greater danger of brain damage. The dilemma that often arises is, How long is too long? After what length of time should the student be taken to the nearest hospital emergency room or doctor's office? If the student is still convulsing after 10 minutes, he or she should be taken to the nearest medical facility and given the proper medication, usually an intravenous medication such as Valium®, to stop the seizure promptly.

The other types of epilepsy need no emergency treatment except to prevent the child from self-harm.

MENINGITIS, ENCEPHALITIS, AND RABIES

Meningitis

Meningitis is a bacterial infection of the membranes covering the brain and spinal cord (meninges). It affects thousands of children each year; 5% to 10% of those affected die from the disease. When it is not fatal, it may leave permanent brain damage in the form of mental retardation, seizures, paralysis, or deafness.

Some types of meningitis are contagious, such as those cases caused by the bacteria *Neisseria meningitidis* and *Haemophilus influenzae* type b (HiB). Bacteria are transmitted from one person to another through upper respiratory secretions, such as a runny nose, during close contact.

Why meningitis develops in one person and not another is not completely understood. Young people with certain underlying disorders such as diabetes, sickle cell anemia, malnutrition, or abnormalities of the immune system are particularly susceptible.

Fever, severe headache, lethargy (drowsiness), and nausea are the earliest symptoms of meningitis. Pain and stiffness of the neck and back soon follow. A stiff neck is nearly always specific to meningitis.

Diagnosis is confirmed by a spinal tap (lumbar puncture). During this procedure, a needle is inserted between two vertebrae of the lower spinal column to sample the cerebrospinal fluid (CSF). Normally, CSF is clear and contains no white blood cells (WBC). In cases of meningitis, however, the CSF contains numerous WBCs, a sign of inflammation of the meninges.

Additional tests (bacterial cultures of blood and CSF) help determine which bacterium is causing the infection so that proper antibiotic therapy can begin. If not treated promptly, a person may lose consciousness and go into a coma. Few survive bacterial meningitis without treatment. Paying attention to early symptoms is very important.

More than half the children over age 3 recover fully from HiB meningitis, although sometimes, permanent complications, such as hearing loss, result.

A vaccine is now routinely given to infants to prevent the meningitis due to the HiB bacteria. Since its use began in 1985, HiB meningitis has decreased dramatically.

Vaccines are also available against selected strains of the meningococcus and pneumococcus bacteria, but they are used only for special groups, such as new military recruits, among whom epidemics are more likely to occur. Unfortunately, these last two vaccines are not always effective in young children.

Persons in close contact with cases of meningococcal meningitis are given preventive (prophylactic) antibiotics. Close contacts include household members and friends who may have shared eating utensils. These also might include close friends at school.

Covering coughs and sneezes, as well as hand washing, also have a role in reducing the spread of bacteria.

Encephalitis

Encephalitis is not one disease, but many. The types are classified by the attacking organisms: viruses.

Like meningitis, encephalitis is an infection within the skull. But unlike meningitis, the organisms attack the substance of the brain. This coupled with there being few specific antiviral drugs makes encephalitis a potentially life-threatening condition. More than 60 percent of those infected with eastern equine (horse) encephalitis die; most survivors suffer permanent neurologic damage.

The symptoms of encephalitis are similar to those of meningitis: headache, fever, and sometimes seizures. Nausea and vomiting are less common in encephalitis than in meningitis. Photophobia (light sensitivity) is common, but mental confusion is the telltale symptom.

As with meningitis, a spinal tap will confirm the diagnosis. Individuals with mumps, measles, or chicken pox occasionally develop encephalitis. Now that vaccines are available for these diseases, this type of encephalitis is rare.

Figure 13-2 compares the various characteristics of encephalitis with meningitis.

	Meningitis	*Encephalitis*
LOCATION	BRAIN COVERINGS (meninges)	BRAIN SUBSTANCE
Cause	Bacteria, usually	Viruses, usually
Vectors	None	Mosquitoes (some types)
Diagnosis	Spinal tap	Spinal tap
Treatment	Antibiotics	Limited antiviral drugs
Prevention	Some vaccines	Insect control; postexposure vaccine for rabies

Figure 13-2. Meningitis versus encephalitis.

Rabies

Rabies is a type of encephalitis caused by a specific virus that can affect many mammals. The most common domestic animals infected are dogs and cats, but horses, cows, and other livestock are susceptible. The largest reservoir is in wild animals: skunks, foxes, coyotes, raccoons, and bats.

Rodents such as squirrels, hamsters, guinea pigs, gerbils, chipmunks, rats, mice, and rabbits are so rarely infected with rabies that health departments often do not test these animals when people report that they were bitten, and their bites almost never require antirabies treatment.

Most commonly, exposure is caused by an animal bite. A nonbite exposure, however, can come from a scratch, abrasion, or other open wound or sore contaminated with animal saliva. Excluding these, casual contact such as petting a rabid animal is not considered an exposure. (Airborne exposure, as in a bat cave, is very rare; only a few cases of rabies from such exposure have been reported.)

Bats are often a cause for concern, but it is extremely rare for a bat to bite. At school, children will frequently pick up a dead bat and play with it. These bats should be sent to the local health department for examination. If rabies virus is found in the bat's brain, each child who played with it must be evaluated individually by a physician to determine the need for rabies vaccine.

Because the disease is fatal, any suspected exposure to rabies must be handled without compromise. Should a student be bitten by a domestic animal on the school grounds, it is important for the animal to be chained or placed in an escape-proof cage and observed for 10 days. The incubation period of rabies in an animal is less than 2 weeks. Therefore, if symptoms do not develop in 10 to 14 days, it is safe to assume that the animal is not rabid. If a previously healthy dog or cat develops rabies, one of the first things it often does is run away. Therefore, if a child has been bitten by an animal that cannot be found, it must be assumed that the child has been exposed to rabies and must receive antirabies vaccine.

CEREBRAL PALSY

Nature of the Condition

Cerebral palsy is a relatively common disorder seen in schools. It is caused by a disease of the brain itself. In most cases, the brain is damaged by disease or injury during fetal life, during the birth process, or shortly after birth.

The nervous system includes the brain, spinal cord, and peripheral nerves. Nerves originate in the brain, pass down the spinal cord, and diverge throughout the body. If a nerve is damaged in the brain or spinal cord, the muscle it supplies becomes fixed in spasm. If that same nerve is damaged after emerging from the spinal cord, the muscle it supplies becomes paralyzed. (Diseases of the peripheral nerves, such as poliomyelitis, produce a flaccid paralysis.)

Because the primary damage is in the brain, the muscles controlled by that part of the brain are fixed in spasm, and the child is said to have a spastic paralysis.

Cerebral palsy results from damage to the motor areas, the parts of the brain that send messages out to the muscles, not the part of the brain that receives messages through the sense organs. This concept is basic to understanding the difficult life of many of these victims, at least half of whom have normal intelligence and an understanding of what is going on around them but have no way of communicating.

Symptoms

The nerves that control the muscles of speech, facial expression, and coordinated arm and leg movement and those that hold the body in an upright position all originate in the motor areas of the brain. With cerebral palsy, these nerves are damaged at their point of origin, and messages transmitted are erratic. A child who wants to smile may grimace; if the child tries to cry, he or she may smile or laugh or emit strange sounds. Drooling is frequent. The child may be completely unable to speak or may speak unintelligibly.

Arm, leg, and trunk muscle movement causes a limping, shuffling gait, unwanted and uncoordinated movements, and falling. Generalized convulsions are common, as are partial seizures of individual arms or legs.

General intelligence or IQ varies considerably; some children with cerebral palsy are of average or superior intelligence, whereas others are severely retarded. Testing is often very difficult and frequently requires special skills and tests.

Classification

Cerebral palsy is divided into the following 10 classifications:

1. *Hemiplegic.* Only one side of the body is involved. The arm is usually less useful than the leg, although the child almost always walks with some limp. This is the most common form of cerebral palsy.
2. *Monoplegic.* Rarely, only one extremity is involved. In most cases, mild involvement of the other extremity on the same side can be demonstrated with tests.
3. *Quadriplegic.* All four extremities are involved, but usually the legs are worse than the arms.

4. *Paraplegic.* Only the legs are involved.
5. *Diplegic.* Paralysis of any two corresponding extremities, usually both legs (but can be both arms).
6. *Athetoid.* Uncontrollable bizarre body, limb, or facial movements that are writhing or wormlike in nature.
7. *Dystonic.* Abnormal muscle tone resulting in abnormal body postures.
8. *Ataxic.* Inability to coordinate the muscles in voluntary movement; often used to describe a staggering gait.
9. *Atonic.* Limpness without muscle tone. This is rare and is seen primarily in infants.
10. *Mixed.* This form includes various combinations of the above.

Treatment

There are five basic forms of treatment for cerebral palsy (not all will be used in every child):

1. *Anticonvulsant medications* are used to control seizures, if present; sometimes, medication will be used to control muscle spasm.
2. *Surgery* is used to lengthen short muscles or tendons and to reinsert tendons into different locations to increase the use of the arms and legs; many other surgical procedures are also beneficial.
3. *Physical therapy (P.T.)* is useful in almost all cases of cerebral palsy. The earlier it is started, the better the results; it should be in place long before a child starts school.
4. *Occupational therapy (O.T.)* helps children learn the skills of daily living, such as eating, dressing, and writing. This should begin almost as early as P.T. begins.
5. *Counseling* is necessary for parents as well as children. Both have a great need for psychological support and for help in school. Counselors who are themselves handicapped often make excellent therapists.

TRAUMATIC BRAIN INJURY (TBI)

In the United States, about one million children each year suffer a serious head injury. Most will have some disability lasting months or years. Nearly half of all head injuries result from motor vehicle accidents. The death rate from auto accidents increases nearly tenfold for young men, but not young women, after driving age. A large portion of the remainder of head injuries result from falls or child abuse. The overall incidence of head injury is about 200 to 300 new cases per year per 100,000 population.

Even though a brain-injured child returns to fully independent and functional living, some subtle deficits that reflect the child's previous injury may be apparent to the experienced eye. Such children may demonstrate problems in organization, emotional control, motivation, judgment, speed of thinking, and memory, as well as irritability and distractibility. School-aged children with TBI most closely resemble students with attention deficit disorder and learning disabilities; thus educational programming is similar (see Section 14).

A few students with severe TBI exhibit behavior changes that include explosive outbursts, extreme anxiety, or intractable indifference. Such students may, of necessity, need to be managed with psychotropic medication and classes for the emotionally disturbed.

For students who have spent time in a postacute residential rehabilitation setting, reintegration into an appropriate school setting requires thoughtful planning, often with one or more transitional phases. These phases usually include part-time attendance and a modified curriculum.

In addition to traumatic or mechanical brain injury, permanent damage to the central nervous system can result from maternal drug use (e.g., cocaine) or inhaled or ingested illicit substances (e.g., glue sniffing).

PROGRESSIVE DISEASES OF THE NERVOUS SYSTEM

The word *progressive* indicates an ongoing disease process during which the symptoms get worse. Examples of such diseases are multiple sclerosis, myasthenia gravis, brain tumor, neurofibromatosis, and a number of other rare degenerative diseases affecting the central nervous system (CNS). Physicians frequently refer to this group of diseases as progressive CNS disorders.

Symptoms

The specific symptoms of progressive disease vary greatly, but most, such as multiple sclerosis, progress slowly. In all cases, the disease becomes steadily worse.

In certain conditions, the earliest symptoms that can be seen are subtle changes in the higher cognitive functions such as short-term memory, arithmetic ability, or abstract reasoning. If the motor area of the brain is involved, a change in writing or athletic ability may be noticed.

Management

Progressive disease is always treated by a physician; the treatment is dependent on the diagnosis, but specific treatments are often not available.

Because progressive nervous system disease of subtle onset is quite rare, caution should be exercised in notifying parents about suggestive symptoms. If a change from previous abilities or behavior occurs, however, it would be well to speak with the parent. This may lead to an early diagnosis and thus render the disease a bit more amenable to appropriate management.

SCHOOL RELEVANCE

Almost every central nervous system dysfunction impacts academic achievement. Because the brain is the organ that controls thinking, movement and emotions, its efficiency determines school performance. Manifestations of CNS disease may be mild, moderate, or severe. For example, a student with well-controlled epilepsy may be an honor student whereas one with significant posttraumatic brain injury may require the most restrictive of special education placements.

The key to optimum educational placement is adequate assessment and management in six areas:

1. General intelligence
2. Receptive and expressive language
3. Academic achievement
4. Motor skills
5. Social and emotional adjustment
6. Special medical needs (equipment, medication, etc.)

For conditions known to change—that is, progressive CNS disease—frequent reassessment will be needed to achieve the best school programming.

ROLE OF THE SCHOOL NURSE

In cases of CNS disorders, the school nurse will obviously need to do more than for the normal child; many cases require special nursing knowledge and procedures. To prevent overlooking an important activity, these four broad areas should be reviewed for each student served:

1. *Charting.* The school nurse can keep a record somewhat similar to a hospital chart that will provide a daily or weekly log. Extra care is be required for medication, physical therapy and special nursing procedures.

2. *Medication.* A large proportion of children with disorders of the brain receive medication; many have difficulty swallowing. The school nurse should give the medication and record each dose. The nurse also needs to be aware of adverse reactions to the medicines; a current copy of the Physician's Desk Reference should be available.

3. *Coordination of physical and occupational therapy.* In many cases, therapy is given only at school or at a medical office. The school nurse can be instrumental in coordinating these services.

4. *Counseling.* In cooperation with the school guidance counselor, the nurse can help the parent accept the child's condition and reinforce management strategies.

HEALTH EDUCATION TIPS

The following questions can be used by the school nurse to stimulate discussion during student or faculty presentations:

1. Differentiate between static and progressive CNS disorders.
2. What percent of children with severe physical problems have normal intelligence?
   a. 10-15%
   b. 20-30%
   c. about 50% (correct answer)
   d. more than 70%
3. Discuss the emotional impact of making fun of physically disabled students.
4. (True or False) Helping physically disabled children succeed in school is mandated by federal law. (True)
5. Differentiate between medicines and drugs.
6. Discuss the transmission of the germs that cause meningitis and encephalitis. Why is rabies different?
7. How do bicycle helmets prevent injury?

The following key points should be brought out when evaluating student answers:

- Permanent or progressive CNS disorders. Help staff and students understand:
  - Children with severe physical problems often have normal intelligence (and feelings).
  - Making fun of physically disabled students is very damaging to the psychological development of both the disabled and the nondisabled child.
  - Helping a physically disabled child is the right thing to do and makes you feel good as well.
- Infectious CNS disorders
  - Germs that cause meningitis and encephalitis are transmitted the same way as cold viruses (rabies is the exception).
  - Encephalitis is often transmitted by a mosquito bite; local health departments have mosquito control programs to reduce the incidence.
  - Early treatment of meningitis is essential for a good outcome.
  - Warn students never to approach stray dogs, cats, or other animals.
- Illicit drugs. Advise students that they should:
  - Know the difference between medicines and drugs.
  - Never inhale or take unknown harmful substances for a "high"; brain damage or death can occur.
  - Take medicine only as prescribed by a doctor or as given to them by a parent.
- Accidents. Tell students to:
  - Wear a helmet if they ride a bicycle or motorcycle.
  - Never take unnecessary risks.

REFERENCES

Adams, R. "Diseases That Attack the Brain." *Current Health* 2 (October 1994): 27–29.

David, R. *Pediatric Neurology.* Norwalk, Conn.: Appleton and Lange, 1992.

Delgado, M. "Discontinuation of Antiepileptic Drug Treatment after Two Seizure-Free Years in Children with Cerebral Palsy." *Pediatrics* 97(2):192–97.

Herskowitz, J. *Pediatrics, Neurology, and Psychiatry—Common Ground.* New York: Macmillan, 1982.

Kinsella, G. "Neuropsychological Deficit and Academic Performance in Children and Adolescents Following Traumatic Brain Injury." *Journal of Pediatric Psychology* 20(6):753–67.

Kne, T. "A Program to Address the Special Needs of Drug Exposed Children." *Journal of School Health* 64(6):251–53.

Merki, M. *A Guide to Wellness.* Mission Hills, Calif.: Glencoe, 1987.

O'Grady, R. "The Prediction of Long-Term Functional Outcomes of Children with Cerebral Palsy." *Developmental Medicine & Child Neurology* 37:997–1005.

Rodgers, G. "Bicycle Helmet Use Patterns among Children." *Pediatrics.* 97(2):166–73.

Wade, S. "Assessing the Effects of Traumatic Brain Injury on Family Functioning." *Journal of Pediatric Psychology* 20(6):737–52.

Wallace, H. "Healthy and Brain Development." Chapter 2 in *Principles and Practices of Student Health*, pp 262–72. Oakland, Calif.: Third Party Publishing, 1994.

Waxman, S. *Correlative Neuroanatomy.* Norwalk, Conn.: Appleton and Lange, 1995.

DISORDERS OF LEARNING

One of psychology's open secrets is the relative inability of grades, IQ or SAT scores to predict unerringly who will succeed in life.

Emotional Intelligence, 1995
Daniel Goldman

The numerous descriptions of the term *learning disability* are proof of the difficulty of defining this elusive disorder. Many categories of specialists deal with this problem, and their approaches differ radically. When controversy exists in a field—whether it be history, science or education—one can assume that no one has a precise answer, or more likely, that there is more than one acceptable answer. Entire library sections are filled with articles on learning disabilities, but here only those aspects that are medically related are discussed.

Physicians first encounter a child with learning disabilities when a parent brings the child in for help. Because few doctors have had training in this subject and because nothing unusual is found on the routine physical examination, the parent may be told that the child is normal. This would not be as likely to happen if proper communication preceded the referral. It is obvious that something is wrong when a bright child with normal vision and hearing, from a well-functioning home, cannot succeed in elementary school. The parents should be urged to get further consultation from a physician specialist or child psychologist knowledgeable about learning problems. There is rarely the need to consult a child psychiatrist at this stage.

SCHOOL READINESS

Delayed School Entrance

Sometimes a school nurse will be asked to help decide if a child is ready for school. More often, the nurse will be asked to participate in the evaluation of a student who is already enrolled, one who seems "immature" for his age. It is more often a male than a female student who has these problems.

Parents of the immature child may ask about delayed enrollment. It is rare that the needs of the "unready" child will be met by simply keeping the child at home. Although developmental skills do improve with time alone, they improve faster in a stimulating educational setting. When we encounter parents (usually high achieving) who want to delay school enrollment so their child "will be competitive," we try to dissuade them. Failing that, we strongly encourage a good preschool setting. At this stage of decision making, developmental testing is not very helpful except for identifying mental retardation. As Black has noted, no test has succeeded in predicting academic skills before those skills are supposed to be present developmentally; that is, our success at forecasting reading ability in 4-year-old children is poor.

Repeating Grades

A concept related to delayed school entrance is repeating a grade. Although frequently recommended, repeating a grade does not help a student gain ground academically and has a negative impact on social adjustment and self-esteem.

It *is* helpful to know how a student compares with peers in terms of motor skills, language, attention, and social-emotional status. This starting point is essential to planning an appropriate program for a student. It has been our experience that kindergarten and first-grade teachers fare as well as formal assessments in spotting students who will need extra help.

The Ideal Kindergarten Classroom

When assessing a kindergarten classroom, the characteristics to look for are the following:

- Different ability levels and learning styles are expected.
- Students select many of their own activities.
- Students are expected to be physically and mentally active.
- Opportunities are provided to see how reading and writing are useful before students are instructed in letter names.
- Learning about math is integrated into meaningful activities such as measuring water when preparing food.
- Group size is limited to 10 to 15 students per adult.

ATTENTION DEFICIT HYPERACTIVITY DISORDER

DSM-IV Diagnostic Criteria

The most common types of learning disabilities are those that are associated with hyperactivity. Because the most significant symptom is a deficit in attention, the official nomenclature is now *attention deficit hyperactivity disorder* (ADHD). In the fourth edition of the *Diagnostic and Statistical Manual of Mental Disorders (DSM-IV)*, published by the American Psychiatric Association, this condition is listed as a single diagnostic entity, attention-deficit hyperactivity disorder. The validity of attention deficit disorder without hyperactivity is now considered questionable.

The symptoms of ADHD vary according to age. Children aged 5 through 9 always "have their motor running"; they are constantly climbing and running. Preadolescents are restless and fidgety. Adolescents tend to have impulsive social behavior.

To make a diagnosis of ADHD, the *DSM-IV* criteria must be present for at least 6 months, begin before age 7, and exist to a greater degree than normal.

These criteria include behaviors that, when taken individually, are not necessarily abnormal; for example, one criterion is "often fails to give close attention to details or makes careless mistakes in school work."

Criteria for either item 1 or item 2 below must be met for a diagnosis of ADHD:

1. Inattention (Six or more of these criteria must be present):
   - Often fails to give close attention to details or makes careless mistakes in schoolwork
   - Often has difficulty sustaining attention in tasks
   - Often does not seem to listen when spoken to
   - Often does not follow through on instructions and fails to finish schoolwork or chores
   - Often has difficulty organizing tasks and activities
   - Often avoids, dislikes, or is reluctant to engage in tasks that require sustained mental effort (such as schoolwork or homework)
   - Often loses things necessary for tasks or activities (pencils, books, or tools)
   - Is often easily distracted by extraneous stimuli
   - Is often forgetful in daily activities
2. Hyperactivity/Impulsivity (six or more):
   - Often fidgets with hands or feet or squirms in seat
   - Often leaves seat in classroom or in other situations in which remaining seated is expected
   - Often runs about or climbs excessively in situations in which it is inappropriate
   - Often has difficulty playing or engaging in leisure activities quietly
   - Is often "on the go" or often acts as if "driven by a motor"
   - Often talks excessively
   - Often blurts out answers before questions have been completed
   - Often has difficulty awaiting turn
   - Often interrupts or intrudes on others

The secondary characteristics which may develop as a result of psychological complications in ADHD include the following:

- Poor self-esteem; childhood depression
- Anxiety neurosis
- Oppositional disorder
- Drug abuse
- Other high-risk behaviors

ADHD occurs most often in boys. Although ADHD has several distinctive features, it is rare that one child will exhibit all the symptoms. For example, some children with ADHD have good learning skills and grow up emotionally healthy, while others do not.

Some experts think that they can recognize a potential ADHD child at 1 year of age, but the younger the child, the more speculative the diagnosis. There is no specific test for ADHD; the diagnosis is a clinical one based on multiple data sources. It is rare that preschool children need medication. Also, children with emotional or hearing problems may appear to have an attention deficit. Their treatment, of course, is entirely different from a child with ADHD.

Some children with ADHD are born with certain innate personality characteristics that interfere with their social adjustment and lead to further maladaptive behavior. Most long-term follow-up studies reveal that children usually get over their hyperactivity by the fifth or sixth grade, but the attention deficit may remain; about half are poor readers, and they often make poor social adjustments. If the child is lucky enough to have good parental, medical, and educational support, however, there is a good chance of making it through the educational system to become a successful adult.

The Conners' behavioral checklist (Figure 14-1) is used to measure hyperactivity. It is a screening instrument only and is meant to be used as a guide. It is especially useful in following a student for changes due to a home or school situation or to assess the effectiveness of drug therapy. Sometimes it is helpful for an impartial observer, other than the student's teacher, to fill out the form after a classroom visit.

Place a check in the appropriate column, then score: each check in column one gets 0 points; in column two, 1 point; in column three, 2 points; and in column four, 3 points. Add the sum of each column.

A total score of 20 or more is abnormal; 15 to 19 is suspect; and under 14 is normal. These cut-off scores were derived from middle-class white populations. In our experience, Hispanic students may have lower cut-off scores and African-American students have higher ones.

CONNERS'
Abbreviated Teacher's School Report

Name _____   School _____

Date _____ Age _____ Grade _____ Birth Date_____

Time of Day _____
A.M.
P.M.
Subject _____

INSTRUCTIONS:

Check the appropriate box for each item, **Not at all, Just a little, Pretty much**, or **Very much**, which best describes your assessment of the child. Please complete all 10 items.

Observation   Degree of Activity|

	0 Not at all	1 Just a little	2 Pretty much	3 Very much
1. Restless or overactive				
2. Excitable, impulsive				
3. Disturbs other children				
4. Fails to finish things he/she starts, short attention span				
5. Constantly fidgeting				
6. Inattentive, easily distracted (interferes with learning)				
7. Demands must be met immediately— easily frustrated				
8. Cries often and easily				
9. Mood changes quickly and drastically				
10. Temper outbursts, explosive and unpredictable behavior				

Initiated by _____   _____
                    Health Professional   Observer's Signature
                                                        Disposition_____
                                                                        Health Professional

COMMENTS:

Figure 14-1. Conners' abbreviated teacher's school report.

Treatment

The usual medical approach to ADHD in the United States is treatment with stimulant medication. The one most often prescribed is Ritalin®. Cylert® and Dexedrine® may also be prescribed. There is much controversy about the use of this type of medication; some people are ardent proponents and some are against it. Researchers have been developing tests to predict which children will improve with Ritalin®. The current thinking, however, is that the best approach is to use all or part of a multidisciplinary team of teacher, doctor, school nurse, and psychologist to treat a hyperactive child. A carefully monitored clinical trial will determine whether the medication is effective. When children are handled in this manner, the results are usually conclusive in a short time. It is most important to have a built-in monitoring system so that dosage can be adjusted or medication stopped if undesired side effects appear if or treatment fails. Stimulant drugs control hyperactivity very well in about 60% of the cases and moderately well in another 20%. The remaining 20% are either unimproved or get worse.

Dosage, of course, must be left up to the prescribing physician. Undesirable side effects are usually not seen until the total daily dose approaches or exceeds 60 milligrams of Ritalin® or 30 milligrams of Dexedrine® for a 5- to 7-year-old child.

Because of the many articles published in the lay press about the undesirable effects of medication, many classroom teachers have strong prejudices against the use of any drug for any child with behavior or learning problems. Although these teachers are undoubtedly well intentioned, they are doing many children a disservice. Even though the teacher knows the student well from daily observation and may well question the diagnosis and argue the case directly with the others involved, a teacher should never undermine the parents' confidence in these professionals through individual biases. The hyperactive child who responds well to a relatively small dose of Ritalin® is being aided in a manner similar to that of a child with diabetes who receives insulin. Although the medication does not cure, it certainly enables the child to lead a more normal life.

Medication

There is still disagreement about the medication of students with ADHD in two areas:

- *Should a child be on medication every day, or just during school hours on school days?* Most doctors prescribe Ritalin® only on school days, not on holidays or weekends, and recommend two doses a day: One at 7:00 A.M. to 8:00 A.M. and another at noon (the noon dose lasts until school is out). Some children have such severe symptoms that the medicine is continued on weekends, holidays, and summer vacation. At times, a 3:00 P.M. to 4:00 P.M. dose is needed to last until bedtime, particularly when concentration on homework is required.

- *Should medication be stopped at the youngest possible age, or should it be continued to young adult life?* Most children stop taking Ritalin® between the sixth and eighth grades. Many physicians recommend it be taken as long as there is any academic or social benefit.

These decisions are made on a case-by-case basis; there can be no blanket rule. We favor the approach that recommends medicine twice a day on school days only, stopping at whatever grade (usually sixth to eighth) the student can do well without it. We have, however, seen students who need to continue their medication through high school and even college.

Standard Ritalin® versus Sustained-Release Ritalin®

For children with attention deficit hyperactivity disorder, the standard, short-acting, 10 mg Ritalin®, twice a day, works better than the sustained-release Ritalin®, 20 mg, given once a day. If a student has difficulty taking a noon dose at school because of psychosocial or scheduling problems, then the long-acting form can be considered. Results are less predictable with all the long-acting forms (SR Ritalin®, SR Dexedrine®, or Cylert®). They occasionally work well and should be continued. Cost is also a factor since none of the long-acting drugs is available in generic form.

Classroom Management Strategies

It is wise never to treat ADHD with medication alone. Classroom management is equally important. When the decision has been made to treat a hyperactive student with medication, it is helpful for the teacher to consider certain behavior modification techniques and minor alterations in instructional methods. The following guidelines are from *A Pediatric Approach to Learning Disorders* by M. L. Levine:

1. Begin and end each day with praise for the student. Many students with attention deficits have a significantly diminished self-image and feel as if there is no chance for success in school.
2. Break work into small units. Avoid lengthy instructions and assignments whose persistence far exceeds the student's working capacity.
3. Have a secret way of signaling a student who is inattentive to the task at hand. It is not helpful to call on a chronically inattentive student who is caught star-

ing out the window. This may be humiliating and is likely to increase anxiety, which will further exaggerate hyperactivity and inattention.

4. Whenever possible, such students should be in small classrooms, and the teacher should try to offer individual attention. There should be an awareness that such students may learn more on a one-to-one basis in 10 minutes than they do in 2 hours in a large classroom.

5. A minimum of background noise and visual stimulation is helpful. A classroom with 50 pictures on the wall, a fish tank, a gerbil cage, two terrariums, and a multicolored mobile may offer more sensory data than an inattentive student can filter out.

6. Following a consistent schedule can help provide organization for such a child. Students with attention deficits generally do not adapt well to major shifts in program content or order.

7. The teacher needs to be sensitive to peer abuse. Students with attention deficits sometimes have associated social ineptness (silliness, grimacing, body posturing, or "coming on too strong" when approaching a new situation or new group of friends) that causes rejection by peers. The impact can be minimized by helping the vulnerable student save face.

8. Motivation can be increased by involving the student in a personal way. Puzzles, finding mistakes in other people's work, and games of concentration can be tried. The student should be helped to plan his or her work through a dialogue with the teacher or other problem-solving strategies.

9. Regular meetings with the students to discuss behavioral and academic progress are important. Offer concrete methods of feedback and monitoring (for example, graphs, scoring systems, diaries).

10. After an understanding is reached between teacher and student with regard to the attention deficit, discussion should center around whether or not the student was "tuned in" and is in control of his or her attention rather than whether he or she was "bad" or "good."

READING DISABILITY

Definitions

Dyslexia (now called specific reading disability) was described in the closing years of the nineteenth century by James Hinshelwood, a British ophthalmologist. The word comes from the Greek *dys* ("abnormal") and *lexis* ("words" or "reading"). It was thought to be a specific entity because the child (or adult) seemed perfectly normal and bright except for this disability. Factors such as hyperactivity, mental retardation, emotional disturbance, poor home environment, and lack of educational opportunity could be ruled out by tests or observation.

Today, confusion reigns because various experts insist on their own definitions. No one can fully agree, and some say there is no disorder called dyslexia. The National Advisory Committee on Dyslexia concluded that in view of the wide divergence of interpretation, the use of the term served no useful purpose; now the term *specific reading disability* (SRD) is used. Any population of reading-deficient children (or adults) rarely shows similar etiology or clinical manifestations, as one would expect if this were a single condition.

In the confusion that has existed, various experts have postulated that individuals with dyslexia actually see words backwards (was for saw; god for dog). Articulate, intelligent dyslexic adults report that their difficulty does not lie in the actual "seeing" of the word or letter, however, but in what their brain does with it after they see it (perception). They speak of difficulty in following a line of print, finishing the end of one line, dropping down one space and beginning the next, keeping their place with small print, and so on. It is becoming increasingly evident that SRD is one of the cerebral processing deficits; it is not a deficit in seeing but rather in associating what is seen with the proper brain connections, resulting in the inability to extract meaning from the printed word.

A subgroup of reading disabled children have auditory deficiencies. These children do not have a hearing loss, but instead have trouble distinguishing similar sounds.

Diagnosis

In our experience in reviewing cases, observing children, and talking to teachers, the following conclusions seem likely:

1. There is an entity that can be called SRD.
2. It affects less than 5% of children.
3. It is distinct from ADHD and requires different management (although about half of ADHD children also have some form of learning disability).
4. SRD can occur in combination with or produce emotional problems.
5. The diagnosis of SRD should be reserved for those children who are obviously of average or above average intelligence and who, at about the age of 7 or 8 (after adequate educational opportunity), still read poorly and are usually very poor spellers. It is in this group of individuals that, with appropriate testing, one can diagnose SRD.

Many children 6 to 10 years of age are poor readers, sometimes to a severe degree, because they have emotional disturbances, hyperactivity, or poor psychosocial environments. Many parents of retarded, emotionally disturbed, or slow-learning children prefer to use the more socially acceptable diagnosis of SRD for their children. (Slow learners have IQs in the range of 70–84.)

Here IQ is determined by the equation

$$\frac{\text{mental age}}{\text{chronological age}} \times 100$$

(Mental age is obtained from any of several standardized tests, e.g., Wechsler Intelligence Scale for Children, Revised).

Alternatives to Printed Materials

Once reading disabled students leave elementary school, the volume of printed material and homework assignments increases. To maintain the flow of academic information to the student, alternatives to print are usually necessary. These "bypass strategies" include the following:

- Recorded lectures
- Untimed tests
- Specific computer software
- Audio tapes or recorded books
- Videos
- Peer note taking (with carbon paper)
- Multiple-choice tests (avoid "fill in the blanks")
- Highlighted texts
- Handouts containing only salient materials
- Abbreviated homework
- "Mini" breaks within each task
- Reduced number of items or tasks

MENTAL RETARDATION AND SLOW LEARNERS

Mental Age versus IQ

Much has been written about mental retardation, but one additional concept bears mentioning: mental age. Although the pitfalls of IQ testing are significant, knowing the approximate mental age of a child is helpful. Figure 14-2 gives the mental ages for children from 5 through 12 years old for IQs between 55 and 80.

These figures can be calculated for any age and IQ by using the formula for the ratio IQ:

$$IQ = \frac{\text{mental age (in months)}}{\text{chronological age (months)}} \times 100$$

Solving for mental age we get

$$\text{mental age (in months)} = IQ \times \frac{\text{chronological age (in months)}}{100}$$

Thus, knowing the IQ and chronological age, a student's approximate mental age can be determined. (Use months for both mental age and chronological age, then divide the answer by 12 to get the mental age in years.)

Armed with the mental age of a student (which correlates reasonably well with receptive language age), a school nurse can pitch questions and instructions at an

	I.Q.	55	60	65	70	75	80
Age							
5 (60 mo.)		2.8	3.0	3.3	3.5	3.8	4.0
6 (72 mo.)		3.3	3.6	4.0	4.2	4.5	4.8
7 (84 mo.)		3.9	4.2	4.6	4.9	5.3	5.6
8 (96 mo.)		4.4	4.8	5.2	5.6	6.0	6.4
9 (108 mo.)		5.0	5.4	5.9	6.0	6.8	7.2
10 (120 mo.)		5.5	6.0	6.5	7.0	7.5	8.0
11 (132 mo.)		6.0	6.5	7.1	7.7	8.2	8.8
12 (144 mo.)		6.5	7.1	7.8	8.4	9.0	9.5

Figure 14-2. Approximate mental age of retarded students, based on simple ratio IQ.

appropriate level. For instance, when trying to explain menstrual care to a 12-year-old student with an IQ of 55, it is clear that it must be done in terms that a 6-1/2-year-old student would understand.

No Place for Slow Learners

Children whose IQs fall between 70 and 84 are described as slow learners. Of course, these numbers are somewhat arbitrary as the progression from mental retardation through slow learner to normal intelligence is a smooth continuum. Students who are slow learners often fall through the cracks because they do not often qualify for special education, yet they have difficulty in the regular classroom. This group is at great risk for emotional problems secondary to multiple academic failures.

UNPROVEN THERAPIES

The chronic handicaps that adversely affect learning and behavior require such prolonged medical and educational intervention that parents are particularly vulnerable to the appeal of any method that offers a quick fix. The history of medicine is replete with such nostrums; there are more in existence today than ever before. It takes a combination of scientifically oriented physicians and well-controlled, double-blind studies (and if medication is involved, the use of placebos) to prove the effectiveness of any therapy. Such safeguards are as important in the educational as in the medical treatment of students with learning disorders and other developmental disabilities.

Most pediatric neurologists, as well as physicians who specialize in behavioral and learning problems of children, favor direct educational remediation methods. It is particularly important that educational demands not add to the student's emotional problems. The student must experience successes through small class size and attainable goals with sensitive, trained teachers.

Nevertheless, parents need to have a role that they feel will ameliorate their child's disability. They do not want to be told that acceptance is their only role; they will resist this by grasping at every available alternative and will see, in any change, evidence that vindicates their faith (even though these changes occur more from elapsed time and parental attention than from the treatment regimen). Therefore, it is important to reassure parents that there is something that can be done and that their participation is necessary. This something is not "curing" the learning disability, but rather using educating techniques that acknowledge the child's limitations and build on the potential present . The parents need medical and educational experts to identify what their particular child has to work with and what techniques to apply to develop these functions fully. Remedial methods that are suspect in their effectiveness are those that are based on various vitamins, diets, and perceptual and optical training methods. These "cures" are akin to many highly questionable medical treatments that have come and gone over the years, and they are based on theories rejected by experts. Many testimonials and anecdotal case studies are offered as evidence, but objective researchers using the same techniques are unable to duplicate claims of effectiveness.

Vitamins

Some professionals still advocate treatment of learning disabilities with large doses of vitamins. Recognized medical authorities agree that this "orthomolecular" or "megavitamin" therapy has no benefit and carries the potential danger of most large-dose vitamin regimes. Vitamins A, C, D, and E have well-known toxic effects: vitamin A may cause increased intracranial pressure, pseudotumor, and liver enlargement; vitamin C may cause kidney stones; vitamin D may cause vomiting, diarrhea, anemia, or a decrease in renal function; and vitamin E may cause fatigue, rash, and increased serum cholesterol.

Minerals

Copper and zinc are two of the various minerals that have been recommended as treatments for learning disability. As with vitamins, minerals provide no proven beneficial effect despite claims to the contrary. Toxic side effects are well documented.

Diets

The Feingold diet enjoyed a brief period of popularity as treatment for hyperactive children. Its theoretical basis is that many foods and food dyes contain salicylates that cause hyperactivity in susceptible children.

Some of the earlier studies were tentatively confirmatory, but all later work has failed to sustain the early optimism. It can now be stated that the diet is not helpful. Besides, it is extremely difficult to prepare. The entire family must eat it if the child is expected to stay with it, and the child who already has a problem with peer relations is segregated even further during parties and snack times.

Hypoglycemia

Low blood sugar has been cited as a cause of learning disability. Although this is also unsubstantiated, hypoglycemia has become a "wastebasket" diagnosis for many common complaints of a vague behavioral or neurologic nature.

All experienced physicians have seen patients with true hypoglycemia. It is both rare and serious. Hypoglycemia must be very carefully diagnosed, usually under hospital conditions, and just as carefully treated. It is not considered a cause of learning disability. (A severe, prolonged episode of hypoglycemia, as with an insulin reaction, can cause brain damage and subsequent mental impairment.)

Allergies

A few allergists believe that some learning disorders are caused by "brain allergies" to certain foods, preservatives, or colorings and have advocated allergic testing and desensitization treatments. They describe what has been called the tension-fatigue syndrome as a type of learning disability.

None of this has been confirmed, and brain allergies are regarded as highly suspect by most medical experts.

Visual Training

One of the most visible and controversial issues is visual training in children with normal eyes. Many optometrists are sincerely dedicated to such treatment, whereas ophthalmologists and neurologists regard it as useless and expensive. The two sides of this controversy are presented in Figure 14-3.

Optometry	*Ophthalmology*
1. Children with reading problems are helped by glasses, eye exercises, or both	1. If a child can see well (no refractive error) without glasses, glasses will not benefit his or her reading ability. Good readers can be cross-eyed, even near blind.
2. Seeing involves the use of eyes. Vision includes what the eyes see plus how the brain interprets this. Glasses can improve vision.	2. There is no difference between seeing and vision. A child without refractive error should not wear glasses. The eyes cannot be contributing to the reading problem.
3. Eye exercises will help a child read because tracking and certain other eye movements are an integral part of reading.	3. Exercises are beneficial only in certain children with abnormal eye muscles, such as strabismus (cross-eye). They do not improve reading ability.

Figure 14-3. Visual training: optometry versus ophthalmology.

The American Academy of Pediatrics and the American Association of Ophthalmology (Pediatrics, vol. 9, July 1992) have issued a joint statement expressing their position:

1. Learning disability and dyslexia . . . require a multidisciplinary approach from medicine, education, and psychology in diagnosis and treatment. Eye care should never be instituted in isolation when a patient has a reading problem.
2. There is no peripheral eye defect which produces dyslexia and associated learning disabilities.
3. No known scientific evidence supports claims for improving the academic abilities of learning-disabled or dyslexic children with treatment based solely on:
   a. visual training (muscle exercise, ocular pursuit, glasses), or
   b. neurologic organization (laterality training, balance board, perceptual training)
4. Excluding correctable refractive errors such as myopia, hyperopia, and astigmatism, glasses have no value in the specific treatment of dyslexia or other learning problems.
5. The teaching of learning-disabled and dyslexic children is a problem for educational science.

Most optometrists do a limited assessment, focusing on visual and visual motor areas of functioning but not on auditory and language areas. Thus, even if an optometric evaluation should indicate a certain type of visual disability, it will not necessarily rule out the possibility of the student having other problems. A full special education evaluation should cover all areas of possible disability. It should also integrate the therapy into the full learning process (like remedial reading or math) to assist the student's performance in the classroom.

Reading is now known to have a significant auditory component.

EEG Biofeedback

Biofeedback techniques are reemerging as a treatment for learning disabilities. Children suspected of having poorly organized alpha waves on an electroencephalogram (EEG) are "taught" through feedback to control their alpha waves, and this is supposed to help their learning disability. A very small segment of psychologists still recommend this treatment. The regimen is long, expensive, and useless.

Sensory Integrative Therapy

Sensory integrative therapy was advocated by a California occupational therapist, A. J. Ayres, in 1965. It was assumed theoretically that "maximum integration of sensory stimuli" would improve classroom performance. Examples of such therapy are involving the sense of balance by postural changes such as spinning or skating, using tactile stimulation like working puzzles, and feeling vibrating brushes.

This therapy is still practiced by some occupational therapists, and in some occupational therapy schools it is taught as a useful technique. Pediatric and neurologic specialists for the most part do not agree that this is a useful technique. We predict it will gradually fall by the wayside.

Perceptual-Motor Exercises

It has been noted that some children with learning disabilities are clumsy. Various researchers have developed physical exercises that are designed to aid the child's perception of his or her body parts (self-image in the anatomical sense). Remedial procedures include balance beams, trampolines, and rhythm exercises. Newell Kephart, an educational researcher, developed a theory that postulates a number of states through which a child must progress to "regain lost ground." Its greatest value lies in getting the reading-disabled student out of the classroom and into an area of the school where he or she can have fun and succeed.

Approach to Unproven Therapies

Caught in the middle of the controversies are the teachers and parents. How do they know who to believe? It is hardly possible for them to study, much less understand, all the literature in the field, so they have no basis for informed decisions. The best course to follow is one of healthy skepticism about any approach, especially if it seems simplistic or is widely disputed.

There is no evidence that approaches to reading that rely solely on visual or kinesthetic training are effective. In fact, they waste precious time that could be used for meaningful academic instruction.

The best lesson to be learned from the foregoing material is that more effective remediation methods will undoubtedly be developed in the future. Educators as well as school nurses and physicians will need to exercise vigilance in their judgment. They will do well to join in a dialogue that pools their areas of expertise.

SCHOOL RELEVANCE

As the epigram at the beginning of this section suggests, IQ can be misleading. But when testing is felt to be accurate, it can serve as a starting point for understanding the child. Many developmental disabilities demonstrate a wide range of intelligence, particularly epilepsy and cerebral palsy. Figure 14-4 illustrates this phenomenon. The narrow band of students who fall in the slow-learner range deserve special atten-

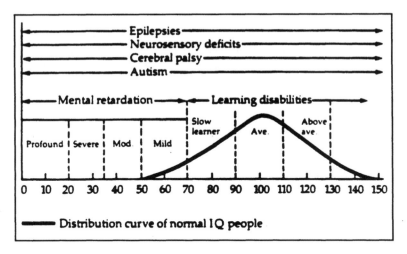

Figure 14-4. IQ distribution in the various developmental disabilities.

tion by school officials because they often go unrecognized and unserved or are mislabeled as mentally retarded.

ROLE OF THE SCHOOL NURSE

The following activities are important for school nurses who serve learning disordered students:

1. Monitor and, if possible, administer prescribed medication.
2. Interpret the medical aspects of the learning or behavior problem to education personnel.
3. Observe classroom behavior. Is there evidence of hyperactivity, aggression, excessive withdrawal, or other unusual behavior?
4. Maintain telephone contact with the physician; he or she usually gets feedback only from the parents. An informed school nurse can furnish accurate medical and nursing information from the school as well. This dual reporting will help the student's physician serve the patient more effectively.
5. Conduct parent conferences. Help parents guard against consultations with too many experts or sort through conflicting recommendations.
6. When appropriate, assist in the development of the student's individual educational plan (IEP).

HEALTH EDUCATION TIPS

Students with learning disorders are generally physically healthy. They are, however, at risk for a number of mental and emotional problems secondary to their primary learning disability. (Section 15 discusses behavioral and emotional problems in more detail.) The following concepts should be kept in mind with each student contact:

1. The learning disabled or retarded child should understand his or her condition to the extent possible; this means providing as much factual information as the child can digest. (Here "retarded" refers to an IQ less than 70 as determined by an appropriate test, such as the Wechsler Intelligence Scale for Children.)

2. Building motivation and self-confidence is the first order of business in managing the learning disordered student.

3. Learning disabled students should be helped to understand that peers may treat them differently because of their learning disorder. They should be taught not to overreact and to develop a repertoire of coping skills.

4. Every learning disordered student should have a specific "safe place" to discuss his or her frustrations, such as the school psychologist's or counselor's office.

5. Educating all school personnel regarding a student's condition is the responsibility of those who know him or her best. Parents should participate.

6. Disciplinary rules may need to be adapted to each student's cognitive and emotional make up.

7. Peers should be taught to understand both obvious and "hidden" disabilities and to respect individual differences.

REFERENCES

Adams, R. *School Nurse's Survival Guide.* Englewood Cliffs, N.J.: Prentice Hall, 1995.

Black, J. "School Readiness." In *Pediatric Basics,* Gerber Medical Service 55 (Summer 1990): 2–5.

Dworkin, P. *Learning and Behavior Problems of School Children.* Philadelphia: W. B. Saunders, 1985.

Herskowitz, J. *Pediatrics, Neurology, and Psychiatry—Common Ground.* New York: Macmillan, 1982.

Hill, Austin. *Why Students Fail.* Waco, Tex.: Davis Brothers Publishing, 1991.

Keele, D. *The Developmentally Disabled Child.* Oradell, N.J.: Medical Economics Books, 1983.

Levine, Melvin. *A Pediatric Approach to Learning Disorders.* New York. John Wiley & Sons, 1990.

Merki, M. *Health—A Guide to Wellness.* Mission Hills, Calif.: Glencoe, 1987.

Roizen, N. "Psychiatric and Developmental Disorders in Families of Children with ADHD." *Archives of Pediatric and Adolescent Medicine* 150:203–8.

Silver, L. Controversial Therapies. *Journal of Child Neurology* 19(1):96–100.

———. *Diagnostic and Statistical Manual of Mental Disorders (DSM),* 4th ed. Washington, D.C.: American Psychiatric Association, 1994.

BEHAVIORAL AND EMOTIONAL PROBLEMS

None of us is alone. We carry everyone inside us—mother, father, teachers,
friends—who gave us a place in the world.

Deepak Chopra
The Return of Merlin, 1995

SCHOOL REFUSAL AND PHOBIA

Many children harbor unexpressed as well as overt fears about school. When the fear is so great that it causes the child to avoid going to school, it is necessary to determine the cause of the extended absence; the management of each case is highly specific.

School Refusal

A child may refuse to go to school for fear of a bully; another may feel unprepared for a test. An older child may simply regard school as irrelevant to his or her entire value system and future life.

Instead of being afraid of the school setting, some children may be fearful of leaving home because of:

1. Parental conflict, causing fear for the mother's safety in the child's absence
2. Fear of abandonment, especially when one parent has recently left
3. Jealousy of a younger sibling at home
4. A recent death in the family, because the child may equate going away with death

Although these children need to learn more productive coping skills, this type of reaction pattern is not altogether abnormal. These reasons for truancy and absenteeism are not considered phobic.

School Phobia (Separation Anxiety Disorder)

Mental health specialists usually reserve the diagnosis of separation anxiety disorder (SAD) for those cases in which there is an abnormally close relationship between the child and the mother; when apart, they both suffer anxiety. Therefore, limiting management to the child always fails; the parents must be equally involved.

School phobia occurs more often in a family with relatively few outside contacts, where many relatives live in close physical proximity, and where the child's parents are often closely involved with the grandparents.

A school-phobic child who is forced to attend school can be expected to have many somatic complaints such as headache, stomachache, and other body aches. Other symptoms are crying, whining, sulking, and running away from school.

Treatment

Management of a school-refusing or school-phobic student requires cooperation from the parents, school nurse, teacher, counselor, therapist, and most important, school principal. The principal's support determines the effectiveness of the school's role in therapy. Insight into the psychodynamics of the family's cultural and religious values aid school personnel in helping the family.

School phobia should be seen as a potentially serious condition, having ramifications beyond school. It affects a student's social relations as well as academics.

All therapy is based on returning the child to school as soon as possible. All studies have shown that the longer a child remains out of school after the onset of symptoms, the longer the necessary treatment, sometimes taking months or years. Suggestions that may be useful in management include the following:

1. The person most likely to be successful in convincing the mother to initiate treatment is often the school person who the child knows (teacher, nurse, counselor, or principal).

2. These mothers are particularly in need of an understanding and reassuring principal who will not become defensive. Such a mother will grasp at any justification to keep a phobic child at home; fear of failure, peer ridicule, or a strict teacher are typical rationalizations for keeping the child at home.

3. The object is to return the child to school. Family counseling may be necessary before this can be initiated. School phobia is more difficult to manage in older children.

4. A suggested technique for reducing anxiety is to have the mother and child visit the school briefly, perhaps to walk down the hall together, and then return home. Insist that the child spend a little more time each visit. Include a friendly greeting from the librarian and the school nurse on a second visit.

5. Adults must be alert to the nurturing needs of these frightened children and should not allowing peers to victimize them.

SLEEPING IN SCHOOL

There are three reasons why students fall asleep in school:

1. In a home in which children are permitted to stay awake too late, having to wake up at 6:00 A.M. or 7:00 A.M. to get to school on time leaves them lacking sufficient sleep to satisfy the developmental needs for their age. They get sleepy during the day, usually right after lunch but sometimes even before noon. The

amount of drowsiness varies from not paying attention to nodding, putting their heads down on their desks, and falling sound asleep.

2. Some children fall asleep as a reaction to stress. This unusual emotional reaction has been reported in adults on the battlefields during actual combat. (A child's most frequent reaction to stress is a stomachache or a headache.) Stress-induced sleep is seen in students who are unhappy in school because of poor academic achievement or poor social adjustment.

3. *Narcolepsy* is an organic disorder with sudden onset of sleep and somewhat related to epilepsy. True narcolepsy is very rare (see below).

Causes

Insufficient Sleep

The following tips often help when dealing with students who get insufficient sleep:

1. Home visits to interview family members, sometimes before or after school hours, are often necessary. The child may stay awake till 11:00 P.M. or midnight, occasionally until 1:00 A.M. or 2:00 A.M.

2. The student usually falls asleep at about the same time each day.

3. The student's mental and emotional health is usually normal in other aspects.

4. Most students in this category will be below the third grade.

Emotional Reaction

If stress is the cause of a student sleeping in school, the following information is helpful:

1. Home visits and other history will reveal that the student gets sufficient sleep at home.

2. The student will fall asleep at a time when he or she is under stress. It may be in the classroom during math (if that is his or her worst subject) or on the playground if he or she has no friends.

3. It may occur at any age but most often in the third to fifth grades.

4. It may occur after school or on weekends.

Narcolepsy

Narcolepsy should be suspected if the following situations are true:

1. The student will fall asleep quite suddenly while doing something interesting.

2. The student may sleep while sitting or standing, but rarely will the student fall to the ground and incur an injury as in an epileptic attack.
3. Each attack lasts about the same length of time.
4. After awakening, the child is drowsy only for a short time.
5. A medical exam often shows an abnormal electroencephalogram (EEG), or brain wave, pattern.
6. The student's academic achievement and social adaptation are usually normal.
7. *Cataplexy*, a sudden loss of muscle tone called *sleep paralysis* (an inability to move while falling asleep), and *hypnagogic hallucinations* (frightening vivid dreams on awakening) occur on rare occasions.

Management

The underlying cause of inappropriate sleeping will naturally suggest the proper treatment and management. Medical treatment is limited to medication and because this is helpful in only a small percentage of cases, it is rarely used.

Educational management consists of special classes, lessening educational demands, and, occasionally, tutoring. If the home situation is completely chaotic and nothing can be done to change it, some principals provide a quiet area where a student in kindergarten or first grade can take a 1- or 2-hour nap after lunch.

Emotional support can be provided by the school nurse, counselor, and teacher. This is always an important addition to any other method of management and often yields good results.

The following steps are essential to appropriate management. The school nurse should be involved in all five steps.

1. Home visits (this is one of the most important diagnostic steps; information gathered will be most helpful)
2. Consultation with parents
3. Referral to a physician
4. Liaison between parents, physician, and school personnel
5. Monitoring or administering medication in those rare cases when it is prescribed for narcolepsy or emotional problems

ENURESIS AND ENCOPRESIS

The involuntary passage of urine or feces (euresis and encopresis) may have their origin in physical or functional/emotional factors. In the pediatric age group both are usually functional.

Enuresis

Urinary incontinence with soiling of clothes can occur during the day or night. Although some children are toilet trained by age 3, so many children have frequent accidents up to age 5 that it can hardly be considered abnormal. Between the ages of 3 and 6, whether it is considered abnormal or not depends on parental expectations. In some families, there is a great deal of parental pressure for early toilet training. If the child, for whatever reason, is not constitutionally ready, or if he or she subconsciously rebels, this parental attitude is apt to cause the child to be labeled as *enuretic*. The label itself can contribute to prolonged wetting. Another child with the same problem in a relaxed household might well become completely toilet trained, day and night, by age 4 or 5. Most pediatricians do not consider bed wetting sufficiently abnormal to require treatment before the child is 6 years old.

Although an occasional child with enuresis will be found to have some infection or abnormality of the urinary tract, the large majority will not. The causes of nonorganic enuresis at school are legion. Examples are too early and too demanding toilet training and fear of going to the school rest room.

Management

Donna Von Merz, a San Antonio school nurse, developed an individual plan for each enuretic student on her campus:

> Kindergarten and first-grade children are often afraid of the large public bathroom in public schools. Debbie had never had 'accidents' at home. She was afraid of two things: the powerful flushing of the school toilets, which was so much louder than the one at home, and at home her mother allowed her to leave the bathroom door open, while at school the other girls always closed it.
>
> This is the schedule I worked out for Debbie. Just before class time, at about 7:50 A.M., Debbie came to the health room (clinic) to urinate in the clinic toilet. For the first week, I had to get her from class; after that, she came on her own. At about 9:30, 11:00, and 12:30, she came again to the clinic to urinate. At 2:00 she came and also had a bowel movement.
>
> After ten days, I began to accompany her to the main rest room and wait for her to finish. I did this three or four times, and then she was willing to go by herself. From that time on, she has remained dry. The whole process took about 4 weeks.

This nurse also emphasizes the importance of keeping spare clothes at schools so that accidents can be handled privately and unobtrusively. Also, holidays or prolonged absences may be followed by regression, so a little "preventive action" is wise *before* accidents recur.

It has always been traditional to rule out urinary tract infection in children with enuresis. Although one cannot argue with this advice, it costs about $40 to visit the doctor's office plus $20 each for two or three urinalyses. Also, it usually means a day off from work for the parent. We see nothing wrong with a school nurse using the above approach for a student with a history like Debbie's, of no wet pants at home and no evidence of ill health.

Almost all kindergarten and first-grade teachers know that many children have "accidents," and they try to protect these children from embarrassment. By the second or third grade, however, repeated urinary soiling is rare enough to be considered abnormal, and the student should be referred to a physician.

When a student is noticeably wet and smells of urine almost every day, management should be the same as for overflow incontinence of the bladder. This happens regularly in certain diseases of the lower spinal cord such as spina bifida. The parents should provide extra clothes so that the child can be helped to change clothes privately.

Encopresis

Habitual fecal soiling occurring past the age of 5 or 6 is known as *encopresis*. Not only are the causes more complicated than those of enuresis, but because of the odor, more adverse social consequences are suffered.

As in children with enuresis, children with encopresis are rarely found to have organic disease or abnormality requiring surgery or specific medication. A notable exception is chronic and severe constipation. Normally, the rectum slowly fills and, at a certain point of stretch, the nerve endings send the proper message to the brain so that the individual has a normal bowel movement. If for some reason the rectum is not evacuated at that time, the urge eventually goes away until a later time. Children who are sufficiently constipated lose the urge altogether and develop a fecal impaction, a large, hard mass of stool that gathers at the lower rectum and causes obstruction. The liquid stool above the impaction often leaks around the impaction (see Figure 15-1). Although the child is completely unaware that this is happening, the underwear is constantly soiled and the fecal odor invites derision from classmates.

Fecal soiling may also occur simply because the student will not take the time to go to the bathroom. In this case, there will be a good-sized mass of stool in the pants, not the lesser amount that is seen in the overflow incontinence just described.

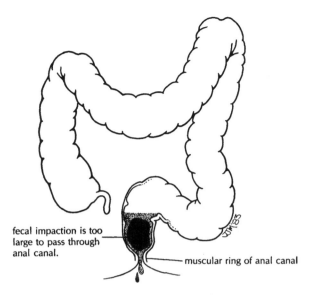

fecal impaction is too
large to pass through
anal canal.

muscular ring of anal canal

Figure 15-1. Fecal impaction.

Management

Treatment of encopresis is administered by a physician. A fecal impaction is easily diagnosed by a digital rectal examination. It can be removed by a gentle water or mineral oil enema, repeated two or three times if necessary, plus mineral oil given by mouth. Each child's oral dose of mineral oil is different; it should be given every night or two in an amount sufficient to cause a full-sized soft stool each day but not enough to cause leaks and stained pants. For children who dislike plain mineral oil, several emulsified flavored products are available. After sufficient time, usually 3 to 6 months, the rectum regains its tone and rhythmicity, and bowel movements can occur normally without mineral oil.

Classroom management is similar to that of the severe enuretic. An extra set of clothes should always be on hand, and the nurse should enlist the aid of the teacher, counselor, and principal to help the student get to the bathroom with as little humiliation as possible.

Children who do not have a fecal impaction yet do have a problem with soiling, may be helped by psychological counseling or behavior management techniques.

ANOREXIA NERVOSA AND BULIMIA

The eating disorders described below are presumed to be of psychologic origin and represent a continuum of manifestations of the same disorder. Both have their onset in adolescence, are more common in females and can be life threatening. A disturbance in perception of body shape and wieght is an essential feature of both anorexia nervosa and bulimia.

Anorexia Nervosa

Anorexia nervosa can be described as a relentless pursuit of excessive thinness. It is not a dislike of food, but simply a pathological desire to be always thinner and thinner. Patients are obsessed with food, and they enjoy preparing it for others. They may collect large numbers of diet cookbooks. When they do eat, they often cut their food up into tiny pieces and chew each one piece slowly so that a meal may last an inordinately long time.

At first, the dieting is mild and intentional, and the patient receives approval. The sinister nature of the disease slowly manifests itself, however, and losing weight becomes an obsession; no matter how thin they become, the patients always want to be thinner. Finally, after sufficient weight loss, symptoms of starvation such as debility, fatigue, and clouding of consciousness begin to take the toll. Some cases have resulted in death.

Symptoms

Ninety to 95% of patients are girls between 15 and 19 years of age who were never overweight to any remarkable degree. Girls who are gymnasts, cheerleaders, or aspiring models are particularly prone to this disorder. The condition sometimes begins as young as 8 years old and as old as 40 years. By the time the patients come to medical attention, they are shockingly thin. As long ago as 1689, a Dr. Richard Martin described a patient: "I do not remember that I did ever in all my practice see one . . . so much wasted . . . (like a skeleton only clad with skin) yet there was no fever but on the contrary a coldness of the whole body."

With anorexia nervosa, there is always intense family involvement and interaction. At first the parents merely tell their daughter that she is thin enough, but they soon discover that she wants to be forever thinner. Sometimes they force the child to eat, but this often leads to induced vomiting, either openly or secretly. The disease may have existed for quite some time before the parents are even aware of it; at this age, parents do not see their children undressed, and the facial fat pads do not disappear until late in the process of starvation.

The daily calorie intake becomes an obsession. A girl who has put herself on a diet of 800 calories per day (already dangerously low) may cut it down to 400 calories per day "just to be sure."

Vomiting, spontaneously or with the help of a finger or spoon down the throat, is a dangerous complication. Some anorexic patients develop bulimia and vomit after a binge of rapid, excessive eating.

Excessive laxatives and diuretics may be used along with induced vomiting. The laxative excess causes burning and pain in the stomach with intestinal cramps. In addition, there is a dangerous loss of minerals, particularly sodium and potassium. Patients who vomit and overuse laxatives and diuretics are in particular danger, and it is in this group of young girls that fatalities may occur.

Exercise excess as a method of burning up calories often occurs in the form of bicycling, running, swimming, and calisthenics. As patients get thinner, they exercise even more.

Mirror gazing occasionally occurs. Patients will stand nude in front of a mirror for long periods of time, never recognizing or acknowledging their thinness, although they may be a mere "bag of bones." This is considered a poor prognostic sign.

Amenorrhea (cessation of menstruation) eventually occurs in all anorexic females, and in about half of the cases, the menstrual periods stop. It is well known that prolonged starvation causes cessation of menstruation; therefore, it was first thought that the amenorrhea of anorexia nervosa was caused only by the severe weight loss. Because about half of the patients stop menstruating before they lose any appreciable weight, it is postulated that there may be some primary disturbance in the hypothalamus, a part of the brain that controls appetite and also, to some extent, menstruation.

The typical patient comes to the doctor about 1 to 2 years after dieting, vomiting or purging, beginning excessive exercises, and disrupting the family. They usually have lost about 20% to 40% of their ideal body weight and are very emaciated, but they do not think of themselves as being excessively thin. They have a characteristic lifestyle that derives satisfaction only from the denial of calories and refusal of outside help from parents, physicians, or other health professionals. When they finally go to the doctor, they reject any suggestions that they should increase their caloric intake.

Psychological Profile

Girls with anorexia nervosa are usually of a compulsive nature. They maintain a neat appearance and are concerned about proper clothing and grooming. They usually get good grades in school, often higher than one would expect from the IQ tests. Yet they seem to be joyless individuals and derive little satisfaction from their good grades. They often have strong feelings of helplessness and unworthiness with a paralyzing sense of ineffectiveness. Parents often describe such a daughter as the perfect child. Adjectives commonly used to describe her are cooperative, obedient, intelligent, thoughtful, considerate, and even-tempered; "she's the last one to cause trouble."

Diagnosis

The diagnostic criteria for anorexia nervosa are:

- Fear of obesity that becomes worse as the patient grows thinner
- Disturbance of body image; feeling fat even when thin
- Loss of at least 25% of original body weight
- Refusal to maintain body weight at normal weight for age and height
- No other physical or mental illness that accounts for weight loss
- Amenorrhea (eventually seen in almost all patients)

Treatment

The earlier anorexia nervosa is recognized and treatment is begun, the better the chances for cure. Most established cases require a period of separation from the family, usually in a hospital. Treatment must be both psychologically and medically oriented. Strict behavior modification with clearly defined goals (such as 1 to 3 pounds of weight gain per week) is the method employed. The diet must be carefully selected so that it will be acceptable to the patient and will also restore minerals, vitamins, and all other nutrients. Only rare, severe cases require tube feeding and intravenous feeding.

Prognosis

Considering all types of cases from mild to severe, the long-term outlook for anorexia nervosa is not particularly favorable. The usual figures quoted are:

Good outcome: 40%

Intermediate outcome: 35%

Poor outcome: 25%

The mortality rate is 2%–5%. Death is usually caused by an infection (such as pneumonia) at a time when the body resources are so depleted that all resistance is gone and no antibodies can be manufactured to fight the disease.

In the 70%–75% of patients who recover, most remain preoccupied with diet and weight for many years. Recurrences are common. Only about 20%–25% of all cases return to perfectly normal health.

A poor prognosis can be guessed at if the following factors exist: long duration, lower weight at beginning of treatment, unsuccessful past treatment, vomiting, and excessive use of laxatives and diuretics.

Bulimia

Pure bulimia consists of episodic and uncontrollable urges to eat excessively and an inability to stop. These episodes are called binges. The food chosen is usually sweet, highly caloric, and capable of being eaten rapidly with little chewing. Binge eating usually occurs in solitude and may stop if interrupted by someone. When the binge is over, patients may go to sleep or vomit either spontaneously or by insertion of a finger or spoon in the back of the throat.

While eating, the binges are pleasurable, but the patient experiences postbinge anguish and depressed mood.

When not combined with anorexia, the weight varies; patients usually do not lose and gain excessively, and the weight losses are never so extreme as to be life-threatening or incapacitating. Bulimia occurs most often as a complication of anorexia nervosa, however. Anorexia nervosa and bulimia are two separate conditions, yet they may coexist in the same person, usually in an older adolescent or young adult.

CHILD ABUSE

Cruelty to children has been practiced in many cultures since the beginning of recorded history and is even a part of the early mythology of many ancient peoples. Infanticide, commercial exploitation, and exorcism of malevolent spirits have all been extensively practiced in "civilized" as well as in "less civilized" societies. The forms of child abuse commonly seen in the United States and Europe today, however, differ in various important ways from the practices described above.

Investigations into the type of child abuse seen in our society began in the mid-1940s with reports by radiologist John Caffey. He speculated that multiple fractures in infants and young children could have been purposefully inflicted by parents. Other reports in the medical and lay press and the involvement of social service agencies led to federal intervention. Slowly, during the 1950s and 1960s, investigations by physicians (led by Dr. Henry Kempe and Dr. Ruth Kempe of Denver, Colorado), social workers, and psychologists led to an understanding of the pathologic dynamics and interactions that are so often seen in families in which an abused or battered child is found.

Classification

There are four categories of child abuse:

1. Physical abuse
2. Sexual abuse
3. Emotional abuse
4. Child neglect or underprotection

All four categories are dealt with by various state laws, and all require reporting to the proper authorities. Definitions vary but are similar in each state. The last two categories—emotional abuse and neglect—are difficult to define, and usually only severe cases are reported and fewer still are investigated.

Description of Abusive Families

It is generally stated that child abuse occurs at all socioeconomic levels of our society. All studies of collected data show that more cases occur among the lower classes, however. There are probably two explanations for this:

1. Most middle- to upper-class individuals utilize private physicians rather than hospital emergency rooms, and therefore cases of child abuse are less likely to be reported.
2. Poor parents cannot afford recreation, babysitters, and other means of relieving the stresses associated with child rearing. Also, at lower socioeconomic levels, more youthful marriages and illegitimate teen pregnancies occur than at higher socioeconomic levels.

Abusive parents have never learned to ask for help or to trust others. Learning to trust begins in infancy with eye contact, touching and cuddling, and voice communication. By experiencing pain instead of pleasure and not receiving normal developmental stimulation, they grow up to be noncommunicative, nonnurturing adults.

Some children are abused because they do not fulfill parental expectations. A particularly difficult child (excessive infantile colic or hyperactive child, for example) is often abused or neglected and becomes the family scapegoat.

The Child as Parent

An abused, neglected, and maltreated child is often the victim of an insidious process by which parents expect the child to take on a nurturing role out of keeping with the child's normal developmental abilities. Some mothers, especially teenagers, have babies out of a need for someone to love them, and they expect the child to fulfill that need. Such a young mother who was herself raised in a stressful situation may lack the ability to nurture. She is apt to respond with anger and to blame the baby when faced with the difficult realities of child rearing. As the years pass, this child will be expected to provide more and more support and nurture to the parent. Unable to fill these unrealistic expectations, the child develops a deep feeling of guilt and may grow to feel that the physical abuse is deserved. Such children become protective of their parents and refuse to divulge information. As adults, they have problems in developing adequate self-esteem. Normally, children are expected to make mistakes; abused children are not allowed to make mistakes and thus develop poor decision-making abilities. They do not learn that they can control their own lives. (It is this feeling of confidence in our own abilities that gives us the ability to control our actions, even though we may not be able to control our feelings. The statement "getting mad at the baby is OK; hitting the baby is not" is an example of this ability.)

Intervention and Reporting

Because its definition is so vague, emotional abuse is almost never reported. This problem can be handled by the school counselor or principal in addition to the nurse, but in such situations, home problems are usually so severe that not much can be done at school.

When a parent refuses to seek treatment for a child with an illness that has potential for serious complications, neglect in school-age children should be reported to child protective services. Common examples are untreated middle ear infections and serious impetigo. Failure to bathe, dirty clothes, or other forms of poor personal hygiene, while regrettable, are not grounds for reporting a case of child neglect.

From the above description, it can readily be seen that merely caring for the injuries or neglect that a maltreated child suffers is a shortsighted approach. All 50 states and the District of Columbia have mandatory reporting requirements. Forty-four states have laws stating that medical treatment by prayer is not a form of abuse or neglect.

Anyone who suspects that a child has been seriously abused is required by law to report the case to the proper authorities. In schools, the teacher or school nurse usually reports suspected cases to the principal, who then makes the official report to the proper social, legal, or medical agency.

School personnel are only required to report. The state department of human services (DHS) is required to investigate. Occasionally, due to personnel shortages, case workers from DHS ask school personnel to investigate. We recommend that school nurses not do this.

The school nurse is in a particularly advantageous position for suspecting child abuse. Any student who does not engage in normal play, is withdrawn, or assumes a nurturing role inappropriate to his or her age should raise some suspicion. Gentle attempts at conversations may reveal a guarded attitude about parents and home. Such students should be watched, not only for the nurture they need, but also for other more overt signs of abuse or neglect.

Most communities have hot lines for children seeking help. A school nurse should devise a means for providing the phone number to suspected victims. Also, many states are connected to computer networks that keep track of child-abuse cases nationwide. Because abusive parents are often mobile and at the same time evasive about the injuries they inflict, a computer database can be most helpful in determining if a child injured under suspicious circumstances has previously been reported as abused.

The school nurse will obviously have a small role in the actual treatment of injuries or specific guidance and counseling of parents. If he or she has a basic understanding of the pathologic, emotional, and social processes underlying child abuse, however, a great deal of support can be given to a very needy student, and some guidance can be provided for school officials concerning the medical aspects of the problem.

AUTISM

Autism is sometimes thought of as infantile or early childhood schizophrenia, but the differences between the autistic child and the preteen or adolescent schizophrenic are so great that the prevailing consensus is that they are separate and distinct conditions.

It was originally believed that autism in children was largely caused by a lack of nurturing and improper parenting; it was thought to exist in the children of cold and aloof parents. Now, however, it is universally agreed that autism is an organic developmental disability whose cause is not related to parental management.

Autism is a unique disorder. It is relatively rare, and some school nurses, especially in the upper grades, have never seen a case. Many nurses would find it beneficial to visit a facility for autistic children or to see a documentary film showing such children at various ages and activities.

Figure 15-2 shows some myths about autism. Although each autistic child is different, most are functioning in the retarded range. Unfortunately, the misconception continues (perpetuated by old school educators and some parent organizations) that there is an "emotionally frozen" normal person inside every autistic child. Implied is that the correct management will release this normal individual. In point of fact, the long term outlook for most children with autism is quite poor.

Symptoms

Symptoms of autism include the following:

* *Aloneness*. Autistic children live in a world of their own. They relate to people as they relate to a table. Occasionally the child will respond to speech, but erratically, infrequently, and often inappropriately. Occasionally they will speak, but with little relationship to what is happening or what they want.
* *Onset at an early age*. Symptoms always appear before 3 years of age. Occasionally, with hindsight, parents can recall that during infancy their baby would not cuddle or snuggle. As toddlers, they did not follow their parents or go to them for comfort.
* *Delayed and deviant language development*. Fully 50% of autistic children never gain useful speech, and those who do often use it in an abnormal fashion.

False	*True*
Autism is an emotional disorder.	It is organic.
Children grow up to be schizophrenic adults.	Genetically different from schizophrenia; adults usually are retarded.
Children do not look retarded and do have normal cognitive potential.	Normal intelligence is very rare; very few enter college.
"Autistic savants" understand what they repeat, say, or draw.	They have rote abilities without understanding.
Untestable or very difficult to test.	Not if test is geared low enough.

Figure 15-2. Myths concerning autism. (From J.M. Farber et al., *Clinical Pediatrics*, April 1984, p. 189. Used with permission.)

There are persistent echolalia (echoing the words of others) of words and phrases and errors in the choice of pronouns. Speech is used in a noncommunicative manner, lacking a give-and-take quality. Only the present exists; what happened earlier is never mentioned. The precursors of oral language, such as "pat-a-cake" or "bye-bye," do not develop. Speech onset is late and comprehension is very poor. There is a lack of appropriate gesture: instead of pointing with the finger, the whole hand is used; if the child wants an object, he or she will take an adult's hand and lead the adult to it rather than ask for it. Simple spoken commands by a parent or teacher require accompanying gestures for complete understanding.

- *Grossly impaired social development with specific characteristics:*
  a. Quality of aloneness described above.
  b. A compulsive insistence on sameness, with resistance to change. Requires the same object at all times. Older children become obsessed with bus routes, colors, or numbers.
  c. Ritualistic behavior such as touching.
  d. Lack of cooperative group play. No imaginative games. Much stereotyped and repetitive behavior.
  e. No friends.
  f. Lack of empathy or ability to perceive feelings of others. Often saying or doing things that are socially inappropriate.
  g. Eye contact deficient and abnormal. "Even when he looks at me, he doesn't seem to be seeing me."
  h. Occasional exceptional rote memory.

Relationship to Mental Retardation

Skillful testing has revealed that autistic children vary greatly in their intellectual capacity and that IQ scores are good predictors of educational attainments. It also appears that IQ scores remain stable over long periods. Thus, it is felt that an autistic child with a very low IQ score is just as functionally retarded as a nonautistic child with a very low IQ score. Autism and mental retardation may coexist.

Most autistic children have a normal physical appearance, but those with concomitant mental retardation may have the facial features commonly seen in nonautistic retarded children. Autistics with a phenomenal rote memory will usually have a high IQ. These children are sometimes called "idiot savant," or more recently, "autistic savant." (Dustin Hoffman's character in *The Rainman* was an autistic savant.)

Those autistic children with lower IQ scores are apt to be less socially competent and are prone to exhibit more bizarre behavior (inflect self-injury, smell other people, etc.) than other children.

Organic Brain Disease

As yet, no specific, localized brain abnormality that is consistent for all autistics has been found. A sizable proportion of autistic children develop neurologic abnormalities such as epilepsy in later life, especially those with lower IQ scores. The consensus is that there is some undetected anatomical or chemical brain abnormality.

Prognosis

Much of the prognosis for an autistic depends on the intellectual level of the particular child. About 75% of autistics with an IQ score above 70 gain competency in basic arithmetic skills and go on to more education or find employment. If the IQ score is below 70, the figure is 20%.

The overall prognosis for the autistic child is generally unfavorable; most eventually reside in institutions. To keep an older autistic child at home requires special physical facilities that most parents do not have. An autistic child with superior intellectual capacity will be educable, and extra effort on his or her behalf is well worth the energy required.

Treatment

Many treatments for autism, rational and otherwise, have been tried. None has succeeded with any consistency. A case is occasionally reported to have improved with vitamins, minerals, manipulations, and so on. Naturally, a parent will not stop using an irrational treatment if it appears to be helping, so unless it is actually harmful, it is usually best to adopt a wait-and-see attitude.

The only "therapy" that consistently yields results is proper behavior modification, often requiring strong aversive methods. This type of therapy only modifies symptoms but is quite effective and necessary to control self-destructive actions such as severe head banging or biting.

Classroom management is extremely difficult. Most often a special facility is required, but if a teacher has an autistic student in class, that teacher has every right to demand expert professional assistance and consultation. Through medical or psychiatric contacts, the school nurse can help in this liaison.

Fenfluramine (Pondimin®) is a relatively new drug that is now used to treat autism. There are conflicting reports as to its effectiveness. Some experts say it is ineffective, and it may have serious adverse side effects. Other autistic children may be helped by the newer serotonin reuptake inhibitors like Prozac® and Zoloft®.

Currently, there is wide interest in a behavioral method that recommends that the patient receive strong body hugging. Time and controlled studies will be necessary to assess the effectiveness of this therapy.

Parents of these children are equally in need of help. Their greatest need is to be able to get away at frequent intervals. In many large cities, respite care facilities are available, but if not, private-duty nurses or tranquilizing medications may be necessary. Parent self-help organizations are useful, and the school nurse can help the parents locate them. Since the passage of the Individuals with Disabilities Education Act (IDEA), P.L. 101-476, more school districts throughout the United States have developed special facilities for autistic children.

CHILDHOOD DEPRESSION

All normal individuals, children and adults, feel depressed at various times in their lives. When mental health specialists speak of depression, however, they do not mean temporarily feeling down; they mean a distinct disease entity that strongly affects the total personality. Depression usually lasts several months or years and often requires specific medical or psychiatric treatment such as psychotherapy or psychoactive medication. Depression is one of the most common psychiatric disorders in adults. It occurs with less frequency in children.

Classification

Depression can be classified into two categories:

1. *Endogenous depression* implies that the patient has a genetic psychological weakness that predisposes him or her to depression.
2. *Reactive depression* is thought to be caused by adverse environmental or situational circumstances. In school children, a suspected cause is continued classroom failure and repeated loss in most of the everyday life struggles that all children face.

Symptoms

Overt symptoms of depression include:

- Feelings of boredom, helplessness, or hopelessness

- Loneliness, isolation, or withdrawal
- Feelings of sadness
- Diminished enthusiasm and physical activity
- Self-deprecatory statements
- Suicidal ideas, expressions, or actual attempts

Masked symptoms are those compensatory or coping mechanisms the depressed child develops to protect his or her self-esteem. Melvine Levine described childhood depression this way:

> The wish to avoid sadness and humiliation is a powerful motivating force and a major determinant of behavior for all school-age- children. If a child cannot measure up to expected school performance, he [or she] often will react with some form of socially maladaptive behavior to save face. Children are forced to participate in activities that expose them to failure and ridicule. Many adults also are engaged in a constant effort to avoid humiliation, but for them the task is an easier one. If they can't dance, they don't go to dances! If they are not good at reading, they can go to movies! Children, however, are required to pursue activities that display weaknesses likely to lead to humiliation.

Depression can be expressed by these masked symptoms:

- Headaches, stomachaches, or other body complaints
- Silliness and clowning
- Aggression, fighting, and rebelliousness
- Poor school performance
- Physical tiredness (often in adolescents)
- Drug use in adolescents. If an adolescent does not know how to communicate fear or anger, the use of drugs eases the emotional discomfort.

Because normal children have these symptoms at various times in their live, long-term studies of large groups of children at various ages are needed to determine the frequency of symptoms of masked depression in a healthy population.

Treatment

Management of the depressed child cannot be generalized; treatment is aimed at the symptoms. School nurses and teachers can be guided by certain principles, however.

1. Never try to manage a depressed student without professional consultation from a psychologist, psychiatrist, or family doctor. Involve the counselor, principal, and parents as much as possible.

2. Depressed children are moody and suffer from low self-esteem. Although it is easier for a teacher to deal with a sad, quiet 6-year-old child than an angry, belligerent 13-year-old adolescent, both need skilled intervention.

3. It is impossible for a classroom teacher to take time to meet all the needs of a depressed student. It is important, however, to have some insight into the underlying problems so as not to unknowingly embarrass the student and perhaps provoke further maladaptive behavior.

4. Maladaptive behavior must not be condoned. Although one cannot be overly strict in every detail, it is important for such students to know that the teacher is aware of what they are doing. Aggression, giving up too easily, poor school performance, and so on should be confronted confidentially and directly.

5. Consistent, sustained academic achievement is not a priority for depressed students. If they can be taught to sublimate their aggression, perform easy-to-complete tasks, relate to peers, and assume some age-appropriate responsibilities, their achievement and self-concept will also improve.

6. Drug treatment of childhood depression with adult-type, mood-elevating medication is controversial. Some children do benefit from its use, however, and a school nurse can make a real contribution to the child's therapy by observing and reporting changes in behavior. Prozac® and Zoloft®, replacing to a degree Tofranil® and Elavil®, are two commonly used medications. (See Section 16 for other psychoactive medications.)

SUICIDE

Suicide is the intentional taking of one's own life. Because it is taboo in our society, suicide is often underreported.

Teenage Suicide

The suicide rate in children and adolescents is unquestionably rising. It is now the fourth leading cause of death in the teenage years, ranking just behind homicide, cancer, and accidents. It is estimated that 5,000 to 6,000 teens between ages 13 and 18 commit suicide each year. This averages to about one suicide per 4,000 teens per year. Thus, a large high school might expect one suicide each year while smaller high schools could expect one every 2 to 3 years.

Attempted suicides are much more common than successful suicides; estimates for attempted suicides range from 100 to 200 for every completed suicide. Girls make about 90% of the attempts, but they are not often successful. Girls usually overdose with pills and can be resuscitated, but in recent years, they have begun to use the same methods as boys. Although boys make fewer attempts than girls, they are more successful because they tend to use more lethal methods, such as guns and hanging, and they seem more intent on being successful. The rate of suicide attempts by white children predominates over Black and Hispanic children, but the differences are less than in previous years. The incidence of both attempts and completions is higher in firstborn.

Increases in suicides have been attributed to many things: increased social and academic pressure on teenagers leading to increased alcohol and drug use, media attention to teen suicide, glamorizing suicide on TV and in movies, less parental supervision than in years past, adult role expectations at younger ages, and an increasing number of families where suicide or an attempt has occurred. Gay teenagers have a suicide rate about three times that of their heterosexual peers.

Preteen Suicide

As with adolescents, the incidence of suicide and attempted suicide is also rising in children under age 12. These young children come from the same types of homes as suicidal teens and also feel hopeless, helpless, and abandoned.

Children develop more complex thought patterns round the age of 10. Before this time, death is perceived as reversible, much like villains in TV programs who are killed one week and reappear the next week. After age 10, death can be perceived as irreversible. Suicide and suicide attempts in children younger than 10 are frequently imitative of someone who seemed to get attention, publicity or notoriety from the suicide, such as a relative, a TV character, or someone mentioned on a news report. Alarmingly, suicide is often an act that the child believes the parent has requested through comments like "I'd be better off without you" or "You should never have been born." Unfortunately, many parents, in jest or anger, tell their children these things. Some children then try to please their parents by dying. In children over age 10, suicide may also be a planned solution to escape a dysfunctional family, to join a deceased relative, or to help rid the world of a "bad" person.

School nurses and teachers need to be alert to the same premonitory signs in younger children as in teenagers, especially in children who have "accidentally" ingested poisons. Many studies have shown that over the age of 6, true accidental poisoning is rare. The occurrence of repetitive "accidents" may also be an indication of suicidal behavior. Children will give as many hints of suicide as teenagers, but the hints are more subtle. The younger the teen or child is, the easier treatment is; early identification is critical.

Identifying the Suicidal Student

It is helpful to think of suicidal behavior as a symptom of a medical condition that can be identified, treated, and often cured. A helpful analogy is diabetes. If properly diagnosed and treated, successful management can be effected. Similarly, suicide is not an isolated event, but rather the last link in a chain of increasingly mortal symptoms of depression. Disregard of the premonitory clues preceding suicide often leads to death, whereas proper diagnosis and treatment can lead to a long and happy life.

Because it is impossible to reverse a completed suicide, attempts to intervene must be made at earlier stages: (1) suicidal ideas or comments, (2) suicidal gestures, and (3) suicidal attempts.

Suicidal Ideas or Comments

Suicidal ideas are the forerunner of suicidal attempts, but they are not easily identified. The student may (1) be embarrassed and downplay or even lie about such thoughts; (2) want attention, esteem, or notoriety and exaggerate the activity; or (3) lie to protect home situations, parent problems, or friends from exposure. The best plan is to take thoughts about suicide seriously.

Idiomatic language has many references to death, such as "I'll kill myself if I fail this history test" or "I would rather die than date that person." These statements are not considered particularly pathological, but other phrases, like "I am going to die," may be pathological depending on their context. It is important to make early appropriate interventions without reacting to every idiomatic expression.

Risk increases in proportion to the frequency of suicidal thoughts. Asking how much one thinks of death or suicide can be a good barometer of the need for intervention. Another risk factor is the degree to which a plan has been developed. A teenager who thinks of suicide without a means or method planned is at low risk, whereas someone who plans to take pills or use a gun in a particular setting and at a particular time should be viewed very seriously, and even more so if the pills or gun are available.

Suicidal Gestures

Suicide gesture is the term applied to *intentionally* nonlethal attempts. These are often small doses of nonlethal medicines, superficial scratches of the wrist, or other means unlikely to be successful. Suicide gestures are really pleas for help and intervention; the teen is asking for increased attention of parents or friends, counseling or therapy, release from unbearable situations, or increased adult guidance. Sometimes "suicide gesture" is used in a very pejorative way: "It was only a suicide gesture!" This is not only unprofessional, but dangerous. A suicide gesture is still a cry for help that is, thankfully, nonlethal.

Not taking a suicide gesture seriously can lead to escalation to a more lethal level to save self-esteem and to prove that at least they can successfully kill themselves. Some children engage in suicidal gestures repeatedly, and although these must be taken seriously, overreaction may provoke more gestures.

Suicide Attempts

Suicide attempt is the term applied to the serious attempt of the teenager to harm himself or herself. The attempt may not be successful for varied reasons: someone unexpectedly intervenes, the gun misfires, the blood vessel constricts and bleeding stops, a lethal dose was thought to be taken but was not, or vomiting occurs. What is clear is that the teenager had the intent to complete a suicide and took action to achieve this goal.

Groups at Risk

Previous Suicide Attempters

Thirty percent of those who successfully complete suicide have made a previous attempt, and 70% have expressed suicidal thoughts to family or friends. Suicidal thoughts or past attempts are the most reliable predictors of future attempts.

Troubled Teenagers

Teenagers who have severe learning problems or conduct disorders (impulsive or aggressive behavior) that continually get them into trouble with family, friends, school, or legal systems have an increased risk of suicidal behavior.

Depression may be present in these youths, but is generally not apparent; teenagers can be very skillful at hiding their depression. Teenagers who are confused about their sexual identity or who are homosexual are clearly at increased risk.

Alcohol and Other Drug Abusers

For some, substance abuse is only a physical addiction. Others use these substances as a method of coping with interpersonal problems. Still others use drugs for the self-medication of a thought disorder or of depression. Although transient improvement can occur, substance use must increase to maintain the effect, causing physical addiction. Because of their physiological effects, both long-term alcohol use or abuse of other substances can make a depression worse. Because alcohol and illegal drugs impair judgment, reduce willpower, and eventually deepen depression, they are high-risk factors for suicide. Further, teenagers may misjudge these drugs and their effects and thus take an unintended lethal dose.

Adolescents with Mental Illness

Major depressive disorders such as bipolar affective disorder (manic-depressive illness) are genetically determined mood disorders associated with an abnormality in levels of neurotransmitters within the brain. Onset of these illnesses often occurs in adolescence. Students from families with a history of affective disorders, alcoholism, or suicide (or all three) have a much increased risk of suicide. In some studies, over 90% of completed suicides have had a diagnosable mental illness and, of these, 70% had sought help prior to the suicide.

Child Abuse Victims

Abused children may think of themselves as bad and responsible for being abused, rather than as being the victim. Older children and teenagers may consider suicide as a response to the feeling of guilt or for having caused their parents so much trouble. Others will consider suicide as a way out of an otherwise hopeless situation. Some feel that "You'll be sorry after I'm dead" and see suicide as a means of getting even.

Rigid, Perfectionistic Personalities

Adolescents with rigid, perfection-seeking personalities have difficulty communicating with peers, experience a great deal of anxiety before tests, and adapt poorly to major life changes. Stress due to either real or perceived parental or school pressure for grade performance may increase their vulnerability.

Precipitating Events

A recent loss can precipitate a suicide attempt in a vulnerable youth. This loss may be real, such as the death of a family member or pet, the loss of a job, failing a test, rejection of a boyfriend or girlfriend, or being arrested. The loss may also be imagined, with a similar loss of self-esteem and an increased suicide risk.

Clusters of suicides have occurred in communities and even in particular schools. Media attention given to a successful suicide can precipitate an attempt in those who have already contemplated suicide or in those teenagers who are personally insecure and who seek to define themselves by doing what others do. It is important to encourage the media to report the death factually, without discussing means or reasons, and without pictures. The media have an obligation to report these events and to report them in a way that does not encourage other attempts.

Help for the Student at Risk

In the Classroom

Rather than presenting classic symptoms of depression, adolescents may instead act out through disruptive classroom behavior. Impulsiveness, aggressiveness, apparent boredom, tardiness or truancy, and failing grades in a previously motivated student should be indications for sympathetic questioning rather than punitive measures. A periodic review of problem students by a team of their teachers might serve to identify students at risk. It should be realized, however, that depression can be well hidden from both family and associates and that suicide is sometimes an impulsive act. Not all cases of suicide can be either predicted or prevented.

In the Principal's Office

Students at risk for suicide who show up in the principal's office are likely to be those who have been abusing drugs or alcohol, who display aggressive or destructive behavior, or who have adjustment problems at home or in school. Some of them may already be known to the juvenile courts in the community. The school may represent the last hope of these students for obtaining adequate help. They should be referred to a mental health center or drug treatment program if there is any suspicion of depression or future suicide.

The threat of school suspension may be used as leverage to induce reluctant students and their parents (who often have a great deal of denial) to accept help from a treatment program, which can be initiated on an outpatient basis with no interruption of school attendance. If hospitalization is necessary to protect the life of the teenager, a phased-in return to school with temporary placement in an alternative class and a gradual return to the regular classroom can be coordinated with successful completion of treatment. This plan implies the need for close cooperation between school authorities and a competent mental health program or drug treatment center designed with the needs of the adolescent in mind. School administrators, counselors, and nurses should be aware of which community programs and private practitioners are well trained and reputable. (See the Role of the School Nurse section later in this section for additional information.)

School Suicide Prevention Program

Referral of Students

Each school system should have a mechanism for the referral of depressed students or those reported by a peer to have talked of committing suicide. Parents should be invited to come to the school where the concern can be discussed.

Should the school be confronted with a crisis situation where a student makes a suicide attempt on school property, the student should be accompanied to an emergency medical center, usually by ambulance. Reputable hospitals require that a psychiatrist provide an evaluation after the acute medical care has been provided. It is recommended that any student who attempts suicide be admitted to the hospital until the family situation can be determined and a treatment plan initiated, unless this can be done safely in the emergency room.

Although many teens remain suicidal after an attempt and need hospitalization, many do not. The attention, pain, and possibly the treatment itself (forced vomiting, gastric tube, sutures) may alleviate the current suicidal ideas. If the family is responsible and will ensure that the teenager will get ongoing care, the teenager may be safely released. If care is promised, but not provided, the teenager will gradually return to suicidal ideas and behavior. School personnel are in a good position to observe this process and intervene in a timely manner. The school psychologist and guidance counselor may need to provide ongoing counseling if these services are not available in the community. Federal law requires each county to provide for the mental health needs of its citizens.

Education

Each school system should have an ongoing program of education for school faculty and administrators in the behavioral manifestations of depression in adolescents and a knowledge of the suicide risk profile. Procedures for referral should be clearly outlined.

Education should be provided to students each school year concerning the symptoms of depression, earmarks of suicidal behavior, knowledge that help is available through psychotherapy and sometimes the use of antidepressant medications, and the resources available at school and in the community to provide that help. The teacher should explain to students the necessity of taking seriously and reporting suicidal thoughts expressed by their friends (or themselves) to the school nurse or a sympathetic teacher. The giving away of treasured possessions should be seen as a particularly ominous sign. This kind of education has been shown to decrease suicide attempts rather than encourage them.

Education of parents through newsletters and parent-teacher association meetings on the symptoms of depression, risks of suicide, and necessity of seeking rapid treatment is also important. It should be stressed that any expression of suicidal intent must be taken seriously. The risk involved in keeping a gun in the home (particularly if parents have a family history of depression or suicide) should be pointed out.

After a Completed Suicide

Unhappily, despite excellent suicide prevention programs, completed suicides still occur. These cases are deeply upsetting for students and teachers alike. The announcement of the death is best made in individual classrooms by teachers or guidance counselors who knew the student rather than in a special assembly or over the public-address system. Care should be taken to downplay the drama of the event. Counseling, both immediate and long term, should be offered to students by guidance counselors and those school psychologists who know the students best; they are more accepted by students than is a team of outside professionals.

Students who are contemplating a similar suicide may display unusual interest in the details of the death of the student, may make more than one visit to the funeral home or grave site, and may seem obsessed with the event even though the student who committed suicide may not have been a close friend. Observance of such behavior by parents or teachers should initiate referral to the counselor, school nurse, or psychologist.

SCHOOL RELEVANCE

Gone are the days when schools could solely teach the three "Rs." Emotional well-being at school is critical to academic achievement. To keep children in class and focused, schools have been forced to deal with myriad emotional, behavioral, and psychosocial problems that are a result of our complex and stressful society. Dealing specifically and appropriately with school refusal, child abuse, depression, suicide prevention, and many other issues has become a major focus of school personnel.

Certainly, schools cannot deal with these problems effectively in isolation; home and community are essential partners. Collaboration among these three elements is a major challenge of education as we approach the twenty-first century. Articulations between helping professionals within and outside the school system must be established, particularly with the mental health community. Consultation with and referral to psychiatrists and psychologists are essential.

School-based mental health services are being tried in many places. In Dallas, for example, County Mental Health and Mental Retardation psychiatrists are seeing children at school, both during and after school hours. Treatment plans are coordinated by school psychologists, counselors, and nurses. These coordinating activities include:

- Giving medication
- Counseling students and parents
- Ensuring that students keep their appointments

This approach has proven to be convenient and mutually beneficial to all parties. Joint funding plus grant applications have sustained the effort and allowed expansion to many campuses.

ROLE OF THE SCHOOL NURSE

School nurses sometimes feel that their expertise does not extend to emotional and behavioral problems. Common sense and caring—plus a willingness to learn and grow in this area—go a long way, however. Two conditions in which the school nurse can play a specific role are child abuse and anorexia. In addition, school nurses can be aware of suicide risks.

Child Abuse

When abuse is suspected all bruises, burns, or other lesions should be measured, described, and recorded as to size, shape, and location. Photographs are very helpful. Any statements the student makes about the origin of the lesion should be recorded.

If sexual abuse is reported by a student, the person who received this trust should interview the student and record details. A physical examination should be done by a doctor, however, not by the school nurse.

Anorexia Nervosa

The school nurse is in a position to integrate the efforts of the parents, school personnel, and physician. Any girl who shows the two most outstanding symptoms—sadness or solitude and weight loss—should be watched for a time to see if the initial suspicions are confirmed.

The physical education teacher should be consulted to see if the girl resists "suiting up" and, if she does, whether she is unusually thin. Because this is usually a growth period, any sustained weight loss should be considered a warning signal, and the other symptoms should be looked for.

Once a diagnosis of anorexia nervosa is established, the school nurse can integrate and support the parents' and physician's efforts. The counselor and physical education teacher can be enlisted to form a team that is actively supportive and thus assist in producing a favorable outcome. There are two concrete steps the school nurse can take to help in therapy:

1. Perform weekly or monthly weighing with support and encouragement.
2. Let the student use the school clinic as a refuge. (Girls with anorexia nervosa, being somewhat depressed and feeling helpless, need support from as many sources as possible.)

Suicide

Adolescents may present classical symptoms of depression such as mood swings, irritability, appetite and sleep disturbances, and fatigue. More often, however, recurrent headaches, abdominal pain, or other physical complaints may be the symptoms that cause their frequent appearance in the school clinic. Because the school nurse is usually perceived as a helping, nonthreatening person, his or her sympathetic questioning may well uncover a teenager's underlying feelings of sadness, emptiness, lack of interest in usually pleasurable activities, and hopelessness and helplessness for future improvement that are the hallmark of a serious depression.

Mental health issues are increasing each year, affecting younger students and creating a greater impact on education. Emotional and behavioral issues should be a focus of professional growth for school nurses and school personnel in general.

HEALTH EDUCATION TIPS

Teaching children about emotional and behavioral problems is probably the most challenging of all health education tasks. Challenging because in most conditions little is known about the cause or prevention,m and treatment is symptomatic rather than specific—few "cures" are seen.

Some time-honored general principles include the following:

1. Always take into account the development age of children in dealing with or teaching about emotional problems.
2. Provide positive reinforcement for healthy behaviors.
3. Support the concept of the individual being in control of their own destiny.
4. Teach coping skills that reduce stress.
5. Model conflict resolution behaviors.
6. Instruct students in the proper use of medication and the harmful effects of illicit drugs.
7. Praise students for thinking through a problem and using decision making strategies.
8. Always acknowledge self-worth and the benefits of having short-term and long-term goals.
9. Be a resource for specialized help when needed.

Regarding number nine, the school nurse should seize each teachable moment, when students are having specific problems to convey the above concepts. These lessons are much better remembered than those taught in the formal classroom setting.

REFERENCES

Adams, R. *School Nurse's Survival Guide* . Englewood Cliffs, N.J.: Prentice Hall, 1995.

Arent, R. *Trust Building with Children Who Hurt*. West Nyack, N.Y.: Center for Applied Research in Education, 1992.

Barker, P. *Basic Child Psychiatry*. London: Blackwell Science, 1995.

Chaplin, J. *Dictionary of Psychology*. New York: Dell, 1985.

Diagnostic and Statistical Manual of Mental Disorders. Washington, D.C.:American Psychiatric Association, 1994.

Erickson, E. *Childhood and Society*. New York: Norton, 1950.

Good, W. *Psychiatry Made Ridiculously Simple*. Miami: MedMaster, 1991.

Hechtman, L. *Do They Grow Out of It? Long-Term Outcomes of Childhood Disorders*. Washington, D.C.: American Psychiatric Press, 1996.

Kendall, P., ed. *Child and Adolescent Therapy: Congnitive-Behavioral Procedures*. New York: Guilford Press, 1991.

Levine, Melvine, Robert Brooks, and Jack Shonkoff. *A Pediatric Approach to Learning Disorders*. New York: Wiley, 1980, p. 249.

Pruitt, B. *Health Skills for Wellness*. Englewood Cliffs, N.J.: Prentice Hall, 1994.

Rapin, I. "Autistic Children: Diagnosis and Clinical Features." *Pediatrics* 87 (Suppl): 751–60.

Roberts, M., ed. *Readings in Pediatric Psychology*. New York: Plenum, 1993.

Singer, M. *Handbook for Screening Adolescents at Psychosocial Risk*. New York: Macmillan, 1993.

PSYCHOACTIVE MEDICATIONS

Approach to Treatment

Stimulants
• Desirable Effects
• Undesirable Effects

Antidepressants

Antianxiety Agents

Antipsychotic Drugs

Mood Stabilizers

Polypharmacy
• School Relevance
• Legal Implications
• Students Carrying Medicine

Role of the School Nurse

Health Education Tips

References

The best cure for the body is to quiet the mind.

Napoleon Bonaparte

The one area of knowledge in which school nurses should excel and far exceed other school personnel is pharmacology. The use and effects of drugs is exclusively their area of expertise. The subcategory of psychoactive medications is particularly challenging.

Psychoactive medications are those that act on the brain and nervous system, to alter mood, anxiety, behavior, or cognitive processes. To understand the actions and side effects of these pharmacologic agents, the functions of the nervous system must be understood. Review the basic anatomy and physiology of the central, peripheral, and autonomic nervous system in a suitable resource, such as Schatsberg's *Textbook of Psychopharmacology.*

APPROACH TO TREATMENT

Psychiatry, particularly child and adolescent psychiatry, has experienced rapid change over in its methods of treatment since the 1970s. The move has been from a largely psychoanalytic orientation toward a more biological one.

As a rule, beneficial outcomes are achieved by simultaneously reducing symptoms and shoring up the capacity of the individual to adapt to life. Although psychotropic medications can exert profound positive effects on mood, behavior, and cognition, they often do not change the underlying disease process that is sensitive to internal and external stressors. A combined approach of drugs and psychoanalytic methods remains essential to adequate outcome.

There are five major categories of psychoactive medications:

- Stimulants
- Antidepressants
- Antianxiety agents
- Antipsychotic drugs
- Mood stabilizers

These medications will be discussed in order, with two or three representative drugs considered in each category.

All the drugs described here require a physician's prescription. They all have multiple adverse side effects. School staff in charge of monitoring them should have ready access to the *Physicians' Desk Reference*, published annually by Medical Economics in Oradell, New Jersey.

The drugs described are only the ones most commonly used. Many more are available and used by some physicians.

In this chapter, the words *drugs* and *medications* are used synonymously. A psychoactive drug is one designed to have a primary effect on brain functioning. Many of them are prescribed for children in school and are designed to have their effects during school hours.

Nonpsychoactive drugs may have psychoactive side effects. For example, an antihistamine used for allergies on occasion make a person sleepy even though it is not classified as a psychoactive drug.

STIMULANTS

The three most commonly used stimulants are:

Ritalin® (generic name: methylphenidate)
Cylert® (generic name: pemoline)
Dexedrine® (generic name: dextroamphetamine)

Stimulants are also mentioned in Section 14. They are prescribed legitimately for attention deficit hyperactivity disorder (ADHD) and narcolepsy (a rare sleep disorder).

Desirable Effects

The desirable effects of stimulants are decreased motor activity, impulsivity, and distractibility and an increased attention span.

Undesirable Effects

Stimulants also cause a number of undesirable effects:

1. Loss of appetite and poor weight gain. Unless severe, nothing needs to be done; the student will regain weight during summer vacation when off medication.
2. Nausea, stomachache, or headache
3. Increased motor activity (usually temporary)
4. Frequent crying spells with little provocation
5. Drowsiness
6. Panda syndrome (dark circles around the eyes)
7. Tremors or tics (rare)

Treatment of the above side effects consists of giving the medication after a meal, reducing the dose, or changing to a different stimulant. If none of these maneuvers relieves the undesirable symptoms, the medication may need to be stopped altogether.

8. Zombielike state (rare). Treatment always consists of reducing the dose or changing the medication.
9. Tics. Whether or not tics can be caused or aggravated by stimulants is controversial. As long as the possibility exists, the school nurse must be watchful and report any new tics or worsening of old ones to the parent, doctor, or both. Ritalin® is particularly prone to accentuate tics and is contraindicated in most cases of Tourette syndrome.
10. Addiction. This has yet to be reported as long as the drug is given in small, controlled doses.

Some of the stimulants are long-acting; one dose given in the morning lasts all day. Examples are Dexedrine® spansules, Cylert®, and Ritalin-SR® (sustained release). Our preference is to start treatment with the short-acting drug to establish a baseline dose and to determine individual tolerance. The short-acting stimulants usually require a morning dose between 7:00 A.M. and 8:00 A.M. and another dose around noon. By the time the student gets home from school, the effects have worn off. Occasionally, a child is so hyperactive that a third dose around 4:00 P.M. will be necessary, especially if there is homework to be done.

ANTIDEPRESSANTS

Depression in adolescents and children differs qualitatively from depression in adults. In addition, symptoms of depression in prepubertal children differ from those in teenagers. Figure 16-1 clarifies the differences in children and adolescents. A quick perusal of this figure reveals that depression in the prepubescent child is more difficult to recognize. They have less anhedonia, which is the inability to enjoy activities that were formerly pleasurable. Children also express hopelessness less often than adolescents but have more physical complaints, anxieties, and phobias. Some may even be "hyperactive." In contrast, adolescents, particularly boys, may not appear depressed because of acting out or aggressive behavior.

Classic antidepressants were originally discovered by accident. In the early 1950s, physicians noted that tuberculosis patients showed elevation of mood when treated with iproniazid. This drug, a *monoamine oxidase inhibitor* (MAOI), turned out

Signs/Symptoms	Children	Adolescents
Anhedonia	Less	More
Hopelessness	Less	More
Sleep	Insomnia	Hypersomnia
Weight	Less likely to change	Increased or decreased
Suicide	Low lethality	Moderate lethality (higher for males)
Appearance	More depressed	less depressed
Somatic complaints	More	Less
Separation anxiety	More	Less
Phobias, hallucinations	More	Less

Figure 16-1. Differences in depression in children and adolescents. (From D. Rosenberg, *Dementia* 3:157-73, 1993.)

to have little or no antituberculous effect, but lead to studies that documented its antidepressant effect.

Next came the tricyclic (three rings) compounds still in use today: Elavil®, Anafranil®, Pertofrane®, Tofranil®, and Aventyl®. Tofranil® (imipramine) is widely used in adolescents and older children for the treatment of both depression and enuresis. Its major drawback is toxicity. An overdose is often fatal due to cardiac arrhythmias. Because depressed individuals are prone to suicide through medication overdose, this is a major disadvantage to the tricyclic antidepressants (TCA).

The newer monoamine oxidase inhibitors (MAOI) are for depression that is refractory to TCAs. *Monoamine oxidase* is an enzyme that inactivates certain neurotransmitters (norepinephrine). Thus, MAOIs exert their effect by reducing the available neurotransmitting chemical in certain areas of the nervous system.

Although MAOIs are not considered first-line therapy for any disorder, they are the most frequent choice for the treatment of depressed adults with anxious or atypical symptoms. *No MAOI compound is currently FDA approved for use in children under 16 years of age.* Certain dietary restrictions are mandatory for patients on MAOIs. Drugs in this category include:

- Nardil® (phenelzine)
- Parnate® (tranylcypromine)
- Marplan® (isocarboxazid)

The newest antidepressants include a mixed bag of medications that cannot be grouped by chemical structure or site of action. They are clinically effective in treating depression. *Prozac*® (fluoxetine) is a very popular antidepressant in adults. Its efficacy and safety have not been established for children and adolescents, but its clinical use in this population is growing. It has fewer side effects than TCAs and is not associated with weight gain. The once-a-day dose improves patient compliance. *Zoloft* ® (sertraline) has a much shorter half-life and even fewer side effects than Prozac®. It is also effective in the treatment of obsessive compulsive disorder. *Paxil* ® (paroxetine) is similar to Zoloft®.

ANTIANXIETY AGENTS

Antianxiety drugs are known as anxiolytics (anxiety dissolving). The term is somewhat deceiving because most serious anxiety is part of depression, especially in prepubescent children. Antidepressants are the long-term treatment of choice for most anxiety disorders. Therefore, anxiolytics do not necessarily represent the current standard of treatment for childhood anxiety disorders over the long haul. They are effective in acute episodes, however.

Historically, barbiturates were used to treat anxiety. The high rate of habituation has caused the discontinuation for this purpose. They are still useful as anticonvulsants and as short-term sedatives, however.

Currently, the term *anxiolytic* has become nearly synonymous with benzodiazepines such as Valium®. A more complete list along with the recommended ages for use is shown in Figure 16-2.

Compound	Age Range
Valium® (diazepam)	Over 6 months
Serax® (oxazepam)	Over 6 years
Librium® (chlordiazepoxide)	Over 12 years
Ativan® (lorazepam)	Over 12 years
Dalmane® (flurazepam)	Over 15 years
Xanax® (alprazolam)	Over 18 years

Figure 16-2. Antianxiety drugs.

ANTIPSYCHOTIC DRUGS

The American Psychiatric Association defines psychosis as follows: "A major mental disorder of organic (physical) or emotional origin in which the individual's ability to think, respond emotionally, remember, communicate, interpret reality, and behave appropriately interferes grossly with his capacity to meet the ordinary demands of life."

The most critical demand of life for a student is school (and sometimes surviving in a dysfunctional family). Adolescents have the added task of dealing with their sexuality and emerging autonomy.

Psychotic disorders include the following:

- Schizophrenia (five subtypes)
  - Paranoid
  - Disorganized
  - Catatonic
  - Undifferentiated (does not meet the criteria for any of the first three subtypes)
  - Residual (an attenuated form)
- Schizophreniform disorder (a cyclic type)
- Schizoaffective disorder (combined with depression, mania, or both)
- Delusional disorder (nonbizarre delusions, e.g., being followed)
- Brief psychotic disorder
- Shared psychotic disorder (*folie à deux:* a delusion develops in an individual in the context of a close relationship with another person who has an established delusion)
- Psychotic disorder due to medical condition (usually with hallucinations)
- Substance induced psychotic disorder (can be due to medication or illicit drugs)
- Psychotic disorder not otherwise specified

Some autistic children are considered psychotic if they are out of touch with reality and appear to have hallucinations (see the discussion on autism in Section 15).

Drugs used to treat psychoses are referred to as antipsychotic agents (also called neuroleptics or major tranquilizers). Although a mainstay of chemotherapy in adults, antipsychotic agents are used far less commonly in child and adolescent psychiatry. Only seven agents have Federal Drug Administration (FDA) approval for psychiatric indications in children younger than 12 years. The main causes for controversy are the potentially severe neurologic and developmental sequelae of long-term use and the risks of short-term side effects that may hamper learning, socialization, and affect. Their use in children is limited to debilitating mental illness and a duration of treatment that is as short as possible.

Other indications for antipsychotic drugs include Tourette syndrome and the short-term treatment of severe self-injurious behavior or aggression. Some agents have also been used for pediatric obsessive compulsive disorder.

The term *childhood schizophrenia* is seldom used today. Various pediatric psychotic syndromes are largely under other diagnostic categories: pervasive developmental disorder, schizoid or schizotypal personality disorders, and to a lesser extent, childhood autism. The diagnosis of schizophrenia in children is now reserved for patients who meet the adult criteria.

The manifestations of schizophrenia are divided into two categories:

1. Positive symptoms: hallucinations, delusions, and thought disorders
2. Negative symptoms: withdrawal, flat affect, and apathy.

Although antipsychotic agents are unequivocally effective against positive symptoms, it is unclear if they improve negative ones.

The first antipsychotic drug, discovered in early 1950s, was Thorazine® (chlorpromazine). Those most in use today are shown in Figure 16-3. All the drugs have

Compound	Age Range	Indications
Mellaril® (thioridazine)	2 years +	Psychosis, SBD,* ADHD†
Stelazine® (trifluoperazine)	6 years +	Psychosis NPA
Compazine® (prochlorperazine)	2 years +	Psychosis NPA
Tractan® (chlorprothixene)	6 years +	Psychosis
Orap® (pimozide)***	2 years +**	Tourette's disorder
Haldol® (haloperidol)	3 years +	Psychosis, SBD, Tourette, ADHD

*Abbreviations:
   SBD = severe behavioral disorders
   NPA = nonpsychotic anxiety
   ADHD = attention deficit hyperactivity disorder
**Parentheses indicate a second choice usage.
***Safety of Orap® in children under 12 years of age is not well established.

Figure 16-3. Antipsychotic drugs.

potentially serious side effects and are reserved for the most severe clinical manifestations; that is, the patient is unable to function without them. Many if not most of these drugs are begun during hospitalization under careful observation.

MOOD STABILIZERS

The term *mood stabilizer* was first applied to lithium salts when it was noted that these compounds were effective in reducing manic excitement and preventing both manic and depressive recurrences in patients with bipolar disorder (formerly called manic-depressive disorder).

More recently, several anticonvulsants (e.g., Tegretol®) have also been shown to be effective in the treatment of manic excitement. These anticonvulsants are currently being studied for their longer-term mood-stabilizing effects.

Lithium is the drug of choice for the treatment of adults with bipolar disorder. Recent studies have shown it to be effective in children and adolescents as well, although it is FDA approved only for patients 12 years of age and older. Other studies are exploring lithium's usefulness in augmenting antidepressants in the treatment of depression and aggressive behaviors and in treating children and adolescents with behavior control problems whose parents have responded to lithium therapy. Lithium is also considered by some to be a "last-line" treatment option in severe pediatric ADHD when all other therapies have failed.

Occasional side effects of lithium include the following:

- Gastrointestinal (nausea/vomiting, diarrhea)
- Tremor
- Elevated white blood cell count
- Malaise (a vague out-of-sorts feeling)

Some of the trade names for lithium preparations are Eskalith®, Lithonate®, Lithotabs®, Lithobid®, and Cibalith®. They are available in tablet and syrup form as well as in slow-release capsules. The dosage is started low (only children 12 and older) and gradually increased with monitoring of the blood level.

Tegretol® (carbamazepine) has been shown to be effective in adults with bipolar disorder and is often used in cases of lithium failure. It is sometimes added to lithium treatment when response has been partial. There are no data on children and adolescents, making this an important area for investigation. Because of its history of relative safety in treating epilepsy, many psychiatrists are trying Tegretol® in individual patients with favorable results.

Other anticonvulsants being tried as mood stabilizers include Depakene® (valproic acid), Dilantin® (phenytoin), and Zaroatin® (ethosuximide).

POLYPHARMACY

It is the hope of all clinicians that their patients will respond to a single psychotherapeutic agent. This may be the exception rather than the rule, however. Although there has been much warranted criticism of polypharmacy (patients receiving too many different types of medications), some individuals do require treatment with two or even three drugs.

There are no studies at all on the long-term consequences of psychiatric drug therapy in childhood on brain function, behavior, or physical health in adult life. The decision to use one or more drugs for a psychiatrically ill child or young adolescent must therefore be based on a clear and urgent clinical need.

SCHOOL RELEVANCE

Only school nurses fully realize how such a simple act as giving a student medication can be fraught with legal problems, administrative complications, and adverse side effects for the child.

Most schools require students to leave their medicines with the school nurse or another designated person and to go get the dose when it is necessary, usually once a day, but occasionally twice. This rule is difficult to enforce strictly.

Each school should use a form to record the date and time medicine is given and the initials of the person giving it. Figure 16-4 gives a sample form. This form should be kept at the site where the medicine is actually given, ideally in the school clinic. It can be attached to the wall to facilitate recording.

Legal Implications

School districts usually require written parental permission and a physician's signed order before allowing medication to be dispensed at school. In lieu of the doctor's order, some states permit medication to be given in school if the medicine is properly labeled and in the original prescription bottle.

Most state nurse practice acts allow nurses to give medicines in or out of school only on a doctor's orders. The requirements for school nurses is the same as for other nurses. Also, no exceptions exist for nonprescription medicines. A teacher can give

DAILY LOG FOR MEDICATION

School	Week of					Week of					Week of					Week of				
	Mon	Tue	Wed	Thu	Fri	Mon	Tue	Wed	Thu	Fri	Mon	Tue	Wed	Thu	Fri	Mon	Tue	Wed	Thu	Fri
Student _____ Dosage _____ Med. _____ Times _____																				
Student _____ Dosage _____ Med. _____ Times _____																				
Student _____ Dosage _____ Med. _____ Times _____																				
Student _____ Dosage _____ Med. _____ Times _____																				
Student _____ Dosage _____ Med. _____ Times _____																				
Student _____ Dosage _____ Med. _____ Times _____																				
Student _____ Dosage _____ Med. _____ Times _____																				

The person dispensing the medication signs his or her name in the block under the corresponding day of the week.

Figure 16-4. Daily log for medication.

a child an aspirin, but if the school nurse does so, she may have acted against the direction of her state nurse practice act.

Students Carrying Medicines

Most principals do not want students to carry their own medicines and be solely responsible for taking it themselves. They give the following reasons:

- Students often trade medicines.
- School authorities may mistake medication for unprescribed or illegal drugs.
- Students are found lethargic or excited with unknown pills in their pocket or purse.
- Students comply poorly with medicine schedules, even when a school nurse is monitoring them.

Whether to allow students to carry their own medicine has always been a difficult decision because doctors, when they make such a request, consider a different set of factors than do principals. The doctor envisions a responsible child and parent and thinks of the medicine's effect on the child's illness. The principal has experienced serious problems resulting from students' carrying their own medicines and is thinking about legal issues, equal treatment of all students, and drug abuse.

Up until 1984, the official statement of the American Academy of Pediatrics was that students should not carry their own medication. In 1984, the statement was changed to recommend that students carry their own medicine if so requested by their doctor. In our opinion, both statements are too dogmatic; these situations call for case-by-case decisions. We know that some students do trade medicines and do carry illegal drugs. On the other hand, some students with certain illnesses should carry their own medicines and can do so safely, but the school nurse should be aware of such an arrangement.

ROLE OF THE SCHOOL NURSE

The school nurse should chart each dose of medication given at school. If the nurse is not at the school every day, the person who is delegated to give the medication should be instructed in the proper way to chart. The nurse should alert school personnel to students holding pills in their mouths and later spitting them out.

When possible, arrange for all the medication to be given at home. The phenothiazine drugs have a longer duration of action and are more amenable to this mode of administration than other drugs. Also, the sustained release amphetamines and Ritalin® for the treatment of ADHD obviate the need for medication to be given at school.

The school nurse must be watchful that a student who is receiving legally prescribed medication is not mistaken for a drug abuser. Adverse side effects may make a student appear drowsy or "stoned".

The school nurse should insist that a copy of the *Physicians' Desk Reference* be available for the nurse and other school personnel. The nurse acts as liaison between parent, student, and physician so that undesirable side effects or lack of therapeutic effects are promptly reported.

HEALTH EDUCATION TIPS

Educating students to the benefits and hazards of prescribed as well as illicit drugs is an ongoing task from kindergarten through twelfth grade. The following core facts should be repeated to students each year in a developmentally appropriate way:

- Take all medicine as directed. Never skip a dose or "double up."
- All medicines are not created equally. Prescription medicines for major diseases often have more serious side effects. Always report any unusual effects from your medicine to the school nurse.
- Never exchange prescription medication with another student or take anyone else's medication.
- Check with a physician or parent before taking nonprescription medication.

REFERENCES

Birmaher, B. "Clozapine for the Treatment of Adolescents with Schizophrenia." *Journal of the American Academy of Child and Adolescent Psychiatry* 31:1609–164, 1992.

Carlson, G. "Lithium in Hospitalized Children." *Journal of Child Psychology and Psychiatry* 33:411–25.

Locascio, J. "Factors Related to Haldoperidol Response in Autistic Children."*Psychopharmacology Bulletin* 27:119–26.

Memmler, R. "The Brain, the Spinal Cord, and the Nerves." In *The Human Body in Health and Disease*, pp. 217-226. Philadelphia: J. B. Lippincott, 1977.

Preston, J. *Clinical Pharmacology Made Ridiculously Simple*. Miami: Med Master, 1995.

Rosenberg, D. *Textbook of Pharmacotherapy for Child and Adolescent Disorders*. New York: Brunner/Mazel, 1994.

Schatzberg, A. *Manual of Clinical Psychopharmacology*. Washington, D.C.: American Psychiatric Press, 1991.

Schatsberg, A. *Textbook of Psychopharmacology*. Washington, D.C.: American Psychiatric Press, 1995.

Strauss, Maurice (Ed.). *Familiar Medical Quotations*. Boston: Little, Brown & Company, 1968, pp. 19-20.

Shrand, J. "Psychopharmacology in Mood and Anxiety Disorders."*Contemporary Pediatrics* 12(2):21–48.

Stewart, J. "A Review of the Pharmacology of Aggression in Children and Adolescents." *Journal of the American Academy of Child and Adolescent Psychiatry* 29:269–77.

Teicher, M. Neuroleptic drugs: Indications and guidelines for their rational use in children and adolescents. *Journal of Child and Adolescent Psychopharmacology* 1:33-56, 1990.

SPECIAL EDUCATION ISSUES

Education is just like everything else. You got to judge it by its results.

Will Rogers

Special education has grown progressively more complex due to legislative changes, technical advances, and expanding numbers of students. Many students are younger and lower functioning developmentally and are thus more labor intensive than in years past. Increasingly, the school nurse's technical expertise is essential to educators as they jointly endeavor to meet the learning and health needs of disabled students.

Although this section focuses largely on mandates and requirements, human caring must not be displaced or minimized. School nurses do this well, so that element must be left to each nurse's professional instincts.

OVERVIEW OF FEDERAL LEGISLATION

Federal legislation protecting the rights of disabled children and adults addresses two broad categories: affirmative duty and access. The legislation on affirmative duty is:

P.L. 94-142: Education of All Handicapped Act of 1975
P.L. 99-457: Amendment to P.L. 94-142 of 1986
P.L. 101-476: Individuals with Disabilities Education Act of 1990

Legislation on access is:

P.L. 93-112 (Section 504 of the Rehabilitation Act of 1973)
P.L. 101-336: Americans with Disabilities Act of 1990

P.L. 94-142, Education of All Handicapped Act (EHA) of 1975, provides for a "free and appropriate public education" (FAPE) for eligible disabled students 3 to 21 years of age in the "least restrictive environment." This act was reauthorized in 1990 as P.L. 101-476, Individuals with Disabilities Education Act (IDEA), with additions to eligibility, related services, and clarification of certain concepts, including transition services.

P.L. 99-457 amended P.L. 94-142 by lowering the age of eligibility to birth. States that desire to initiate programs for disabled children birth to 3 years old would receive supplementary funds, but this amendment is not mandatory. P.L. 93-112: Rehabilitation Act of 1973 (Section 504) states:

No otherwise qualified handicapped individual in the United States shall, solely by reason of his handicap. be excluded from the participation in, be denied the benefits of, or be subjected to discrimination under any program or activity receiving Federal financial assistance.

P.L. 101-336, Americans with Disabilities Act (ADA) of 1990, is a comprehensive statute designed to prohibit discrimination against the handicapped in a wide range of activities managed by both public and private entities. ADA impacts the private sector because its provisions are patterned after Section 504.

INDIVIDUALS WITH DISABILITIES EDUCATION ACT (IDEA)

IDEA (PL 101-476) ensures a free and appropriate educational program for eligible disabled students 3 to 21 years of age. States accomplish this by developing implementation plans based on the components of the law (for which they receive federal funding).

Schools have an affirmative duty to locate and offer educational services to all eligible children. Students at home, in institutions, or in public or private facilities, if school age, may be eligible for services. Schools must also develop a procedure for identifying disabled students attending school but not receiving appropriate educational services.

Following identification, the question of whether a disability exists and to what extent it interferes with education must be addressed. This requires a multidisciplinary evaluation. State policy makers have developed varied criteria for this evaluation. In general, all children receive basic intelligence and achievement testing and some form of family history taking followed by specialized evaluations regarding the presumed deficit.

Before special education services can be initiated, eligibility must be established. The disability categories are:

1. Mental retardation
2. Hearing impairment (including deafness)
3. Speech or language impairment
4. Visual impairment (including blindness)
5. Serious emotional disturbance
6. Physical handicap (including orthopedic and other health impairment)
7. Autism
8. Deaf-blindness
9. Learning disabled

10. Multiple disabilities
11. Traumatic brain injury

If a student is eligible for placement, the multidisciplinary team is responsible for development of an individual education plan (IEP). The decisions on how to provide educational services to a student must be adapted to that student's unique needs and are made by a team that includes the parents. Eligibility, instructional program, placement, and related services must be addressed by the team. Educational programs and services are be provided in the least restrictive environment, that is, with nondisabled peers to the extent possible.

Schools must provide procedural safeguards under the federal mandates by notifying students or their parents of the school's responsibility and the procedures to be followed. If parents and schools are unable to agree on specifics on the general education program of the disabled student, either party may seek redress in a formal hearing.

ELIGIBILITY CRITERIA

To be eligible to receive special education and related services under IDEA, a student must have been determined to have one or more of the disabilities listed in federal regulation or in state law and that condition must adversely affect educational performance. There are 11 categories:

1. *Physical disability* includes:
   - *Orthopedic impairment* such as congenital anomalies, impairments caused by disease, and other conditions including cerebral palsy, fractures, or burns with resultant contractures.
   - *Other health impairment* is an acute or chronic health problem that limits vitality, alertness, or strength such as a heart condition, tuberculosis, rheumatic fever, nephritis, asthma, sickle-cell anemia, hemophilia, leukemia, and diabetes.
   A licensed physician must confirm that the student falls in one of the above categories.
2. *Auditory impairment* is a serious hearing loss, even after corrective medical treatment or use of amplification. Determination of this disability requires an otological and audiological evaluation.
3. *Visual impairment* is a serious visual loss even after correction. This determination requires a comprehensive visual examination and a functional vision assessment that includes assistive devices.

4. *Deaf-blind* is a combination of severe hearing and visual losses after best correction.

5. *Mental retardation* refers to a student who is functioning two or more standard deviations below the mean on individually administered scales of verbal and nonverbal ability plus deficits in adaptive behavior.

6. *Emotionally disturbed* refers to a condition exhibiting one or more of the following characteristics over a long period of time and to a marked degree:

   • An inability to learn that cannot be explained by intellectual, sensory, or health deficits

   • An inability to build or maintain satisfactory interpersonal relationships with peers and teachers

   • Inappropriate types of behavior or feelings

   • A pervasive mood of unhappiness or depression

   • A tendency to develop physical symptoms or fears associated with personal or school problems

   The term *emotionally disturbed* includes children who are schizophrenic, but not children who are merely socially maladjusted.

7. *Learning disabled* refers to a severe discrepancy between achievement and intellectual ability that is not the result of another disability. Deficiencies are noted in one or more of the following areas: listening, thinking, speaking, reading, writing, spelling, mathematical calculations, or reasoning.

8. *Speech impairment* refers to a communication disorder such as stuttering, impaired articulation, a language impairment, or a voice impairment.

9. *Autism* refers to a markedly abnormal or impaired development in social interaction and communication and a severely restricted repertoire of activities and interests. Manifestations of this disorder vary greatly, depending on the child's developmental level and chronological age. The presence of autism must be established by a multidisciplinary team. The team is usually composed of a licensed physician (preferably a psychiatrist) or school psychologist; a certified speech and hearing therapist; and an educational diagnostician.

10. *Multiple disabilities* refers to a student who has a combination of disabilities included in this section with the following additional criteria:

    • The student's disability is expected to continue indefinitely.

    • The disabilities severely impair performance in two or more of the following areas:

      - Psychomotor skills
      - Self-care skills

        - Communication

        - Social and emotional development

        - Cognition

11. *Traumatic brain injury* defines an injury to the brain caused by an external physical force resulting in total or partial functional disability, psychosocial impairment, or both. The term does not apply to brain injuries that are congenital or degenerative or to injuries induced by birth trauma.

Figure 17-1 gives an overview of the necessary medical data and personnel for determination of the presence of disabilities.

Under IDEA, students are eligible under one or more of the 11 categories previously mentioned. Specially designed individual education programs are planned for each student by IEP teams. These students are also eligible under Section 504.

Eligibility under Section 504 is less restrictive than IDEA. It stipulates "a substantial mental or physical impairment that limits one or more major life activities: caring for oneself, performing manual tasks, walking, seeing, hearing, speaking, breathing, learning and working."

Special accommodations in the student's program may be required. A 504 accommodation plan is designed for each student according to individual need. Potential disability conditions under Section 504 not typically covered under IDEA include:

- Communicable diseases such as HIV/AIDS, tuberculosis
- Temporary medical conditions such as injuries or short-term illness
- Medical conditions such as asthma, diabetes, and heart disease that do not limit strength, vitality or alertness
- Attention deficit hyperactivity disorder
- Behavior disorders
- Treatment for drug or alcohol addiction

ASSESSMENT AND PROGRAM PLANNING

Referral of students for possible special education services should be a part of the district's overall regular education program. Students experiencing difficulty in the classroom should be considered for all support services available to students (tutorial or remedial, compensatory, and other services).

Central to the special education process is the development of an IEP that provides for the student's unique educational needs based on a comprehensive individual evaluation. Cognitive and achievement status are determined by individual psy-

DISABILITIES	Vision/Hearing Screening Health History	Otological and Audiological	Eye Specialist Exam[1]	Psychiatrist/Psychologist	Physician Report	Type & Severity of Impairment	Functional Implications
1. Orthopedically Impaired	X				X	X	X
2. Other Health Impaired	X				X	X[2]	
3. Auditorily Impaired	X	X			X	X	X[4]
4. Visually Impaired	X		X		X	X	X[5]
5. Deaf-Blind	X	X	X		X	X	X
6. Mentally Retarded	X						
7. Emotionally Disturbed	X			X		X	X
8. Learning Disabled	X						
9. Speech Impaired	X					X	X
10. Autistic	X			X		X	X
11. Multi-Disabled	X				X[3]	X	X
12. Traumatic Brain Injury	X				X		

(1) Ophthalmologist/Optometrist

(2) Report for OHI specifies limited strength, vitality or alertness due to chronic or acute health problems.

(3) Depends on Disability

(4) Audiologist addresses functional implications.

(5) Teacher of VI addresses functional implications.

Figure 17-1. Special education eligibility medical data summary chart.

choeducational testing (see Figure 17-2 for commonly used instruments). Health, behavioral, and family information is usually completed by parental interview and review of medical records. Other information concerning the student's discipline and attendance, grades, group test scores, and observations from those who work with the student, particularly classroom teachers, should be reviewed as well.

Upon completion of the comprehensive individual assessment, the IEP team must meet to begin framing the individualized educational plan. This process includes:

- Reviewing all data from the comprehensive individual evaluation, including information from parents, school personnel, and other appropriate sources
- Establishing eligibility for special education services
- Developing the individual educational plan
- Providing placement in the least restrictive environment
- Reviewing services annually

INTELLIGENCE
- Slossen Intelligence Test (4.5 years to adult)
- Stanford-Binet Intelligence Scale (2 years to adult)
- Wechsler Intelligence Scale for Children (6 to 16 years)

ACHIEVEMENT
- Wide-Range Achievement Test (5 years to adult)
- Kaufmann Assessment Battery for Children (2-1/2 to 12.5 years)
- Woodcock-Johnson Psychoeducational Battery (3 years to adult)
- Peabody Individual Achievement Test (5 years to adult)

ADAPTIVE BEHAVIOR
- Vineland Adaptive Behavior Scale

DEVELOPMENT
- Bayley Scales of Infant Development (3 to 30 months)

LANGUAGE
- Receptive: Peabody Picture Vocabulary Test
- Expressive: Receptive-Expressive Emergent Language Scale

Figure 17-2. Common psychoeducational assessment tools with age range.

- Ensuring that minority group students are not placed in special education based solely on English proficiency
- Ensuring that students are not placed because of cultural difference or lack of educational opportunity

A comprehensive review of each student's progress is mandated every 3 years. This review serves as the foundation for assessing the student's ongoing eligibility and need for special education as well as provides information for updating the IEP.

RELATED SERVICES

Related services are those supportive services that may be required to assist a child with a disability to benefit from special education instruction. Federal regulations list the following services: transportation; speech therapy and audiology; psychological services; occupational and physical therapy, recreation, including therapeutic recreation; early identification and assessment of disabilities in children; counseling services, including rehabilitation counseling; medical services for diagnostic and evaluation purposes; school health services; social work services; and parent counseling and training.

Many states have added to the list: art therapy, corrective therapy, music therapy, and orientation and mobility training. The list of related services in the state and federal regulations is not exhaustive. Related services may include items that are not specifically identified, *if the service is required to assist a child with a disability to benefit from special education.* Assistive technology services and devices, such as closed-circuit television units to enlarge print for the visually impaired, may qualify as a related service.

Occupational therapy and physical therapy (OT/PT) deserve special mention because these services emerged in the hospital setting. With the advent of federal mandates, a considerable amount of OT/PT services are now provided in the educational setting, which has created two separate models for the provision of services: the *medical model* emphasizing patient health and the *school-based model* emphasizing student learning.

The school-based model seeks to assist students in achieving optimally in the school. Direct therapy as well as consultation with the student and teacher, program equipment consultation, individual and classroom equipment modifications, and training for various school staff may qualify as related services.

Educationally relevant OT/PT services may include intervention in the following areas:

- Functional mobility: maximum student accessibility to the instructional environment
- Self-help: Maximal student independence in the management of personal care needs
- Positioning: Safe, learning-ready postures for physically impaired students
- Fine motor: Maximal student participation in instructional activities requiring manipulation of educational tools (includes written communication)
- Sensory-motor: Facilitates a student's ability to process and respond to basic sensory and motor information

The IEP planning team must deliberate the need for related services. Many services may benefit a student with a disability, but the law does not require such services to be provided. The legal duty to provide related services applies only when the student could not benefit from the educational program without the service. In deciding whether a related service is necessary, schools must depend on a related service assessment. Services such as speech therapy and occupational and physical therapy, which are utilized as part of a medical regime, must serve some educational goal before schools are required to provide the service as a related service.

Federal regulations contain requirements regarding qualifications and the function of related service personnel, such as "school health services shall be provided or supervised by a licensed physician or by a registered nurse (RN) with or without a bachelor's degree."

INSTRUCTIONAL ARRANGEMENTS

Under IDEA, special education means specially designed instruction, at no cost to the parent, to provide for the unique needs of a child with a disability. This includes instruction conducted in the classroom, in the home, in hospitals, in institutions, and in other settings and instruction in physical education.

Children eligible for special education services ought to be educated in the least-restrictive environment possible, that is, interaction with nondisabled peers to the extent possible given the nature and severity of the disability. Various models exist for the provision of instructional services based on a continuum from least restrictive (regular classes) to most restrictive (residental placement, home, or hospital instruction). Examples of models include regular class with support, resource room, self-contained, self-contained on separate campus, partial school attendance plus homebound, homebound only, residential, and nonpublic day contract.

School health professionals considering student placement needs must be knowledgeable about the school's resources. Every effort should be made to integrate children as fully as possible.

TRANSITION SERVICES

Transition services were added to P.L. 101-476 as a new service by Congress to ensure planning for a successful move to life outside the public school system. Transition services are defined in federal regulations as

> "a set of activities for a student, designed within an outcome-oriented process, that promotes movement from school to post-school activities, including post-secondary education, vocational training, integrated employment (including supported employment), continuing and adult education, adult services, independent living or community participation."

These activities must be based on the individual needs, taking into account the student's preferences and interests; must include needed activities in the areas of instruction, community experiences, and the development of employment and other postschool adult living objectives; and if appropriate, must include the acquisition of daily living skills and functional vocational evaluation.

The following issues should be considered when initiating transition planning:

- What does the student want to do after graduation?
- What skills are needed?
- Where will the student live?
- What support or services will be necessary to achieve optimal integration into the community?
- What assistive technology might be used to enable the student to function at his or optimum level?

The planning should focus on education, employment, leisure and recreation, housing, adult responsibilities (i.e., voter registration, selective service, social security, driver's license), support services (guardianship, family planning, day activities, etc.), transportation, income and resources, and medical services (personal assistive devices, group insurance, special therapies, etc.).

Some states require a written plan when the student is 16 years old. The transition plan should be separate from the individualized education plan and be reviewed at least annually, with updates based on the needs and preferences of the student.

SCHOOL RELEVANCE

Advances in medical science are allowing more children, with what were once life-threatening conditions, to live relatively stable and active lives and to attend school. This trend has generated litigation on the provision of health services at school.

Under IDEA, school health services are defined as a related service, those provided to eligible students in addition to those routinely available to all students. School health services are provided or supervised by a licensed physician or a registered nurse with or without a bachelor's degree. These services may include:

* Screening and referral for health needs
* Monitoring medication needed by students during school hours
* Consultations with physicians, parents, and staff regarding the effects of medication, and emergency care training for staff and parents
* Counseling with students and their families concerning health care practices and services

Major litigation regarding school health services has included the following cases:

* *Irving ISD v. Tatro* (1984): The Supreme Court held that clean intermittent catheterization is a related service; that "medical services" are those services that must be provided by a physician.
* *Detsel v. Board of Education of Auburn Enlarged School District* (1987): The Second Circuit Court ruled that schools do not have to provide a full-time health professional to monitor a student's health needs on a continuous basis.
* *Department of Education v. Katherine D.* (9th Cir., 1983): The court ruled that suctioning and replacement of a tracheotomy tube is a related service and that the school must provide this service.

- *Bevin H. by Michael H. v. Wright* (W.D. Pa. 1987): The court ruled that the school does not have to provide full-time nursing to enable a child to attend school.

In making decisions about school health services as a related service, several questions must be addressed:

- Is the service necessary to enable the student to benefit from special education?
- Who must provide the service?
- What amount of time and resources are required to perform the service?
- What is the cost to schools?

The student's educational right to attend school must be balanced against the burden on the school of performing the service.

ROLE OF THE SCHOOL NURSE

There are several roles for the school nurse regarding the provision of services to students with disabilities:

1. First aid and assessment of illness
2. Health screening
3. Participating in the assessment process for special education by utilizing existing health information in making decisions
4. Assisting with the multidisciplinary evaluation by generating new information regarding hearing and vision; also a comprehensive health history (see Figure 17-3) should be obtained from the parent and from health records with particular attention to the referral problem
5. Collaborating with development of the IEP by discussing the need for school health services or medical services with school staff or with the primary health care provider
6. Communicating with the primary health care provider after the IEP and related services have been decided to monitor progress (provide and receive feedback)
7. Advocating for all children

HEALTH HISTORY
(School Nurse's Worksheet)

I. Student Profile:

NAME _____

DATE _____AGE_____

D.O.B.: _____SEX: M   F

GRADE_____

SCHOOL _____

Date of History _____

RECORDER:_____

INFORMANT: _____

INTERVIEWER:_____

HEALTH CARE PROVIDER: _____

MEDICAID: NO   YES   _____
                                                Number

II. Referred for evaluation of: (circle)   Referred by_____
                                                                        (relationship to pupil)
   A. Low academic progress or academic problem
   B. Attention deficit
   C. Hyperactivity
   D. Behavior
   E. Related health problem(s)
   F. Developmental delay
   G. Other

III. Health Problem(s), during past 12 months: (list and describe management/treatment) Are there other known health problems?

IV. Past History: (list with date and age)

   A. Hospitalizations — (include reason) overnight stay, emergency room visit, outpatient, day surgery

   B. Illness — (Including contagious diseases, high fever, etc.)

   C. Injuries — accidents, ingestions, head injury, sequale

   D. Medications —

   E. Allergies —

   F. Last Health Care Visit_____Name of Provider _____

     Purpose of visit (acute care) (Routine P.E.) _____

     Dental Care   Date of last visit _____Purpose _____Provider _____

   G. Prenatal: Maternal age_____Length of pregnancy _____# of pregnancy _____
     # of living children_____ # of miscarriages_____Prenatal care — (where and what month
     begun_____ Habits: (circle)   smoking, drinking, drugs, pica, other_____
     (Explain) _____

     High Risks: (circle) Infections, bleeding, high blood pressure, anemia, fever, RH factor, trauma, inherited
     disease(s), medications, weight gain, chronic disease, hospitalization, other: _____

Figure 17-3. Health history.

(2)   Name _____

H. Labor and Delivery: Place_____
   Length of Labor —
   Type of Delivery —
   Condition of mother —
   Problems: (circle) breathing, forceps, C-section, other _____
   Birth weight_____

I. Neonatal:
   Problems: (circle) breathing, infections, RH factor, jaundice, transfusions, bleeding, congenital anomaly, feeding, other.
   (Explain)

J. Post natal:
   Home from the Hospital — Baby in _____days. Mother in _____days. Complications —
   (explain)

K. Development: (state age, if known)
   1. sat alone   5. combined words
   2. crawled   6. toilet trained
   3. stood   7. other (Big Wheel, bike, roller skates, etc.)
   4. walked alone   8. school performance
   Development is (circle) faster, slower, equal to siblings or peers.
   Comments:

V. Family History:

Biological Mother — Age: _____ Health_____

Biological Father — Age: _____ Health _____

Siblings: Name   Sex   Age   Health
   1. _____
   2. _____
   3. _____
   4. _____

Maternal Grandparents:
                                        Paternal Grandparents:

1. Grandmother — Age:_____ Health _____ 1. Grandmother — Age:_____ Health _____

2. Grandfather — Age:_____ Health _____ 2. Grandfather — Age:_____ Health _____

Familial Diseases: (circle) Heart Disease, stroke, hypertension, diabetes, asthma, allergy, anemia, sickle cell disease or trait, arthritis, cancer, epilepsy, cataracts, glaucoma, kidney disease, tuberculosis, mental problems, mental retardation, learning problems, other.

(Explain)_____   _____

VI. Social History;

Household members:

Housing: Others caring for child:

(3)   Name _____

VII. Habits — (sleep, thumb sucking, nightmares, sleepwalking, rocking)

VIII. Any problems parent or child wishes to discuss —

IX. Review of Systems (circle)

1. General — Changes in weight, appetite, activity level, bowel habits, resistance to disease, other. (Explain) Birth defects — congenital anomalies

2. Skin — Rashes, easy bruising, changes in skin color or texture, eczema, impetigo, growths, or tumors. (Explain)

3. Head — Headache, trauma, infections (Explain)

4. Eyes — Vision changes, trauma, infections, cataracts, glaucoma, other (Explain)

5. Ears, Nose, Throat — Infections (specify), trauma, epistaxis, allergies, hearing changes, voice changes, caries, speech problems. (Explain)

6. Neck — Trauma, swollen lymph nodes, limitation of movement. (Explain)

7. Respiratory — Infections, breathing problems, trauma, wheezing, cough, asthma (Explain)

8. Cardiovascular — murmur, fatigue with exertion, cyanosis (Explain)

9. Gastrointestinal — Abdominal pain, nausea, jaundice, vomiting, diarrhea, constipation, ulcer, (Explain)

10. Genitourinary — Infections, enuresis, encopresis, discharge, rashes, menstruation, sexual development (Explain)

11. Musculosketal — Trauma, limitation of movement, joint pain or swelling, growths or tumor, curvature of the spine, braces, corrective shoes (Explain)

12. Neurological — Birth injury, trauma, seizures (febrile vs afebrile), staring spells, poor coordination or balance, dizziness, syncope, developmental evaluation (Explain)

13. Endocrine — increased thirst, appetite, urination, diabetes, thyroid problems (Explain)

14. Hematologic — Anemia, blood transfusions, blood dyscrasias, sickle cell (Explain)

15. Psychosocial — Changes in activity level, behavior, relationships, punishment, rewards (Explain)

16. Nutrition — (24 hour recall including snacks)

(4)   Name _____

X. Summary of pertinent history (List in Priority)

    1.

    2.

    3.

    4.

    5.

    6.

XI. Records Request(s)   Needed from (Secure 2.1 for Parent Release):

    1.

    2.

    3.

    4.

XII. Physical Examination (circle one number)

    1. Has been requested from physician or health care facility (see IV-6).

    2. On file, see attached current medical records.

    3. Needed, refer to private physician due to _____

    4. Needed, schedule exam by DISD practitioner.

By participating in the interdisciplinary efforts for children with disabilities and maintaining knowledge of the legal issues, the school nurse can focus on the whole child and improve the coordination of services and care.

REFERENCES

Adams, R. M. *School Nurse's Survival Guide.* Englewood Cliffs, N.J.: Prentice Hall, 1995.

Aylward, G. *Practitioners Guide to Developmental and Psychological Testing.* New York: Plenum Medical Book Company, 1994.

Batshan, M. L., and Y. M. Perret. *Children with Disabilities: A Medical Primer,* 3rd ed. Baltimore: Paul Brookes Publishing, 1992.

Behrman, R., ed. "Special Education for Students with Disabilities." *Future of Children* 6(1):25–53.

Canning, R. "Factors Predicting Distress among Caregivers to Children with Chronic Medical Conditions." *Journal of Pediatric Psychology* 21(5):735–50.

Code of Federal Regulations. Title 34, Part 300.

Graham, S. B. "Related Services: Enabling Students with Disabilities to Benefit from Special Education." *Texas School Administrator's Legal Digest* 12 (Feb. 1996): 1–6.

Lewis, R. L., P. Herring, and R. M.Adams. "Coordinating Services for the Young Developmentally Disabled Patient." *Physician Assistant* 16(10):65–75.

Nader, P. ed., *School Health: Policy and Practice,* 5th ed. Elk Grove Village, Ill.: American Academy of Pediatrics, 1993.

Patterson, J. "Risk and Resilience among Children and Youth with Disabilities." *Archives of Pediatric and Adolescent Medicine* 150 (1996): 692–98.

Position Statement: The School Nurse and Specialized Health Care Services. National Association of School Nurses, revised June 16, 1996.

Public Law 101-476, 1990. *Individuals with Disabilities Education Act.*

Walsh, J. "Medical or Educational: Hospitalizations and Related Services." TCASE Legal Seminar; Austin, Tex., Apr. 15, 1988.

TEEN PREGNANCY

The best contraceptive is a real future.

Marion Wright Edelman
Children's Defense Fund

The numbers of adolescent parents are increasing. Statistics indicate that when teens become pregnant or when they are parents, they are at greater risk of dropping out of school and becoming dependent on welfare than other students. Schools that offer programs and personnel to help these student parents find and obtain quality health care and social services and to prepare them to enter the work force are more likely to see these students finish their basic education. When school districts and communities combine their efforts, the complex needs of pregnant teens and adolescent parents are more completely met.

IS IT ALWAYS A PROBLEM?

Some families have a tradition of early marriage and childbearing. Some teenage girls make a decision to have a child and do an adequate job of parenting. Some young men make efforts to become good fathers and to provide emotional and financial support for their child.

How much should agencies and adult professionals interfere with the process in the above cases? Do we give the teen parent what we think they need regardless of their wishes? Do we do so without consulting their parents? The answer is, probably not.

In the school setting, the primary goal is to support teen parents so that they can complete school and become independent. In reaching this goal, the school nurse may be asked to help find child care, teach parenting skills, provide academic tutoring, facilitate well-baby appointments, and a number of other things. In addition, if a second child would interfere with the students established goals and she wishes it, resources that help defer a second pregnancy can be provided.

Teen pregnancy is not always a problem, but it never fails to create challenges of major proportions.

THE NUMBERS AND THE CHOICES

Several sources agree that approximately one million adolescent pregnancies occur in the United States annually. Half of these result in live births, whereas the other half end in miscarriages or abortions. Teen pregnancy is, by any definition, an epidemic.

Once a young person experiences sexual intercourse, she or he acquires "risk status." Unquestionably, young people who are not sexually active are not at risk of pregnancy, unless they are forced to have sex (not a rare event). Once the decision is made to initiate sexual activity, the risk of pregnancy is high for those who do not use contraception consistently. Once pregnant, a young woman must decide whether to carry the pregnancy to term. She may decide on an abortion, if that option is available to her. If a child is born, the mother may decide to give the child up for adoption.

Although this series of decisions seems relatively straightforward, there is little consensus in our society about how to intervene and prevent the negative consequences. One set of conflicts centers on the morality of premarital sex. Some people believe that the only response to the issue of adolescent pregnancy is to promote abstention. Others believe that premarital sexual activity has become the norm and therefore interventions should focus on teaching responsible sexual behavior and providing access to contraception. A second set of conflicts is focused on the abortion issue. Once pregnant, should a girl be required to maintain a pregnancy and encouraged to put the baby up for adoption if she cannot care for it, or should she be assisted to obtain an abortion if that is what she wants?

PRECURSORS

The target behaviors considered high risk are (1) early sexual activity, (2) nonuse or inconsistent use of contraceptives, and (3) early childbearing. Many of the precursors are the same for each of these three high-risk behaviors. A tabulation of precursors of early childbearing shows this similarity (see Figure 18-1).

African-American young people, especially boys, are more likely than other young people to have intercourse at very early ages. Early pubertal development has some influence on age of initiation. Young people from low-income families with uneducated parents who are not supportive or communicative are much more likely to initiate sex at early ages than others their age. Children who are not engaged in school activities, who have low expectations for school achievement, and who hang around with friends in similar situations are more prone to early sex than those who do not. This behavior is often preceded by other high-risk behaviors, such as early substance use (tobacco, alcohol, or other drugs) and truancy. Such young people are often drawn into gangs, prostitution, and the underground economy of stolen goods and drug trafficking.

The living room couch has long since displaced the back seat of the car or the beach as the place of intercourse. The use of contraception follows a pattern that is linked to early initiation of intercourse and other behaviors. Hispanic teens are less likely to use contraception either initially or subsequently. Young, sexually active

Precursor	Early Coitus	Contraceptive Nonuse
Educational expectations	Low	Low
Perception of life options	Poor	Poor
School grades	Low	Low
Conduct	Truancy	———
Religiosity	Low attendance	Variable
Peer influence	Heavy	———
Peer use	———	Imitative
Beliefs about risk	———	Unconcerned
Other high-risk behaviors	Early delingquency; Substance use	———
Psychological factors	———	Impulsive
Self-esteem	Variable	Lack locus of control
Relationship to partner	———	Uncommitted

Figure 18-1. Precursors of early childbearing. (Dryfoos, J., Adolescents at Risk: Prevalence and Prevention. New York: Oxford University Press, 1990)

teens who do not use contraception are more impulsive than other teens and lack an internalized locus of control; they are poor planners. They are more likely to have casual sex and not be in committed relationships with partners. Their parents often have limited education and are less likely to communicate with them than other parents do or may have been early parents themselves.

Girls who bear children early appear to have limited basic life skills; pregnancy just seems to happen to them. Some are less cognitively able than their peers; some are submissive and depressed. Others use marriage or pregnancy as a way to escape an unsupportive family and create someone who will love them. And, most sadly, many early pregnancies are the result of sexual abuse.

FATHERS

Our knowledge of the role of young men in sexuality and pregnancy behaviors is incomplete. Much of the published information on adolescent pregnancy ignores males, except to acknowledge that they are "perpetrators" of the outcomes.

Information about almost 40% of the fathers of babies born to teenage mothers is missing from vital statistics. Close to 70% of the identified fathers are over the age of 19. No data are available about the age of the male partners in teen pregnancies that terminate in abortions, but it is probable that those males are younger than the fathers of live births. In any case, young men must be included in target populations for pregnancy prevention programs.

Teen fathers attain less education than teenagers who are not fathers. Many of the teen fathers are school dropouts, unemployed, or both. From studies of pregnancy among urban teenagers, even the older fathers involved in a teenage pregnancy appear to be disadvantaged in education and employment fields as compared with men whose partners are women age 20 and older. Young men who become fathers as teenagers continue to have an educational and occupational disadvantage as they age when compared with their peers who delay childbearing.

Financial responsibility, relationship issues, school, and work are among the immediate concerns of most young men involved in the pregnancy. Involvement of the young man in the pregnancy and with the child can have a positive effect on the child's development and provide greater personal satisfaction for the father and the young mother.

CONSEQUENCES OF EARLY PREGNANCY

Early sexual intercourse places young women at very high risk of negative health consequences. The younger the age at which a girl first enters into sexual relationships, the more likely that negative consequences will follow. Early sexual initiates have more frequent acts of sexual intercourse and multiple partners and are less likely to use effective methods of contraception than those who wait. The most deleterious consequences, other than pregnancy, are sexually transmitted diseases and their related side effects (infertility, cervical cancer, ectopic pregnancy, and infections passed on to newborns). AIDS is the most life-threatening consequence; young people who are involved in an array of high-risk behaviors, such as drug use, prostitution, and frequent sex with multiple partners, are extremely vulnerable to this disease.

The most direct consequences of early pregnancy relate to childbearing. The birth of a child impacts both the mother and the baby—and ultimately the father, family, and community—with immediate, long-term, and often lifetime consequences. Recent studies show that adolescents 15 years old or under are at increased risk of anemia, toxemia, cephalopelvic disproportion, hypertension, and vaginal infections. They are also at risk for prolonged labor, premature labor, and maternal death.

Adolescents over 15 have a higher incidence of anemia but no higher incidence of hypertensive disorders or abnormal deliveries than older mothers. Those who receive early, thorough prenatal care are believed to have no greater physiological risks of pregnancy than women over 20 years old. Unfortunately, many adolescents do not seek early prenatal care, and those that do may fail to cooperate with recommendations, especially those focusing on dietary practices.

Additional risks for the pregnant adolescent girl include premature infants and low-birth-weight infants. Even when the pregnant student initiates prenatal care early in the pregnancy, complications, such as bleeding and threatened abortion of the fetus, may occur. Iron-deficiency anemia is a problem in many pregnant women. The adolescent who begins her pregnancy already anemic is at even greater risk. She must be followed closely and counseled carefully regarding nutrition during pregnancy.

In the years following early childbearing, mothers suffer several disadvantages: reduced educational achievement, unstable marriages and high divorce rates or no marriage, more subsequent births closer together and unintended, lower-status jobs and lower income than their peers, and in some cases, long-term welfare dependency. Adverse effects on children of teen parents include lower achievement and many more behavioral and emotional problems than other children, high risk of becoming teenage parents themselves, and often a lifetime of poverty.

Adoption is a decision that teenagers rarely make following unplanned pregnancies. No studies have been identified that document the psychological consequences of adoption, such as depression or regret, although such consequences undoubtedly occur in some cases. There is no evidence in the psychological literature that abortion produces depression or guilt. Most anecdotal reports refer to feelings of relief.

Of the one million adolescents who become pregnant each year, it is estimated that 50% give birth, 40% choose to have an abortion, and 10% miscarry. Adolescents under 20 years of age account for about 26% of the abortions in the United States. A 1993 study by the Advocates for Youth found that, of teenagers under 18 who chose to have an abortion, 54% were white, 30% were black, 12% were Hispanic, and 4% were of other races.

PREVENTION

Family Interventions

There is no substitute for a supportive, involved family when it comes to primary prevention of teen pregnancy. Strong evidence upholds the theory that good parent-child communication helps children develop decision-making skills and delay intercourse. Schools can give suggestions to parents for involvement and communication with their children and can reinforce good parenting.

School-Based Interventions

The school's role in minimizing the negative impact of teen pregnancy comes under three headings: *curriculum, counseling,* and *school-based clinics.*

It is well documeted that sexuality education improves knowledge, but there is little evidence that behavior is influenced by taking courses. The rate of sexual activity does not appear to change as a result of information, nor does contraceptive use. *There is no evidence that pregnancies have been prevented as an outcome of any specific sex education curriculum.* Sex educators have responded to these disappointing research results by developing new approaches, such as decision-making skills, goal setting, effective communication, enhanced self-esteem, parenting, child development, conflict resolution, and life planning. As yet, the success of these programs cannot be measured, but this broader approach holds promise.

The term *counseling* encompasses a wide variety of activities, from advice for an individual to generic "preventive" sessions for groups of people. The essential element for success seems to be a one-on-one relationship between a student and an adult. Such a relationship must be ongoing so that rapport and trust can be developed. The "one-minute psychologist" approach does not work; written handouts and a pat on the back are valueless unless followed up. The adult must truly care what happens to the child and show it frequently.

The number of *school-based* and *school-linked health clinics* is increasing, as is their acceptance. In the context of sexually active adolescents, these clinics have the most documentable track record of reducing teen pregnancy, especially second and third pregnancies. The success of school-based clinics seems to hinge on them being comprehensive health centers that see adolescents for any number of problems, not just family planning. Such clinics reach a higher percentage of youth in a given population, especially males, than family-planning clinics. Most school-based clinics report that student visits related to family planning constitute only about 15% of visits. No stigma accompanies a school clinic visit; peers need not know the reason. A student's confidential problems are often unknown to school personnel unless there is a need to know, such as schedule adjustment. Sharing of information between the school and an on-campus clinic run by another agency must be worked out at the local level on an individual basis that is acceptable to both the school, the clinic, and the parents.

Contraception

Because condoms are often forgotten or not used in the "heat of the moment" and daily pills are difficult to remember and have side effects, more health care professionals are prescribing long-acting contraceptives. Any student who requests information is referred to their physician by the school health care provider.

SCHOOL MANAGEMENT

Prenatal Care

Health problems the school-age mother faces during pregnancy are often the result of not consulting a physician early in the pregnancy. The school health care provider may need to assist the student in finding a resource to determine pregnancy or to obtain prenatal care. To assess, monitor, and advise the student as well as to ensure that the student is making and keeping appointments at regular interval, the school nurse can develop the health management plan (individualized health care plan) that includes scheduled visits to the school clinic midway between prenatal clinic or physician visits. At this time, the school nurse or other health care provider may also evaluate the pregnant adolescent's weight, blood pressure, and general well-being. The school nurse will want to use special health record during the student's pregnancy (see Figure 18-2).

Collaboration with the school counselor, school social worker, home economics teacher (family and parenting classes), and other appropriate personnel in the school and in community agencies will help the student obtain social services, counseling, and family and parenting classes during this time of increased need for assistance. Clarification of the responsibilities of the team may be aided with a chart similar to the one shown in Figure 18-3.

Educational Issues

Federal legislation passed in 1972 prohibits schools from excluding students because they are pregnant. Keeping the student in school during pregnancy, providing home instruction or limited classes (2 to 4 hours per week) following the birth of the infant, and encouraging the return to school as soon as possible have a positive influence on the students continuation of her education.

In many school districts, pregnant students have the option of attending the home school or transferring to a special school for pregnant students. In either location, students should receive prenatal and postnatal counseling and health monitoring (see Figure 18-2) by the school nurse between scheduled visits to their personal health care provider (physician, midwife, or clinic). In most cases, additional social services and counseling are needed for the young student. Special schools for pregnant students generally provide a comprehensive education program, expanded counseling, and social services.

A modified schedule for the pregnant teen may be necessary. Some health care providers do not allow the pregnant teen to participate in certain physical activities

HEALTH CARE MONITORING AND COUNSELING RECORD FOR PREGNANT STUDENTS

Demographic Data:

Name _____ Date _____ Home School _____

Married _____ Husband's Name _____

Address _____ Home Phone _____

Mother's Name _____ Work Phone _____

Address _____

Father's Name _____ Work Phone _____

Address _____

Age ____ D.O.B. _____ LMP _____ EDC _____ Week or Month of Pregnancy _____

Clinic or Physician _____ Phone _____ First Appointment _____

Routine prenatal health care visits are scheduled:

Every four (4) weeks up to 32 weeks (end of this period _____) *write in pencil*

Every two (2) weeks up to 36 weeks (end of this period _____) *write in pencil*

Then every week until delivery. Record dates for future medical prenatal care. When the appointment has been kept or changed, record the new date. Student to be seen by school nurse approximately midway between physician/clinic visits.

Medical Prenatal Appointments   School Prenatal Appointments

1.____ 2.____ 3.____ 4.____ 5.____   1.____ 2.____ 3.____ 4.____ 5.____

6.____ 7.____ 8.____ 9.____ 10.____   6.____ 7.____ 8.____ 9.____ 10.____

11.____ 12.____ 13.____ 14.____ 15.____   11.____ 12.____ 13.____ 14.____ 15.____

HISTORY

I. Health Problems(s), during past 12 months: (list and describe management/treatment) Are there other known health problems?

II. Past History: (list with date and age)

A. Hospitalizations — (Include reason) overnight stay, emergency room visit, outpatient, day surgery

B. Illness — (Including contagious diseases, high fever, etc.)

C. Injuries — accidents, ingestions, head injury, sequalae

D. Medications —

E. Allergies —

F. Last Health Care Visit _____ Name of Provider _____

Purpose of visit (acute care) (Routine P.E.) _____

Figure 18-2. Health care monitoring and counseling record for pregnant students.

Dental Care Date of last visit _____ Purpose _____ Provider _____

III. Family History:

Biological Mother— Age:_____   Biological Father — Age: :_____ Health _____

Maternal Grandparents: Paternal Grandparents:

1. Grandmother — Age: :_____   Health _____ 1. Grandmother Age: :_____   Health _____

2. Grandfather — Age: :_____   Health _____ 2. Grandfather Age: :_____   Health _____

Familial Diseases: (circle) Heart Disease, stroke, hypertension, diabetes, asthma, allergy, anemia, sickle cell disease or trait, arthritis, cancer, epilepsy, cataracts, glaucoma, kidney disease, tuberculosis, mental problems, mental retardation, learning problems, other. (Explain)

IV. Social History:

Household members:

Housing:

Plans for future:

Child: Adoption   Self: Education
          Keep Child   Parenting Classes
          Child Care Plans   Prenatal Classes
                                             High School
                                             Trade School
                                               College
                                             Marriage

V. Postdelivery History:

Labor and Delivery: Place —

Length of Labor —

Type of Delivery —

Condition of Mother —

Problems: (circle) breathing, infections, RH factors, jaundice, transfusions, bleeding, congenital anomaly, feeding, other.
(Explain)

Postnatal:

Home from the Hospital — Baby in _____ days. Mother in _____ days.
Complications —
(Explain)

Return to school   Postpartum Check Up

Child care arrangements   Lives with

III. Past OB History (if applicable):

Gravida   Para   AB

(# of Pregnancies)   (# of Live Babies)

Delivery: Vaginal   C-Section

Date

If C-Section, state reason:

Prenatal: Maternal age   Length of pregnancy   # of pregnancies

\# of living children   # of miscarriages

Prenatal care — (where and what month begun)

(Explain)

High Risks: (circle) Infections, bleeding, high blood pressure, anemia, fever, RH factor, trauma, inherited disease(s), medications, weight gain, chronic disease, hospitalization, other:

VII. Review of Systems (circle)

1. General — Changes in weight, appetite, activity level, bowel habits, resistance to disease, other. (Explain) Birth defects — congenital anomalies

2. Skin — Rashes, easy bruising, changes in skin color or texture, eczema, impetigo, growths, or tumors. (Explain)

3. Head — Headache, trauma, infections. (Explain)

4. Eyes — Vision changes, trauma, infections, cataracts, glaucoma, other. (Explain)

5. Ears, Nose, Throat — Infections (specify), trauma, epistaxis, allergies, hearing changes, voice changes, canes, speech problems. (Explain)

6. Neck — Trauma, swollen lymph nodes, limitation of movement. (Explain)

7. Respiratory — Infections, breathing problems, trauma, wheezing, cough, asthma. (Explain)

8. Cardiovascular — murmur, fatigue with exertion, cyanosis. (Explain)

9. Gastrointestinal — Abdominal pain, nausea, jaundice, vomiting, diarrhea, constipation, ulcer. (Explain)

10. Genitourinary — Infections, enuresis, encopresis, discharge, rashes, menstruation, sexual development. (Explain)

11. Musculoskeletal — Trauma, limitation of movement, joint pain or swelling, growths of tumor, curvature of the spine, braces, corrective shoes. (Explain)

12. Neurological — Birth injury, trauma, seizures (febrile vs. afebrile), staring spells, poor coordination or balance, dizziness, syncope, developmental evaluation. (Explain)

13. Endocrine — Increased thirst, appetite, urination, diabetes, thyroid problems. (Explain)

14. Hematologic — Anemia, blood transfusions, blood dyscrasias, sickle cell. (Explain)

15. Psychosocial — Changes in activity level, behavior, relationships, punishment, rewards. (Explain)

16. Nutrition — (24-hour recall including snacks).

Prepregnant Weight _____ Date _____ Prepregnant B _____ Date _____

MONITORING — COUNSELING

DATE	WT.	B.P.	VISITS WITH SCHOOL NURSE — COMMENTS: Inquire specifically re: nutrition, headache, altered vision, abdominal pain, nausea, vomiting, bleeding, fluid or secretions from vagina, dysuria. Comment about health, nutrition, any classes re: labor, delivery, etc. being taken by student.	LEARNING MODULE

RESPONSIBILITY CHART SERVICES
FOR PREGNANT AND PARENTING STUDENTS

Activity	School Social Worker	School Counselor	School Home Economics Teacher	School Nurse
• Identify client population in school/community and refer them to the Social Worker.	X	X	X	X
• Complete/contribute to the assessment or data on each pregnant or parenting student .	X	X	X	X
• Define/agree upon anticipated client outcomes, including time frames.	X	X	X	X
• Negotiate/implement and coordinate an Individual Education Career Plan (IECP) with the pregnant and/or parenting student, family, school nurse, home economics teacher, school counselor, and appropriate others:	X			X
Counseling services	X	X		X
Health services	X			X
Transportation services (self and child)	X	X		
Assistance in obtaining governmental/social services	X	X	X	X
Parenting skill training, job training	X	X	X	
Child care	X			
Case management	X			X
Compensatory education Home Instruction		X		
• Monitor and evaluate the clients status specifically using each part of the plan (above) and anticipated outcomes in a timely way.	X	X	X	X

Figure 18-3. Responsibility chart: services for pregnant and parenting students.

or sports. Physical discomforts such as frequent urination or morning sickness may require the school health care provider to intervene on behalf of the student. The extra weight of the baby and the stretching that accompanies pregnancy frequently cause severe backaches and may serve to keep the student out of school if collaboration between the school nurse and the classroom teacher does not take place. Climbing stairs, caring heavy book bags, and fitting comfortably behind stationary desks may also pose problems. Modified schedules to help the pregnant adolescent attend school regularly are the result of school interdisciplinary team planning. School personnel who are committed to keeping students enrolled and attending classes can be generally supportive and can help to accommodate special needs.

Prenatal and parenting classes and hands-on baby care skills are often included in the curriculum of the home economic classes in secondary schools. In most communities, social agencies have parenting classes and provide additional services to assist pregnant teens. During pregnancy, motivation for learning about parenting and infant care is generally higher than previously. Providing this opportunity in the school is strongly encouraged.

When health problems with pregnancy prevent an adolescent from attending classes, most schools provide home or hospital instruction by a qualified teacher. Students are required to provide physician verification of the need for this arrangement. In some programs, lessons are sent home weekly, other programs provide homebound teachers who go to the student's home and guide student learning for 4 or more hours per week. This allows the student time with the teacher and encourages her to complete her classwork.

SCHOOL RELEVANCE

To meet the needs of the growing adolescent population of teenage pregnancies, programs that focus on prevention, education, health, social and emotional needs, career development, and vocational training are needed. Additionally, a case management system can be implemented to ensure that the students remain in school and receive placement in programs that meet their needs. Child care, transportation, and tuition for summer and evening classes are often cited as student needs. Many state and community agencies currently provide services for pregnant and parenting teens enrolled in schools. Increased collaboration of school and agency personnel often provides students with services in the community they would otherwise have difficulty obtaining.

ROLE OF THE SCHOOL NURSE

School nurses can recommend community agency programs for elementary, middle, and high school students as an effort to help prevent or delay pregnancy. Many comprehensive programs seek to provide young women information and the self-confidence to deal with peer pressures and society's confusing sexual messages. One excellent nationally known program is Girls, Inc. This organization develops curriculum and teaches young women to make personal decisions based on what is best for each individual. Classes start at age 9, with sessions for the parent and daughter to encourage communication. Classes for older students focus on assertiveness, emphasize education and career planning, and help teens to see what they miss if they become mothers at a young age. Programs of Girls, Inc. include:

- *Growing Together* (girls and boys aged 9 to 11, and parent or trusted adult): A four-session Saturday workshop designed to increase positive communication between parents and children about sexual information and values
- *Will Power/Won't Power* (youth aged 12 to 14): An eight-session workshop in assertiveness training with the specific goal of encouraging young people to delay engaging in sexual intercourse
- *Taking Care of Business* (youth aged 15 to 18): An eight-session workshop designed to increase education and career planning skills as well as motivation to avoid pregnancy.
- *Health Seminars* (all ages): Additional program topics that support the pregnancy prevention curriculum, such as AIDS and other sexually transmitted diseases, rape, and sexual harassment.

Other programs to actively involve all teens in decision-making, self confidence, and communication are available in community agencies, organizations, or churches. The school nurse is the health resource specialist in the school and, in an effort to prevent early pregnancy and parenting, has the opportunity and responsibility to find resources for young students.

REFERENCES

Adams, R. *School Nurse's Survival Guide.* Englewood Cliffs, N.J.: Prentice Hall, 1995.
Archives of Pediatric and Adolescent Medicine, vol. 150, 1996.

Olds, S. B., M. L. London, and P. W. Ladwig."The Adolescent Mother." In *Maternal Newborn Nursing*, 4th ed., edited by P. Cleary, J. Northway, and C. Lewis, pp. 384–85. Redwood City, Calif.: Benjamin/Cummings Publishing Co. Inc., 1992.

"Pregnancy Related Services." Section IX in *Student Attendance Accounting Handbook*, p. 1. Austin: Texas Education Agency, 1996.

Robinson, K. "Support Needs of Pregnant and Parenting High School Students." *Journal of School Nursing*, 9(4):12-15.

Stanhope, Marcia, and Jeanette Lancaster. *Community Health Nursing: Promoting Health of Aggregates, Families and Individuals,* 4th ed. St. Louis: Mosby-Year Book,1996.

Texas Education Agency. *Successful Planning for School Age Parents.* Austin, Tex.: Home Economics Education, 1993.

Wallace, H. *Principals and Practices of Student Health.* Oakland, Calif.: Third Party Publishing, 1992.

EMERGING CONCEPTS

It is what we think we know already that often prevents us from learning.

Claude Bernard

THE ELECTRONIC SCHOOL NURSE

A Paperless School Clinic?

Computerized school clinic records are not as far away as one might think. Many hospitals have abandoned patient charts in favor of total computerization while retaining the ability to print hard copies when needed. In terms of computerized school clinics, the pros far outweigh the cons, with a few exceptions. Two of these exceptions are the limitations of the software chosen and the modifications that can be made.

These exceptions notwithstanding, there are a number of reasons for computerizing the school clinic. The nature of the data collected makes a school clinic ideal for the application of computer technology, since the data are repetitive, often hard to read, enormous in volume and gathered, kept, revised, and retrieved frequently. Specifically, new information can be added where it is relevant, rather than at the end of a record. Any part of a student's record can be accessed, or any facet of the collected data can be sorted or tabulated. For example, screening rosters for hearing and vision can be printed in minutes rather than handwritten. Existing rosters and documents can also be scanned into the computer if there is scanning attachment (about $250 at press time).

Other advantages of computerized records and data are that they (1) facilitate creating, editing, rearranging, and storing text; (2) enable the nurse to personalize memos to teachers, school district personnel, parents, students, and referrals to doctors; and (3) offer the opportunity to sort and summarize data regarding frequency and types of accidents at school, students needing boosters, students requiring serial weights, and so forth.

Along with the other computers in a school, the clinic computer can make the exchange of health, curricular, and social information easier and more efficient.

Software and Hardware

First, the needs of a school clinic must be determined. What results are wanted and can reasonably be expected from computerizing a school clinic? Next, software should be selected to meet the desired goals, understanding that the program may need to be adapted.

Finally, the school nurse should determine which hardware will run the selected software and will be able to access the local area network (LAN), if there is one. If the school district has computer technologists, they can be asked what computer brands and models can be serviced and maintained before the hardware is chosen. Whatever hardware is chosen will become obsolete shortly after delivery. Choosing hardware that can be *updated* is essential. Figure 19-1 is a glossary of computer terms.

Networks

Intradistrict or LANs have a central "server" that stores all demographic data on each student. To access the server, clinics must be hardwired (through fiber optics) or have a dedicated phone line for a modem.

City and county immunization records and data, as well as statewide immunization data in some states, are available on networks. Local, state, national, university, and commercial resources, such as child abuse reporting, the Centers for Disease Control and Prevention, research results, counseling and health education bulletin boards, are available via local and toll calls, 800 numbers, local Freenets, the Internet, Fidonet, and BITNET. The Internet address for the School Nurse Forum (sponsored by the *School Health Alert* newsletter) is:
http://www.onr.com/ user/schnurse.

Selling the Idea

Computers appeal to most school nurses because they can be used to (1) simplify input and retrieve immunization data; (2) facilitate the compilation of monthly and yearly reports; (3) create memos, newsletters, and referrals; (4) print health management plans for individual students; (5) record and monitor student health problems of individual students; and (6) generate screening rosters.

If the above information is in a database, the school nurse can answer questions in minutes that might otherwise require hours of searching paper files. Spreadsheets are useful for doing monthly and yearly statistical reports, tracking absenteeism, and keeping inventories. Nurses can also generate height and weight charts, posters, and so on using graphics programs.

To convince administrators to computerize school clinics, one must show that the use of a computer in the clinic will help the nurse use his or her time more efficiently. Most administrators and other funding sources want to know how clinic computers will impact education. Will students receive services sooner? Will their health and therefore their learning ability be positively affected?

Like any field, computer networking has its own terminology. Listed below are brief definitions of commonly used terms.

1. **Communications software:** A program you install on your computer to enable it to exchange information with another computer via a modem.

2. **File server:** A specially equipped computer that contains files and data that can be used by everyone connected to a network.

3. **Modem:** The equipment used to link a computer to a telephone line. A modem may be either internal to the computer or a separate piece of hardware.

4. **Network:** A group of interconnected computers that can communicate with each other. Computers on a local area network (LAN) are on the same floor or in the same building, are directly connected to a file server, and share equipment such as printers. Wide-area networks (WANs) link computers or LANs over a greater distance. Computers may be wired directly or have remote, dial-up access to a network node.

5. **Server:** A program on the information side of the network that retrieves items and transmits the results to clients.

6. **Cyberspace:** A term coined by William Gibson in his 1984 science fiction novel *Neuromancer* used to explain the theoretical boundaries of the Internet and other on-line services.

7. **Hypertext:** A way of organizing and linking information that allows users to access related text, images, or sounds from a single computer screen. For example, a user reading an encyclopedia entry on jazz on any hypertext-capable system could also hear excerpts from recordings and look up biographical facts about musicians. Hypertext is the basis of the World Wide Web.

8. **Information superhighway:** Often used as a synonym for the Internet, this theoretical concept is actually much broader, encompassing cable, video, and other communication channels expected to be linked together in the future and easily accessible from homes, schools, and workplaces.

9. **Internet:** A worldwide collection of computer networks that serves as a conduit for the transfer of messages and files. It is operated most commonly from education and research institutions; individuals have accounts on nodes.

10. **World Wide Web (also called the Web):** A hypertext system for finding and accessing Internet resources organized by colorful, graphics-oriented "home pages." The Web links objects seamlessly so users can go directly to particular items located anywhere in cyberspace. To access the Web, users need a modem, an Internet connection, and a special client program.

11. **Download:** To transfer information from computer network to a personal computer.

12. **E-mail:** Electronic mail in which messages are sent through a network. To send e-mail, you need an e-mail address, which is a combination of letters, numbers, and symbols you select when you get an account on the Internet or subscribe to a commercial on-line service.

13. **Upload:** To transfer information from a personal computer to a computer network.

Figure 19-1. Computer glossary.

If persuaded of the value of computerizing the school clinic, principals may be the best source of funds. Other sources of funding might be the school PTA, a local school business adopter, service organizations (such as Kiwanis), grants, foundations, and Title I Medicaid or other federal funding. Also, local businesses or parents may donate used computers.

Training the Users

Acquiring the computer is the first step, followed by learning all the impressive capabilities of computers and software programs. The possibilities are almost infinite and will take time and effort to explore.

The ideal situation is to have technical assistance (real people, both in person and on the phone). Networking with other school nurses (on the computer, by phone or electronic mail, or at meetings, etc.) might also give this kind of assistance.

The manuals that come with hardware and software are often too technical to be user-friendly; there are simple guidebooks available at bookstores for both hardware and software.

The school nurse should read about computers and information management in magazines and newspapers. Workshops, in-service training, and courses on specific software (from community colleges, computer retailers, companies that teach the use of programs, etc.) are also available. The school nurse should try to have input into decisions about computerizing and networking that are made in that school district so that health applications will be included. Especially in secondary schools, students are often computer experts and can give valuable assistance.

Hardware Maintenance

Like automobiles, computers eventually require maintenance. Regular attention and care such as screen and mouse cleaning, protection from dust and other pollutants, use of plastic keyboard protectors, and careful handling of cords and plugs will lessen the need for repairs.

The computer distributor may provide hardware maintenance during the warranty period. If the school district has computer technologists, they can advise on what brands and models can be serviced.

Updating Systems

A computer (hardware) becomes obsolete shortly after purchase, so try to buy the *latest model*. Software becomes obsolete in about 90 days. If software designed specifically for school health clinics is purchased, *updates* should be part of the contract. When buying software, the school nurse should remember to focus on individual information needs. It is acceptable to make suggestions to the program's producer about items to be included in updating, based on discoveries made while reviewing other software.

Final Thought

Computers will change school clinics for the better! The transition from the "paper" way of doing things to a computerized method is a rewarding challenge to meet. Computers vastly improve the management of data necessary in the delivery and monitoring of health care to students, freeing the school nurse for more hands-on services.

SCHOOL-BASED AND SCHOOL-LINKED CLINICS

Managed Care

In an effort to control costs and improve cost effectiveness, government agencies and the business world have assumed progressively greater control of health care. It is in fact referred to as the health care *industry*, having literally become big business; Labor Department statistics show that health care is the largest employer in the United States. Solo medical practitioners are becoming less common than they used to be. Health maintenance organizations (HMOs) and preferred provider organizations (PPOs) that operate under state regulations (and possibly federal, in the future) are here to stay. Unfortunately, cost-cutting measures of most HMOs have reduced either services or the quality of care offered. Their gatekeepers (primary physicians and triage nurses) guard specialists jealously because it means more money in the gatekeeper's pocket. That is to say, front-line physicians are financially rewarded for holding down the number of specialty referrals, which is a potential conflict of interest.

Although health insurance premium costs are being held down by some employer and HMO partnerships, to be covered one must be employed and earn a wage that permits paying health premiums. Non HMO systems are more costly.

A certain percentage of people are always unemployed, but the segment of the "working poor" is increasing rapidly. Minimum wage earners may be eligible for Medicaid, but when they receive a raise, benefits are cut; they have enough money to cover food and shelter but not health insurance. If present influences continue, the number of uninsured adults and their children will continue to grow dramatically. For example, in the Dallas public schools, 70% of the students are on free or reduced-price lunch, but only 28% are eligible for Medicaid.

By default, schools have increasingly assumed various health care roles. If they are to fend off health obstacles to learning and protect sacred in-class time, schools have no choice but to participate to some degree in the health care of its students. It is well and good to say that health care is the parents' responsibility, but if health problems are sinking the educational ship, then educators must at least help plug the holes. The most popular (and logical) hole-plugging activity of schools has been to cooperate in the creation of school-based or school-linked clinics.

Clinic Models

Three basic models of school-based or school-linked clinics exist:

- The stand-alone clinic on campus is the most expensive model and perhaps the ideal clinic. It has all the advantages of being on campus and being accessible to students with none of the disadvantages of being inside the building. In this case, the clinic staff, who may be from the county hospital, health department, or medical or nursing school, may maintain their distance and autonomy as a separate entity and not become entangled in the school bureaucracy.
- A second model, which is probably the most cost-effective and easiest to implement, is the visiting team. An itinerant health team minimally consists of a nurse practitioner or physician's assistant, a social worker, and a paraprofessional who doubles as a medical assistant and clerk. The team has telephone consultation and occasional on-site visits with a pediatrician or adolescent specialist. The cost of this team varies, depending on salaries, but averages $115,000–$130,000 per year.
- Off-campus clinics have existed for many years with varying linkages to schools. It is harder to get students and parents to go to these sites, particularly when the clinics do not have evening hours.

Regardless of which model is chosen, it is important to ensure that the school nurse is carefully integrated into the system. Generally, the school nurse should be the referral originator to the school-based clinic and often the case manager for the students referred. Even if the parent or student bypass the school nurse, this person is the one who will need to implement or monitor any treatment plan in the school setting (e.g., giving medications).

Mental Health

There is no question that mental health has been given short shrift within the overall health care system, both in terms of availability and affordability. Schools cannot afford to emulate this approach. With discipline problems often out of control, schools must be creative and vocal in reversing this trend. Although at times it may be necessary to deal with high school violence in adult and drastic ways for the protection of all, the only long-term solution lies in the prevention of violence. Schools can exert only a limited influence toward primary prevention; the family does that (or fails to do it) in the first 5 or 6 years of life. What schools can do is teach and model appropriate behavior and secure mental health assessment for those who get too far beyond the norm to function in school. Granted, it is a large-mesh safety net, but it is what schools can do.

Adding a mental health component to the school-based clinic is long overdue. Even normal adolescents have a difficult time becoming well-adjusted adults. In addition, signs of societal stress are now showing up in elementary students. Several options of incorporating mental health into the existing school health program exist:

- Adding a paid psychiatric consultant (to organize the program and see the worst cases)
- Adding a cadre of psychiatric social workers or licensed professional counselors (to triage and provide group and family therapy)
- Having a mental health agency, such as Metal Health and Mental Retardation (MHMR) assume responsibility in the school setting
- Referring all students to an outside source

COMMUNITY AND SCHOOL PARTNERSHIPS

Schools cannot and should not bear the total burden for the health care of its students. They should be creative in developing partnerships with community agencies, however. The essential steps in promoting a community-school health partnership are the following:

- Create a community vision
- Define partnership parameters
- Identify barriers
- Agree on goals (include all stakeholders, especially parents and students)
- Examine models
- Develop trust (allow time)
- Identify funding sources
- Implement a pilot model
- Evaluate and revise

- Implement a schoolwide program

Funding

In its broadest sense, funding may include providing space, lending employees or recruiting volunteers, and donating equipment as well as committing actual dollars. Until such time as the investment in comprehensive school health activities is seen to produce affordable results, the financing of such operations will be a patchwork of sources.

The following is a generic list of organizations and agencies that have helped support school-based clinics:

1. Possible agency sponsors (various combinations):
   Schools of nursing
   Hospitals
   Medical schools
   Community-based organizations (profit and nonprofit)
   Public health departments
   Community health clinic
   Mental health agencies
2. Budget support (including in-kind support):
   Federal:
   - Early Periodic Screening Diagnosis and Treatment (EPSDT)
   - School Health and Related Services (Medicaid reimbursement to schools for services to special education students)
   - Medicaid Administrative Claiming (Medicaid reimbursement to schools for case management and administrative activities on behalf of eligible students)
   - Maternal and child health block grants
   - Title X—Improving America's Schools Act (PL 103-382)—Programs of National Significance
   - Title I—Improving America's Schools Act (PL 103-382)—Helping Disadvantaged Children Meet High Standards
   State
   - General funds
   - Health departments
   - Human Services department
   - Education department

Local

- County and city governments
- School districts
- Client fees
- Private insurance
- Private foundations
- Community health centers

The same obstacles encountered in any project where two or more agencies are attempting to collaborate are some of the obstacles to developing functioning school-community partnerships, such as:

- Differences in philosophy: Many agencies have a narrow focus in terms of their delivery system. They may focus on one physical illness or only on mental illness, with a limited ability to consider a holistic approach.
- Territory and control
- Budget constraints
- Accessibility (weekends and summer)
- Lack of unanimous community support

Even the most carefully designed program will fail if funding is not sustained. Grants and private sector funds serve as excellent seed money but rarely provide stable funding. Federal categorical funding is exceedingly complex and contains strict eligibility criteria. The decentralization of selected federal programs now occurring should bring greater flexibility to states in servicing children and families.

There is no sure solution to funding problems, but the goal must be to secure a reliable, continuing source. In some communities, county hospital districts have established satellite clinics that they see as the wave of the future. These satellites can be located on school campuses, and county tax dollars can become a continuing source of funding. Local health departments and state health departments are another source because of their commitment to prevention.

The Bottom Line

Ninety-five percent of the 55 million children in the United States aged 5 to 18 attend school. Therefore, school is the logical place for health resources that espouse illness prevention and wellness promotion.

Although student health needs are increasing in number and complexity, basic health and social services remain fragmented, inaccessible, or simply unavailable. Clearly, comprehensive, integrated service delivery approaches that are community wide and coordinate various services—including education, health, social service, and family support—are needed. Changes in health care delivery and educational restructuring are setting the stage for ever-increasing school-community linkages.

THE SCHOOL CRISIS TEAM

Occasionally, outside help for the local school is warranted for catastrophic events such as the following:

- An accident with severe injuries
- Violence between ethnic groups
- The assault of a student on campus
- A community/political protest
- An accusation against school personnel
- A suicide attempt or threat
- The death of student, on or off campus

When a student dies, all students are affected, even those who did not personally know the deceased individual. To respond to these and other catastrophic occurrences, many school districts have put together crisis teams that can be dispatched to a school on a few minutes' notice. These crisis teams are usually composed of a psychologist, a counselor, a social worker, a nurse, and a specialist in the particular type of event to which the team is responding.

Their mission is first to identify the students most impacted—perhaps the deceased individual's homeroom—and spend the day with the teacher and students to facilitate the grieving process. The steps usually go something like this:

1. Acknowledge the death along with whatever amount of detail is appropriate considering the age of peers and the circumstances of the death. This is best done by the teacher. The principal should never announce a death over the public address system!

2. Next, a psychologist or counselor usually takes over and acknowledges the sadness brought on by the event. Students are allowed to cry, ask questions, or otherwise vent their emotions. Particular care should be exercised to include withdrawn students; they may be candidates for individual counseling.

3. After sufficient, unstructured emoting time, the facilitator should ask the class to share what they liked most about their deceased peer, to remember the good things. (If the death followed a sustained and possibly painful illness, it is appropriate to point out that the individual is no longer suffering.)

4. In parochial schools, certain religious topics may be discussed. This is a difficult area for public schools. A moment of silent remembrance is often the best solution.

5. At this point, the teacher may want to echo some of the students' observations about "the good times."

6. The date and time of the funeral and whether it is for family only or if friends may attend should be announced.

7. The facilitator should close the group counseling session with an open invitation for individual students to drop by the counselor's or psychologist's office "at any time."

8. Finally, the teacher should say that there will be no homework that evening, but should give the students a preview of what to expect in class the following day. This gives a sense of continuity and returning to normal.

In the ensuing days, the teacher must be alert for deeply grieving or disturbed students who do not self-refer to the counselor or psychologist.

The above example addressed the death of a single student. Different types of events require different levels of intervention, both in nature and extent. Figure 19-2 on pages 365-366 outlines three intervention levels by type of event.

DO NOT RESUSCITATE ORDERS

Litigation and new state legislation are forcing more school districts to honor do not resuscitate (DNR) requests. These orders from a student's parents and physician accompany some students with severe and profound developmental disabilities or a terminal illness. They instruct the school to make no effort at resuscitating a student who appears to be dying, nor to call emergency medical services.

Many school officials feel that children who are that fragile should not be in school. Parents may disagree, claiming that their child should be allowed to lead as normal a life as possible.

Although hospitals and hospices have been comfortable in carrying out DNR orders for some time, school staff members, including many nurses, oppose allowing a child to die at school without an effort to resuscitate. Many school nurses feel they are trained to support life rather than do nothing, whereas hospital nurses are accustomed to dealing with death and are more accepting of this response.

LEVEL I: Personal Tragedy or Threatening Incidents Affecting a Student, Teacher or Administrator

Such incidents might involve:

> Local crisis team
>
> Security personnel
>
> Psychological/Social services

Examples:

> Death of a parent, guardian, or significant family member
>
> Suicide threat
>
> Suicide attempt off campus
>
> Serious contagious disease (meningitis)
>
> Violent or bizarre behavior of a student
>
> Dangerous or irate person on campus
>
> Serious illness of a student or faculty member
>
> Assault of a student on campus
>
> Evidence of suspected cult activity
>
> Community or political protest activity
>
> Bomb threat
>
> Child abuse or neglect
>
> Weapons on campus

LEVEL II: Major Personal Crisis or Threatening Incident at Single School or Major Disaster Elsewhere That Indirectly Impacts Students and Teachers

Such incidents might involve:

> Local crisis team
>
> Security personnel
>
> Psychological and social services
>
> Central administrators
>
> Employee relations
>
> Community relations
>
> Community emergency services
>
> News media

Examples:

> Accusation against school personnel involved in illegal activities such as child abuse/molestation
>
> Death of a teacher or student off campus
>
> National incident or declaration of war

Figure 19-2. Levels of crises: The framework for a comprehensive crisis management system.

Undercover police work disclosed

Accident with several severe injuries

Suicide attempt at school

Altercation or violence between ethnic groups or gang members

School bus accident with injuries

Abduction

Level III: Terrorism, Disaster, or Threatened Disaster, Directly and Profoundly Affecting One or More Schools

Such incidents might involve:

Local crisis team

Security personnel

Psychological and social services crisis team

Central crisis team and area administrators

Employee relations

Community relations

Health services department

Community emergency services

News media

Examples:

Tornado, hurricane, severe windstorm, flood

Taking of hostages or sniper gunfire

Airplane crash, explosion, fire

Cluster suicides

Death at a school

Serious environmental hazard (gas leak, etc.)

Figure 19-2. (continued)

School Issues

School issues of do not resuscitate orders include the following:

- The effect on other students (lack of a place to keep the body so that students will not see a hearse come to the school); most emergency medical services do not transport bodies.
- Who will pronounce the student dead? (Nurses can do this.)

- Can a funeral home be called before the student is pronounced dead?

Nevertheless, some school districts have arranged to carry out DNR orders. In one school, the body of the deceased student was kept at school until school was ended for the day.

Nurses report that the attorney general of one state has ruled that the schools must follow DNR orders, whereas another state ruled that schools must not follow these orders. In yet another state, nurses were told by an official of their state board of nurse examiners that performing resuscitation despite written orders to the contrary could be considered an assault on the child.

The Texas legislature passed a law effective November 1996 providing that out-of-hospital facilities must follow doctors' DNR orders. It is being widely construed that this includes schools. The law provides details about the format of the DNR order, including student identification procedures.

Today's prevailing attitudes bear some resemblance to the situation in the late 1970s after P.L. 94-142 (Education for All Handicapped Children Act) required acceptance of severe and profoundly disabled students. Although it was then widely thought that caring for these children in standard public schools was an impossibility, procedures and facilities were gradually developed to accommodate them. It appears that DNR is headed down this same path.

Some state offices of education may eventually take the lead in developing official guidelines for schools to follow. Although some states have convened task forces and have developed guidelines, only Tennessee and Texas have published them. For the present, each district is left to develop their own guidelines.

Items for a DNR Protocol

When a student has a DNR order, the following procedures should be followed:
- Notify the medical examiner's/coroner's office that a student with a DNR order is enrolled in school and prearrange with that office in case they need to send someone to that school to confirm death.
- Make arrangements with the local emergency medical service if they will agree to transport a body.
- Verify that the DNR order has been executed in proper compliance with any existing law, such as the student having to wear an identification bracelet.
- Designate a place at school to hold the body temporarily.
- Arrange with the family which mortuary is to be called if parents cannot be reached.

EMPLOYEE ASSISTANCE PROGRAMS

Discipline versus Support

Until recently, only disciplinary procedures were used by most school districts to "keep employees in line." Studies from the business world show that a helping mode is more effective in keeping employees on the job, whether the problem is alcohol abuse, undue stress, or a physical health issue. Support programs that restore productivity are more effective than pure disciplinary models. Such programs are referred to as employee assistance programs (EAPs).

EAPs allow employees to present themselves and their problems to a neutral, supportive person (often an EAP coordinator) for assessment and help. As illustrated in Figure 19-3, this new step is interposed between flagging performance or attendance and ordinary discipline procedures. Urban school districts have larger EAPs than smaller districts, but one individual can constitute such an office. The EAP head can be a psychologist, counselor, nurse, social worker, or other helping professional. The primary qualification is experience with the types of problems handled. Out-of-district mental health professionals are also desirable for the assessment and treatment of more difficult problems, although this can sometimes be managed through the employee's individual health plan. Because most employees want to be well and do a good job, they are usually willing to sign a contract to follow the prescribed rehabilitation plan. Failure to do so causes action to revert back to disciplinary procedures and sometimes dismissal; the employee has a choice.

Serious psychiatric disorders do not always respond to treatment, and dismissal may still be necessary. Schizophrenia and multiple personality disorder fall in this group. Either way, a school district and its students are better off for having made the effort to assist the troubled employee; many are salvaged and returned to productivity, and others who might have a negative impact on students are removed.

EAP records should be kept separately from personnel files until such time as disciplinary action or dismissal is necessary. This provision facilitates both self- and administrative referrals and promotes the helping relationship.

The employee without health insurance, most often a paraprofessional, poses a particular challenge because he or she may have no primary physician or medical home; the school district must then spend consultation funds. For this reason, schools should make every effort to provide universal health coverage.

Wellness Programs

Thus far, problems that are already interfering with job performance or attendance have been discussed. Ideally, EAPs should be proactive and preventive in their approach. Programs in this category are the following:

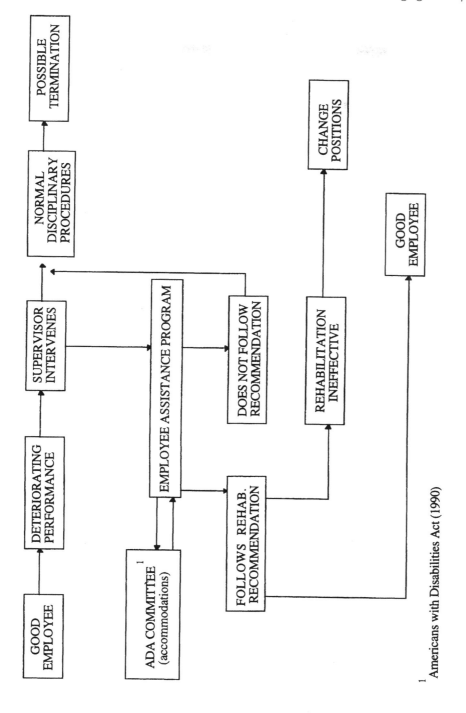

[1] Americans with Disabilities Act (1990)

Figure 19-3. Employee assistance program.

- Smoking cessation
- Weight reduction
- Exercise (aerobics, etc.)
- Mammograms
- Stress reduction
- Cardiac risk screening

Making these activities available at work accomplishes three things:

1. It sends a positive message about the employer.
2. It allows the employee to take charge of health behaviors.
3. It increases employee productivity through better physical and mental well-being.

Numerous studies have documented the cost-effectiveness of such wellness programs. Although it may take up to 3 years to document the overall savings to a school district, the goodwill generated will produce immediate benefits.

RISK MANAGEMENT

Risk management is composed of all measures to control costs related to employee injury and illness as well as damage or theft of property. The risk management division of a school district usually administers workers' compensation, the program responsible for financing the medical care of injured employees and paying the employee for lost time. Risk management focuses on financial liability awareness. It is the centralization of loss control operations and the search for wall-to-wall insurance coverage for property. Employee safety is a key concern of risk management, but the primary mission is to safeguard corporate assets.

Core activities of a typical risk management program include the following:

- Coordinating safety programs, loss prevention, and injury claims control
- Processing employee injury claims
- Purchasing cost-effective property insurance
- Ensuring compliance with laws and government agencies (e.g., Environmental Protection Agency)
- Analyzing accident data to identify risk exposure

Getting injured workers back to work as soon as possible reduces cost; timely evaluation and appropriate treatment must be arranged. Although employees have a choice of treatment resources (from a family physician to a hospital emergency room), it is best to prearrange care with a professional or agency with experience in work-related injuries. Delay in evaluation and treatment often prolongs morbidity and impedes an early return to work. Hospital emergency rooms constitute the most expensive form of care and should be reserved for the more serious or life-threatening injuries. School nurses called to see injured employees can influence the triage process.

EDUCATION OF THE SCHOOL NURSE

Schools of Nursing

School nursing is a growing professional specialty characterized by expanded responsibilities. Changes in the health care delivery system and the changing roles of nurses within those systems make adequate preparation and continuing education mandatory for nurses practicing in the schools. The quality of health care for students is clearly influenced by the knowledge, skills, and attitudes of the caregiver.

Graduates from a variety of nursing education programs are currently practicing professional nursing in schools: hospital (diploma) programs; associate degree programs; nursing programs at the bachelor, master's, and doctoral levels; and combinations of undergraduate degrees with master's degrees in related fields (i.e., health education, special education, guidance and counseling, or education). In 1983, the National Association of School Nurses adopted a position statement on school nurse education and certification indicating that a baccalaureate degree from an accredited college or university is the appropriate preparation for entry into school nursing (see Figure 19-4).

In addition to basic nursing education, advanced education for the school nurse should cover:

- Community resources and networking
- Special education
- Legal issues
- Counseling
- Crisis intervention
- Interdisciplinary and intradisciplinary teams
- Environmental hazards

Description of issue: The ability to learn at school is directly related to the status of a student's health. Identification of health-related barriers to learning are crucial to the provision of an appropriate educational plan for every student. The school nurse serves as the health advocate for all school children, focusing on the promotion of healthful living styles and the prevention of illness and disability.

Rationale: School nurses strengthen and facilitate the education process by improving and protecting the health status of children and staff by identifying and assisting in the removal or modification of health-related barriers to the learning and teaching process for individual children. The school nurse has the educational background, experience, and competencies to provide preventative health, health assessment, and referral services to students.

Professional education: Nursing is a unique discipline and service with its own knowledge base and area of responsibility. Nursing includes the diagnosis and treatment of human responses to actual or potential health problems. The practice of nursing is an art and an applied science that assists the individual to achieve maximum health within his or her own capacity. The uniqueness of school nursing stems from its perspective of care, concern for the whole person, respect for individual rights, and the promotion of wellness and growth.

Professional Nursing education is based upon and combines a liberal education with the study of nursing science and practice. This forms the basis of making sound nursing decisions and a framework for consistent use of critical thinking. Professional nursing is built upon knowledge from natural science, behavioral sciences, and nursing science and theory.

Certification and licensure: School nursing is a separate and distinct specialty within the nursing and educational professions, and therefore competence in specified areas of health and education is needed for school nurses to act as health advocates for school-age children.

Accountability: School nurses adhere to the standards of school nursing practice as established by the National Association of School Nurses.

Functions: The practice of nursing by school nurses occurs within the complex and unpredictable setting of the school agency. The school nurse acts as a care provider, advocate, change agent, teacher, manager, and educator. The school nurse collaborates with other education and health care professionals to provide optimal school nursing care to the school community.

The functions of the specialized school nurse include, but are not limited to, the following:

1. Promotes and protects the optimal health status of children.
2. Provides health assessments.
   a. Obtains a health and developmental history.
   b. Screens and evaluates findings of deficits in vision, hearing, scoliosis, and growth, and so forth.

Figure 19-4. Position statement on the professional school nurse roles and responsibilities: education, certification, and licensure.

    c. Observes the child for development and health patterns in making nursing assessment and nursing diagnosis.

    d. Identifies deviant health findings.

3. Develops and implements a health plan.

    a. Interprets the health status of pupils to parents and school personnel.

    b. Initiates referrals to parents, school personnel, and community health resources for intervention, remediation, and follow-through.

    c. Provides ongoing health counseling with pupils, parents, school personnel, and health agencies.

    d. Recommends and helps to implement modification of school programs to meet students' health needs.

    e. Utilizes existing health resources to provide appropriate care of students.

4. Maintains, evaluates, and interprets cumulative health data to accommodate the individual needs of students.

5. Participates as the health team specialist on the child education evaluation team to develop the individual education plan (IEP).

6. Plans and implements school health management protocols for the child with special health needs, including the administration of medication.

7. Participates in home visits to assess the family's needs as related to the child's health.

8. Develops procedures and provides for crisis intervention for acute illness, injury, and emotional disturbances.

9. Promotes and assists in the control of communicable diseases through preventative immunization programs, early detection, surveillance, and reporting and follow-up of contagious diseases.

10. Recommends provisions for a school environment conducive to learning.

11. Provides health education.

    a. Teaches parenting skills as they relate to child development and the health needs of children.

    b. Provides direct health education and health counseling to assist students and families in making decisions on health and lifestyles that affect health.

    c. Participates in health education directly and indirectly for the improvement of health by teaching people to become more assertive health consumers and to assume greater responsibility for their own health.

    d. Counsels students concerning chronic health conditions, mental health issues and problems such as pregnancy, sexually transmitted diseases, and substance abuse to facilitate responsible decision-making.

    e. Serves as a resource person to the classroom teacher and administrator in health instruction and as a member of the health curriculum development committee.

Figure 19-4. (continued)

12. Coordinates school and community health activities and serves as a liaison person between the home, school, and community.
13. Acts as a resource person in promoting health careers.
14. Provides health counseling for staff.
15. Provides leadership, support, or both for staff wellness programs.
16. Engages in research and evaluation of school health services to act as a change agent for school health programs and school nursing practices.
17. Assists in the formation of health policies, goals, and objectives for the school district.

Conclusion: It is the position of the National Association of School Nurses that professional school nurses should be employed to provide quality health care to students in the school setting. School nurses should be registered nurses licensed to practice nursing by the state board of nursing, and the certification and licensure of school nurses must be established by the regular certifying and licensing agency in the appropriate state education agency. School nurses are accountable to practice in accordance with current standards as stated by the National Association of School nurses.

NASN promotes, supports, and represents the school nurse who has a high level of academic preparation. NASN believes that a baccalaureate degree from an accredited college or university is suitable preparation for entry into school nursing.

Resolution: The School Nurse
Adopted 1982
Position statement: Education of the Professional School Nurse
Adopted 1983
Resolution: The School Nurse: Certification and Licensure
Adopted 1969
Revised June 1996

Figure 19-4. (continued)

- Chronically ill, medically fragile, and technologically dependent students
- Leadership roles (planning, developing, evaluating and managing a school health program)

Graduate nursing programs for master's and doctoral degrees in nursing provide courses to meet these requirements. National leaders in school health are acknowledging and supporting the need for school nurses to be prepared at the master's level.

Continuing Education

Depending on the clinical specialty area, the "half-life" of nursing knowledge ranges from 2 to 5 years. To prevent becoming outdated, school nurses and their employers must carefully plan for the renewal of staff knowledge and nursing practice skills.

Continuing nursing education programs build on previous education and experience to enhance the practice of nursing and thus improve the health of clients. The increasing complexity and severity of health problems of school-age children, social changes, the medical knowledge explosion, advances in technology, and the increased need for accountability underscore the need for continuing education.

A variety of continuing education programs for school nurses are available in community hospitals, agencies, schools of nursing, and commercial companies. Many school nurses are in school districts that provide professional growth programs. In addition, professional associations and organizations hold a variety of meetings, seminars, workshops, and presentations to update information on the school nursing practice.

Certifications

The Council on Certification of the American Nurses Association (ANA) defines certification as the "documented validation of specific qualifications demonstrated by the individual registered nurse in the provision of professional nursing care in a defined area of practice." Several professional nursing organizations offer this recognition for nurses who have gained knowledge through educational and clinical experience in a specific area of practice. The National Association of School Nurses (NASN) recognizes school nurses who meet specific criteria and successfully complete a national examination by granting them the title of certified school nurse (CSN). The ANA offers certification for school nurses and titles successful candidates as registered nurse, certified (RN-C).

Most nurses who are practicing in the expanded role of primary caregiver in school-based and school-linked clinics are certified nurse practitioners. Nurse practitioners are registered nurses with advanced practice in primary health care.

REFERENCES

Adams, R. *School Nurse's Survival Guide,* Englewood Cliffs, N.J.: Prentice Hall, 1995.

Bergren, Martha Dewy, and Robert Mehl. "Help! Where to Find It (Information Management and the Computer)." In *Computer Technology for School Health Nurses,* pp. 17–18. Scarborough, Maine: National Association of School Nurses, 1995.

————. "To Compute or Not to Compute (Information Management and the Computer)." In *Computer Technology for School Health Nurses*, pp. 10–12. Scarborough, Maine: National Association of School Nurses, 1995.

————. "You Decide To Computerize, Now What? (Information Management and the Computer)." In *Computer Technology for School Health Nurses,* pp. 13–14. Scarborough, Maine: National Association of School Nurses, 1995.

Bruininks, R. "Integrating Services: The Case for Better Links to Schools." *Journal of School Health* 64(6):242.

Dryfoos, J. "Research and Evaluation in School-Based Health Care." In *Adolescent Medicine: State of the Art Reviews* 7(2):207–20.

Ellis, Janice K., and Hartley, Cellia A. *Nursing in Today's World: Challenges, Issues and Trends,* 5th ed. Philadelphia: J. B. Lippincott, 1995.

Emmett, A. "Health Care Trends That Will Reshape Nursing." *Nursing 94,* Vol. 68. April 1994, pp. 1701-1704.

Expanding School Health Services to Serve Families in the 21st Century.

Gibbons, Linda. "Health Records Simplified by Computer." *School Nurse,* Vol. 26, February 1990, pp. 7–8.

Greenspan, A., ed. *Medical Employer's Guide.* Bedford, Tex.: Business Publishing, 1993.

Hacker, K. "A Nationwide Survey of School Health Services Delivery in Urban Schools." *Journal of School Health* 64(7):279.

Igoe, J. *National Survey of School Nurses and School Nurse Supervisors.* Scarborough, Maine: National Association of School Nurses, 1994.

Joel, L. "Closing the School Health Safety Net." *American Journal of Nursing,* Vol 47, September 1994, pp. 317-322.

Kozinetz, Claudia A. "Using Administrative Data to Identify Elementary Schools at Increased Risk for Student Absences." *Journal of School Health* 65(7):262–64.

Lowe, B. "Integrated School Health Services." *Pediatrics* 94(3):400.

Meyerson, A. *Psychiatric Disability.* Washington, D.C.: American Psychiatric Press, 1996.

Position Statements. Scarborough, Maine: National Association of School Nurses, 1990.

Passarelli, Carole. *School Nursing: Trends for the Future.* National Health/Education Consortium, November 1993.

Rienzo, B. "The Politics of School-Based Clinics: A Community-Level Analysis." *Journal of School Health* 64(6):266.

Sedlacek, Karen K., and Martha Dewey Bergren. "Computer Use in the Health Office (NASN Survey on Technology/Management Systems)." In *Computer Technology for School Health Nurses,* pp. 7–9. Scarborough, Maine: National Association of School Nurses, 1995.

Siri, D. "Community-School Partnerships: A Vision for the Future." In *The Comprehensive School Health Challenge—Promoting Health through Education*, pp. 19-21. Scotts Valley, Calif.: ETR Associates, 1994.

Stanhope, Marcia, and Jeanette Lancaster. *Community Health Nursing, Promoting Health of Aggregates, Families And Individuals*, 4th ed. St. Louis: Mosby-Year Book, 1996.

U.S. Equal Employment Opportunity Commission. *The Americans with Disabilities Act: Questions and Answers*. Washington, D.C.: September 1992.

Wallace, H., et al., eds. "Employee Health in Schools." In *Principles and Practices of Student Health,* vol. 2, pp. 360–68. Oakland, Calif.: Third Party Publishing, 1992.

Zakarya, Sally Banks, ed. "Electronic School." Booklet published by *American School Board Journal*, June 1996.

INDEX